The Light of Reason

FONTANA PHILOSOPHY CLASSICS

GENERAL EDITOR
A. M. Quinton, New College, Oxford

Russell's Logical Atomism
Edited by David Pears

A Treatise of Human Nature
David Hume
Books II and III edited by P. S. Árdal

A Guide to the British Moralists
Selected and edited by D. H. Monro

A list of volumes in this series published under the general editorship of G. J. Warnock, Magdalen College, Oxford, is given on p. 379.

The Light of Reason

Rationalist Philosophers of the 17th Century

Selected and edited by

MARTIN HOLLIS

FONTANA/COLLINS

This selection first issued in Fontana 1973

Printed in Great Britain for the publishers
William Collins Sons & Co Ltd
14 St James's Place, London, SW1
by Richard Clay (The Chaucer Press), Ltd,
Bungay, Suffolk

Contents

Acknowledgments

The extract from Antoine Arnauld, *The Art of Thinking*, translated by James Dickoff and Patricia James, copyright © 1964 by the Bobbs-Merrill Company, Inc., is reprinted by permission of the publisher. The extract from M. H. Carré's translation of Herbert of Cherbury's *De Veritate* is reprinted by permission of M. H. Carré and Bristol University. The extracts from *The Philosophical Works of Descartes*, translated by E. S. Haldane and G. R. T. Ross, © 1911 Cambridge University Press, are reprinted by permission of the publisher. The extracts from Descartes' *Philosophical Letters*, translated by Anthony Kenny, are reprinted by permission of The Clarendon Press, Oxford. The extracts from *Leibniz Selections*, edited by Philip Wiener, are reprinted by permission of Charles Scribner's Sons. Copyright © 1951 Charles Scribner's Sons.

Introduction

Martin Hollis

'In the beginning God created the heaven and the earth.' Of that there could be no doubt. But, of all the possible worlds, which did He actually choose? It is no use replying '*this* one', since our immediate knowledge extends only to a small corner of it and embraces the merest fraction of its history. The question has always been which world is this world. Is it one where the laws of matter determine the actions of men? Is it one where populations expand faster than food supplies? Is it finite in size and will it one day come to an end? What are the properties of lead and can it be turned into gold? Will copper salts cure rheumatism and what makes men live together in peace? Almost any question can be seen as one about which world God created and science as the construction of a systematic catechism about the ways of God.

From time to time science has to start again. It inherits a structure of methods and answers which then collapses, leaving a void. Then, as Castellio says in his *De Arte Dubitandi*, 'it is necessary to search for a principle by which the truth will be so manifest, so well recognised by all, that no force in the universe, that no probability can ever make the alternative possible' (I.23). The seventeenth century succeeded one of these intellectual earthquakes and Rationalism offered an answering principle. The story of Rationalism is the story of a method for restoring order to the study of God's universe. It is also the first chapter in the history of modern philosophy, and many of its ideas and enigmas are still with us. It presents a new spirit of enquiry, a new scientific strategy and a new, infinite universe.

Since grand systems of thought become coherent and agreed only when they are dead, the new, rational universe cannot be neatly described. The Rationalists agreed only about the method which philosophy and science were to follow and their results were in flat contradiction to each other. Nevertheless, prompted by Descartes' *Meditations*, let us risk a sketch, to show the sort of Cartesian world which took shape and to introduce the sort of riddles it produced.

Let us suppose that the natural sciences all study aspects of a single system, which we may call Nature or Matter. That is the real, physical world of science and all events in it happen according to iron laws of cause and effect. It is like a perfectly constructed watch and its succession of states from moment to moment is inexorable. Its workings are silent, not in the sense that it is perfectly oiled but in the more philosophical and doubtful sense that noise is a human interpretation of sound-waves. By the same token there are no colours, textures, tastes or smells in the strictly mechanical world of Nature. Instead there is only the logic of perfect machinery, embodied in the tireless motions of matter. This is the common stuff of everything physical, as God knows it without any distorting veil of human sense-perception.

The other general ingredient of the universe is Mind. Having no position in the shifting world of matter, each mind or rational soul or spirit is immaterial and, having no separable parts, immortal. Each contains its own world of objects of consciousness or, as the seventeenth century put it, of 'ideas'. These mental objects are as they appear to the mind, rich in colour, texture, sound, scent and taste; but need not correspond to anything more solid in the world of physical nature. They have the qualities of objects in a varied and broadly coherent dream. The mind aware of them is a pure self, whose surest datum is *cogito ergo sum*.

This universe of mind and matter is the work of God. He created it and presides over its workings in smallest detail. He is wholly wise, powerful and good and there is a reason for whatever He has done. His cosmos is not only utterly orderly but also a work of beauty and of love. The rational universe is the realm not only of scientific causal laws but also of harmony and design. For God has all these attributes and science or philosophy is the study of what He has chosen.

The notion that the universe forms a rational whole is an old one. Indeed the belief that the ways of nature are the ways of God is more ancient than modern. The novelty of Rationalism lies in its method of enquiry, which owed more to logic and mathematics and, at the same time, to scientific experiment than any before. The results of the method, however, often owed more to the past than the Rationalists admitted. Presumptions were made about God, about human nature and about the character of rational order which need to be made explicit, if we are to understand the claims made for the new method.

The Collapse of the Old World

In a universe created by an all-wise, all-powerful and all-good God, there ought to be no conflict between science and religion. As St Thomas Aquinas pointed out in the thirteenth century:

> The natural dictates of reason must certainly be true; it is impossible to think of their being otherwise. Nor again is it permissible to believe that the tenets of faith are false, being so evidently confirmed by God. Since therefore falsehood alone is contrary to truth, it is impossible for the truth of faith to be contrary to the principles known by natural reason. *Summa Contra Gentiles* I.7

Indeed faith and reason had then co-operated to depict a world where everything had been set in scientific order for a divine purpose and that co-operation had lasted, under growing strain, for three hundred years. The Bible, interpreted by the Catholic Church, contained the truths of faith. Nature, interpreted in Aristotelian categories, yielded to the dictates of reason. In the integrated cosmos, everything was animate, or endowed with a divine form, to some degree. The Bible was rich in scientific lessons and scientific categories like substance and essence, matter and form, quality and quantity, action and passion, efficient and final cause were equipped to confirm what the Bible taught.

This harmony did not last and, before picking out what survives into the seventeenth century, we might note what did not. In the realm of faith, the Reformation began with a destructive dispute about the mysteries of the Christian religion – the Trinity, the Incarnation, Grace and the Sacraments. The dispute soon spread to the interpretation of the Bible and to the canons of rational theology. On the Catholic side lay the tradition of fathers, popes, councils or, in a word, of Authority and centuries of intricate work by scholastic theologians. On the Protestant side the arbiter was individual conscience, imperfectly supported by a more recent and fragile structure of scholastic argument.

Meanwhile the scholastics of both parties were opposed by the mystics, who denied the power of Reason to reveal truth and so united with sceptics of all kinds in attacking the very possibility of rational religious knowledge.[1] In this many-handed battle, a famous old engine of Pyrrhonian scepticism could be unleashed with tremendous effect:

> In order to decide the dispute which has arisen about the criterion, we must first possess an accepted criterion by which we shall be able to judge the dispute; in order to possess an accepted criterion, the dispute about the criterion must first be decided. Sextus Empiricus: *Outlines of Pyrrhonism* (II.4.xx)

The weapon has a recoil as devastating as its thrust, since whatever removes reason from the realm of faith, also removes faith from the realm of reason. Since agreement to compromise between science and religion by allowing each a separate sphere did not become general until the eighteenth or even nineteenth century, pious but scientific Rationalists were to see fideism as a dangerous path to atheism, and one which scholastic argument was unable to bar.

The collapse of the old scientific world was more stark and complete. In the mediaeval story, the universe had comprised a set of crystal spheres with the earth at its centre. Within the sphere of the moon lay the terrestrial realm, composed of compounds of earth, water, air and fire. Matter was corruptible and corrupting and so the sublunary region was the place of decay and evil. The compounds of elements were distinguished into varieties by having material forms superimposed on them, for instance those of rocks, liquids, plants and animals and it was the task of Aristotelian science to define and classify them by essence and attributes and, by applying the categories men-

1. Extreme statements are easily found from both Catholics and Protestants, e.g.

> We know that reason is the Devil's harlot, and can do nothing but slander and harm all that God says and does . . . Therefore keep to revelation and do not try to understand. Luther: *De Servo Arbitrio*

> That we may be altogether of the same mind and in conformity with the Church herself, if she shall have defined anything to be black which to our eyes appears to be white, we ought in the like manner to pronounce it to be black. St Ignatius Loyola: *Rules for Thinking with the Church* 13 (St Ignatius founded the Jesuits in 1534)

tioned earlier, to discover their purpose or function. Beyond the moon came the spheres of the sun, of the planets (seven of them), of the fixed stars and of the *primum mobile*, which God spun in the beginning to set the rest moving. Beyond that lay the empyrean, outside space and time, eternal, infinite and the home of the blessed spirits . This imaginative *tour de force* was upheld by an astronomy of great ingenuity, which survived the first findings of the telescope and indeed retained eminent defenders into the eighteenth century.

Nevertheless the invention of the telescope (and the microscope) brought the old world down. As it was put later, Copernicus, Kepler and Galileo smashed the crystal spheres as if they had been windows. Our earth was presently reduced to a satellite of a sun, which was one of many suns and the cosmos expanded. We can now realise with only a tremor that our tiny solar system of planets, appendages, asteroids, comets and meteors is barely 7,350,000,000 miles across and is embedded in a medium sized galaxy of some 100 billion stars, itself but one in a universe of galaxies, to which our greatest telescopes can find no end. The first hints of this were news in the sixteenth and seventeenth centuries and they reduced the old story of the heavens to nonsense. The microscope also revealed a world which had no business to be there and travellers sailing westward from Spain found another. Equally the blood had no business to circulate nor iron filings to dance to a magnet. These and other scientific discoveries were too much for the old fabric and overthrew the former scientific methods along with their results.

The collapse was only gradual and the attackers should not be thought of as dispassionate, value-neutral, objective modern scientists, blessed with conclusive evidence. Kepler, for example, wanted the sun at the centre of the solar system partly because it symbolically embodied God the Father. The world was still rich in demons, powers, essences, virtues, humours, potencies and cabalistic forces. Nor was the clash with religious authority direct or immediate. For instance the Inquisition had sound scientific objections to Galileo and, in the course of examining him for heresy, offered him the option of declaring his theory a provisional device for predicting celestial motions, in return for being let alone. Scientists were in any case inclined to caution, for fear of being classed as purveyors of the 'forbidden knowledge' of the Christian tradition, along with sorcerers, witches, magicians and others needing redemption by force and fire. But, despite these complications, the old world could not last.

Faith and reason had also combined to produce an account of man's place in the scheme. Alone of all God's creatures, man had been given knowledge of good and evil and the power to choose between them. In the Great Chain of Being, ascending from minerals to planets, to animals, to angels and to the feet of God, he was the highest of the animals and lowest of the spirits; as it were, the first angel and last ape. He was linked by his bodily nature to the elemental, vegetative, animal and corrupt and by his intellectual soul to the life of the heavens. In a geocentric universe, he could see himself as the core of God's design. The thought is well captured by Sir Francis Bacon in *De Sapientia Veterum*:

> Man, if we look to final causes, may be regarded as the centre of the world; inasmuch that if man were taken away from the world, the rest would seem to be all astray, without aim or purpose . . . and leading to nothing. For the whole world works together in the service of man; and there is nothing from which he does not derive use and fruit . . . insomuch that all things seem to be going about man's business and not their own.

Man was special in the animate, integrated cosmos, partly because he was at the very centre of the visible world, partly because, with his unique power of choice, he was the focus of development and aspiration in the spiritual.

This self-portrait could not survive the new science. The Renaissance too, although it offered him a new autonomy and self-respect, supplied a corroding humanism and individualism. The pervasive scepticism of men like Montaigne found an easy target. And, as we shall see, when Nature came to be thought mechanical in the seventeenth century, he was finally caught on an impossible frontier between matter and spirit. Of all the problems exercising the Rationalists, that of human nature owed most to the past and still most commands the interest of the modern mind.

There are other ingredients in the prehistory of Rationalism which no scholar could neglect. But enough has been said to point out the fall of a cosmic edifice. For enquirers forced to doubt all the traditional orthodoxies, it was time to start again.

Yet, although the method of science was new, the old world had not vanished without trace.

The Geometrical Method

Thinkers like Galileo, Bacon, Hobbes and Descartes did not simply scrap the old account and begin afresh with a *tabula rasa*. Despite their own claims to novelty, they inherited presumptions from the past, which shaped intellectual strategies for at least another century. Novelty consists in asking new questions, whereas the seventeenth century more often provided new answers to old questions. It remained central that the universe was God's handiwork and so had a single rationally discernible design. Design meant order and therefore apparent disorder signified only imperfect human understanding. There still had to be a reason for everything, since, as the old tag has it, 'Nature does nothing in vain'. The study of Nature was still the study of the ways of God and so a scientist, whose theories revealed nothing of God, was still tainted with heresy no less than with error. Every event still had the sort of cause which displayed the glory and goodness of God and there was still no principle of distinction between rational theology, science and philosophy. (We owe the now orthodox belief that philosophical questions are *sui generis* to Kant.)

Such presumptions prompt questions which fall oddly on the modern ear. Why, for instance, are there fishes? There must be an answer since God created them and found them good. But why exactly are actual fish better then merely possible fish? And why exactly did God find them good? Well, there are 'principles of natural light', like 'the greater the variety the more complete the creation' or 'the more real a thing is, the greater its degree of perfection'. The deliverances of natural light are guides for judging and ordering claims to knowledge and so are to be counted as scientific. The general premise of Rationalism is that whatever exists is the work of an all-wise, all-powerful and all-good God. If there is anything beyond the scope of reason, God could permit it only to prevent man from understanding everything. But, mysteries of faith aside, God is no deceiver and wishes men to understand His ways.[2] Or, to put the point obli-

2. cf. 'Even if God should abandon himself to chance only in some cases

quely, the limits of what is rationally explicable are the limits of what can be known by Reason and so the limits of science. Science must proceed therefore on the assumption of a rational world; otherwise it cannot proceed at all.

The Rationalists were thus heirs of the past as well as pioneers. They still needed principles of reason, even though they were ready to discard Aristotelian categories. Of all the new ventures, the one which best satisfied the demands of reason at the frontier of knowledge was mathematics. Galileo had already set the tone, evocatively put in a letter to Cesarini:

> Philosophy is written in that great book which ever lies before our eyes – I mean the universe – but we cannot understand it, if we do not first learn the language and grasp the symbols in which it is written. This book is written in the mathematical language, and the symbols are triangles, circles and other geometrical figures, without whose help it is impossible to comprehend a single word of it, without which one wanders in vain through a dark labyrinth.

A mathematical truth, elegantly proved, is so manifest that 'no force in the universe . . . can ever make the alternative possible'; mathematical models have the sublime reasonableness needed to appeal to a supremely rational God; mathematical techniques were charting a novel world. And so a mathematical fever gripped seventeenth-century thinkers.

The mathematical world, it was claimed, contained only objective properties. Objects were deemed to have shape, size, motion and number but to lack colour, texture, smell, taste and sound. This is the sort of view which makes laymen despair of philosophy, even when they turn out to hold it themselves. Are roses not red, lemons acid and klaxons shrill? But the affront to common sense is less than it seems. The receiving sense organs can plausibly be said to contribute something to the process of perception. White looks yellow to the man with jaundice and who knows how it looks to the bee or the frog. Different groups are repelled by different smells and tastes. Tepid water is cool to the fevered brow and hot to the cold foot.

---

and some respects . . . he would be imperfect, as would the object of his choice; he would not deserve to be wholly trusted; he would act without reason in those cases and the government of the universe would be like certain games, half a matter of chance, half of reason.' Leibniz: *Theodicy*

A host of well-worn examples can be used to suggest a subjective element in perception.

One stock account of the mechanism of perception has it that our information about the world is all presented to us in code in the brain. For example, it is as if we saw the world only on television, in that our data of sight are always on our retinas and never at a distance from our eyes. In other words, objects around us cause us to have the sense-experiences we do and the sense-experiences are not identical with the objects. The effects of being presented with objects depend partly on the state of our sense-organs. Having thus distinguished cause and effect, we can ask what exactly the percipient contributes in the way of intermediate causes. How different is the world when these influences are allowed for? Galileo's answer is still quite widely accepted:

> To excite tastes, odours and sounds, I believe nothing is required in external bodies except shapes, numbers and slow or rapid movements. I think that if ears, tongues and noses were removed, shapes and numbers would remain but not odours or tastes or sounds.

We can thus try to contrast the world as it is independently of sense perception with the world as we experience it. The contrast can be put in various ways (which do not necessarily come to the same thing). If experience is thought of as subjective, it contrasts with the objective world which caused it. If experience is inner awareness of what is outside, then the internal world contrasts with the external. These contrasts made, we soon find ourselves contrasting the world as it appears to us with the world as it really is, appearance with reality. In what sense is the external world objective or real? Well, it is the world of science and things in it can be weighed and measured. By contrast, our internal data are qualitative – there is no deciding how tall an imaginary tower seen in a dream really is. The real world is quantitative; whatever is only qualitative belongs to the world of appearances. And that leads us to say that objects have shape, size, motion and number independently of perception but lack colour, texture, smell, taste and sound.

The snag of distinguishing appearance from reality is that everything we experience then presumably belongs to the world of appearance. If all sense-perception is at the receiving end of a transmission, how do we know what is at the transmitting end? If we see only the television screen, how do we know that there is anything at all in the studio? The question is posed in Descartes' *Meditations* – perhaps a malignant demon is constantly causing us to have experiences which correspond to nothing outside – and has never lost its fascination. Our awareness is of objects in our own consciousness, or, to use the seventeenth-century term, of 'ideas'. Which of our 'ideas' are true and how do we know?

Those reared on the Empiricist tradition will have traced one answer from Locke's primary and secondary qualities, to Berkeley's '*esse est percipi*', to Hume's fictions of identity, to Mill's 'permanent possibilities of sensation' to the Logical Positivist's sense-data and Verification Theory of meaning. The Rationalist tradition is very different. In it, sense-perception is not our only access to the external world. (Indeed, in echo of Plato, it may not be an access at all.) There is also Intellectual Perception, which yields to our understanding truths about how the world must be. By Intellectual Perception we grasp substance and essence, detect the laws of nature and discover why things must happen as they do. Sense-perception informs us about appearance; Intellectual Perception about reality.

But what is Intellectual Perception and how does it answer the problem about how we know what is in the studio? The first part of the question is best left to Descartes' *Meditations*. The second turns on a feature of mathematical truths which hypnotised seventeenth-century philosophers. Mathematical truths are necessarily true. As Leibniz put it:

> There are also two kinds of truth, those of reasoning and those of fact. Truths of reasoning are necessary and their opposite impossible, and those of fact are contingent and their opposite is possible. *Monadology* § 33

For instance, when I claim to observe a square tower on the horizon or to know by induction that all white cats are deaf, I cannot guarantee that I am right. The tower may actually be round and my acquaintance with cats too limited. Indeed I cannot even guarantee that I am not dreaming or systematically fooled by a demon. But I can guarantee that Euclidean 3″, 4″, 5″ triangles are right-angled, in the sense that the proof of a theorem rules out all possibility of error. The findings of observation and induction are only provisional and, at best, probable. Those of the mathematician's understanding are demon-proof.

At this point, however, we must tread warily, because Descartes, the arch-methodologist, is somewhat at odds with the rest. Moreover Descartes' exact view is still disputed among scholars. The strategy of Rationalism, as it looks to a distant modern eye, is the strategy of axioms and theorems, typified by Euclidean Geometry. Spinoza's *Ethics* or Hobbes' *Leviathan* spring to mind and Hobbes put it in a nutshell when he remarked:

> For though in all places of the world, men should lay the foundation of their houses on the sand, it could not thence be inferred that so it ought to be. The skill of making and maintaining commonwealths consisteth in certain rules, as doth arithmetic and geometry: not, as tennis-play, on practice only: which rules, neither poor men have the leisure, nor men that have had the leisure, have hitherto had the curiosity, or the method to find out. *Leviathan* XX

Use of the axiomatic method, however, raises two immediate questions, one about the status of the axioms, the other about the role of logic in securing the theorems. The Rationalists all saw that proof of a theorem did not make the theorem true. A theorem is true because what it states is true. It is not true because it can be proved but, rather, it can be proved because it is true. So no theorem is true because it follows from an axiom. Equally the grounds of truth of axioms have nothing to do with the fact that theorems follow. Consequently the axioms must be known true by some sort of intuition (perhaps aided by attempts to state real definitions) and the role of logic is to help the enquirer to notice other truths. This is more or less common ground to the other Rationalists. But Descartes made more of the point. Early in the *Meditations* he let himself call logic and mathematics into question and did not renew his faith in them until he was certain of the existence of God. Also he maintained in his letters (included in the selections given later) that God created the necessary truths no less than anything in the world. Furthermore he regarded the axiomatic method as no very useful guide even for discovering truths. There is no space here to assess the significance of this for understanding either Descartes or his relation to the others but the reader may wish to be aware that the ground is tricky.

Descartes is indeed a Rationalist, however, and he speaks for all when he says, 'In our search for the direct road to truth, we should not occupy ourselves with any object about which we are unable to have a certitude equal to that of arithmetical and geometrical demonstration.' In general the mathematicians' understanding illustrates the kind of epistemic certainty required by Rationalists and necessary truths or 'eternal verities' are proof against even hyperbolic doubt.

Yet that hardly seems to answer the question. It is widely believed today (at any rate by non-philosophers) that necessary truths have to do with the meanings of terms and not with facts; that they are tautologies and lack all factual content. If this is right, the guarantee that being necessary stamps on mathematical truths is an empty one. But, right or not, it is not at all the Rationalists' view. The Rationalists held that there are necessary facts; that, in at least some ways, the world could not possibly be otherwise than it is. For example, when Hobbes assures us that men are essentially material creatures driven by a selfish lust for power, he intends to announce a truth as certain as that all bachelors are unmarried and as informative as that sugar is soluble in water. The Rationalists looked to necessary truths to provide an indisputable account and explanation of the workings of the universe.

Of all the branches of mathematics, geometry was held to be most basic and instructive. Geometry is the study of spatial relations or, more boldly, of the properties of space. Any pair of physical objects must share one common characteristic, that of occupying space. Study of the properties of space is therefore study of the essence of all physical objects. Geometry, Descartes argued, was the key to physics and therefore to all knowledge of the physical world. (This unconvincing equation between matter and space partly accounts for the common refusal to admit that there can be a vacuum. If there is no matter between two objects, then there is no space between them, and, if there is no space, then they are touching.) The true method of science is the 'geometrical method'. Intellectual Perception is the geometer's understanding. The world of nature is an embodiment of geometrical principles. The God who created it is, in the Freemasons' phrase, the Grand Geometer.

For all its debt to the past, rationalism produced a novel scientific method, and got striking results without appeal to traditional authority or universal consent. The new authority was reason and the consent that of rational men. The mathematical language is free of idiom and science was ready to adopt its modern character. Nevertheless it would be misleading to say that Rationalism substituted 'how?' questions for 'why?' questions or science for metaphysics. The world remained God's handiwork and its furniture was still there for a reason. Even Spinoza, who urged the removal of final causes from physics, saw the history of the universe in moral terms and Leibniz is explicit about the utility of final causes in science (*Discourse on Metaphysics* 19). The seventeenth century at most exchanged a metaphysics based on Aristotelian categories for a metaphysics based on mathematics. The attraction of mathematics was that it satisfied the scientist's faith as well as his reason.[3] The idea that the universe is a collection of contingencies, accessible only to observation and induction, is an eighteenth-century novelty.

If necessary truths describe necessary facts, then the history of a world describable by use of necessary truths is pre-determined. What happens by mathematical principles, it was held, is bound to happen. To know that something is so, it is not enough merely to believe truly that it is. It is to understand why it must be. Any state of the physical world can continue in only one way.

3. The geometrical spirit is well caught by the twentieth-century rationalist A. N. Whitehead:

> Faith in reason is the trust that the ultimate natures of things lie together in a harmony which excludes mere arbitrariness. It is the faith that at the base of things we shall not find mere arbitrary mystery. The faith in the order of nature which has made possible the growth of science is a particular example of a deeper faith. This faith cannot be justified by any inductive generalisation. It springs from direct inspection of the nature of things as disclosed in our immediate present experience. There is no parting from your own shadow. To experience this faith is to know that in being ourselves we are more than ourselves: to know that our experience, dim and fragmentary as it is, yet sounds the ultimate depths of reality: to know that detached details merely in order to be themselves demand that they should find themselves in a system of things: to know that this system includes the harmony of logical rationality, and the harmony of aesthetic achievement: to know that, while the harmony or logic lies upon the universe as an iron necessity, the aesthetic harmony stands before it as a living ideal moulding the general flux in its broken progress towards finer subtler issues. *Science and the Modern World* ch. 1.

In more formal terms, any statement describing a state of the world is deducible from any statement describing an earlier state, with the help of statements of the laws of nature. For instance, given Newton's laws of motion, the setting of a billiard table and the angle and momentum of one ball, the behaviour of all other balls struck is in principle exactly predictable. As in school mechanics textbooks, the answer is fully calculable; and the explanation of why the answer is right is contained in the setting of the problem and elicited by the calculation. In the recurrent seventeenth-century image, the world is a watch.

Hence Descartes (typically for Rationalism in general, even if perhaps expressive of only some of his own work) could declare:

> The whole of philosophy is like a tree, whose roots are metaphysics, whose trunk is physics, and whose branches are all the other sciences, which can be reduced to three principal ones, namely medicine, mechanics and morals. *The Principles of Philosophy* (Preface)

An axiomatic method is ideally apt for tracing the roots, trunk and branches. Descartes' claims are ambitious:

> These long chains of perfectly simple and easy reasonings by means of which geometers are accustomed to carry out their most difficult demonstrations had led me to fancy that everything that can fall under human knowledge forms a similar sequence, and that so long as we avoid accepting as true what is not so, and always preserve the right order for deduction of one thing from another, there can be nothing too remote to be reached in the end, or too well hidden to be discovered. *Discourse of Method* (Part II)

De Fontenelle in his charming work for enquiring ladies, is more modest:

> Madam, *said I*, since we are in the humour of mixing amorous follies with our most serious Discourses, I must tell you that in Love and the Mathematics People reason alike. Allow never so little to a Lover, yet presently you must grant him more, nay more and more, which will at last go a great way. In like manner, grant but a Mathematician one little Principle, he immediately draws a consequence from it, to which you must necessarily assent; and from this consequence another, till he

> leads you so far (whether you will or no) that you have much ado to believe him. *A Plurality of Worlds* (Fifth Evening)

but ambition was the order of the day and men were now equipped to start 'a-guessing the riddle of the universe'.

Riddles of the Rational Universe: God, Matter and Mind

We have now outlined the strategy for rescuing God's universe from doubt and dispute and sketched the new picture which was to emerge. The method and the metaphysics seem well matched. A deductive system based on clear and distinct ideas was to describe a determined world where everything happened for a reason, which can be expressed as a set of logical connections between states of the world in the model. It was to be a world without mysteries, contingencies, accidents or Uncertainty Principles, where cause precedes effect in a continuous chain whose first link is in the hand of God. But there turned out to be snags in the scheme of epic proportions. Let us briefly see what some of them were.

Descartes' cosmos has three 'substances' or general orders of being. They are God, Matter and Mind. God is the Grand Geometer; Matter is the stuff or essence of everything in the world of physical nature; Mind is the realm of all immaterial creatures, or, for purposes of this Introduction, men conceived of as rational souls. There turned out not to be room in the cosmos for all three.

First, God. If the universe is to be accessible to Reason and acceptable to Faith, it must be both wholly rational and wholly dependent on God. God created it from nothing freely, rationally and for the best. Very well – what was the scope of His choice? Is the world we live in the only possible one, the best possible one, or merely one among those possible? If it is the only possible world, can God be truly said to have chosen it? If it is not the only possible world, how is Reason to discover which one has been chosen?

Descartes insisted that God had an open choice. Indeed, as just noted, he implied in the *Meditations* and stated in letters that the principles of mathematics and logic depend on God no less than the law of gravity or the existence of mice and men. So the original choice presumably included worlds we would call contradictory. Yet, since the geometrical method depends on being able to take some principles of proof for granted, the effect of divine anomie would be to make all ultimate premisses contingent on an act of will and so to deprive Reason of its guarantee of truth. Descartes himself may have accepted this, relying on the fact that 'God is no deceiver' to ensure that what we humans take to be impossible (because contradictory) was also rejected at the creation. But the other Rationalists firmly reasserted the old doctrine that 'Whatever implies contradiction does not come within the scope of the divine essence because it cannot have the aspect of possibility' (Aquinas: *Summa* Ia 253). If the geometrical method is to do any epistemological work, God's choice is restricted at least to the possible worlds.[4]

In that case, which was in fact chosen? The answer needs to be a 'mathematical' formula which generates the known history of our world expressed in the language of physics from a unique statement of initial conditions. But even that would not be enough. There is always more than one formula which generates a given series of data and we shall need to know why God chose, in order to know which formula to rely on, when different formulae suggest different future continuations. Leibniz, treading the delicate edge between fatalism and unreason, proposed that 'God has chosen that world which is most perfect, that is to say, which is at the same time simplest in its laws and richest in its phenomena' (*Discourse on Metaphysics* sec.6). In other words God is under a moral necessity to create the best possible world, which, in scientific terms, means maximum effect at minimum cost. Some such moral necessity (or synthetic *a priori* principle) is a prerequisite for any inductive reasoning or hypothetico-deductive method of science.

4. It is notable that Descartes sometimes echoed Luther and St Ignatius. For instance:

> Above all we should impress on our memory as an infallible rule that what God has revealed to us is incomparably more certain than anything else and that we ought to submit to the Divine authority rather than to our judgement even though the light of reason may seem to us to suggest, with the utmost clearness and distinctness, something opposite. *Principles of Philosophy* I.76

This sort of remark can be construed as an orthodox piety but it is also suggestive when comparing Descartes with the other Rationalists.

But is God not then bound to create the best possible world? Taking God's rational goodness into account, the best possible seems to be the only possible. Spinoza was more ruthless than Descartes or Leibniz and argued firmly that the very notion of God's choosing or creating anything was anthropomorphic and absurd. God (or Nature) is simply the name of whatever has to be. This can be argued either frontally, as Spinoza does in the *Ethics*, or obliquely, on the grounds that the geometrical method gives a single solution, only if all statements can be proved or disproved. Hence if anything is freely chosen, there is no way of knowing what choice has been made. Some of Leibniz' finest philosophy is an attempt to evade this conclusion without either slipping into heresy or destroying the pretensions of Rationalism.

Having created the world, is God to play a further part in its history? Can His creation be both wholly rational and wholly dependent on Him? The perfect watch-maker presumably creates a perfect watch. A perfect watch needs no adjusting and no repairs. So either God intervenes in the running of His machine or He does not. If He does, then He lacked the wisdom or the power or the will to create the best possible machine. If He does not, then the machine is perfectly able to run without Him, and He is there only to supply the final cause why it runs at all. God is apparently either an eternal busybody or, having once declared the universe open, redundant.

The dilemma, at least when posed less crudely, has been crucial to relations between religion and science. Descartes took God to be not only the creator of the world but also the reason for its continued existence from moment to moment. This follows the Christian tradition, in which God's primary concern, so to speak, is with the internal life of the Trinity. But the question of God's role in history came alive with the advent of a mechanical and apparently self-contained system of Nature. God's office is either an arduous one or it is not. If it is not, God is still redundant. If it is, then how do we know that the machinery will continue to run on rational principles? Spinoza traced the difficulty to the notion that God was separate from the world and chose whether to intervene in it. He and Leibniz both realised that science could not cope with miracles.[5] Spinoza offered an immanent God in place of a transcendent one, thus

5. A complete anticipation of Hume's famous argument about miracles (*Enquiries* X), which so upset anglican theologians in the nineteenth century.

removing all possibility of conflict between science and religion. Leibniz argued that the dilemma was bogus, since a perfect governor is indeed idle, and thus unwittingly gave the signal for removing God wholly from science.[6] Religious contemporaries took Spinoza for an atheist but applauded Leibniz, who has since turned out much more of a threat to religion's claims to relevance in science and life.

Secondly, the seventeenth-century concept of Matter was a troublesome one. The relation of Cartesian geometry to Newtonian mechanics and the gradual transformation of Matter into Energy belong to the history of science and are too technical to discuss here. But the question of how we know what the world really contains should perhaps be pursued a little further. We have already seen how objects are shorn of their non-mathematical properties, to leave them endowed only with shape, size, motion and number. We have seen also that geometry, the key to all science, is the study of spatial properties. What, then, is the relation of one object to another and of objects to properties?

The seventeenth-century answer is in terms of 'substance', 'essence', 'attribute' and 'mode'. The key notion is that of 'substance', meaning roughly what we would now call a self-contained system. It was variously used but Spinoza captured the core of it, when he defined it as 'that which is in itself, and is conceived through itself: in other words that of which a conception can be formed independently of any other conception'. (*Ethics* I.def.3). Implicit, or at least related, theses are that all properties of a substance (or self-contained system) can be understood and all changes explained without reference beyond the substance (system); that a substance is what persists through change in its properties; that it can exist alone in the universe, whereas its parts cannot; that it cannot be destroyed (since such a change would be inexplicable from within); that it is the reference of a logical subject, whereas whatever is the reference of a predicate is no more than a property; that different substances must differ in their properties (cannot differ *solo numero*). These criteria may not be wholly consistent and, at least to the twentieth-century eye, involve ambiguities. For instance the single term 'substance' is used by Descartes to

6. He states his case most clearly in correspondence with Clarke, which can usefully be read in conjunction with the *Monadology* and the *Theodicy* (see Alexander (ed): *The Leibniz–Clarke Correspondence*).

refer to the uncaused cause, to the primary stuff of everything physical and (sometimes) to a special sort of concrete particular. Moreover it is very much Rationalist strategy to identify logical connections between truths with causal connections between states, giving the notions of dependence and independence an apparent ambiguity. But, in outline, it is clear that the Rationalists regarded particular things not as substances but as sub-systems or 'modes' within a larger system. Since all particular things can influence each other, all belong to the same system. This led Descartes to say that the natural world formed a single substance, composed of 'prime matter', whose essence is to occupy space. Matter is the universal stuff of which everything physical is made. A complete geometrical tree of knowledge would be a complete account of it and we know its properties by mathematical understanding or intellectual intuition.

Such a substance is a Frankenstein's monster. Taken seriously as defined, it crowds both God and free will out of the universe. If we need never look outside the system to explain changes within it, then neither God nor man can ever intervene in its workings. Consequently Descartes held that matter was not fully a substance, since it depended causally-cum-logically on God, thus raising the problems already discussed. He also tried to budget for human interventions by allowing men to affect the direction but not the quantity of matter (or motion of matter); but this does not meet the point that *all* changes in a self-contained system must be explicable from within. Spinoza argued that the universe could contain only one complete substance, which he called 'God or Nature'. Leibniz, reasoning very like Spinoza, declared that there were infinitely many substances, each with a degree of autonomous activity and independent of all the rest, which he called 'monads'. (Spinoza and Leibniz were also objecting to Descartes' distinction between mental and physical, which will be discussed presently.)

The notion that matter is a substance or an attribute of a substance raises several sorts of question. How, for instance, are we to conceive of time or change, seeing that it is eternally true of every property and mode that it is contained in the complete account of the substance? How are we to conceive of relations between substances or is Spinoza right to deem a plurality of substances inconceivable? Do terms like 'logical subject' from philosophical logic allow us to talk about substances or is a substance an indescribable 'we know not what'? Can we dispense with substances altogether and treat the natural order as consisting of bundles of properties? Can we admit more than one kind of explanation of natural events or must human action fall equally under the laws of matter? Is there a basic stuff of which everything material is composed? Are there general categories for classifying all that exists and how much sense does it make to distinguish 'essence' and 'accident'? Even allowing for ambiguities which stem from taking matter now as a substance now as an attribute, many of these questions are perennial. But the Rationalists' conceptions of nature gave them a new twist and created problems about physics and perception, matter and activity, categories and explanation which plague us still.

Thirdly, Mind could not be fitted into the cosmos. Descartes reduced the subject to a heroic muddle, which we have not yet escaped. His theory seems simple at first. The bodies of men and of animals are material bodies and so part of the unified system of matter and subject to its inexorable laws. Animals, indeed, are machines, in that they are fully describable in physical terms and cannot behave otherwise than they do. They have no rational souls. As there is no room for rational souls in the busy world of nature, whatever has one inhabits another world where the laws of mathematics do not hold sway. Not everything is essentially physical and spatial; we are creatures, whose essence is to think.

Each man is an epistemological island. Each is a consciousness dependent only on God, and so a substance. Each consciousness is a self-contained world furnished with 'ideas' or 'thoughts' (whatever it is directly aware of). Having no position in the physical world, each rational soul is immortal and free. Each man's perception of his own existence is the demon-proof foundation of all his rational knowledge and the truth that he is a thinking thing (*res cogitans*) is both accessible to reason and acceptable to faith.

This plea for an immaterial self gives the demon huge scope. In return for being king in his own castle, Descartes cedes everything outside to the demon and then has to wrest it painfully back. The moat is the dividing line between the world of inner awareness and the physical world. Within the moat, each man knows what his own 'ideas' or 'thoughts' are and the demon cannot deceive him about these objects of awareness. But the inner world includes beliefs about the other, or, in our earlier metaphor, television pictures purporting to represent the outer world. The demon's influence reaches from studio to screen. So Descartes knows what appears on his screen, in the sense that his description of the picture is privileged. But only the demon knows in the first instance whether the picture is an accurate one or whether it has been produced by fiddling with the input signals. The problem of perception becomes one of knowing when output corresponds to ultimate input. As suggested earlier, if we do not guarantee some correspondence by invoking the necessities of mathematics and separating intellectual from sense perception, then we must either, with Hobbes and Berkeley, dispense with one world altogether, or query the posing of the problem.

Spinoza and Leibniz take the latter line. Before sketching their strategy, let us glance at the closely-related mind–body problem. The popular contemporary version of Descartes' account of man is memorably caught by Sir Thomas Browne:

> Thus is man that great and true Amphibium whose nature is disposed to live, not only like other creatures in divers elements, but in divided and distinguished worlds.

A great and true Amphibium satisfies the claims of Faith and fills the right gap in the Great Chain of Being. But Descartes' problems are not so easily dismissed. It is not strictly true that Cartesian man inhabits divided and distinguished worlds, since he has his headquarters in only one of them and his headquarters are the ground of his identity. He is, rather, a sort of Metaphysical Motorist, who stands to his body as a driver to his car. The driver makes the decisions and the car has the engine. The car responds to the driver's will; the driver is restricted by the make and condition of the car and by the state of the traffic. The driver is who he is independently of the car, and, to sermonise a little, when that one last nightfall comes, he parks the car in its earthly garage and departs to his celestial home with ego undamaged.

Descartes, although explicit about the distinctness of mind and body, was also wont to declare that there is a more intimate connection than this:

> Nature also teaches me by these sensations of pain, hunger, thirst etc that I am not merely lodged in my body as a pilot

> in a vessel but that I am very closely united to it, and so to speak intermingled with it that I seem to compose with it one whole. *VIth Meditation*

Elsewhere he speaks of a 'substantial union' of mind and body, presumably implying that a person is more than a temporarily embodied thinking thing. But he cannot consistently claim so much. The essence of matter is to occupy space, that of mind to think and Descartes insists that nothing material thinks. A thing which was both essentially material and thinking would have a contradictory essence. Since much in the *Meditations* depends on an inference from 'I am a thinking thing' to 'I am not a material thing', and since matter is held to be a substance or self-contained system, a 'substantial union' would be an epistemological disaster.

The Metaphysical Motorist scarcely fares better, however. Matter being a self-contained system, physical events are fully explicable by other physical events and the laws of matter. The motorist cannot intervene. If he is the explanation of any behaviour of his car, then he belongs to the physical system.[7] If he could intervene freely, the world of nature would no longer be an ironly determined system whose whole past and future history is in principle deducible at any moment and the whole Rationalist method of science would collapse.

Descartes did try asserting that the motorist had a sort of steering wheel, sited in the pineal gland, which lets him affect the direction of motion in the world without affecting its quantity. But that suspicious hypothesis would, if successful, again destroy the method of science. At best the motorist has an illusion of free choice and of control over his car, if he happens to will what is in any case just about to occur from its own physical causes. In the same way a sorcerer's apprentice might be lucky enough to will the sun to be darkened just before an eclipse. (Indeed, whereas an isolated case might count as a specific miracle, a regular coincidence of will with physical effect perhaps comes nearer to a proof that God is busy. This ingenious notion, under the name of Occasionalism, is Malebranche's contribution to philosophy.)

7. Materialism was a very scandalous doctrine at the time. Hobbes was roundly denounced for espousing it. So too was Spinoza, although it is plain enough from the *Ethics* that he was not a materialist.

The difficulty of connecting separate self-contained systems is thus both epistemological and ontological. Epistemologically, the question is how Descartes knows even that he has a body, seeing that his world of ideas is apparently complete whether he has one or not? Ontologically, how is any interaction even possible?

Spinoza and Leibniz both accepted that there was no connecting substance. Accordingly both avoided having to try. For Spinoza, the universe forms a single system, describable in two ways. Everything can be seen either as a link in a complete chain of causes and effects or as a stage in a complete scheme of inferences, rather as every state of a flawless computer can be seen either as a caused physical state of its circuits or as a step in the working of its programme. Particular consciousnesses stand to mind in general as particular bodies stand to matter; and mind is related to matter as programme to circuits. There is no question of interaction but it can be made to seem that interaction occurs, if one state of a person is described in mental terms and the next in physical. The human mind is simply from one point of view what the human body is from another.

Leibniz is less chillingly unconcerned with the demands of orthodox religion and everyday belief. He made two attempts to budget for free choice without destroying the rationalist method of science. The more Cartesian is known as psycho-physical parallelism, or, more popularly, as the two-clock theory. Like Malebranche, he asserted that the connection of mind and body was not like that of a signalman's lever but that of a coincidence. But, instead of making God attend to acts of will as they arose, he included a systematic programme of coincidences in the original creation of the world and its laws. It was as if God had created two synchronised clocks, giving the uninformed the impression that the movements of one were causing the behaviour of the other. Leibniz was vastly proud of this flight of celestial daring and referred to it as his doctrine of Pre-established Harmony. Preposterous as it seems at first, it in effect makes the analysis of the notion of 'cause', for which Hume has been so often applauded.

The other attempt depends on denying the distinction of mental and physical. Monads, the infinitely small and numerous substances which compose the universe, vary in their degree of activity. The more active and perceptive they are, the less like

Cartesian physical objects they are. The more passive and purely receptive they are, the less like Cartesian rational souls they are. But none is either wholly active (except perhaps God, if He counts as a monad) or wholly passive. (The explanation of this masterly but obscure thesis is best left to Leibniz himself in the *Discourse* and *Monadology*.)

The Rationalists found themselves trying to assemble a sort of Japanese puzzle. They thought they had the bits and knew the rules of construction. But try as they might, there were always bits left over. If a rational God was made to create a perfect machine, neither God nor man could intervene in it. If the machine responded to acts of will, then it could not be known *a priori* what it would do. If human beings were substances, inhabiting a complete world of ideas and in communion with God, the world of nature was superfluous and knowledge of it impossible. If there were more than one substance there was no interaction and, if only one, no choice. The rational universe never yielded wholly to reason, and the demons of mystery, chance, contingency and doubt were never fully expelled.

This hasty sketch has done the subtleties of rationalism scant justice. Questions about the nature of space, time, logic, truth, change, existence, physics, emotions and ethics have not been discussed and those of God, matter and mind have been debated without detail. But the Rationalists are well able to speak for themselves and this introduction is hoped only to sharpen the gaze of the distant twentieth-century reader. In case the distance seems too great and Rationalism too outrageous, let us finally ask what we still owe to the seventeenth century.

The Significance of Rationalism

The influence of Descartes and the geometrical method needs no argument. His hand is visible in the development of empiricism from Hume to the Vienna Circle, no less than in the history of Kantian and Absolute Idealism. But recent work in Britain and America has usually been hostile. The most striking examples are perhaps Ryle's exorcism of the Ghost in the Machine and J. L. Austin's assault on the very idea that knowledge needs foundations; but scepticism about Cartesian egos, about the method of doubt, about rationalism (and indeed all theories of knowledge) has been almost universal. In the last decade philosophic ambitions have revived and metaphysics is regaining some ground. Descartes is being treated with more sympathy and Leibniz and Spinoza are commanding more attention. But at most this means that Rationalism is seen with pity rather than scorn. Despite Chomsky and Lévi-Strauss, Anglo-Saxon philosophy of science remains unrepentantly empiricist and in epistemology traditional methods remain out of favour.

Yet the case for insisting on foundations of knowledge remains strong. Suppose I list all the propositions which I believe I know to be true and then set myself to overhaul my list, in order to expunge those which, on reflection, I cannot warrantably regard as known truths. Some of the entries require inference. For example knowledge that there were once dodos on Mauritius is inferential. An inferred entry is conditional, in the sense that it is warranted, only if some other entry is warranted. So suppose I put a star against all conditional entries on the list. Now, what justifies my retaining a starred entry? Well, the premisses I inferred it from must also be on the list and some of them must be unstarred. For, however sound the inference, its conclusion is not a known truth, unless its premisses are known truths. And, suppose the list contains a subset of entries complete in itself, in the sense that all are starred and all depend only on each other. (A subset asserting the effectiveness of witchcraft, oracles and magic might be an example.) It would then follow that I knew the truth of none of these entries. For, if I know the truth of *P*, only if I know the truth of *Q* and if, moreover, my warrant for claiming to know *Q* is *P* itself (or else *R*, whose warrant is *P*), then I know the truth of neither *P* nor *Q*. The diameter of the circle is irrevelant and if my whole list forms such a complete subset of itself, then (without relying on a coherence theory of truth) I know nothing at all. Hence there must be some unstarred entries. There must be entries whose truth I know without proof or evidence and these are my foundations of knowledge.

The argument is a general one and gives no licence to insist that sense-data, for instance, and the deliverances of sense-perception are the only possible foundations. It applies equally to knowledge of logical, mathematical or other *a priori* truths. The philosopher's task is to produce a list with genuine unstarred entries; the demon's to show that the unstarred should have been starred or at least that most of the starred should not have been included. The empiricist demon has never shown that there are no unstarred *a priori* truths.

Talk of empiricist demons raises a point about the relation of epistemology to metaphysics which also supports the Rationalists. Pyrrhonian sceptics are exceedingly rare but every thinker is sceptical about his rivals and the job of a theory of knowledge is to make an honest woman of metaphysics. Metaphysics then becomes ontology. Epistemology and ontology are related as evidence to verdict, or tactics to strategy. The success of the method depends on the merit of its results. So there are two ways of going about it. Either the ontology is specified in advance and the theory of knowledge required to justify it. Or criteria of knowledge are set up and we agree to settle for whatever ontology they allow. In practice it is usual to specify something of both method and results; and in practice the two then turn out to conflict. This fate befell the Rationalists, but it has also befallen all other thinkers since.

If there is play in the rules of evidence and the criteria of knowledge, how can the demon be kept at bay? Does he not always have other criteria of knowledge, just as warranted but much more damaging? The Rationalist answer has claims to being the only one. It is in effect, that even the demon needs an absolute relation between a given criterion and its results. No less than the epistemologist, he cannot allow any verdict whatever to be proper from any evidence whatever. These absolute relations can be stated as propositions in 'if . . . then' form, about which there can be no further argument. But, since the foundations of knowledge argument applies equally to *a priori* truths, this means admitting *a priori* self-evidence or, in other words, scope for intellectual perception.

It will hardly be disputed that particular stretches of Rationalist argument are of perennial value. To pick almost at random, Descartes' discussions of sense-perception, Spinoza's account of freedom and of scientific knowledge, Hobbes' materialism and Leibniz' distinction of necessary and contingent are still storm-centres. Even their less plausible doctrines are essential to understanding how modern philosophical problems have developed and a student who has not read widely in seventeenth-century thought remains philosophically illiterate. But the modern reader may be inclined to object that the Rationalists are 'God-intoxicated' and require too great a suspension of secular disbelief to be taken altogether seriously. Several replies spring to mind. First, God enters the argument at points which are still crucial even for conceptual analysis and certainly for epistemology. For instance, Descartes reasons, in effect, that there is no escaping solipsism without some *a priori* guarantee that news does not come from nowhere; Leibniz insists that philosophy or grand theory is futile without a 'necessary being' to act as 'a sufficient reason with which we could stop'. Even after changing the criterion of empirical knowledge, empiricists are still left with similar conceptual gaps and have failed to bridge them by appealing to notions like 'the most economical theory', 'inference to the best explanation' or 'the grammar of our talk'. Leibniz' Pre-established Harmony may be a bit much to swallow – but can the analysis of Cause as constant conjunction do without it? Secondly, if God looms large, it is not because of the paragraphs explicitly devoted to the topic but because the arguments advance so insidiously from their premisses that the secular reader sees too late where they are tending. Ours is almost the first age to suppose that belief in God need not make any difference to philosophy or science and it does us no harm to wonder whether the deist compromise is more convenient than defensible. Thirdly, God answers a particular sort of ontological question about what there is beyond the veil of sense-perception. If that sort of question is not to be asked or cannot be answered, the onus is on the objector to show why.

But the Rationalists' final claim on our attention is their systematic theorising. When Leibniz retorted that the mind was not a *tabula rasa*, since it comprised 'being, substance, unity, identity, cause, perception, reason and many other notions which the senses cannot give', he was assigning to thought a positive role in the interpretation of experience. Scientifically, the Rationalist suggestion was that facts are to be explained by bringing them under *a priori* laws and Leibniz was probably willing to allow that facts so explained could nevertheless remain contingent. It is not fanciful to see in Rationalist epistemology and philosophy of science a reasoned rejection of some recent versions of empiricism and of some uses of the analytic-synthetic distinction. The relationship between 'empirical' laws and mathematics is much in dispute at present and the Rationalists made a persuasive case for their views. There are still grounds for holding that laws of nature are instances of necessary connections between descriptions of states of the world. Although Kant made some of the points more clearly, earlier thinkers differed from Kant in ways which can still lay claim to truth.

'Reason is the pace; increase of science the way; and the benefit of mankind the end', Hobbes remarks in *Leviathan* (ch.5). We are less ambitious now and have lost the will to systematise. We no longer expect nature to yield all her secrets at once, and especially not to a Geometrical method. But are we nearer to guessing the riddles of existence and identity, reason and experience, mind and body or appearance and reality? Have we really shown that the riddles do not exist? Those, who, like Milton, 'cannot praise a fugitive and cloistered virtue', will relish an encounter with the subtle, flamboyant and systematic intellects of the seventeenth century. Even those, who practise a modern philosophical humility, will find much sharp and vivid argument. There are still problems of epistemology, science, religion and metaphysics and even the most modern cloister is haunted by seventeenth-century ghosts.

EDITOR'S NOTE

The theme of this anthology is 'The Geometrical Method and its Results'. Since snippets seem to me tendentious and, unless the reader shares the editor's prejudices, useless, I have usually chosen whole works and, for the sake of the general reader, famous ones. This has meant omitting much that is too little available, like Leibniz' *New Essays* or Malebranche's *Search After Truth.* The decisions to confine Hobbes to a chapter of *De Corpore* and to ignore the later books of Spinoza's (very long) *Ethics* were reluctant and I was tempted to include some of the Rationalism prominent (indeed arguably predominant) in Locke. Moreover Galileo, Bacon, Newton and Pascal are thinkers with enough of the Geometrical spirit (despite their own reservations) to warrant more than a dismissive mention, and I must also apologise to a host of other theological, scientific and literary figures with philosophical leanings for their exclusion. But the main line of Rationalism is complex enough for one anthology and considerations of general usefulness have prevailed.

The Rationalists all had the gift of expression and the difficulties they raise are of thought rather than words. Besides they have been well translated and I have been happy to rely on standard editions.

My warm thanks are due to Dr P. M. Hacker of St John's College, Oxford and to Dr A. J. P. Kenny of Balliol College for skimming off errors in a previous draft of the introduction and for their useful comments. Even after their help, any attempt to present the Rationalists in a few pages is bound to be tendentious and I am responsible for the remaining distortions.

Prologue: The New Philosophy

Bernard de Fontenelle, 1657–1757

To set the scene, there follows an extract from *The Plurality of Worlds* by Bernard de Fontenelle (1657–1757), written to edify young ladies with those parts of contemporary astronomy and philosophy which were most 'Uniform, Probable and Diverting'. As the author explains, 'In these Discourses, I have introduced a Woman, to be instructed in things of which she never heard; and I have made use of this Fiction, to render the Book the more acceptable, and to give encouragement to Ladies, by the Example of one of their own Sex, who without any supernatural parts, or tincture of Learning, understands what is said to her; . . . I shall desire no more of the fair Ladies, than that they will read this System of Philosophy, with the same application that they do a Romance or a Novel.'[1]

From *The Plurality of Worlds*, 1686

FIRST EVENING

All Philosophy, said I, Madam, is founded upon two things, either that we are too short sighted, or that we are too curious; for if our eyes were better than they are, we should soon see whether the Stars were worlds or not; and if on the other side we were less curious, we should not care whether the Stars are Worlds or not, which I think is much to the same purpose. But the business is, we have a mind to know more than we see. And again, if we could discern well what we do see, it would be so much known to us. But we see things quite otherwise than they are. So that your true Philosopher will not believe what he doth see, and is always conjecturing at what he doth not, which is a Life I think not much to be envy'd. Upon this I fancy to my

1. In John Glanvill's enchanting translation of 1688, last reprinted by the Nonesuch Press in 1929.

self, that Nature very much resembleth an Opera, where you stand, you do not see the Stage as really it is; but it is plac'd with advantage, and all the Wheels and Movements are hid, to make the Representation the more agreeable. Nor do you trouble your self how, or by what means the Machines are moved, though certainly an Engineer in the Pit is affected with what doth not touch you; he is pleas'd with the motion, and is demonstrating to himself on what it depends, and how it comes to pass. This Engineer then is like a Philosopher, though the difficulty is greater on the Philosopher's part, the Machines of the Theatre being nothing so curious as those of Nature, which disposeth her Wheels and Springs so out of sight, that we have been long a-guessing at the movement of the Universe.

Suppose then the Sages at an Opera, the Pithagoras, the Platos, the Aristotles, and all the Wise Men who have made such a noise in the World, for these many Ages. We will suppose 'em at the Representation of Phaeton, where they see the aspiring Youth lifted up by the Winds, but do not discover the Wires by which he mounts, nor know they any thing of what is done behind the Scenes. Would you have all these Philosophers own themselves to be stark Fools, and confess engenuously they know not how it comes to pass: No, no, they are not called Wise Men for nothing; tho', let me tell you, most of their Wisdom depends upon the ignorance of their Neighbours. Every man presently gives his Opinion, and how improbable so ever, there are Fools enough of all sorts to believe 'em: One tells you Phaeton is drawn up by a hidden Magnetick Vertue, no matter where it lies; and perhaps the grave Gentleman will take pet, if you ask him the Question. Another says, Phaeton is compos'd of certain Numbers that make him mount, and after all, the Philosopher knows no more of those numbers than a sucking Child of Algebra. A third tells you, Phaeton hath a secret love for the top of the Theatre, and like a true Lover cannot be at rest out of his Mistress's Company, with an hundred such extravagant fancies, that a Man must conclude the Old Sages were very good Banterers.

But now comes Monsieur Descartes, with some of the Moderns, and they tell you Phaeton ascends because a greater weight than he descends; so that now we do not believe a Body can move without it is push'd and forced by another body, and as it were drawn by Cords, so that nothing can rise or fall but by means of a Counterpoise; he then that will see Nature really as she is must stand behind the Scenes at the Opera.

I perceive, said the Countess, Philosophy is now become very Mechanical.

So mechanical, said I, that I fear we shall quickly be asham'd of it; they will have the World to be in great, what a Watch is in little; which is very regular, and depends only upon the just disposing of the several parts of the movement. But pray tell me, Madam, had you not formerly a more sublime Idea of the Universe? Do you not think you did then honour it more than it deserv'd? For most have the less esteem of it since they have pretended to know it.

I am not of their opinion, said she, I value it more since I know it resembles a Watch, and the whole order of Nature the more plain and easy it is, to me it appears the more admirable.

1. Natural Instinct and the Common Notions

Herbert of Cherbury, 1583–1648

De Veritate, published in 1624, sets itself to distinguish Truth from Revelation, Probability, Possibility and Error. Lord Herbert steers delicately between dogma and scepticism with the help of Common Notions. 'The whole aim of the work is the common nature of the search for truth which exists in every normal human being', he says in the Preface, and its intended result is to mark out a clear role for Reason in establishing religious truths which do not rest on Faith.

The attempt is clever, original and splendidly bombastic. Herbert is by no means the dull dog occasionally mentioned in footnotes to histories of thought. Elder brother to George Herbert and himself a poet, soldier, diplomat, scholar and philosopher, he lived a varied life with panache. The *De Veritate* was his proudest achievement (and the only one recorded on the tombstone he designed for himself). It has been unjustly neglected.

Those seeking the target of Locke's attack on innate ideas and struck by the close general accord between Locke and Descartes, occasionally suggest Lord Herbert as a long shot. This is perhaps as much as most readers know of him. Yet his Common Notions anticipate much of what Descartes says about axioms and simple natures and his analysis of truth, into *veritas apparentiae*, *veritas rei*, *veritas conceptus* and *veritas intellectus*, is subtler than Descartes'. Admittedly he makes much play with the idea of Universal Consent, which Locke ridicules. But his use of it anticipates Leibniz' retort to Locke and his general account of Common Notions even hints at some of Kant's concerns in the *Critique of Pure Reason*. At the same time much of what he says finds echoes in the later Scottish philosophy of Common Sense.

His best known passages deal with the Common Notions Concerning Religion – that there is a Sovereign Deity, that the Deity should be worshipped, that virtue and piety are the roots of religious practice, that sin must be expiated by repentance and that there is reward and punishment after this life. But this section of the work is so unsatisfactory and accords so ill with the earlier epistemology that I have preferred to quote some of his remarks on Natural Instinct and its relation to discursive thought.[1]

From *De Veritate*, 1624

NATURAL INSTINCT AND THE COMMON NOTIONS

I treat first of natural instinct, or the faculty which conforms with Common Notions.

Whatever is believed by universal consent must be true and must have been brought into conformity in virtue of some internal faculty. No argument would ever convince us of its falsity. And man has no other faculty to which we can attribute this truth. I therefore define natural instinct as the faculty which conforms. I do so with the understanding that any who find this term antiquated may demand another of me so long as the truths which we expect from universal consent are preserved. Universal consent, then, will be found to be the final test of truth. It is of the highest importance to distinguish these Common Notions and to allot each of these indubitable truths to its proper position. This has never been so necessary as now. For men are now not only exhorted with every device that language can employ by arguments from the pulpit, but are tormented in spite of the protests of conscience and the inner consciousness, by the belief that all who are outside their particular Church are condemned, whether through ignorance or error, to undergo instantly or with the concession of a short postponement, eternal punishment after death. The wretched terror-stricken mass have no refuge, unless some immovable foundations of truth resting on universal consent are established, to which they can turn amid the doubts of theology or of philosophy. All races require law, that is to say the Common Notions possessed by them arranged in due order. Yet different versions of this law have been given by different law givers. But while among legal codes differences exist on many points, there is the closest agreement concerning religion or civic and political justice as such. I hold,

1. From M. H. Carre's translation, J. W. Arrowsmith, 1937, pp. 116–18, 139–42.

therefore, that this universal consent is the teaching of Natural Instinct and is essentially due to Divine Providence. It is extraordinary, however, how persistently weak mortals alternate between total acceptance of the theories of the authorities and total rejection of them. They have no criterion, but dully immersing themselves in a naïve credulity, they become incapable of using their own faculties; and not having the heart to confront the terrors with which they are threatened, they fall back on fear and hate. These popular creeds are not, however, entirely true nor entirely false, for there has never been a religion or a philosophy so barbarous which has not contained some measure of truth. If it has been contaminated with error, as often happens, it can only be restored to its true glory by the analysis proposed in my method. While truth possesses the witness of some faculty, falsity will have no such witness. In my view, then, Universal Consent must be taken to be the beginning and end of theology and philosophy. And to this end Divine Providence signally contributes, in so far as it has now revealed to the whole world what was unknown to preceding ages, so that no knowledge of any value need be withheld from our grasp.

* * *

Now I distinguish Common Notions which arise from pure natural instinct from those which are brought into conformity only with the aid of discursive thought; in other words, the first order of notions from those of the second order. I put forward six characteristics by which the first order of Notions may be recognised. In the first place they are distinguished by their priority. Natural Instinct occupies the first position among our faculties, discursive reason the last. Thus this faculty promotes self-preservation in the elements, the zoophytes, and even the embryo, and applying itself gradually to objects, forestalls at every point the processes of reason. In the same way Natural Instinct anticipates reason in perceiving the beauty of the proportions of a house built according to architectural principles; for reason reaches its conclusion by a laborious consideration of the proportions, first severally and then as a whole, and even in the process itself is constrained to rely on Common Notions. And the same point can be noticed in judging beautiful features, or graceful form, or harmony in music. For it is not necessary to call any plain man who takes immediate pleasure in such things a mathematician or a musician.

The second characteristic consists in independence. For if a principle is derived from some Common Notion it does not belong to the first order, but to the second, however true it may be. So when there is no further fundamental Common Notion to which we can refer, we must hold it to belong to the first class; and upon it the entire chain of inference depends.

The third characteristic is universality. Accordingly I take the chief criterion of Natural Instinct to be universal consent (putting aside persons who are out of their minds or mentally incapable). For I have always viewed particular principles with suspicion as savouring of deception, or at least as mingled with error. In a word, pure Common Notions are universals, distilled as it were from the wisdom of Nature itself; though they may be broken up into particular forms by discursive reason.

The fourth mark is certainty; for these Notions exercise an authority so profound that anyone who were to doubt them would upset the whole natural order and strip himself of his humanity. These principles may not be disputed. As long as they are understood it is impossible to deny them. It has been well said that while the understanding recognises principles the will recognises the end.

The fifth characteristic is necessity. Every Common Notion is directed towards man's preservation. These Notions contain such an abundance of secret power that when they are arranged systematically they reflect the eternal wisdom of the universe. There exists no more striking conception of it within us or in the external world. We are guided by our own judgment and Destiny gives support to our free will, so that while God alone directs the wisdom of the fool, both God and himself govern in the sage. Thus we must arrange these notions in our minds and endeavour not to be false to ourselves by a reckless confidence in reason, as though these notions lay in some region outside ourselves; but reverting to our own faculties, we must retrace the steps which led the all-wise Artificer to ourselves.

The sixth characteristic consists in the method of conformation. Common Notions are brought into conformity immediately, provided that the meaning of the facts or words is grasped; while discursive reason works slowly by means of species and its Questions, moving for ever to and fro, without any recourse to apprehension. This is the source of countless errors among the schoolmen. They often rely on reason in describing the characters of the elements in spite of the doubtful evidence even of perception. They fail to notice that what belongs to some form of perception has been wrongly attributed to reason and *vice versa* and that each single faculty has its own province, beyond which it functions vainly or fails to function at all. It is important further to observe that the beliefs which rest on Natural Instinct may also be recommended by false theories. For they rest on pure faith. Thus the worship of God may be supported by a false theology. I attribute this error to discursive reason, for true religion has no need of it.

The truths of Natural Instinct are then not only distinguished from those of discursive reason by priority, independence, universality, certainty and necessity, but also by their manner of conformation. It follows that unless Natural Instinct sets a limit to its range, reason remains undecided and will raise such a host of images and scruples of its own that it will never reach any conclusion. The master-physician therefore erred when in order to destroy the sacred doctrine of Natural Instinct which governs reason he insisted on using reason, a lower kind of power, to prove those beliefs which belong by right to natural instinct. It is not then permissible to raise objections when all these criteria of natural instinct are present together. The question, however, may still be asked what these Common Notions are. I answer that in so far as they are common they must be found in ourselves, so that those notions that lie hidden within us, though vague, confused and mixed with error, yet enable us to grasp what we endeavour to acquire with vast effort from laws, religions, and the whole body of treatises; provided that we clearly distinguish between these notions and reduce them to order, always enquiring according to my test what faculty is used in proving them. In truth I hold that every age, place and person, Greek or barbarian, ancient or modern, has had this knowledge fully in possession. Thus men have for the most part overstepped the due bounds of truth, in other words the proper conformation of the faculties, and failed to remain within its confines. Now the Reader has a twofold means at his disposal for discovering these Common Notions. When he lights upon them, let him pay due respect to them and place each in its appropriate rank. For so far from feeling burdened by them he will be filled with extraordinary pleasure and experience an intimate harmony of the faculties through which the notions are brought into conformity. He need not labour to extract these notions from the views of the authorities. Whenever he is aware of some faculty active within him, let him refer whatever assertion is recognised by his inner sense to its fundamental Common Notion and then to its conforming faculty and adopt it as a first principle. If he perceives this there will be no need for him to waste further time. For if the same objects and the same faculties are present to everyone, why should anyone turn out wiser than he? If he finds it too heavy a business to draw up a list of these Common Notions, it is my purpose to relieve him of this labour. I pray that this book may bring enlightenment to its readers; nor do I desire any other reward for the trouble and time that I have spent on it except their judgment that, apart from what is due to God's grace or special Providence, it possesses some merit. I do not wish to recommend anything in nature or common Providence which cannot or ought not to be anticipated or even surpassed by Grace or special Providence. This, then, is the single intention of my argument, that what is Divine should appear, however much it may be corrupted, a daily effect of universal Providence, either through its own worth or by means of its power of salvation; and secure from blasphemies, shine forth in its genuine splendour. Accordingly the task I undertake is the cause of God.

2. The Light of Nature

René Descartes, 1596–1650

The Giaconda smile on Descartes' most famous portrait bids us beware. His lucid style and bold reasonings still delight students and destroy scholars. His works still provoke a deep shiver of excitement, which rereading does nothing to dispel. Even when the finest commentators have finished, there is still room for further research and reflection. For philosophers he is the first modern immortal.

All his writings are marked by a concern with method. It is the core of his first major study, the *Rules for the Direction of the Mind* (written in 1628 or 9), is given its fullest exposition in the *Discourse on the Method* (published 1637) and is applied most famously in the *Meditations* (published 1641). The model throughout is mathematical intuition, which could be generalised he hoped, to all rational enquiry. There are three aspects to be distinguished. The first is epistemological, indeed ontological: our knowledge rests and can only rest on 'clear and distinct perceptions' for which neither proof nor evidence is needed. The second is heuristic: we can arrive at these intuitions, as in the opening Meditations, by systematic suspension of belief in everything dubitable or not self-evident. The third is expository: axiomatic geometry is a paradigm of how a developed system of knowledge can be ordered and exhibited. For Descartes himself the first or intuitive aspect was crucial. But he also found it the hardest to express. Hence Leibniz could say teasingly that the rule is 'take what you need, do what you should and you will get what you want'. Nevertheless Cartesian philosophy is based on 'the undoubting conception of an unclouded and attentive mind' and not on the reasoned (and more easily understood) interplay between the thinking Ego, the malignant demon and the God who is no deceiver.

The main selections given here are accordingly from the *Discourse* (slightly abridged) and the *Meditations*. But I have also included the Geometrical Appendix to the Second Reply and should perhaps emphasise that it is not typical of Descartes and that he himself attached little importance to it. The *Meditations* provoked Objections from many learned contemporaries, seven of which, together with Descartes' courteous Replies were published in 1641. The Geometrical Appendix is a sketch of how Descartes' philosophy would look in the axiomatic manner and illustrates only what has just been called the expository aspect of the method. Nevertheless it is of great interest to the student of Rationalism, partly for its useful definitions of terms like 'thought', 'idea' and 'substance' and partly because other Rationalists, notably Spinoza, took the Geometrical method far more seriously, as the best way of acquiring Adequate Ideas. A similar *caveat* should be entered for the brief selection given from Descartes' letters. Descartes is very silent in his published work about whether God created the Eternal Truths and I have included his rare remarks on the subject because of their intrinsic importance in examining the method of doubt. The remarks on the self, the mind-body problem and freewill are included to show how Descartes himself might have tried to resolve some hideous difficulties in his philosophy of mind.[1]

There is no space here to recount the views on God, Man and Nature for which he is best known. But the *Meditations* contain a matchless general statement of them, and I especially recommend the *Principles of Philosophy* (published 1644) to newcomers, who wish to pursue Descartes' thoughts further.

Discourse on the Method of Rightly Conducting the Reason and Seeking for Truth in the Sciences, 1637

If this Discourse appears too long to be read all at once, it may be separated into six portions. And in the first there will be found various considerations respecting the sciences; in the second, the principal rules regarding the Method which the author has sought

1. Translation of the *Discourse, Meditations* and Geometrical Appendix by E. S. Haldane and G. T. Ross, Cambridge University Press, 1911 and of the letters by A. J. P. Kenny, Oxford, Clarendon Press, 1970.

out; while in the third are some of the rules of morality which he has derived from this Method. In the fourth are the reasons by which he proves the existence of God and of the human soul, which form the foundation of his Metaphysic. In the fifth, the order of the questions regarding physics which he has investigated, and particularly the explanation of the movement of the heart, and of some other difficulties which pertain to medicine, as also the difference between the soul of man and that of the brutes. And in the last part the questions raised relate to those matters which the author believes to be requisite in order to advance further in the investigation of nature, in addition to the reasons that caused him to write.

PART ONE

Good sense is of all things in the world the most equally distributed, for everybody thinks himself so abundantly provided with it, that even those most difficult to please in all other matters do not commonly desire more of it than they already possess. It is unlikely that this is an error on their part; it seems rather to be evidence in support of the view that the power of forming a good judgment and of distinguishing the true from the false, which is properly speaking what is called Good sense or Reason, is by nature equal in all men. Hence too it will show that the diversity of our opinions does not proceed from some men being more rational than others, but solely from the fact that our thoughts pass through diverse channels and the same objects are not considered by all. For to be possessed of good mental powers is not sufficient; the principal matter is to apply them well. The greatest minds are capable of the greatest vices as well as of the greatest virtues, and those who proceed very slowly may, provided they always follow the straight road, really advance much faster than those who, though they run, forsake it.

For myself I have never ventured to presume that my mind was in any way more perfect than that of the ordinary man; I have even longed to possess thought as quick, or an imagination as accurate and distinct, or a memory as comprehensive or ready, as some others. And besides these I do not know any other qualities that make for the perfection of the human mind. For as to reason or sense, inasmuch as it is the only thing that constitutes us men and distinguishes us from the brutes, I would fain believe that it is to be found complete in each individual, and in this I follow the common opinion of the philosophers, who say that the question of more or less occurs only in the sphere of the *accidents* and does not affect the *forms* or natures of the *individual* in the same *species*.

But I shall not hesitate to say that I have had great good fortune from my youth up, in lighting upon and pursuing certain paths which have conducted me to considerations and maxims from which I have formed a Method, by whose assistance it appears to me I have the means of gradually increasing my knowledge and of little by little raising it to the highest possible point which the mediocrity of my talents and the brief duration of my life can permit me to reach. For I have already reaped from it fruits of such a nature that, even though I always try in the judgments I make on myself to lean to the side of self-depreciation rather than to that of arrogance, and though, looking with the eye of a philosopher on the diverse actions and enterprises of all mankind, I find scarcely any which do not seem to me vain and useless, I do not cease to receive extreme satisfaction in the progress which I seem to have already made in the search after truth, and to form such hopes for the future as to venture to believe that, if amongst the occupations of men, simply as men, there is some one in particular that is excellent and important, that is the one which I have selected.

It must always be recollected, however, that possibly I deceive myself, and that what I take to be gold and diamonds is perhaps no more than copper and glass. I know how subject we are to delusion in whatever touches ourselves, and also how much the judgments of our friends ought to be suspected when they are in our favour. But in this Discourse I shall be very happy to show the paths I have followed, and to set forth my life as in a picture, so that everyone may judge of it for himself; and thus in learning from the common talk what are the opinions which are held of it, a new means of obtaining self-instruction will be reached, which I shall add to those which I have been in the habit of using.

Thus my design is not here to teach the Method which everyone should follow in order to promote the good conduct of his Reason, but only to show in what manner I have endeavoured to conduct my own. Those who set about giving precepts must esteem themselves more skilful than those to whom they advance them, and if they fall short in the smallest matter they must of course take the blame for it. But regarding this Treatise simply as a history, or, if you prefer it, a fable in which, amongst certain things which may be imitated, there are possibly others also which it would not be right to follow, I hope that it will be of use to some without being hurtful to any, and that all will thank me for my frankness.

I have been nourished on letters since my childhood, and since I was given to believe that by their means a clear and certain knowledge could be obtained of all that is useful in life, I had an extreme desire to acquire instruction. But so soon as I had achieved the entire course of study at the close of which one is usually received into the ranks of the learned, I entirely changed my opinion. For I found myself embarrassed with so many doubts and errors that it seemed to me that the effort to instruct myself had no effect other than the increasing discovery of my own ignorance. And yet I was studying at one of the most celebrated Schools in Europe, where I thought that there must be men of learning if they were to be found anywhere in the world. I learned there all that others learned; and not being satisfied with the sciences that we were taught, I even read through all the books which fell into my hands, treating of what is considered most curious and rare. Along with this I knew the judgments that others had formed of me, and I did not feel that I was esteemed inferior to my fellow-students, although there were amongst them some destined to fill the places of our masters. And finally our century seemed to me as flourishing, and as fertile in great minds, as any which had preceded. And this made me take the liberty of judging all others by myself and of coming to the conclusion that there was no learning in the world such as I was formerly led to believe it to be.

I did not omit, however, always to hold in esteem those exercises which are the occupation of the Schools. I knew that the Languages which one learns there are essential for the understanding of all ancient literature; that fables with their charm stimulate the mind and histories of memorable deeds exalt it; and that, when read with discretion, these books assist in forming a sound judgment. I was aware that the reading of all good books is indeed like a conversation with the noblest men of past centuries who were the authors of them, nay a carefully studied conversation, in which they reveal to us none but the best of their thoughts. I deemed Eloquence to have a power and beauty beyond compare; that Poesy has most ravishing delicacy and sweetness; that in Mathematics there are the subtlest discoveries and inventions which may accomplish much, both in satisfying the curious, and in furthering all the arts, and in diminishing man's labour; that those writings that deal with Morals contain much that is instructive, and many exhortations to virtue which are most useful; that Theology points out the way to Heaven; that Philosophy teaches us to speak with an appearance of truth on all things, and causes us to be admired by the less learned; that Jurisprudence, Medicine and all other sciences bring honour and riches to those who cultivate them; and finally that is is good to have examined all things, even those most full of superstition and falsehood, in order that we may know their just value, and avoid being deceived by them.

But I considered that I had already given sufficient time to languages and likewise even to the reading of the literature of the ancients, both their histories and their fables. For to converse with those of other centuries is almost the same thing as to travel. It is good to know something of the customs of different peoples in order to judge more sanely of our own, and not to think that everything of a fashion not ours is absurd and contrary to reason, as do those who have seen nothing. But when one employs too much time in travelling, one becomes a stranger in one's own country, and when one is too curious about things which were practised in past centuries, one is usually very ignorant about those which are practised in our own time. Besides, fables make one imagine many events possible which in reality are not so, and even the most accurate of histories, if they do not exactly misrepresent or exaggerate the value of things in order to render them more worthy of being read, at least omit in them all the circumstances which are basest and least notable; and from this fact it follows that what is retained is not portrayed as it really is, and that those who regulate their conduct by examples which they derive from such a source, are liable to fall into the extravagances of the knights-errant of Romance, and form projects beyond their power of performance.

I esteemed Eloquence most highly and I was enamoured of Poesy, but I thought that both were gifts of the mind rather than fruits of study. Those who have the strongest power of reasoning, and who most skilfully arrange their thoughts in order to render them clear and intelligible, have the best power of persuasion even if they can but speak the language of Lower

Brittany and have never learned Rhetoric. And those who have the most delightful original ideas and who know how to express them with the maximum of style and suavity, would not fail to be the best poets even if the art of Poetry were unknown to them.

Most of all was I delighted with Mathematics because of the certainty of its demonstrations and the evidence of its reasoning; but I did not yet understand its true use, and, believing that it was of service only in the mechanical arts, I was astonished that, seeing how firm and solid was its basis, no loftier edifice had been reared thereupon. On the other hand I compared the works of the ancient pagans which deal with Morals to palaces most superb and magnificent, which are yet built on sand and mud alone. They praise the virtues most highly and show them to be more worthy of being prized than anything else in the world, but they do not sufficiently teach us to become acquainted with them, and often that which is called by a fine name is nothing but insensibility, or pride, or despair, or parricide.

I honoured our Theology and aspired as much as anyone to reach to heaven, but having learned to regard it as a most highly assured fact that the road is not less open to the most ignorant than to the most learned, and that the revealed truths which conduct thither are quite above our intelligence, I should not have dared to submit them to the feebleness of my reasonings; and I thought that, in order to undertake to examine them and succeed in so doing, it was necessary to have some extraordinary assistance from above and to be more than a mere man.

I shall not say anything about Philosophy, but that, seeing that it has been cultivated for many centuries by the best minds that have ever lived, and that nevertheless no single thing is to be found in it which is not subject of dispute, and in consequence which is not dubious, I had not enough presumption to hope to fare better there than other men had done. And also, considering how many conflicting opinions there may be regarding the self-same matter, all supported by learned people, while there can never be more than one which is true, I esteemed as well-nigh false all that only went as far as being probable.

Then as to the other sciences, inasmuch as they derive their principles from Philosophy, I judged that one could have built nothing solid on foundations so far from firm. And neither the honour nor the promised gain was sufficient to persuade me to cultivate them, for, thanks be to God, I did not find myself in a condition which obliged me to make a merchandise of science for the improvement of my fortune; and, although I did not pretend to scorn all glory like the Cynics, I yet had very small esteem for what I could not hope to acquire, excepting through fictitious titles. And, finally, as to false doctrines, I thought that I already knew well enough what they were worth to be subject to deception neither by the promises of an alchemist, the predictions of an astrologer, the impostures of a magician, the artifices or the empty boastings of any of those who make a profession of knowing that of which they are ignorant.

This is why, as soon as age permitted me to emerge from the control of my tutors, I entirely quitted the study of letters. And resolving to seek no other science that that which could be found in myself, or at least in the great book of the world, I employed the rest of my youth in travel, in seeing courts and armies, in intercourse with men of diverse temperaments and conditions, in collecting varied experiences, in proving myself in the various predicaments in which I was placed by fortune, and under all circumstances bringing my mind to bear on the things which came before it, so that I might derive some profit from my experience. For it seemed to me that I might meet with much more truth in the reasonings that each man makes on the matters that specially concern him, and the issue of which would very soon punish him if he made a wrong judgment, than in the case of those made by a man of letters in his study touching speculations which lead to no result, and which bring about no other consequences to himself excepting that he will be all the more vain the more they are removed from common sense, since in this case it proves him to have employed so much the more ingenuity and skill in trying to make them seem probable. And I always had an excessive desire to learn to distinguish the true from the false, in order to see clearly in my actions and to walk with confidence in this life.

It is true that while I only considered the manners of other men I found in them nothing to give me settled convictions; and I remarked in them almost as much diversity as I had formerly seen in the opinions of philosophers. So much was this the case that the greatest profit which I derived from their study was that, in seeing many things which, although they seem to us very extravagant and ridiculous, were yet commonly received and approved by other great nations, I learned to believe nothing too certainly of which I had only been convinced by example and custom. Thus little by little I was delivered from many errors which might have obscured our natural vision and rendered us less capable of listening to Reason. But after I had employed several years in thus studying the book of the world and trying to acquire some experience, I one day formed the resolution of also making myself an object of study and of employing all the strength of my mind in choosing the road I should follow. This succeeded much better, it appeared to me, than if I had never departed either from my country or my books.

PART TWO

I was then in Germany, to which country I had been attracted by the wars which are not yet at an end. And as I was returning from the coronation of the Emperor to join the army, the setting in of winter detained me in a quarter where, since I found no society to divert me, while fortunately I had also no cares or passions to trouble me, I remained the whole day shut up alone in a stove-heated room, where I had complete leisure to occupy myself with my own thoughts. One of the first of the considerations that occurred to me was that there is very often less perfection in works composed of several portions, and carried out by the hands of various masters, than in those on which one individual alone has worked. Thus we see that buildings planned and carried out by one architect alone are usually more beautiful and better proportioned than those which many have tried to put in order and improve, making use of old walls which were built with other ends in view. In the same way also, those ancient cities which, originally mere villages, have become in the process of time great towns, are usually badly constructed in comparison with those which are regularly laid out on a plain by a surveyor who is free to follow his own ideas. Even though, considering their buildings each one apart, there is often as much or more display of skill in the one case than in the other, the former have large buildings and small buildings indiscriminately placed together, thus rendering the streets crooked and irregular, so that it might be said that it was chance rather than the will of men guided by reason that led to such an arrangement. And if we consider that this happens despite the fact that from all time there have been certain officials who have had the special duty of looking after the buildings of private individuals in order that they may be public ornaments, we shall understand how difficult it is to bring about much that is satisfactory in operating only upon the works of others. Thus I imagined that those people who were once half-savage, and who have become civilized only by slow degrees, merely forming their laws as the disagreeable necessities of their crimes and quarrels constrained them, could not succeed in establishing so good a system of government as those who, from the time they first came together as communities, carried into effect the constitution laid down by some prudent legislator. Thus it is quite certain that the constitution of the true Religion whose ordinances are of God alone is incomparably, better regulated than any other. And, to come down to human affairs, I believe that if Sparta was very flourishing in former times, this was not because of the excellence of each and every one of its laws, seeing that many were very strange and even contrary to good morals, but because, being drawn up by one individual, they all tended towards the same end. And similarly I thought that the sciences found in books – in those at least whose reasonings are only probable and which have no demonstrations, composed as they are of the gradually accumulated opinions of many different individuals – do not approach so near to the truth as the simple reasoning which a man of common sense can quite naturally carry out respecting the things which come immediately before him. Again I thought that since we have all been children before being men, and since it has for long fallen to us to be governed by our appetites and by our teachers (who often enough contradicted one another, and none of whom perhaps counselled us always for the best), it is almost impossible that our judgments should be so excellent or solid as they should have been had we had complete use of our reason since our birth, and had we been guided by its means alone.

It is true that we do not find that all the houses in a town are rased to the ground for the sole reason that the town is to be rebuilt in another fashion, with streets made more beautiful; but at the same time we see that many people cause their own houses to be knocked down in order to rebuild them, and that sometimes they are forced so to do where there is danger of the houses falling of themselves, and when the foundations are not secure.

From such examples I argued to myself that there was no plausibility in the claim of any private individual to reform a state by altering everything, and by overturning it throughout, in order to set it right again. Nor is it likewise probable that the whole body of the Sciences, or the order of teaching established by the Schools, should be reformed. But as regards all the opinions which up to this time I had embraced, I thought I could not do better than endeavour once for all to sweep them completely away, so that they might later on be replaced, either by others which were better, or by the same, when I had made them conform to the uniformity of a rational scheme. And I firmly believed that by this means I should succeed in directing my life much better than if I had only built on old foundations, and relied on principles of which I allowed myself to be in youth persuaded without having inquired into their truth. For although in so doing I recognised various difficulties, these were at the same time not unsurmountable, nor comparable to those which are found in reformation of the most insignificant kind in matters which concern the public. In the case of great bodies it is too difficult a task to raise them again when they are once thrown down, or even to keep them in their places when once thoroughly shaken; and their fall cannot be otherwise than very violent. Then as to any imperfections that they may possess (and the very diversity that is found between them is sufficient to tell us that these in many cases exist) custom has doubtless greatly mitigated them, while it has also helped us to avoid, or insensibly corrected a number against which mere foresight would have found it difficult to guard. And finally the imperfections are almost always more supportable than would be the process of removing them, just as the great roads which wind about amongst the mountains become, because of being frequented, little by little so well-beaten and easy that it is much better to follow them than to try to go more directly by climbing over rocks and descending to the foot of precipices.

This is the reason why I cannot in any way approve of those turbulent and unrestful spirits who, being called neither by birth nor fortune to the management of public affairs, never fail to have always in their minds some new reforms. And if I thought that in this treatise there was contained the smallest justification for this folly, I should be very sorry to allow it to be published. My design has never extended beyond trying to reform my own opinion and to build on a foundation which is entirely my own. If my work has given me a certain satisfaction, so that I here present to you a draft of it, I do not so do because I wish to advise anybody to imitate it. Those to whom God has been most beneficent in the bestowal of His graces will perhaps form designs which are more elevated; but I fear much that this particular one will seem too venturesome for many. The simple resolve to strip oneself of all opinions and beliefs formerly received is not to be regarded as an example that each man should follow, and the world may be said to be mainly composed of two classes of minds neither of which could prudently adopt it. There are those who, believing themselves to be cleverer than they are, cannot restrain themselves from being precipitate in judgment and have not sufficient patience to arrange their thoughts in proper order; hence, once a man of this description had taken the liberty of doubting the principles he formerly accepted, and had deviated from the beaten track, he would never be able to maintain the path which must be followed to reach the appointed end more quickly, and he would hence remain wandering astray all through his life. Secondly, there are those who having reason or modesty enough to judge that they are less capable of distinguishing truth from falsehood than some others from whom instruction might be obtained, are right in contenting themselves with following the opinions of these others rather than in searching better ones for themselves.

For myself I should doubtless have been of these last if I had never had more than a single master, or had I never known the diversities which have from all time existed between the opinions of men of the greatest learning. But I had been taught, even in my College days, that there is nothing imaginable so strange or so little credible that it has not been maintained by one philosopher or other, and I further recognised in the course of my travels that all those whose sentiments are very contrary to ours are yet not necessarily barbarians or savages, but may be possessed of reason in as great or even a greater degree than ourselves. I also considered how very different the self-same man, identical in mind and spirit, may become, according as he is brought up from childhood amongst the French or Germans, or has passed his whole life amongst Chinese or cannibals. I likewise noticed how even in the fashions of one's clothing the same thing that pleased us ten years ago, and which will perhaps please us once again before ten years are passed, seems at the present time extravagant and ridiculous. I thus concluded that it is much more custom and example that persuade us than any certain knowledge, and yet in spite of this the voice of the majority does not afford a proof of any value in truths a little difficult to discover, because such truths are much more likely to have been discovered by one man than by a nation. I could not, however, put my finger on a single person whose opinions seemed preferable to those of others, and I found that I was, so to speak, constrained myself to undertake the direction of my procedure.

But like one who walks alone and in the twilight I resolved to go so slowly, and to use so much circumspection in all things, that if my advance was but very small, at least I guarded myself well from falling. I did not wish to set about the final rejection of any single opinion which might formerly have crept into my beliefs without having been introduced there by means of Reason, until I had first of all employed sufficient time in planning out the task which I had undertaken, and in seeking the true Method of arriving at a knowledge of all the things of which my mind was capable.

Among the different branches of Philosophy, I had in my younger days to a certain extent studied Logic; and in those of Mathematics, Geometrical Analysis and Algebra – three arts of sciences which seemed as though they ought to contribute something to the design I had in view. But in examining them I observed in respect to Logic that the syllogisms and the greater part of the other teaching served better in explaining to others those things that one knows (or like the art of Lully, in enabling one to speak without judgment of those things of which one is ignorant) than in learning what is new. And although in reality Logic contains many precepts which are very true and very good, there are at the same time mingled with them so many others which are hurtful or superfluous, that it is almost as difficult to separate the two as to draw a Diana or a Minerva out of a block of marble which is not yet roughly hewn. And as to the Analysis of the ancients and the Algebra of the moderns, besides the fact that they embrace only matters the most abstract, such as appear to have no actual use, the former is always so restricted to the consideration of symbols that it cannot exercise the Understanding without greatly fatiguing the

Imagination; and in the latter one is so subjected to certain rules and formulas that the result is the construction of an art which is confused and obscure, and which embarrasses the mind, instead of a science which contributes to its cultivation. This made me feel that some other Method must be found, which, comprising the advantages of the three, is yet exempt from their faults. And as a multiplicity of laws often furnishes excuses for evil-doing, and as a State is hence much better ruled when, having but very few laws, these are most strictly observed; so, instead of the great number of precepts of which Logic is composed, I believed that I should find the four which I shall state quite sufficient, provided that I adhered to a firm and constant resolve never on any single occasion to fail in their observance.

The first of these was to accept nothing as true which I did not clearly recognise to be so: that is to say, carefully to avoid precipitation and prejudice in judgments, and to accept in them nothing more than what was presented to my mind so clearly and distinctly that I could have no occasion to doubt it.

The second was to divide up each of the difficulties which I examined into as many parts as possible, and as seemed requisite in order that it might be resolved in the best manner possible.

The third was to carry on my reflections in due order, commencing with objects that were the most simple and easy to understand, in order to rise little by little, or by degrees, to knowledge of the most complex, assuming an order, even if a fictitious one, among those which do not follow a natural sequence relatively to one another.

The last was in all cases to make enumerations so complete and reviews so general that I should be certain of having omitted nothing.

Those long chains of reasoning, simple and easy as they are, of which geometricians make use in order to arrive at the most difficult demonstrations, had caused me to imagine that all those things which fall under the cognizance of man might very likely be mutually related in the same fashion; and that, provided only that we abstain from receiving anything as true which is not so, and always retain the order which is necessary in order to deduce the one conclusion from the other, there can be nothing so remote that we cannot reach to it, nor so recondite that we cannot discover it. And I had not much trouble in discovering which objects it was necessary to begin with, for I already knew that it was with the most simple and those most easy to apprehend. Considering also that of all those who have hitherto sought for the truth in the Sciences, it has been the mathematicians alone who have been able to succeed in making any demonstrations, that is to say producing reasons which are evident and certain, I did not doubt that it had been by means of a similar kind that they carried on their investigations. I did not at the same time hope for any practical result in so doing, except that my mind would become accustomed to the nourishment of truth and would not content itself with false reasoning. But for all that I had no intention of trying to master all those particular sciences that receive in common the name of Mathematics; but observing that, although their objects are different, they do not fail to agree in this, that they take nothing under consideration but the various relationships or proportions which are present in these objects, I thought that it would be better if I only examined these proportions in their general aspect, and without viewing them otherwise than in the objects which would serve most to facilitate a knowledge of them. Not that I should in any way restrict them to these objects, for I might later on all the more easily apply them to all other objects to which they were applicable. Then, having carefully noted that in order to comprehend the proportions I should sometimes require to consider each one in particular, and sometimes merely keep them in mind, or take them in groups, I thought that, in order the better to consider them in detail, I should picture them in the form of lines, because I could find no method more simple nor more capable of being distinctly represented to my imagination and senses. I considered, however, that in order to keep them in my memory or to embrace several at once, it would be essential that I should explain them by means of certain formulas, the shorter the better. And for this purpose it was requisite that I should borrow all that is best in Geometrical Analysis and Algebra, and correct the errors of the one by the other.

As a matter of fact, I can venture to say that the exact observation of the few precepts which I had chosen gave me so much facility in sifting out all the questions embraced in these two sciences, that in the two or three months which I employed in examining them – commencing with the most simple and general, and making each truth that I discovered a rule for helping me to find others – not only did I arrive at the solution of many questions which I had hitherto regarded as most difficult, but, towards the end, it seemed to me that I was able to determine in the case of those of which I was still ignorant, by what means, and in how far, it was possible to solve them. In this I might perhaps appear to you to be very vain if you did not remember that having but one truth to discover in respect to each matter, whoever succeeds in finding it knows in its regard as much as can be known. It is the same as with a child, for instance, who has been instructed in Arithmetic and has made an addition according to the rule prescribed; he may be sure of having found as regards the sum of figures given to him all that the human mind can know. For, in conclusion, the Method which teaches us to follow the true order and enumerate exactly every term in the matter under investigation contains everything which gives certainty to the rules of Arithmetic.

But what pleased me most in this Method was that I was certain by its means of exercising my reason in all things, if not perfectly, at least as well as was in my power. And besides this, I felt in making use of it that my mind gradually accustomed itself to conceive of its objects more accurately and distinctly; and not having restricted this Method to any particular matter, I promised myself to apply it as usefully to the difficulties of other sciences as I had done to those of Algebra. Not that on this account I dared undertake to examine just at once all those that might present themselves; for that would itself have been contrary to the order which the Method prescribes. But having noticed that the knowledge of these difficulties must be dependent on principles derived from Philosophy in which I yet found nothing to be certain, I thought that it was requisite above all to try to establish certainty in it. I considered also that since this endeavour is the most important in all the world, and that in which precipitation and prejudice were most to be feared, I should not try to grapple with it till I had attained to a much riper age than that of three and twenty, which was the age I had reached. I thought, too, that I should first of all employ much time in preparing myself for the work by eradicating from my mind all the wrong opinions which I had up to this time accepted, and accumulating a variety of experiences fitted later on to afford matter for my reasonings, and by ever exercising myself in the Method which I had prescribed, in order more and more to fortify myself in the power of using it.

PART THREE

And finally, as it is not sufficient, before commencing to rebuild the house which we inhabit, to pull it down and provide materials and an architect (or to act in this capacity ourselves, and make a careful drawing of its design), unless we have also provided ourselves with some other house where we can be comfortably lodged during the time of rebuilding, so in order that I should not remain irresolute in my actions while reason obliged me to be so in my judgments, and that I might not omit to carry on my life as happily as I could, I formed for myself a code of morals for the time being which did not consist of more than three or four maxims, which maxims I should like to enumerate to you.

The first was to obey the laws and customs of my country, adhering constantly to the religion in which by God's grace I had been instructed since my childhood, and in all other things directing my conduct by opinions the most moderate in nature, and the farthest removed from excess in all those which are commonly received and acted on by the most judicious of those with whom I might come in contact. For since I began to count my own opinions as nought, because I desired to place all under examination, I was convinced that I could not do better than follow those held by people on whose judgment reliance could be placed. And although such persons may possibly exist amongst the Persians and Chinese as well as amongst ourselves, it seemed to me that it was most expedient to bring my conduct into harmony with the ideas of those with whom I should have to live; and that, in order to ascertain that these were their real opinions, I should observe what they did rather than what they said, not only because in the corrupt state of our manners there are few people who desire to say all that they believe, but also because many are themselves ignorant of their beliefs. For since the act of thought by which we believe a thing is different from that by which we know that we believe it, the one often exists without the other. And amongst many opinions all equally received, I chose only the most moderate, both because these are always most suited for putting into practice, and probably the best (for all excess has a tendency to be bad), and also because I should have in a less degree turned aside from the right path, supposing that I was wrong, than if, having chosen an extreme course, I found that I had chosen amiss. I also made a point of counting as excess all the engagements by means of which we limit in some degree our liberty. Not that I hold in low esteem those laws which, in order to remedy the inconstancy of feeble souls, permit, when we have a good object in our view, that certain vows be taken, or contracts made, which oblige us to carry out that object. This sanction is even given for security in commerce where designs are wholly indifferent. But because I saw nothing in all the world remaining constant, and because for my own part I promised myself gradually to get my judgments to grow better and never to grow worse, I should have thought that I had committed a serious sin against commonsense if, because I approved of something at one time, I was obliged to regard it similarly at a later time, after it had possibly ceased to meet my approval, or after I had ceased to regard it in a favourable light.

My second maxim was that of being as firm and resolute in my actions as I could be, and not to follow less faithfully opinions the most dubious, when my mind was once made up regarding them, than if these had been beyond doubt. In this I should be following the example of travellers, who, finding themselves lost in a forest, know that they ought not to wander first to one side and then to the other, nor, still less, to stop in one place, but understand that they should continue to walk as straight as they can in one direction, not diverging for any slight reason, even though it was possibly chance alone that first determined them in their choice. By this means if they do not go exactly where they wish, they will at least arrive somewhere at the end, where probably they will be better off than in the middle of a forest. And thus since often enough in the actions of life no delay is permissible, it is very certain that, when it is beyond our power to discern the opinions which carry most truth, we should follow the most probable; and even although we notice no greater probability in the one opinion than in the other, we at least should make up our minds to follow a particular one and afterwards consider it as no longer doubtful in its relationship to practice, but as very true and very certain, inasmuch as the reason which caused us to determine upon it is known to be so. And henceforward this principle was sufficient to deliver me from all the penitence and remorse which usually affect the mind and agitate the conscience of those weak and vacillating creatures who allow themselves to keep changing their procedure, and practise as good, things which they afterwards judge to be evil.

My third maxim was to try always to conquer myself rather than fortune, and to alter my desires rather than change the order of the world, and generally to accustom myself to believe that there is nothing entirely within our power but our own thoughts: so that after we have done our best in regard to the things that are without us, our ill-success cannot possibly be failure on our part. And this alone seemed to me sufficient to prevent my desiring anything in the future beyond what I could actually obtain, hence rendering me content; for since our will does not naturally induce us to desire anything but what our understanding represents to it as in some way possible of attainment, it is certain that if we consider all good things which are outside of us as equally outside of our power, we should not have more regret in resigning those goods which appear to pertain to our birth, when we are deprived of them for no fault of our own, than we have in not possessing the kingdoms of China or Mexico. In the same way, making what is called a virtue out of a necessity, we should no more desire to be well if ill, or free, if in prison, than we now do to have our bodies formed of a substance as little corruptible as diamonds, or to have wings to fly with like birds. I allow, however, that to accustom oneself to regard all things from this point of view requires long exercise and meditation often repeated; and I believe that it is principally in this that is to be found the secret of those philosophers who, in ancient times, were able to free themselves from the empire of fortune, or, despite suffering or poverty, to rival their gods in their happiness. For, ceaselessly occupying themselves in considering the limits which were prescribed to them by nature, they persuaded themselves so completely that nothing was within their own power but their thoughts, that this conviction alone was sufficient to prevent their having any longing for other things. And they had so absolute a mastery over their thoughts that they had some reason for esteeming themselves as more rich and more powerful, and more free and more happy than other men, who, however favoured by nature or fortune they might be, if devoid of this philosophy, never could arrive at all at which they aim.

And last of all, to conclude this moral code, I felt it incumbent on me to make a review of the various occupations of men in this life in order to try to choose out the best; and without wishing to say anything of the employment of others I thought that I could not do better than continue in the one in which I found myself engaged, that is to say, in occupying my whole life in cultivating my Reason, and in advancing myself as much as possible in the knowledge of the truth in accordance with the method which I had prescribed myself. I had experienced so much satisfaction since beginning to use this method, that I did not believe that any sweeter or more innocent could in this life be found, – every day discovering by its means some truths which seemed to me sufficiently important, although commonly ignored by other men. The satisfaction which I had so filled my mind that all else seemed of no account. And, besides, the three preceding maxims were founded solely on the plan which I had formed of continuing to instruct myself. For since God has given to each of us some light with which to distinguish truth from error, I could not believe that I ought for a single moment to content myself with accepting the opinions held by others unless I had in view the employment of my own judgment in examining them at the proper time; and I could not have held myself free of scruple in following such opinions, if nevertheless I had not intended to lose no occasion of finding superior opinions, supposing them to exist; and finally, I should not have been able to restrain my desires nor to remain content, if I had not followed a road by which, thinking that I should be certain to be able to acquire all the knowledge of which I was capable, I also thought I should likewise be certain of obtaining all the best things which could ever come within my power. And inasmuch as our will impels us neither to follow after nor to flee from anything, excepting as our understanding represents it as good or evil, it is sufficient to judge wisely in order to act well, and the best judgment brings the best action – that is to say, the acquisition of all the virtues and all the other good things that it is possible to obtain. When one is certain that this point is reached, one cannot fail to be contented.

Having thus assured myself of these maxims, and having set them on one side along with the truths of religion which have always taken the first place in my creed, I judged that as far as the rest of my opinions were concerned, I could safely undertake to rid myself of them. And inasmuch as I hoped to be able to reach my end more successfully in converse with man than in living longer shut up in the warm room where these reflections had come to me, I hardly awaited the end of winter before I once more set myself to travel. And in all the nine following years I did nought but roam hither and thither, trying to be a spectator rather than an actor in all the comedies the world displays. More especially did I reflect in each matter that came before me as to anything which could make it subject to suspicion or doubt, and give occasion for mistake, and I rooted out of my mind all the errors which might have formerly crept in. Not that indeed I imitated the sceptics, who only doubt for the sake of doubting, and pretend to be always uncertain; for, on the contrary, my design was only to provide myself with good ground for assurance, and to reject the quicksand and mud in order to find the rock or clay. In this task it seems to me, I succeeded pretty well, since in trying to discover the error or uncertainty of the propositions which I examined, not by feeble conjectures, but by clear and assured reasonings, I encountered nothing so dubious that I could not draw from it some conclusion that was tolerably secure, if this were no more than the inference that it contained in it nothing that was certain. And just as in pulling down an old house we usually preserve the debris to serve in building up another, so in destroying all those opinions which I considered to be ill-founded, I made various observations and acquired many experiences, which have since been of use to me in establishing those which are more certain. And more than this, I continued to exercise myself in the method which I had laid down for my use; for besides the fact that I was careful as a rule to conduct all my thoughts according to its maxims, I set aside some hours from time to time which I more especially employed in practising myself in the solution of mathematical problems according to the Method, or in the solution of other problems which though pertaining to other sciences, I was able to make almost similar to those of mathematics, by detaching them from all principles of other sciences which I found to be not sufficiently secure. You will see the result in many examples which are expounded in this volume. And hence, without living to all appearance in any way differently from those who, having no occupation beyond spending their lives in ease and innocence, study to separate pleasure from vice, and who, in order to enjoy their leisure without weariness, make use of all distractions that are innocent and good, I did not cease to prosecute my design, and to profit perhaps even more in my study of Truth than if I had done nothing but read books or associate with literary people.

These nine years thus passed away before I had taken any definite part in regard to the difficulties as to which the learned are in the habit of disputing, or had commenced to seek the foundation of any philosophy more certain than the vulgar. And the example of many excellent men who had tried to do the same before me, but, as it appears to me, without success, made me imagine it to be so hard that possibly I should not have dared to undertake the task, had I not discovered that someone had spread abroad the report that I had already reached its conclusion. I cannot tell on what they based this opinion; if my conversation has contributed anything to it, this must have arisen from my confessing my ignorance more ingenuously than those who have studied a little usually do. And perhaps it was also due to my having shown forth my reasons for doubting many things which were held by others to be certain, rather than from having boasted of any special philosophic system. But being at heart honest enough not to desire to be esteemed as different from what I am, I thought that I must try by every means in my power to render myself worthy of the reputation which I had gained. And it is just eight years ago that this desire made me resolve to remove myself from all places where any acquaintances were possible, and to retire to a country such as this,[2] where the long-continued war has caused such order to be established that the armies which are maintained seem only to be of use in allowing the inhabitants to enjoy the fruits of peace with so much the more security; and where, in the crowded throng of a great and very active nation, which is more concerned with its own affairs than curious about those of others, without missing any of the conveniences of the most populous towns, I can live as solitary and retired as in deserts the most remote.

PART FOUR

I do not know that I ought to tell you of the first meditations there made by me, for they are so metaphysical and so unusual that they may perhaps not be acceptable to everyone. And yet at the same time, in order that one may judge whether the foundations which I have laid are sufficiently secure, I find myself

2. i.e. Holland, where Descartes settled in 1629.

constrained in some measure to refer to them. For a long time I had remarked that it is sometimes requisite in common life to follow opinions which one knows to be most uncertain, exactly as though they were indisputable, as has been said above. But because in this case I wished to give myself entirely to the search after Truth, I thought that it was necessary for me to take an apparently opposite course, and to reject as absolutely false everything as to which I could imagine the least ground of doubt, in order to see if afterwards there remained anything in my belief that was entirely certain. Thus, because our senses sometimes deceive us, I wished to suppose that nothing is just as they cause us to imagine it to be; and because there are men who deceive themselves in their reasoning and fall into paralogisms, even concerning the simplest matters of geometry, and judging that I was as subject to error as was any other, I rejected as false all the reasons formerly accepted by me as demonstrations. And since all the same thoughts and conceptions which we have while awake may also come to us in sleep, without any of them being at that time true, I resolved to assume that everything that ever entered into my mind was no more true than the illusions of my dreams. But immediately afterwards I noticed that whilst I thus wished to think all things false, it was absolutely essential that the 'I' who thought this should be somewhat, and remarking that this truth '*I think, therefore I am*' was so certain and so assured that all the most extravagant suppositions brought forward by the sceptics were incapable of shaking it, I came to the conclusion that I could receive it without scruple as the first principle of the Philosophy for which I was seeking.

And then, examining attentively that which I was, I saw that I could conceive that I had no body, and that there was no world nor place where I might be; but yet that I could not for all that conceive that I was not. On the contrary, I saw from the very fact that I thought of doubting the truth of other things, it very evidently and certainly followed that I was; on the other hand if I had only ceased from thinking, even if all the rest of what I had ever imagined had really existed, I should have no reason for thinking that I had existed. From that I knew that I was a substance the whole essence or nature of which is to think, and that for its existence there is no need of any place, not does it depend on any material thing; so that this 'me', that is to say, the soul by which I am what I am, is entirely distinct from body, and is even more easy to know than is the latter; and even if body were not, the soul would not cease to be what it is.

After this I considered generally what in a proposition is requisite in order to be true and certain; for since I had just discovered one which I knew to be such, I thought that I ought also to know in what this certainty consisted. And having remarked that there was nothing at all in the statement '*I think, therefore I am*' which assures me of having thereby made a true assertion, excepting that I see very clearly that to think it is necessary to be, I came to the conclusion that I might assume, as a general rule, that the things which we conceive very clearly and distinctly are all true – remembering, however, that there is some difficulty in ascertaining which are those that we distinctly conceive.

Following upon this, and reflecting on the fact that I doubted, and that consequently my existence was not quite perfect (for I saw clearly that it was a greater perfection to know than to doubt), I resolved to inquire whence I had learnt to think of anything more perfect than I myself was; and I recognised very clearly that this conception must proceed from some nature which was really more perfect. As to the thoughts which I had of many other things outside of me, like the heavens, the earth, light, heat, and a thousand others, I had not so much difficulty in knowing whence they came, because, remarking nothing in them which seemed to render them superior to me, I could believe that, if they were true, they were dependencies upon my nature, in so far as it possessed some perfection; and if they were not true, that I held them from nought, that is to say, that they were in me because I had something lacking in my nature. But this could not apply to the idea of a Being more perfect than my own, for to hold it from nought would be manifestly impossible; and because it is no less contradictory to say of the more perfect that it is what results from and depends on the less perfect, than to say that there is something which proceeds from nothing, it was equally impossible that I should hold it from myself. In this way it could but follow that it had been placed in me by a Nature which was really more perfect than mine could be, and which even had within itself all the perfections of which I could form any idea – that is to say, to put it in a word, which was God. To which I added that since I knew some perfections which I did not possess, I was not the only being in existence (I shall here use freely, if you will allow, the terms of the School); but that there was necessarily some other more perfect Being on which I depended, or from which I acquired all that I had. For if I had existed alone and independent of any others, so that I should have had from myself all that perfection of being in which I participated to however small an extent, I should have been able for the same reason to have had all the remainder which I knew that I lacked; and thus I myself should have been infinite, eternal, immutable, omniscient, all-powerful, and, finally, I should have all the perfections which I could discern in God. For, in pursuance of the reasonings which I have just carried on, in order to know the nature of God as far as my nature is capable of knowing it, I had only to consider in reference to all these things of which I found some idea in myself, whether it was a perfection to possess them or not. And I was assured that none of those which indicated some imperfection were in Him, but that all else was present; and I saw that doubt, inconstancy, sadness, and such things, could not be in Him considering that I myself should have been glad to be without them. In addition to this, I had ideas of many things which are sensible and corporeal, for, although I might suppose that I was dreaming, and that all that I saw or imagined was false, I could not at the same time deny that the ideas were really in my thoughts. But because I had already recognised very clearly in myself that the nature of the intelligence is distinct from that of the body, and observing that all composition gives evidence of dependency, and that dependency is manifestly an imperfection, I came to the conclusion that it could not be a perfection in God to be composed of these two natures, and that consequently He was not so composed. I judged, however, that if there were any bodies in the world, or even any intelligences or other natures which were not wholly perfect, their existence must depend on His power in such a way that they could not subsist without Him for a single moment.

After that I desired to seek for other truths, and having put before myself the object of the geometricians, which I conceived to be a continuous body, or a space indefinitely extended in length, breadth, height or depth, which was divisible into various parts, and which might have various figures and sizes, and might be moved or transposed in all sorts of ways (for all this the geometricians suppose to be in the object of their contemplation), I went through some of their simplest demonstrations, and having noticed that this great certainty which everyone attributes to these demonstrations is founded solely on the fact that they are conceived of with clearness, in accordance with the rule which I have just laid down, I also noticed that there was nothing at all in them to assure me of the existence of their object. For, to take an example, I saw very well that if we suppose a triangle to be given, the three angles must certainly be equal to two right angles; but for all that I saw no reason to be assured that there was any such triangle in existence, while on the contrary, on reverting to the examination of the idea which I had of a Perfect Being, I found that in this case existence was implied in it in the same manner in which the equality of its three angles to two right angles is implied in the idea of a triangle; or in the idea of a sphere, that all the points on its surface are equidistant from its centre, or even more evidently still. Consequently it is at least as certain that God, who is a Being so perfect, is, or exists, as any demonstration of geometry can possibly be.

What causes many, however, to persuade themselves that there is difficulty in knowing this truth, and even in knowing the nature of their soul, is the fact that they never raise their minds above the things of sense, or that they are so accustomed to consider nothing excepting by imagining it, which is a mode of thought specially adapted to material objects, that all that is not capable of being imagined appears to them not to be intelligible at all. This is manifest enough from the fact that even the philosophers in the Schools hold it as a maxim that there is nothing in the understanding which has not first of all been in the senses, in which there is certainly no doubt that the ideas of God and of the soul have never been. And it seems to me that those who desire to make use of their imagination in order to understand these ideas, act in the same way as if, to hear sounds or smell odours, they should wish to make use of their eyes: excepting that there is indeed this difference, that the sense of sight does not give us less assurance of the truth of its objects, than do those of scent or of hearing, while neither our imagination nor our senses can ever assure us of anything, if our understanding does not intervene.

If there are finally any persons who are not sufficiently persuaded of the existence of God and of their soul by the reasons which I have brought forward, I wish that they should know that all other things of which they perhaps think themselves more assured (such as possessing a body, and that there are stars and an earth and so on) are less certain. For, although we have a moral assurance of these things which is such that it seems that it would be extravagant in us to doubt them, at the same time no one, unless he is devoid of reason, can deny, when a metaphysical certainty is in question, that there is sufficient cause for our not having complete assurance, by observing the fact that when asleep we may similarly imagine that we have another body, and that we see other stars and another earth, without there being anything of the kind. For how do we know that the thoughts that come in dreams are more false than those that we have when we are awake, seeing that often enough the former are not less lively and vivid than the latter? And though the wisest minds may study the matter as much as they will, I do not believe that they will be able to give any sufficient reason for removing this doubt, unless they presuppose the existence of God. For to begin with, that which I have just taken as a rule, that is to say, that all the things that we very clearly and very distinctly conceive of are true, is certain only because God is or exists, and that He is a Perfect Being, and that all that is in us issues from Him. From this it follows that our ideas or notions, which to the extent of their being clear or distinct are ideas of real things issuing from God, cannot but to that extent be true. So that though we often enough have ideas which have an element of falsity, this can only be the case in regard to those which have in them somewhat that is confused or obscure, because in so far as they have this character they participate in negation – that is, they exist in us as confused only because we are not quite perfect. And it is evident that there is no less repugnance in the idea that error or imperfection, inasmuch as it is imperfection, proceeds from God, than there is in the idea of truth or perfection proceeding from nought. But if we did not know that all that is in us of reality and truth proceeds from a perfect and infinite Being, however clear and distinct were our ideas, we should not have any reason to assure ourselves that they had the perfection of being true.

But after the knowledge of God and of the soul has thus rendered us certain of this rule, it is very easy to understand that the dreams which we imagine in our sleep should not make us in any way doubt the truth of the thoughts which we have when awake. For even if in sleep we had some very distinct idea such as a geometrician might have who discovered some new demonstration, the fact of being asleep would not militate against its truth. And as to the most ordinary error in our dreams, which consists in their representing to us various objects in the same way as do our external senses, it does not matter that this should give us occasion to suspect the truth of such ideas, because we may be likewise often enough deceived in them without our sleeping at all, just as when those who have the jaundice see everything as yellow, or when stars or other bodies which are very remote appear much smaller than they really are. For, finally, whether we are awake or asleep, we should never allow ourselves to be persuaded excepting by the evidence of our Reason. And it must be remarked that I speak of our Reason and not of our imagination nor of our senses; just as though we see the sun very clearly, we should not for that reason judge that it is of the size of which it appears to be; likewise we could quite well distinctly imagine the head of a lion on the body of a goat, without necessarily concluding that a chimera exists. For Reason does not insist that whatever we see or imagine thus is a truth, but it tells us clearly that all our ideas or notions must have some foundation of truth. For otherwise it could not be possible that God, who is all perfection and truth, should have placed them within us. And because our reasonings are never so evident nor so complete during sleep as during wakefulness, although sometimes our imaginations are then just as lively and acute, or even more so, Reason tells us that since our thoughts cannot possibly be all true, because we are not altogether perfect, that which they have of truth must infallibly be met with in our waking experience rather than in that of our dreams.

PART FIVE

I should be very glad to proceed to show forth the complete chain of truths which I have deduced from these first, but because to do this it would have been necessary now to speak of many matters of dispute among the learned, with whom I have no desire to embroil myself, I think that it will be better to abstain. I shall only state generally what these truths are, so that it may be left to the decision of those best able to judge whether it would be of use for the public to be more particularly informed of them or not. I always remained firm in the resolution which I had made, not to assume any other principle than that of which I have just made use, in order to demonstrate the existence of God and of the Soul, and to accept nothing as true which did not appear to be more clear and more certain than the demonstrations of the geometricians had formerly seemed. And nevertheless I venture to say that not only have I found the means of satisfying myself in a short time as to the more important of those difficulties usually dealt with in philosophy, but I have also observed certain laws which God has so established in Nature, and of which He has imprinted such ideas on our minds, that, after having reflected sufficiently upon the matter, we cannot doubt their being accurately observed in all that exists or is done in the world. Further, in considering the sequence of these laws, it seems to me that I have discovered many truths more useful and more important than all that I had formerly learned or even hoped to learn.

But because I tried to explain the most important of these in a Treatise[3] which certain considerations prevented me from publishing, I cannot do better, in making them known, than here summarise briefly what that Treatise contains. I had planned to comprise in it all that I believed myself to know regarding the nature of material objects, before I set myself to write. However, just as the painters who cannot represent equally well on a plain surface all the various sides of a solid body, make selection of one of the most important, which alone is set in the light, while the others are put in shadow and made to appear only as they may be seen in looking at the former, so, fearing that I could not put in my Treatise all that I had in my mind, I undertook only to show very fully my conceptions of light. Later on, when occasion occurred, I resolved to add something about the sun and fixed stars, because light proceeds almost entirely from them; the heavens would be dealt with because they transmit light, the planets, the comets and the earth because they reflect it, and more particularly would all bodies which are on the earth, because they are either coloured or transparent, or else luminous; and finally I should deal with man because he is the spectator of all. For the very purpose of putting all these topics somewhat in shadow, and being able to

3. i.e. 'Le Monde,' suppressed on hearing of Galileo's condemnation.

express myself freely about them, without being obliged to adopt or to refute the opinions which are accepted by the learned, I resolved to leave all this world to their disputes, and to speak only of what would happen in a new world if God now created, somewhere in an imaginary space, matter sufficient wherewith to form it, and if He agitated in diverse ways, and without any order, the diverse portions of this matter, so that there resulted a chaos as confused as the poets ever feigned, and concluded His work by merely lending His concurrence to Nature in the usual way, leaving her to act in accordance with the laws which He had established. So, to begin with, I described this matter and tried to represent it in such a way, that it seems to me that nothing in the world could be more clear or intelligible, excepting what has just been said of God and the Soul. For I even went so far as expressly to assume that there was in it none of these forms or qualities which are so debated in the Schools, nor anything at all the knowledge of which is not so natural to our minds that none could even pretend to be ignorant of it. Further I pointed out what are the laws of Nature, and, without resting my reasons on any other principle than the infinite perfections of God, I tried to demonstrate all those of which one could have any doubt, and to show that they are of such a nature that even if God had created other worlds, He could not have created any in which these laws would fail to be observed. After that, I showed how the greatest part of the matter of which this chaos is constituted, must, in accordance with these laws, dispose and arrange itself in such a fashion as to render it similar to our heavens; and how meantime some of its parts must form an earth, some planets and comets, and some others a sun and fixed stars. And, enlarging on the subject of light, I here explained at length the nature of the light which would be found in the sun and stars, and how from these it crossed in an instant the immense space of the heavens, and how it was reflected from the planets and comets to the earth. To this I also added many things touching the substance, situation, movements, and all the different qualities of these heavens and stars, so that I thought I had said enough to make it clear that there is nothing to be seen in the heavens and stars pertaining to our system which must not, or at least may not, appear exactly the same in those of the system which I described. From this point I came to speak more particularly of the earth, showing how, though I had expressly presupposed that God had not placed any weight in the matter of which it is composed, its parts did not fail all to gravitate exactly to its centre; and how, having water and air on its surface, the disposition of the heavens and of the stars, more particularly of the moon, must cause a flux or reflux, which in all its circumstances is similar to that which is observed in our seas, and besides that, a certain current both of water and air from east to west, such as may also be observed in the tropics. I also showed how the mountains, seas, fountains and rivers, could naturally be formed in it, how the metals came to be in the mines and the plants to grow in the fields; and generally how all bodies, called mixed or composite, might arise. And because I knew nothing but fire which could produce light, excepting the stars, I studied amongst other things to make very clear all that pertains to its nature, how it is formed, how nourished, how there is sometimes only heat without light, and sometimes light without heat; I showed, too, how different colours might by it be induced upon different bodies and qualities of diverse kinds, how some of these were liquefied and others solidified, how nearly all can be consumed or converted into ashes and smoke by its means, and finally how of these ashes, by the intensity of its action alone, it forms glass. Since this transformation of ashes into glass seemed to me as wonderful as any other process in nature, I took particular pleasure in describing it.

I did not at the same time wish to infer from all these facts that this world has been created in the manner which I described; for it is much more probable that at the beginning God made it such as it was to be. But it is certain, and it is an opinion commonly received by the theologians, that the action by which He now preserves it is just the same as that by which He at first created it. In this way, although He had not, to begin with, given this world any other form than that of chaos, provided that the laws of nature had once been established and that He had lent His aid in order that its action should be according to its wont, we may well believe, without doing outrage to the miracle of creation, that by this means alone all things which are purely material might in course of time have become such as we observe them to be at present; and their nature is much easier to understand when we see them coming to pass little by little in this manner, than were we to consider them as all complete to begin with.

From a description of inanimate bodies and plants I passed on to that of animals, and particularly to that of men. But since I had not yet sufficient knowledge to speak of them in the same style as of the rest, that is to say, demonstrating the effects from the causes, and showing from what beginnings and in what fashion Nature must produce them, I contented myself with supposing that God formed the body of man altogether like one of ours, in the outward figure of its members as well as in the interior conformation of its organs, without making use of any matter other than that which I had described, and without at the first placing in it a rational soul, or any other thing which might serve as a vegetative or as a sensitive soul; excepting that He kindled in the heart one of these fires without light, which I have already described, and which I did not conceive of as in any way different from that which makes the hay heat when shut up before it is dry, and which makes new wine grow frothy when it is left to ferment over the fruit. For, examining the functions which might in accordance with this supposition exist in this body, I found precisely all those which might exist in us without our having the power of thought, and consequently without our soul – that is to say, this part of us, distinct from the body, of which it has just been said that its nature is to think – contributing to it, functions which are identically the same as those in which animals lacking reason may be said to resemble us. For all that, I could not find in these functions any which, being dependent on thought, pertain to us alone, inasmuch as we are men; while I found all of them afterwards, when I assumed that God had created a rational soul and that He had united it to this body in a particular manner which I described.[4]

* * *

I had explained all these matters in some detail in the Treatise which I formerly intended to publish. And afterwards I had shown there, what must be the fabric of the nerves and muscles of the human body in order that the animal spirits therein contained should have the power to move the members, just as the heads of animals, a little while after decapitation, are still observed to move and bite the earth, notwithstanding that they

4. There follows a long passage, mainly about the circulation of the blood and of merely historical interest.

are no longer animate; what changes are necessary in the brain to cause wakefulness, sleep and dreams; how light, sounds, smells, tastes, heat and all other qualities pertaining to external objects are able to imprint on it various ideas by the intervention of the senses; how hunger, thirst and other internal affections can also convey their impressions upon it; what should be regarded as the 'common sense' by which these ideas are received, and what is meant by the memory which retains them, by the fancy which can change them in diverse ways and out of them constitute new ideas, and which, by the same means, distributing the animal spirits through the muscles, can cause the members of such a body to move in as many diverse ways, and in a manner as suitable to the objects which present themselves to its senses and to its internal passions, as can happen in our own case apart from the direction of our free will. And this will not seem strange to those, who, know how many different *automata* or moving machines can be made by the industry of man, without employing in so doing more than a very few parts in comparison with the great multitude of bones, muscles, nerves, arteries, veins, or other parts that are found in the body of each animal. From this aspect the body is regarded as a machine which, having been made by the hands of God, is incomparably better arranged, and possesses in itself movements which are much more admirable, than any of those which can be invented by man. Here I specially stopped to show that if there had been such machines, possessing the organs and outward form of a monkey or some other animal without reason, we should not have had any means of ascertaining that they were not of the same nature as those animals. On the other hand, if there were machines which bore a resemblance to our body and imitated our actions as far as it was morally possible to do so, we should always have two very certain tests by which to recognise that, for all that, they were not real men. The first is, that they could never use speech or other signs as we do when placing our thoughts on record for the benefit of others. For we can easily understand a machine's being constituted so that it can utter words, and even emit some responses to action on it of a corporeal kind, which brings about a change in its organs; for instance, if it is touched in a particular part it may ask what we wish to say to it; if in another part it may exclaim that it is being hurt, and so on. But it never happens that it arranges its speech in various ways, in order to reply appropriately to everything that may be said in its presence, as even the lowest type of man can do. And the second difference is, that although machines can perform certain things as well as or perhaps better than any of us can do, they infallibly fall short in others, by the which means we may discover that they did not act from knowledge, but only from the disposition of their organs. For while reason is a universal instrument which can serve for all contingencies, these organs have need of some special adaptation for every particular action. From this it follows that it is morally impossible that there should be sufficient diversity in any machine to allow it to act in all the events of life in the same way as our reason causes us to act.

By these two methods we may also recognise the difference that exists between men and brutes. For it is a very remarkable fact that there are none so depraved and stupid, without even excepting idiots, that they cannot arrange different words together, forming of them a statement by which they make known their thoughts; while, on the other hand, there is no other animal, however perfect and fortunately circumstanced it may be, which can do the same. It is not the want of organs that brings this to pass, for it is evident that magpies and parrots are able to utter words just like ourselves, and yet they cannot speak as we do, that is, so as to give evidence that they think of what they say. On the other hand, men who, being born deaf and dumb, are in the same degree, or even more than the brutes, destitute of the organs which serve the others for talking, are in the habit of themselves inventing certain signs by which they make themselves understood by those who, being usually in their company, have leisure to learn their language. And this does not merely show that the brutes have less reason than men, but that they have none at all, since it is clear that very little is required in order to be able to talk. And when we notice the inequality that exists between animals of the same species, as well as between men, and observe that some are more capable of receiving instruction than others, it is not credible that a monkey or a parrot, selected as the most perfect of its species, should not in these matters equal the stupidest child to be found, or at least a child whose mind is clouded, unless in the case of the brute the soul were of an entirely different nature from ours. And we ought not to confound speech with natural movements which betray passions and may be imitated by machines as well as be manifested by animals; nor must we think, as did some of the ancients, that brutes talk, although we do not understand their language. For if this were true, since they have many organs which are allied to our own, they could communicate their thoughts to us just as easily as to those of their own race. It is also a very remarkable fact that although there are many animals which exhibit more dexterity than we do in some of their actions, we at the same time observe that they do not manifest any dexterity at all in many others. Hence the fact that they do better than we do, does not prove that they are endowed with mind, for in this case they would have more reason than any of us, and would surpass us in all other things. It rather shows that they have no reason at all, and that it is nature which acts in them according to the disposition of their organs, just as a clock, which is only composed of wheels and weights is able to tell the hours and measure the time more correctly than we can do with all our wisdom.

I had described after this the rational soul and shown that it could not be in any way derived from the power of matter, like the other things of which I had spoken, but that it must be expressly created. I showed, too, that it is not sufficient that it should be lodged in the human body like a pilot in his ship, unless perhaps for the moving of its members, but that it is necessary that it should also be joined and united more closely to the body in order to have sensations and appetites similar to our own, and thus to form a true man. In conclusion, I have here enlarged a little on the subject of the soul, because it is one of the greatest importance. For next to the error of those who deny God, which I think I have already sufficiently refuted, there is none which is more effectual in leading feeble spirits from the straight path of virtue, than to imagine that the soul of the brute is of the same nature as our own, and that in consequence, after this life we have nothing to fear or to hope for, any more than the flies and ants. As a matter of fact, when one comes to know how greatly they differ, we understand much better the reasons which go to prove that our soul is in its nature entirely independent of body, and in consequence that it is not liable to die with it. And then, inasmuch as we observe no other causes capable of destroying it, we are naturally inclined to judge that it is immortal.

PART SIX

It is three years since I arrived at the end of the Treatise which contained all these things; and I was commencing to revise it in order to place it in the hands of a printer, when I learned that certain persons, to whose opinions I defer, and whose authority cannot have less weight with my actions than my own reason has over my thoughts, had disapproved of a physical theory published a little while before by another person.[5] I will not say that I agreed with this opinion, but only that before their censure I observed in it nothing which I could possibly imagine to be prejudicial either to Religion or the State, or consequently which could have prevented me from giving expression to it in writing, if my reason had persuaded me to do so: and this made me fear that among my own opinions one might be found which should be misunderstood, notwithstanding the great care which I have always taken not to accept any new beliefs unless I had very certain proof of their truth, and not to give expression to what could tend to the disadvantage of any person. This sufficed to cause me to alter the resolution which I had made to publish. For, although the reasons for my former resolution were very strong, my inclination, which always made me hate the profession of writing books, caused me immediately to find plenty of other reasons for excusing myself from doing so. And these reasons, on the one side and on the other, are of such a nature that not only have I here some interest in giving expression to them, but possibly the public may also have some interest in knowing them.

I have never made much of those things which proceed from my own mind, and so long as I culled no other fruits from the Method which I use, beyond that of satisfying myself respecting certain difficulties which pertain to the speculative sciences, or trying to regulate my conduct by the reasons which it has taught me, I never believed myself to be obliged to write anything about it. For as regards that which concerns conduct, everyone is so confident of his own common sense, that there might be found as many reformers as heads, if it were permitted that others than those whom God has established as the sovereigns of his people, or at least to whom He has given sufficient grace and zeal to be prophets, should be allowed to make any

5. i.e. Galileo.

changes in that. And, although my speculations give me the greatest pleasure, I believed that others also had speculations which possibly pleased them even more. But so soon as I had acquired some general notions concerning Physics, and as, beginning to make use of them in various special difficulties, I observed to what point they might lead us, and how much they differ from the principles of which we have made use up to the present time, I believed that I could not keep them concealed without greatly sinning against the law which obliges us to procure, as much as in us lies, the general good of all mankind. For they caused me to see that it is possible to attain knowledge which is very useful in life, and that, instead of that speculative philosophy which is taught in the Schools, we may find a practical philosophy by means of which, knowing the force and the action of fire, water, air, the stars, heavens and all other bodies that environ us, as distinctly as we know the different crafts of our artisans, we can in the same way employ them in all those uses to which they are adapted, and thus render ourselves the masters and possessors of nature. This is not merely to be desired with a view to the invention of an infinity of arts and crafts which enable us to enjoy without any trouble the fruits of the earth and all the good things which are to be found there, but also principally because it brings about the preservation of health, which is without doubt the chief blessing and the foundation of all other blessings in this life. For the mind depends so much on the temperament and disposition of the bodily organs that, if it is possible to find a means of rendering men wiser and cleverer than they have hitherto been, I believe that it is in medicine that it must be sought. It is true that the medicine which is now in vogue contains little of which the utility is remarkable; but, without having any intention of decrying it, I am sure that there is no one, even among those who make its study a profession, who does not confess that all that men know is almost nothing in comparison with what remains to be known; and that we could be free of an infinitude of maladies both of body and mind, and even also possibly of the infirmities of age, if we had sufficient knowledge of their causes, and of all the remedies with which nature has provided us. But, having the intention of devoting all my life to the investigation of a knowledge which is so essential, and having discovered a path which appears to me to be of such a nature that we must by its means infallibly reach our end if we pursue it, unless, indeed, we are prevented by the shortness of life or by lack of experience, I judged that there was no better provision against these two impediments than faithfully to communicate to the public the little which I should myself have discovered, and to beg all well-inclined persons to proceed further by contributing, each one according to his own inclination and ability, to the experiments which must be made, and then to communicate to the public all the things which they might discover, in order that the last should commence where the preceding had left off; and thus, by joining together the lives and labours of many, we should collectively proceed much further than any one in particular could succeed in doing.

I remarked also respecting experiments, that they become so much the more necessary the more one is advanced in knowledge, for to begin with it is better to make use simply of those which present themselves spontaneously to our senses, and of which we could not be ignorant provided that we reflected ever so little, rather than to seek out those which are more rare and recondite; the reason of this is that those which are more rare often mislead us so long as we do not know the causes of the more common, and the fact that the circumstances on which they depend are almost always so particular and so minute that it is very difficult to observe them. But in this the order which I have followed is as follows: I have first tried to discover generally the principles or first causes of everything that is or that can be in the world, without considering anything that might accomplish this end but God Himself who has created the world, or deriving them from any source excepting from certain germs of truths which are naturally existent in our souls. After that I considered which were the primary and most ordinary effects which might be deduced from these causes, and it seems to me that in this way I discovered the heavens, the stars, an earth, and even on the earth, water, air, fire, the minerals and some other such things, which are the most common and simple of any that exist, and consequently the easiest to know. Then, when I wished to descend to those which were more particular, so many objects of various kinds presented themselves to me, that I did not think it was possible for the human mind to distinguish the forms or species of bodies which are on the earth from an infinitude of others which might have been so if it had been the will of God to place them there, or consequently to apply them to our use, if it were not that we arrive at the causes by the effects, and avail ourselves of many particular experiments. In subsequently passing over in my mind all the objects which have ever been presented to my senses, I can truly venture to say that I have not there observed anything which I could not easily explain by the principles which I had discovered. But I must also confess that the power of nature is so ample and so vast, and these principles are so simple and general, that I observed hardly any particular effect as to which I could not at once recognise that it might be deduced from the principles in many different ways; and my greatest difficulty is usually to discover in which of these ways the effect does depend upon them. As to that, I do not know any other plan but again to try to find experiments of such a nature that their result is not the same if it has to be explained by one of the methods, as it would be if explained by the other. For the rest, I have now reached a position in which I discern, as it seems to me, sufficiently clearly what course must be adopted in order to make the majority of the experiments which may conduce to carry out this end. But I also perceive that they are of such a nature, and of so great a number, that neither my hands nor my income, though the latter were a thousand times larger than it is, could suffice for the whole; so that just in proportion as henceforth I shall have the power of carrying out more of them or less, shall I make more or less progress in arriving at a knowledge of nature. This is what I had promised myself to make known by the Treatise which I had written, and to demonstrate in it so clearly the advantage which the public might receive from it, that I should induce all those who have the good of mankind at heart – that is to say, all those who are really virtuous in fact, and not only by a false semblance or by opinion – both to communicate to me those experiments that they have already carried out, and to help me in the investigation of those that still remain to be accomplished.

But I have since that time found other reasons which caused me to change my opinion, and consider that I should indeed continue to put in writing all the things which I judged to be of importance whenever I discovered them to be true, and that I should bestow on them the same care as I should have done had I wished to have them printed. I did this because it would give me so much the more occasion to examine them carefully (for there is no doubt that we always scrutinize more closely what we think will be seen by many, than what is done simply for ourselves, and often the things which have seemed true to me when I began to think about them, seemed false when I tried to place them on paper); and because I did not desire to lose any opportunity of benefiting the public if I were able to do so, and in order that if my works have any value, those into whose hands they will fall after my death, might have the power of making use of them as seems best to them. I, however, resolved that I should not consent to their being published during my lifetime, so that neither the contradictions and controversies to which they might possibly give rise, nor even the reputation, such as it might be, which they would bring to me, should give me any occasion to lose the time which I meant to set apart for my own instruction. For although it is true that each man is obliged to procure, as much as in him lies, the good of others, and that to be useful to nobody is popularly speaking to be worthless, it is at the same time true that our cares should extend further than the present time, and that it is good to set aside those things which may possibly be adapted to bring profit to the living, when we have in view the accomplishment of other ends which will bring much more advantage to our descendants. In the same way I should much like that men should know that the little which I have learned hitherto is almost nothing in comparison with that of which I am ignorant, and with the knowledge of which I do not despair of being able to attain. For it is much the same with those who little by little discover the truth in the Sciences, as with those who, commencing to become rich, have less trouble in obtaining great acquisitions than they formerly experienced, when poorer, in arriving at those much smaller in amount. Or we might compare them to the Generals of our armies, whose forces usually grow in proportion to their victories, and who require more leadership in order to hold together their troops after the loss of a battle, than is needed to take towns and provinces after having obtained a success. For he really gives battle who attempts to conquer all the difficulties and errors which prevent him from arriving at a knowledge of the truth, and it is to lose a battle to admit a false opinion touching a matter of any generality and importance. Much more skill is required in order to recover ths position that one beforehand held, than is necessary to make great progress when one already possesses principles which are assured. For myself, if I have succeeded in discovering certain truths in the Sciences (and I hope that the matters contained in this volume will show that I have discovered some), I may say that they are resultant from, and dependent on, five or six principal difficulties which I have surmounted, and my encounter with these I look upon as so many battles in which I have had fortune on my side. I will not even hesitate to say that I think I shall have no need to win more than two or three other victories similar in kind in order to reach the accomplishment of my plans. And my age is not so advanced but that, in the ordinary course of nature, I may still have sufficient leisure for this end. But I believe myself to be so much the more bound to make the most of the time which remains, as I have the greater hope of being able to employ it well. And without doubt I should have many chances of being robbed of it, were I to publish the foundations of my Physics; for though these are nearly all so evident that it is only necessary to understand them in order to accept them, and although there are none of them as to which I do not believe myself capable of giving demonstration, yet because it is impossible that they should accord with all the various opinions of other men, I foresee that I should often be diverted from my main design by the opposition which they would bring to birth.

We may say that these contradictions might be useful both in making me aware of my errors, and, supposing that I had reached some satisfactory conclusion, in bringing others to a fuller understanding of my speculations; and, as many can see more than can a single man, they might help in leading others who from the present time may begin to avail themselves of my system, to assist me likewise with their discoveries. But though I recognise that I am extremely liable to err, and though I almost never trust the first reflections that I arrive at, the experience which I have had of the objections which may be made to my system prevents my having any hope of deriving profit from them. For I have often had experience of the judgments both of those whom I have esteemed as my friends, and of some others to whom I believed myself to be indifferent, and even, too, of some whose ill-feeling and envy would, I felt sure, make them endeavour to reveal what affection concealed from the eyes of my friends. But rarely has it happened that any objection has been made which I did not in some sort foresee, unless where it was something very far removed from my subject. In this way hardly ever have I encountered any censor of my opinions who did not appear to be to be either less rigorous or less judicial than myself. And I certainly never remarked that by means of disputations employed by the Schools any truth has been discovered of which we were formerly ignorant. And so long as each side attempts to vanquish his opponent, there is a much more serious attempt to establish probability than to weigh the reasons on either side; and those who have for long been excellent pleaders are not for that reason the best judges.

As to the advantage which others may receive from the communication of my reflections, it could not be very great, inasmuch as I have not yet carried them so far as that it is not necessary to add many things before they can be brought into practice. And I think I can without vanity say that if anyone is capable of doing this, it should be myself rather than another – not indeed that there may not be in the world many minds incomparably superior to my own, but because no one can so well understand a thing and make it his own when learnt from another as when it is discovered for himself. As regards the matter in hand there is so much truth in this, that although I have often explained some of my opinions to persons of very good intelligence, who, while I talked to them appeared to understand them very clearly, yet when they recounted them I remarked that they had almost always altered them in such a manner that I could no longer acknowledge them as mine. On this account I am very glad to have the opportunity here of begging my descendants never to believe that what is told to them proceeded from myself unless I have myself divulged it. And I do not in the least wonder at the extravagances attributed to all the ancient philosophers whose writings we do not possess, nor do I judge from these that their thoughts were very unreasonable, considering that theirs were the best minds of the time they lived in, but only that they have been imperfectly represented to us. We see, too, that it hardly ever happens that any of their disciples surpassed them, and I am sure that those who most passionately follow Aristotle now-a-days would think themselves happy if they had as much knowledge of nature as he had, even if this were on the condition that they should never attain to any more. They are like the ivy that never tries to mount above the trees which give it support, and which often even descends again after it has reached their summit; for it appears to me that such men also sink again – that is to say, somehow render themselves more ignorant than they would have been had they abstained from study altogether. For, not content with knowing all that is intelligibly explained in their author, they wish in addition to find in him the solution of many difficulties of which he says nothing, and in regard to which he possibly had no thought at all. At the same time their mode of philosophising is very convenient for those who have abilities of a very mediocre kind, for the obscurity of the distinctions and principles of which they make use, is the reason of their being able to talk of all things as boldly as though they really knew about them, and defend all that they say against the most subtle and acute, without any one having the means of convincing them to the contrary. In this they seem to me like a blind man who, in order to fight on equal terms with one who sees, would have the latter to come into the bottom of a very dark cave. I may say, too, that it is in the interest of such people that I should abstain from publishing the principles of philosophy of which I make use, for, being so simple and evident as they are, I should, in publishing them, do the same as though I threw open the windows and caused daylight to enter the cave into which they have descended in order to fight. But even the best minds have no reason to desire to be acquainted with these principles, for if they wish to be able to talk of everything and acquire a reputation for learning, they will more readily attain their end by contenting themselves with the appearance of truth which may be found in all sorts of things without much trouble, than in seeking for truth which only reveals itself little by little in certain spheres, and which, when others come into question, obliges one to confess one's ignorance. If, however, they prefer the knowledge of some small amount of truth to the vanity of seeming to be ignorant of nothing, which knowledge is doubtless preferable, or if they desire to follow a course similar to my own, it is not necessary that I should say any more than what I have already said in this Discourse. For if they are capable of passing beyond the point I have reached, they will also so much the more be able to find by themselves all that I believe myself to have discovered; since, not having examined anything but in its order, it is certain that what remains for me to discover is in itself more difficult and more recondite than anything that I have hitherto been able to meet with, and they would have much less pleasure in learning from me than from themselves. Besides, the habit which they will acquire of seeking first things that are simple and then little by little and by degrees passing to others more difficult, will be of more use than could be all my instructions. For, as regards myself, I am persuaded that if from my youth up I had been taught all the truths of which I have since sought the demonstrations, or if I had not had any difficulty in learning them, I should perhaps never have known any others, or at least I should never have acquired the habit or facility which I think I have obtained, of ever finding them anew, in proportion as I set myself to seek for them. And, in a word, if there is any work at all which cannot be so well achieved by another as by him who has begun it, it is that at which I labour.

It is true as regards the experiments which may conduce to this end, that one man could not possibly accomplish all of them. But yet he could not, to good advantage, employ other hands than his own, excepting those of artisans or persons of that kind whom he could pay, and whom the hope of gain – which is a very effectual incentive – might cause to perform with exactitude all the things they were directed to accomplish. As to those who, whether by curiosity or desire to learn, might possibly offer him their voluntary assistance, not only are they usually more ready with promises than with performance, planning out fine sounding projects, none of which are ever realised, but they will also infallibly demand payment for their trouble by requesting the explanation of certain difficulties, or at least by empty compliments and useless talk, which could not occupy any of the student's time without causing it to be lost. And as to the experiments already made by others, even if they desired to communicate these to him – which those who term them secrets would never do – they are for the most part accompanied by so many circumstances or superfluous matter, that it would be very difficult for him to disentangle the truth. In addition to this he would find nearly all so badly explained, or even so false (because those who carried them out were forced to make them appear to be in conformity with their principles), that if there had been some which might have been of use to him, they would hardly be worth the time that would be required in making the selection. So true is this, that if there were anywhere in the world a person whom one knew to be assuredly capable of discovering matters of the highest importance and those of the greatest possible utility to the public, and if for this reason all other men were eager by every means in their power to help him in reaching the end which he set before him, I do not see that they could do anything for him beyond contributing to defray the expenses of the experiments which might be requisite, or, for the rest, seeing that he was not deprived of his leisure by the importunities of anyone. But, in addition to the fact that I neither esteem myself so highly as to be willing to promise anything extraordinary, nor give scope to an imagination so vain as to conceive that the public should interest itself greatly in my designs, I do not yet own a soul so base as to be willing to accept from anyone whatever a favour which it might be supposed I did not merit.

All those considerations taken together were, three years ago, the cause of my not desiring to publish the Treatise which I had on hand, and the reason why I even formed the resolution of not bringing to light during my life any other of so general a kind, or one by which the foundations of Physics could be understood. But since then two other reasons came into operation which compelled me to bring forward certain attempts, as I have done here, and to render to the public some account of my actions and designs. The first is that if I failed to do so, many who knew the intention I formerly had of publishing certain writings, might imagine that the causes for which I abstained from so doing were more to my disadvantage than they really were; for although I do not care immoderately for glory, or, if I dare say so, although I even hate it, inasmuch as I judge it to be antagonistic to the repose which I esteem above all other things, at the same time I never tried to conceal my actions as though they were crimes, nor have I used many precautions against being known, partly because I should have thought it damaging to myself, and partly because it would have given me a sort of disquietude which would again have militated against the perfect repose of spirit which I seek. And forasmuch as having in this way always held myself in a condition of indifference as regards whether I was known or was not known, I have not yet been able to prevent myself from acquiring some sort of reputation, I thought that I should do my best at least to prevent myself from acquiring an evil reputation. The other reason which obliged me to put this in writing is that I am becoming every day more and more alive to the delay which is being suffered in the design which I have of instructing myself, because of the lack of an infinitude of experiments, which it is impossible that I should perform without the aid of others: and although I do not flatter myself so much as to hope that the public should to any large degree participate in my interest, I yet do not wish to be found wanting, both on my own account, and as one day giving occasion to those who will survive me of reproaching me for the fact that I might have left many matters in a much better condition than I have done, had I not too much neglected to make them understand in what way they could have contributed to the accomplishment of my designs.

And I thought that it was easy for me to select certain matters which would not be the occasion for many controversies, nor yet oblige me to propound more of my principles than I wish, and which yet would suffice to allow a pretty clear manifestation of what I can do and what I cannot do in the sciences. In this I cannot say whether I have succeeded or have not succeeded, and I do not wish to anticipate the judgment of any one by myself speaking of my writings; but I shall be very glad if they will examine them. And in order that they may have the better opportunity of so doing, I beg all those who have any objections to offer to take the trouble of sending them to my publishers, so that, being made aware of them, I may try at the same time to subjoin my reply. By this means, the reader, seeing objections and reply at the same time, will the more easily judge of the truth; for I do not promise in any instance to make lengthy replies, but just to avow my errors very frankly if I am convinced of them; or, if I cannot perceive them, to say simply what I think requisite for the defence of the matters I have written, without adding the exposition of any new matter, so that I may not be endlessly engaged in passing from one side to the other.

If some of the matters of which I spoke in the beginning of the *Dioptrics* and *Meteors* should at first sight give offence because I call them hypotheses and do not appear to care about their proof, let them have the patience to read these in entirety, and I hope that they will find themselves satisfied. For it appears to me that the reasonings are so mutually interwoven, that as the later ones are demonstrated by the earlier, which are their causes, the earlier are reciprocally demonstrated by the later which are their effects. And it must not be imagined that in this

I commit the fallacy which logicians name arguing in a circle, for, since experience renders the greater part of these effects very certain, the causes from which I deduce them do not so much serve to prove their existence as to explain them; on the other hand, the causes are explained by the effects. And I have not named them hypotheses with any other object than that it may be known that while I consider myself able to deduce them from the primary truths which I explained above, yet I particularly desired not to do so, in order that certain persons may not for this reason take occasion to build up some extravagant philosophic system on what they take to be my principles, and thus cause the blame to be put on me. I refer to those who imagine that in one day they may discover all that another has arrived at in twenty years of work, so soon as he has merely spoken to them two or three words on the subject; while they are really all the more subject to err, and less capable of perceiving the truth as they are the more subtle and lively. For as regards the opinions that are truly mine I do not apologise for them as being new, inasmuch as if we consider the reasons of them well, I assure myself that they will be found to be so simple and so conformable to common sense, as to appear less extraordinary and less paradoxical than any others which may be held on similar subjects. And I do not even boast of being the first discoverer of any of them, but only state that I have adopted them, not because they have been held by others, nor because they have not been so held, but only because Reason has persuaded me of their truth.

Even if artisans are not at once able to carry out the invention explained in the *Dioptrics*, I do not for that reason think that it can be said that it is to be condemned; for, inasmuch as great address and practice is required to make and adjust the mechanism which I have described without omitting any detail, I should not be less astonished at their succeeding at the first effort than I should be supposing some one were in one day to learn to play the guitar with skill, just because a good sheet of musical notation were set up before him. And if I write in French which is the language of my country, rather than in Latin which is that of my teachers, that is because I hope that those who avail themselves only of their natural reason in its purity may be better judges of my opinions than those who believe only in the writings of the ancients; and as to those who unite good sense with study, whom alone I crave for my judges, they will not, I feel sure, be so partial to Latin as to refuse to follow my reasoning because I expound it in a vulgar tongue.

For the rest, I do not desire to speak here more particularly of the progress which I hope in the future to make in the sciences, nor to bind myself as regards the public with any promise which I shall not with certainty be able to fulfil. But I will just say that I have resolved not to employ the time which remains to me in life in any other matter than in endeavouring to acquire some knowledge of nature, which shall be of such a kind that it will enable us to arrive at rules for Medicine more assured than those which have as yet been attained; and my inclination is so strongly opposed to any other kind of pursuit, more especially to those which can only be useful to some by being harmful to others, that if certain circumstances had constrained me to employ them, I do not think that I should have been capable of succeeding. In so saying I make a declaration that I know very well cannot help me to make myself of consideration in the world, but to this end I have no desire to attain; and I shall always hold myself to be more indebted to those by whose favour I may enjoy my leisure without hindrance, than I shall be to any who may offer me the most honourable position in all the world.

Meditations on First Philosophy, 1641

TO THE MOST WISE AND ILLUSTRIOUS THE DEAN AND DOCTORS OF THE SACRED FACULTY OF THEOLOGY IN PARIS

The motive which induces me to present to you this Treatise is so excellent, and, when you become acquainted with its design, I am convinced that you will also have so excellent a motive for taking it under your protection, that I feel that I cannot do better, in order to render it in some sort acceptable to you, than in a few words to state what I have set myself to do.

I have always considered that the two questions respecting God and the Soul were the chief of those that ought to be demonstrated by philosophical rather than theological argument. For although it is quite enough for us faithful ones to accept by means of faith the fact that the human soul does not perish with the body, and that God exists, it certainly does not seem possible ever to persuade infidels of any religion, indeed, we may almost say, of any moral virtue, unless, to begin with, we prove these two facts by means of the natural reason. And inasmuch as often in this life greater rewards are offered for vice than for virtue, few people would prefer the right to the useful, were they restrained neither by the fear of God nor the expectation of another life; and although it is absolutely true that we must believe that there is a God, because we are so taught in the Holy Scriptures, and, on the other hand, that we must believe the Holy Scriptures because they come from God (the reason of this is, that, faith being a gift of God, He who gives the grace to cause us to believe other things can likewise give it to cause us to believe that He exists), we nevertheless could not place this argument before infidels, who might accuse us of reasoning in a circle. And, in truth, I have noticed that you, along with all the theologians, did not only affirm that the existence of God may be proved by the natural reason, but also that it may be inferred from the Holy Scriptures, that knowledge about Him is much clearer than that which we have of many created things, and, as a matter of fact, is so easy to acquire, that those who have it not are culpable in their ignorance. This indeed appears from the Wisdom of Solomon, chapter xiii, where it is said '*Howbeit they are not to be excused; for if their understanding was so great that they could discern the world and the creatures, why did they not rather find out the Lord thereof?*' and in Romans, chapter i, it is said that they are '*without excuse*'; and again in the same place, by these words '*that which may be known of God is manifest in them,*' it seems as though we were shown that all that which can be known of God may be made manifest by means which are not derived from anywhere but from ourselves, and from the simple consideration of the nature of our minds. Hence I thought it not beside my purpose to inquire how this is so, and how God may be more easily and certainly known than the things of the world.

And as regards the soul, although many have considered that it is not easy to know its nature, and some have even dared to say that human reasons have convinced us that it would perish with the body, and that faith alone could believe the contrary, nevertheless, inasmuch as the Lateran Council held under Leo X (in the eighth session) condemns these tenets, and as Leo expressly ordains Christian philosophers to refute their arguments and to employ all their powers in making known the truth, I have ventured in this treatise to undertake the same task.

More than that, I am aware that the principal reason which causes many impious persons not to desire to believe that there is a God, and that the human soul is distinct from the body, is that they declare that hitherto no one has been able to demonstrate these two facts; and although I am not of their opinion but, on the contrary, hold that the greater part of the reasons which have been brought forward concerning these two questions by so many great men are, when they are rightly understood, equal to so many demonstrations, and that it is almost impossible to invent new ones, it is yet in my opinion the case that nothing more useful can be accomplished in philosophy than once for all to seek with care for the best of these reasons, and to set them forth in so clear and exact a manner, that it will henceforth be evident to everybody that they are veritable demonstrations. And, finally, inasmuch as it was desired that I should undertake this task by many who were aware that I had cultivated a certain Method for the resolution of difficulties of every kind in the Sciences – a method which it is true is not novel, since there is nothing more ancient than the truth, but of which they were aware that I had made use successfully enough in other matters of difficulty – I have thought that it was my duty also to make trial of it in the present matter.

Now all that I could accomplish in the matter is contained in this Treatise. Not that I have here drawn together all the different reasons which might be brought forward to serve as proofs of this subject: for that never seemed to be necessary excepting when there was no one single proof that was certain. But I have treated the first and principal ones in such a manner that I can venture to bring them forward as very evident and very certain demonstrations. And more than that, I will say that these proofs are such that I do not think that there is any way open to the human mind by which it can ever succeed in discovering better. For the importance of the subject, and the glory of God to which all this relates, constrain me to speak here somewhat more freely of myself than is my habit. Nevertheless, whatever certainty and evidence I find in my reasons, I cannot persuade myself that all the world is capable of understanding them. Still, just as in Geometry there are many demonstrations that have been left to us by Archimedes, by Apollonius, by Pappus, and others, which are accepted by everyone as perfectly certain and evident (because they clearly contain nothing which, considered by itself, is not very easy to understand, and as all through that which follows has an exact connection with, and dependence on that which precedes), nevertheless, because they are somewhat lengthy, and demand a mind wholly devoted to their consideration, they are only taken in and understood by a very limited number of persons. Similarly, although I judge that those of which I here make use are equal to, or even surpass in certainty and evidence, the demonstrations of Geometry, I yet apprehend that they cannot be adequately understood by many, both because they are also a little lengthy and dependent the one on the other, and principally because they demand a mind wholly free of prejudices, and one which can be easily detached from the affairs of the senses. And, truth to say, there are not so many in the world who are fitted for metaphysica speculations as there are for those of Geometry. And more than that; there is still this difference, that in Geometry, since each one is persuaded that nothing must be advanced of which there is not a certain demonstration, those who are not entirely adepts more frequently err in approving what is false, in order to give the impression that they understand it, than in refuting the true. But the case is different in philosophy where everyone believes that all is problematical, and few give themselves to the search after truth; and the greater number, in their desire to acquire a reputation for boldness of thought, arrogantly combat the most important of truths.

That is why, whatever force there may be in my reasonings, seeing they belong to philosophy, I cannot hope that they will have much effect on the minds of men, unless you extend to them your protection. But the estimation in which your Company is universally held is so great, and the name of SORBONNE carries with it so much authority, that, next to the Sacred Councils, never has such deference been paid to the judgment of any Body, not only in what concerns the faith, but also in what regards human philosophy as well: everyone indeed believes that it is not possible to discover elsewhere more perspicacity and solidity, or more integrity and wisdom in pronouncing judgment. For this reason I have no doubt that if you deign to take the trouble in the first place of correcting this work (for being conscious not only of my infirmity, but also of my ignorance, I should not dare to state that it was free from errors), and then, after adding to it these things that are lacking to it, completing those which are imperfect, and yourselves taking the trouble to give a more ample explanation of those things which have need of it, or at least making me aware of the defects so that I may apply myself to remedy them – when this is done and when finally the reasonings by which I prove that there is a God, and that the human soul differs from the body, shall be carried to that point of perspicuity to which I am sure they can be carried in order that they may be esteemed as perfectly exact demonstrations, if you deign to authorise your approbation and to render public testimony to their truth and certainty, I do not doubt, I say, that henceforward all the errors and false opinions which have ever existed regarding these two questions will soon be effaced from the minds of men. For the truth itself will easily cause all men of mind and learning to subscribe to your judgment; and your authority will cause the atheists, who are usually more arrogant than learned or judicious, to rid themselves of their spirit of contradiction or lead them possibly themselves to defend the reasonings which they find being received as demonstrations by all persons of consideration, lest they appear not to understand them. And, finally, all others will easily yield to such a mass of evidence, and there will be none who dares to doubt the existence of God and the real and true distinction between the human soul and the body. It is for you now in your singular wisdom to judge of the importance of the establishment of such beliefs [you who see the disorders produced by the doubt of them].[6] But it would not become me to say more in consideration of the cause of God and religion to those who have always been the most worthy supports of the Catholic Church.

PREFACE TO THE READER

I have already slightly touched on these two questions of God and the human soul in the Discourse on the Method of rightly conducting the Reason and seeking truth in the Sciences, published in French in the year 1637. Not that I had the design of

6. When it is thought desirable to insert additional readings from the French version this will be indicated by the use of square brackets.

treating these with any thoroughness, but only so to speak in passing, and in order to ascertain by the judgment of the readers how I should treat them later on. For these questions have always appeared to me to be of such importance that I judged it suitable to speak of them more than once; and the road which I follow in the explanation of them is so little trodden, and so far removed from the ordinary path, that I did not judge it to be expedient to set it forth at length in French and in a Discourse which might be read by everyone, in case the feebler minds should believe that it was permitted to them to attempt to follow the same path.

But, having in this Discourse on Method begged all those who have found in my writings somewhat deserving of censure to do me the favour of acquainting me with the grounds of it, nothing worthy of remark has been objected to in them beyond two matters: to these two I wish here to reply in a few words before undertaking their more detailed discussion.

The first objection is that it does not follow from the fact that the human mind reflecting on itself does not perceive itself to be other than a thing that thinks, that its nature or its essence consists only in its being a thing that thinks, in the sense that this word *only* excludes all other things which might also be supposed to pertain to the nature of the soul. To this objection I reply that it was not my intention in that place to exclude these in accordance with the order that looks to the truth of the matter (as to which I was not then dealing), but only in accordance with the order of my thought [perception]; thus my meaning was that so far as I was aware, I knew nothing clearly as belonging to my essence, excepting that I was a thing that thinks, or a thing that has in itself the faculty of thinking. But I shall show hereafter how from the fact that I know no other thing which pertains to my essence, it follows that there is no other thing which really does belong to it.

The second objection is that it does not follow from the fact that I have in myself the idea of something more perfect than I am, that this idea is more perfect than I, and much less that what is represented by this idea exists. But I reply that in this term *idea* there is here something equivocal, for it may either be taken materially, as an act of my understanding, and in this sense it cannot be said that it is more perfect than I; or it may be taken objectively, as the thing which is represented by this act, which, although we do not suppose it to exist outside of my understanding, may, none the less, be more perfect than I, because of its essence. And in following out this Treatise I shall show more fully how, from the sole fact that I have in myself the idea of a thing more perfect than myself, it follows that this thing truly exists.

In addition to these two objections I have also seen two fairly lengthy works on this subject, which, however, did not so much impugn my reasonings as my conclusions, and this by arguments drawn from the ordinary atheistic sources. But, because such arguments cannot make any impression on the minds of those who really understand my reasonings, and as the judgments of many are so feeble and irrational that they very often allow themselves to be persuaded by the opinions which they have first formed, however false and far removed from reason they may be, rather than by a true and solid but subsequently received refutation of these opinions, I do not desire to reply here to their criticisms in case of being first of all obliged to state them. I shall only say in general that all that is said by the atheist against the existence of God, always depends either on the fact that we ascribe to God affections which are human, or that we attribute so much strength and wisdom to our minds that we even have the presumption to desire to determine and understand that which God can and ought to do. In this way all that they allege will cause us no difficulty, provided only we remember that we must consider our minds as things which are finite and limited, and God as a Being who is incomprehensible and infinite.

Now that I have once for all recognised and acknowledged the opinions of men, I at once begin to treat of God and the human soul, and at the same time to treat of the whole of the First Philosophy, without however expecting any praise from the vulgar and without the hope that my book will have many readers. On the contrary, I should never advise anyone to read it excepting those who desire to meditate seriously with me, and who can detach their minds from affairs of sense, and deliver themselves entirely from every sort of prejudice. I know too well that such men exist in a very small number. But for those who, without caring to comprehend the order and connections of my reasonings, form their criticisms on detached portions arbitrarily selected, as is the custom with many, these, I say, will not obtain much profit from reading this Treatise. And although they perhaps in several parts find occasion of cavilling, they can for all their pains make no objection which is urgent or deserving of reply.

And inasmuch as I make no promise to others to satisfy them at once, and as I do not presume so much on my own powers as to believe myself capable of foreseeing all that can cause difficulty to anyone, I shall first of all set forth in these Meditations the very considerations by which I persuade myself that I have reached a certain and evident knowledge of the truth, in order to see if, by the same reasons which persuaded me, I can also persuade others. And, after that, I shall reply to the objections which have been made to me by persons of genius and learning to whom I have sent my Meditations for examination, before submitting them to the press. For they have made so many objections and these so different, that I venture to promise that it will be difficult for anyone to bring to mind criticisms of any consequence which have not been already touched upon. This is why I beg those who read these Meditations to form no judgment upon them unless they have given themselves the trouble to read all the objections as well as the replies which I have made to them.

SYNOPSIS OF THE SIX FOLLOWING MEDITATIONS

In the first Meditation I set forth the reasons for which we may, generally speaking, doubt about all things and especially about material things, at least so long as we have no other foundations for the sciences than those which we have hitherto possessed. But although the utility of a Doubt which is so general does not at first appear, it is at the same time very great, inasmuch as it delivers us from every kind of prejudice, and sets out for us a very simple way by which the mind may detach itself from the senses; and finally it makes it impossible for us ever to doubt those things which we have once discovered to be true.

In the second Meditation, mind, which making use of the liberty which pertains to it, takes for granted that all those things of whose existence it has the least doubt, are non-existent, recognises that it is however absolutely impossible that it does not itself exist. This point is likewise of the greatest moment, inasmuch as by this means a distinction is easily drawn between the things which pertain to mind

– that is to say to the intellectual nature – and those which pertain to body.

But because it may be that some expect from me in this place a statement of the reasons establishing the immortality of the soul, I feel that I should here make known to them that having aimed at writing nothing in all this Treatise of which I do not possess very exact demonstrations, I am obliged to follow a similar order to that made use of by the geometers, which is to begin by putting forward as premises all those things upon which the proposition that we seek depends, before coming to any conclusion regarding it. Now the first and principal matter which is requisite for thoroughly understanding the immortality of the soul is to form the clearest possible conception of it, and one which will be entirely distinct from all the conceptions which we may have of body; and in this Meditation this has been done. In addition to this it is requisite that we may be assured that all the things which we conceive clearly and distinctly are true in the very way in which we think them; and this could not be proved previously to the Fourth Meditation. Further we must have a distinct conception of corporeal nature, which is given partly in this Second, and partly in the Fifth and Sixth Meditations. And finally we should conclude from all this, that those things which we conceive clearly and distinctly as being diverse substances, as we regard mind and body to be, are really substances essentially distinct one from the other; and this is the conclusion of the Sixth Meditation. This is further confirmed in this same Meditation by the fact that we cannot conceive of body excepting in so far as it is divisible, while the mind cannot be conceived of excepting as indivisible. For we are not able to conceive of the half of a mind as we can do of the smallest of all bodies; so that we see that not only are their natures different but even in some respects contrary to one another. I have not however dealt further with this matter in this treatise, both because what I have said is sufficient to show clearly enough that the extinction of the mind does not follow from the corruption of the body, and also to give men the hope of another life after death, as also because the premises from which the immortality of the soul may be deduced depend on an elucidation of a complete system of Physics. This would mean to establish in the first place that all substances generally – that is to say all things which cannot exist without being created by God – are in their nature incorruptible, and that they can never cease to exist unless God, in denying to them his con-

currence, reduce them to nought; and secondly that body, regarded generally, is a substance, which is the reason why it also cannot perish, but that the human body, inasmuch as it differs from other bodies, is composed only of a certain configuration of members and of other similar accidents, while the human mind is not similarly composed of any accidents, but is a pure substance. For although all the accidents of mind be changed, although, for instance, it think certain things, will others, perceive others, etc., despite all this it does not emerge from these changes another mind: the human body on the other hand becomes a different thing from the sole fact that the figure or form of any of its portions is found to be changed. From this it follows that the human body may indeed easily enough perish, but the mind [*or soul of man (I make no distinction between them)*] *is owing to its nature immortal.*

In the third Meditation it seems to me that I have explained at sufficient length the principal argument of which I make use in order to prove the existence of God. But none the less, because I did not wish in that place to make use of any comparisons derived from corporeal things, so as to withdraw as much as I could the minds of readers from the senses, there may perhaps have remained many obscurities which, however, will, I hope, be entirely removed by the Replies which I have made to the Objections which have been set before me. Amongst others there is, for example, this one, 'How the idea in us of a being supremely perfect possesses so much objective reality [*that is to say participates by representation in so many degrees of being and perfection*] *that it necessarily proceeds from a cause which is absolutely perfect'. This is illustrated in these Replies by the comparison of a very perfect machine, the idea of which is found in the mind of some workman. For as the objective contrivance of this idea must have some cause, i.e. either the science of the workman or that of some other from whom he has received the idea, it is similarly impossible that the idea of God which is in us should not have God himself as its cause.*

In the fourth Meditation it is shown that all these things which we very clearly and distinctly perceive are true, and at the same time it is explained in what the nature of error or falsity consists. This must of necessity be known both for the confirmation of the preceding truths and for the better comprehension of those that follow. (But it must meanwhile be remarked that I do not in any way there treat of sin – that is to say of the error which is committed in the pursuit of good and evil, but only of that which arises in the deciding between the true and the false. And I do not intend to speak of matters pertaining to the Faith or the conduct of life, but only of those which concern speculative truths, and which may be known by the sole aid of the light of nature.)

In the fifth Meditation corporeal nature generally is explained, and in addition to this the existence of God is demonstrated by a new proof in which there may possibly be certain difficulties also, but the solution of these will be seen in the Replies to the Objections. And further I show in what sense it is true to say that the certainty of geometrical demonstrations is itself dependent on the knowledge of God.

Finally in the Sixth I distinguish the action of the understanding from that of the imagination; the marks by which this distinction is made are described. I here show that the mind of man is really distinct from the body, and at the same time that the two are so closely joined together that they form, so to speak, a single thing. All the errors which proceed from the senses are then surveyed, while the means of avoiding them are demonstrated, and finally all the reasons from which we may deduce the existence of material things are set forth. Not that I judge them to be very useful in establishing that which they prove, to wit, that there is in truth a world, that men possess bodies, and other such things which never have been doubted by anyone of sense; but because in considering these closely we come to see that they are neither so strong nor so evident as those arguments which lead us to the knowledge of our mind and of God; so that these last must be the most certain and most evident facts which can fall within the cognizance of the human mind. And this is the whole matter that I have tried to prove in these Meditations, for which reason I here omit to speak of many other questions with which I dealt incidentally in this discussion.

Meditations on the First Philosophy in which the Existence of God and the Distinction between Mind and Body are Demonstrated

MEDITATION I: *Of the things which may be brought within the sphere of the doubtful*

It is now some years since I detected how many were the false beliefs that I had from my earliest youth admitted as true, and how doubtful was everything I had since constructed on this basis; and from that time I was convinced that I must once for all seriously undertake to rid myself of all the opinions which I had formerly accepted, and commence to build anew from the foundation, if I wanted to establish any firm and permanent structure in the sciences. But as this enterprise appeared to be a very great one, I waited until I had attained an age so mature that I could not hope that at any later date I should be better fitted to execute my design. This reason caused me to delay so long that I should feel that I was doing wrong were I to occupy in deliberation the time that yet remains to me for action. Today, then, since very opportunely for the plan I have in view I have delivered my mind from every care [and am happily agitated by no passions] and since I have procured for myself an assured leisure in a peaceable retirement, I shall at last seriously and freely address myself to the general upheaval of all my former opinions.

Now for this object it is not necessary that I should show that all of these are false – I shall perhaps never arrive at this end. But inasmuch as reason already persuades me that I ought no less carefully to withhold my assent from matters which are not entirely certain and indubitable than from those which appear to me manifestly to be false, if I am able to find in each one some reason to doubt, this will suffice to justify my rejecting the whole. And for that end it will not be requisite that I should examine each in particular, which would be an endless undertaking; for owing to the fact that the destruction of the foundations of necessity brings with it the downfall of the rest of the edifice, I shall only in the first place attack those principles upon which all my former opinions rested.

All that up to the present time I have accepted as most true and certain I have learned either from the senses or through the senses; but it is sometimes proved to me that these senses are deceptive, and it is wiser not to trust entirely to any thing by which we have once been deceived.

But it may be that although the senses sometimes deceive us concerning things which are hardly perceptible, or very far away, there are yet many others to be met with as to which we cannot reasonably have any doubt, although we recognise them by their means. For example, there is the fact that I am here, seated by the fire, attired in a dressing gown, having this paper in my hands and other similar matters. And how could I deny that these hands and this body are mine, were it not perhaps that I compare myself to certain persons, devoid of sense, whose cerebella are so troubled and clouded by the violent vapours of black bile, that they constantly assure us that they think they are kings when they are really quite poor, or that they are clothed in purple when they are really without covering, or who imagine that they have an earthenware head or are nothing but pumpkins or are made of glass. But they are mad, and I should not be any the less insane were I to follow examples so extravagant.

At the same time I must remember that I am a man, and that consequently I am in the habit of sleeping, and in my dreams representing to myself the same things or sometimes even less probable things, than do those who are insane in their waking moments. How often has it happened to me that in the night I dreamt that I found myself in this particular place, that I was dressed and seated near the fire, whilst in reality I was lying undressed in bed! At this moment it does indeed seem to me that it is with eyes awake that I am looking at this paper; that this head which I move is not asleep, that it is deliberately and of set purpose that I extend my hand and perceive it; what happens in sleep does not appear so clear nor so distinct as does all this. But in thinking over this I remind myself that on many occasions I have in sleep been deceived by similar illusions, and in dwelling carefully on this reflection I see so manifestly that there are no certain indications by which we may clearly distinguish wakefulness from sleep that I am lost in astonishment. And my astonishment is such that it is almost capable of persuading me that I now dream.

Now let us assume that we are asleep and that all these particulars, e.g. that we open our eyes, shake our head, extend our hands, and so on, are but false delusions; and let us reflect that possibly neither our hands nor our whole body are such as they appear to us to be. At the same time we must at least confess that the things which are represented to us in sleep are like painted representations which can only have been formed as the counterparts of something real and true, and that in this way those general things at least, i.e. eyes, a head, hands, and a whole body, are not imaginary things, but things really existent. For, as a matter of fact, painters, even when they study with the greatest skill to represent sirens and satyrs by forms the most strange and extraordinary, cannot give them natures which are entirely new, but merely make a certain medley of the members of different animals; or if their imagination is extravagant enough to invent something so novel that nothing similar has ever before been seen, and that then their work represents a thing purely fictitious and absolutely false, it is certain all the same that the colours of which this is composed are necessarily real. And for the same reason, although these general things, to wit, [a body], eyes, a head, hands, and such like, may be imaginary, we are bound at the same time to confess that there are at least some other objects yet more simple and more universal, which are real and true; and of these just in the same way as with certain real colours, all these images of things which dwell in our thoughts, whether true and real or false and fantastic, are formed.

To such a class of things pertains corporeal nature in general, and its extension, the figure of extending things, their quantity or magnitude and number, as also the place in which they are, the time which measures their duration, and so on.

That is possibly why our reasoning is not unjust when we conclude from this that Physics, Astronomy, Medicine and all other sciences which have as their end the consideration of composite things, are very dubious and uncertain; but that Arithmetic, Geometry and other sciences of that kind which only treat of things that are very simple and very general, without taking great trouble to ascertain whether they are actually existent or not, contain some measure of certainty and an element of the indubitable. For whether I am awake or asleep, two and three together always form five, and the square can never have more than four sides, and it does not seem possible that truths so clear and apparent can be suspected of any falsity [or uncertainty].

Nevertheless I have long had fixed in my mind the belief that an all-powerful God existed by whom I have been created such as I am. But how do I know that He has not brought it to pass that there is no earth, no heaven, no extended body, no magnitude, no place, and that nevertheless [I possess the perceptions of all these things and that] they seem to me to exist just exactly as I now see them? And, besides, as I sometimes imagine that others deceive themselves in the things which they think they know best, how do I know that I am not deceived every time that I add two and three, or count the sides of a square, or judge of things yet simpler, if anything simpler can be imagined? But possibly God has not desired that I should be thus deceived, for He is said to be supremely good. If, however, it is contrary to His goodness to have made me such that I constantly deceive myself, it would also appear to be contrary to His goodness to permit me to be sometimes deceived, and nevertheless I cannot doubt that He does permit this.

There may indeed be those who would prefer to deny the existence of a God so powerful, rather than believe that all other things are uncertain. But let us not oppose them for the present, and grant that all is here said of a God is a fable; nevertheless in whatever way they suppose that I have arrived at the state of being that I have reached – whether they attribute it to fate or to accident, or make out that it is by a continual succession of antecedents, or by some other method – since to err and deceive oneself is a defect, it is clear that the greater will be the probability of my being so imperfect as to deceive myself ever, as is the Author to whom they assign my origin the less powerful. To these reasons I have certainly nothing to reply, but at the end I feel constrained to confess that there is nothing in all that I formerly believed to be true, of which I cannot in some measure doubt, and that not merely through want of thought or through levity, but for reasons which are very powerful and maturely considered; so that henceforth I ought not the less carefully to refrain from giving credence to these opinions than to that which is manifestly false, if I desire to arrive at any certainty [in the sciences].

But it is not sufficient to have made these remarks, we must also be careful to keep them in mind. For these ancient and commonly held opinions still revert frequently to my mind, long and familiar custom having given them the right to occupy my mind against my inclination and rendered them almost masters of my belief; nor will I ever lose the habit of deferring to them or of placing my confidence in them, so long as I consider them as they really are, i.e. opinions in some measure doubtful, as I have just shown, and at the same time highly probable, so that there is much more reason to believe in than to deny them. That is why I consider that I shall not be acting amiss, if, taking of set purpose a contrary belief, I allow myself to be deceived, and for a certain time pretend that all these opinions are entirely false and imaginary, until at last, having thus balanced my former prejudices with my latter [so that they cannot divert my opinions more to one side than to the other], my judgment will no longer be dominated by bad usage or turned away from the right knowledge of the truth. For I am assured that there can be neither peril nor error in this course, and that I cannot at present yield too much to distrust, since I am not considering the question of action, but only of knowledge.

I shall then suppose, not that God who is supremely good and the fountain of truth, but some evil genius not less powerful than deceitful, has employed his whole energies in deceiving me; I shall consider that the heavens, the earth, colours, figures, sound, and all other external things are nought but the illusions and dreams of which this genius has availed himself in order to lay traps for my credulity; I shall consider myself as having no hands, no eyes, no flesh, no blood, nor any senses, yet falsely believing myself to possess all these things; I shall remain obstinately attached to this idea, and if by this means it is not in my power to arrive at the knowledge of any truth, I may at least do what is in my power [i.e. suspend my judgment], and with firm purpose avoid giving credence to any false thing, or being imposed upon by this arch deceiver, however powerful and deceptive he may be. But this task is a laborious one, and insensibly a certain lassitude leads me into the course of my ordinary life. And just as a captive who in sleep enjoys an imaginary liberty, when he begins to suspect that his liberty is but a dream, fears to awaken, and conspires with these agreeable illusions that the deception may be prolonged, so insensibly of my own accord I fall back into my former opinions, and I dread awakening from this slumber, lest the laborious wakefulness which would follow the tranquillity of this repose should have to be spent not in daylight, but in the excessive darkness of the difficulties which have just been discussed.

MEDITATION II: *Of the Nature of the Human Mind; and that it is more easily known than the Body*

The Meditation of yesterday filled my mind with so many doubts that it is no longer in my power to forget them. And yet I do not see in what manner I can resolve them; and, just as if I had all of a sudden fallen into very deep water, I am so disconcerted that I can neither make certain of setting my feet on the bottom, nor can I swim and so support myself on the surface. I shall nevertheless make an effort and follow anew the same path as that on which I yesterday entered, i.e. I shall proceed by setting aside all that in which the least doubt could be supposed to exist, just as if I had discovered that it was absolutely false; and I shall ever follow in this road until I have met with something which is certain, or at least, if I can do nothing else, until I have learned for certain that there is nothing in the world that is certain. Archimedes, in order that he might draw the terrestrial globe out of its place, and transport it elsewhere, demanded only that one point should be fixed and immoveable; in the same way I shall have the right to conceive high hopes if I am happy enough to discover one thing only which is certain and indubitable.

I suppose, then, that all the things that I see are false; I persuade myself that nothing has ever existed of all that my fallacious memory represents to me. I consider that I possess no senses; I imagine that body, figure, extension, movement and place are but the fictions of my mind. What, then, can be esteemed as true? Perhaps nothing at all, unless that there is nothing in the world that is certain.

But how can I know there is not something different from those things that I have just considered, of which one cannot have the slightest doubt? Is there not some God, or some other being by whatever name we call it, who puts these reflections into my mind? That is not necessary, for is it not possible that I am capable of producing them myself? I myself, am I not at least something? But I have already denied that I had senses and body. Yet I hesitate, for what follows from that? Am I so dependent on body and senses that I cannot exist without these? But I was persuaded that there was nothing in all the world, that there was no heaven, no earth, that there were no minds, nor any bodies: was I not then likewise persuaded that I did not exist? Not at all; of a surety I myself did exist since I persuaded myself of something [or merely because I thought of something]. But there is some deceiver or other, very powerful and very cunning, who ever employs his ingenuity in deceiving me. Then without doubt I exist also if he deceives me, and let him deceive me as much as he will, he can never cause me to be nothing so long as I think that I am something. So that after having reflected well and carefully examined all things, we must come to the definite conclusion that this proposition: I am,

I exist, is necessarily true each time that I pronounce it, or that I mentally conceive it.

But I do not yet know clearly enough what I am, I who am certain that I am; and hence I must be careful to see that I do not imprudently take some other object in place of myself, and thus that I do not go astray in respect of this knowledge that I hold to be the most certain and most evident of all that I have formerly learned. That is why I shall now consider anew what I believed myself to be before I embarked upon these last reflections; and of my former opinions I shall withdraw all that might even in a small degree be invalidated by the reasons which I have just brought forward, in order that there may be nothing at all left beyond what is absolutely certain and indubitable.

What then did I formerly believe myself to be? Undoubtedly I believed myself to be a man. But what is a man? Shall I say a reasonable animal? Certainly not; for then I should have to inquire what an animal is, and what is reasonable; and thus from a single question I should insensibly fall into an infinitude of others more difficult; and I should not wish to waste the little time and leisure remaining to me in trying to unravel subtleties like these. But I shall rather stop to consider the thoughts which of themselves spring up in my mind, and which were not inspired by anything beyond my own nature alone when I applied myself to the consideration of my being. In the first place, then, I considered myself as having a face, hands, arms, and all that system of members composed of bones and flesh as seen in a corpse which I designated by the name of body. In addition to this I considered that I was nourished, that I walked, that I felt, and that I thought, and I referred all these actions to the soul: but I did not stop to consider what the soul was, or if I did stop, I imagined that it was something extremely rare and subtle like a wind, a flame, or an ether, which was spread throughout my grosser parts. As to body I had no manner of doubt about its nature, but thought I had a very clear knowledge of it; and if I had desired to explain it according to the notions that I had then formed of it, I should have described it thus: By the body I understand all that which can be defined by a certain figure: something which can be confined in a certain place, and which can fill a given space in such a way that every other body will be excluded from it; which can be perceived either by touch, or by sight, or by hearing, or by taste, or by smell: which can be moved in many ways not, in truth, by itself, but by something which is foreign to it, by which it is touched [and from which it receives impressions]: for to have the power of self-movement, as also of feeling or of thinking, I did not consider to appertain to the nature of body: on the contrary, I was rather astonished to find that faculties similar to them existed in some bodies.

But what am I, now that I suppose that there is a certain genius which is extremely powerful, and, if I may say so, malicious, who employs all his powers in deceiving me? Can I affirm that I possess the least of all those things which I have just said pertain to the nature of body? I pause to consider, I revolve all these things in my mind, and I find none of which I can say that it pertains to me. It would be tedious to stop to enumerate them. Let us pass to the attributes of soul and see if there is any one which is in me? What of nutrition or walking [the first mentioned]? But if it is so that I have no body it is also true that I can neither walk nor take nourishment. Another attribute is sensation. But one cannot feel without body, and besides I have thought I perceived many things during sleep that I recognised in my waking moments as not having been experienced at all. What of thinking? I find here that thought is an attribute that belongs to me; it alone cannot be separated from me. I am, I exist, that is certain. But how often? Just when I think; for it might possibly be the case if I ceased entirely to think, that I should likewise cease altogether to exist. I do not now admit anything which is not necessarily true: to speak accurately I am not more than a thing which thinks, that is to say a mind or a soul, or an understanding, or a reason, which are terms whose significance was formerly unknown to me. I am, however, a real thing and really exist; but what thing? I have answered: a thing which thinks.

And what more? I shall exercise my imagination [in order to see if I am not something more]. I am not a collection of members which we call the human body: I am not a subtle air distributed through these members, I am not a wind, a fire, a vapour, a breath, nor anything at all which I can imagine on conceive; because I have assumed that all these were nothing. Without changing that supposition I find that I only leave myself certain of the fact that I am somewhat. But perhaps it is true that these same things which I supposed were non-existent because they are unknown to me, are really not different from the self which I know. I am not sure about this, I shall not dispute about it now; I can only give judgment on things that are known to me. I know that I exist, and I inquire what I am, I whom I know to exist. But it is very certain that the knowledge of my existence taken in its precise significance does not depend on things whose existence is not yet known to me; consequently it does not depend on those which I can feign in imagination. And indeed the very term *feign* in imagination proves to me my error, for I really do this if I image myself a something, since to imagine is nothing else than to contemplate the figure or image of a corporeal thing. But I already know for certain that I am, and that it may be that all these images, and, speaking generally, all things that relate to the nature of body are nothing but dreams [and chimeras]. For this reason I see clearly that I have as little reason to say, 'I shall stimulate my imagination in order to know more distinctly what I am,' than if I were to say, 'I am now awake, and I perceive somewhat that is real and true: but because I do not yet perceive it distinctly enough, I shall go to sleep of express purpose, so that my dreams may represent the perception with greatest truth and evidence.' And, thus, I know for certain that nothing of all that I can understand by means of my imagination belongs to this knowledge which I have of myself, and that it is necessary to recall the mind from this mode of thought with the utmost diligence in order that it may be able to know its own nature with perfect distinctness.

But what then am I? A thing which thinks. What is a thing which thinks? It is a thing which doubts, understands, [conceives], affirms, denies, wills, refuses, which also imagines and feels.

Certainly it is no small matter if all these things pertain to my nature. But why should they not so pertain? Am I not that being who now doubts nearly everything, who nevertheless understands certain things, who affirms that one only is true, who denies all the others, who desires to know more, is averse from being deceived, who imagines many things, sometimes indeed despite his will, and who perceives many likewise, as by the intervention of the bodily organs? Is there nothing in all this which is as true as it is certain that I exist, even though I should always sleep and though he who has given me being employed all his ingenuity in deceiving me? Is there likewise any one of these attributes which can be distinguished from my thought, or which might be said to be separated from myself? For it is so evident of itself that it is I who doubts, who understands, and who desires, that there is no reason here to add anything to explain it. And I have certainly the power of imagining likewise; for although it may happen (as I formerly supposed) that none of the things which I imagine are true, nevertheless this power of imagining does not cease to be really in use, and it forms part of my thought. Finally, I am the same who feels, that is to say, who perceives certain things, as by the organs of sense, since in truth I see light, I hear noise, I feel heat. But it will be said that these phenomena are false and that I am dreaming. Let it be so; still it is at least quite certain that it seems to me that I see light, that I hear noise and that I feel heat. That cannot be false; properly speaking it is what is in me called feeling; and used in this precise sense that is no other thing than thinking.

From this time I begin to know what I am with a little more clearness and distinction than before; but nevertheless it still seems to me, and I cannot prevent myself from thinking, that corporeal things, whose images are framed by thought, which are tested by the senses, are much more distinctly known than that obscure part of me which does not come under the imagination. Although really it is very strange to say that I know and understand more distinctly these things whose existence seems to me dubious, which are unknown to me, and which do not belong to me, than others of the truth of which I am convinced, which are known to me and which pertain to my real nature, in a word, than myself. But I see clearly how the case stands: my mind loves to wander, and cannot yet suffer to be retained within the just limits of truth. Very good, let us once more give it the freest rein, so that, when afterwards we seize the proper occasion for pulling up, it may the more easily be regulated and controlled.

Let us begin by considering the commonest matters, those which we believe to be the most distinctly comprehended, to wit, the bodies which we touch and see; not indeed bodies in general, for these general ideas are usually a little more confused, but let us consider one body in particular. Let us take, for example, this piece of wax: it has been taken quite freshly from the hive, and it has not yet lost the sweetness of the honey which it contains; it still retains somewhat of the odour of the flowers from which it has been culled; its colour, its figure, its size are apparent; it is hard, cold, easily handled, and if you strike it with the finger, it will emit a sound. Finally all the things which are requisite to cause us distinctly to recognise a body, are met with in it. But notice that while I speak and approach the fire what remained of the taste is exhaled, the smell evaporates, the colour alters, the figure is destroyed, the size increases, it becomes liquid, it heats, scarcely can one handle it, and when one strikes it, no sound is emitted. Does the same wax remain after this change? We must confess that it remains; none would judge otherwise. What then did I know so distinctly in this piece of wax? It could certainly be nothing of all that the senses brought to my notice, since all these things which fall under taste, smell, sight, touch, and hearing, are found to be changed, and yet the same wax remains.

Perhaps it was what I now think, viz. that this wax was not that sweetness of honey, nor that agreeable scent of flowers, nor that particular whiteness, nor that figure, nor that sound, but simply a body which a little while before appeared to me as perceptible under these forms, and which is now perceptible under others. But what, precisely, is it that I imagine when I form such conceptions? Let us attentively consider this, and, abstracting from all that does not belong to the wax, let us see what remains. Certainly nothing remains excepting a certain extended thing which is flexible and movable. But what is the meaning of flexible and movable? Is it not that I imagine that this piece of wax being round is capable of becoming square and of passing from a square to a triangular figure? No, certainly it is not that, since I imagine it admits of an infinitude of similar changes, and I nevertheless do not know how to compass the infinitude by my imagination, and consequently this conception which I have of the wax is not brought about by the faculty of imagination. What now is this extension? Is it not also unknown? For it becomes greater when the wax is melted, greater when it is boiled, and greater still when the heat increases; and I should not conceive [clearly] according to truth what wax is, if I did not think that even this piece that we are considering is capable of receiving more variations in extension than I have ever imagined. We must then grant that I could not even understand through the imagination what this piece of wax is, and that it is my mind alone which perceives it. I say this piece of wax in particular, for as to wax in general it is yet clearer. But what is this piece of wax which cannot be understood excepting by the [understanding or] mind? It is certainly the same that I see, touch, imagine, and finally it is the same which I have always believed it to be from the beginning. But what must particularly be observed is that its perception is neither an act of vision, nor of touch, nor of imagination, and has never been such although it may have appeared formerly to be so, but only an intuition of the mind, which may be imperfect and confused as it was formerly, or clear and distinct as it is at present, according as my attention is more or less directed to the elements which are found in it, and of which it is composed.

Yet in the meantime I am greatly astonished when I consider [the great feebleness of mind] and its proneness to fall [insensibly] into error; for although without giving expression to my thoughts I consider all this in my own mind, words often impede me and I am almost deceived by the terms of ordinary language. For we say that we see the same wax, if it is present, and not that we simply judge that it is the same from its having the same colour and figure. From this I should conclude that I knew the wax by means of vision and not simply by the intuition of the mind; unless by chance I remember that, when looking from a window and saying I see men who pass in the street, I really do not see them, but infer that what I see is men, just as I say that I see wax. And yet what do I see from the window but hats and coats which may cover automatic machines? Yet I judge these to be men. And similarly solely by the faculty of judgment which rests in my mind, I comprehend that which I believed I saw with my eyes.

A man who makes it his aim to raise his knowledge above the common should be ashamed to derive the occasion for doubting from the forms of speech invented by the vulgar; I prefer to pass on and consider whether I had a more evident and perfect conception of what the wax was when I first perceived it, and when I believed I knew it by means of the external senses or at least by the common sense as it is called, that is to say by the imaginative faculty, or whether my present conception is clearer now that I have most carefully examined what it is, and in what way it can be known. It would certainly be absurd to doubt as to this. For what was there in this first perception which was distinct? What was there which might not as well have been perceived by any of the animals? But when I distinguish the wax from its external forms, and when, just as if I had taken from it its vestments, I consider it quite naked, it is certain that although some error may still be found in my judgment, I can nevertheless not perceive it thus without a human mind.

But finally what shall I say of this mind, that is, of myself, for up to this point I do not admit in myself anything but mind? What then, I who seem to perceive this piece of wax so distinctly, do I not know myself, not only with much more truth and certainty, but also with much more distinctness and clearness? For if I judge that the wax is or exists from the fact that I see it, it certainly follows much more clearly that I am or that I exist myself from the fact that I see it. For it may be that what I see is not really wax, it may also be that I do not possess eyes with which to see anything; but it cannot be that when I see, or (for I no longer take account of the distinction) when I think I see, that I myself who think am nought. So if I judge that the wax exists from the fact that I touch it, the same thing will follow, to wit, that I am; and if I judge that my imagination, or some other cause, whatever it is, persuades me that the wax exists, I shall still conclude the same. And what I have here remarked of wax may be applied to all other things which are external to me [and which are met with outside of me]. And further, if the [notion or] perception of wax has seemed to me clearer and more distinct, not only after the sight or the touch, but also after many other causes have rendered it quite manifest to me, with how much more [evidence] and distinctness must it be said that I now know myself, since all the reasons which contribute to the knowledge of wax, or any other body whatever, are yet better proofs of the nature of my mind! And there are so many other things in the mind itself which may contribute to the elucidation of its nature, that those which depend on body such as these just mentioned, hardly merit being taken into account.

But finally here I am, having insensibly reverted to the point I desired, for, since it is now manifest to me that even bodies are not properly speaking known by the senses or by the faculty of imagination, but by the understanding only, and since they are not known from the fact that they are seen or touched, but only because they are understood, I see clearly that there is nothing which is easier for me to know than my mind. But because it is difficult to rid oneself so promptly of an opinion to which one was accustomed for so long, it will be well that I should halt a little at this point, so that by the length of my meditation I may more deeply imprint on my memory this new knowledge.

MEDITATION III: *Of God: that He exists*

I shall now close my eyes, I shall stop my ears, I shall call away all my senses, I shall efface even from my thoughts all the images of corporeal things, or at least (for that is hardly possible) I shall esteem them as vain and false; and thus holding converse only with myself and considering my own nature, I shall try little by little to reach a better knowledge of and a more familiar acquaintanceship with myself. I am a thing that thinks, that is to say, that doubts, affirms, denies, that knows a few things, that is ignorant of many [that loves, that hates], that wills, that desires, that also imagines and perceives; for as I remarked before, although the things which I perceive and imagine are perhaps nothing at all apart from me and in themselves, I am nevertheless assured that these modes of thought that I call perceptions and imaginations, inasmuch only as they are modes of thought, certainly reside [and are met with] in me.

And in the little that I have just said, I think I have summed up all that I really know, or at least all that hitherto I was aware that I knew. In order to try to extend my knowledge further, I shall now look around more carefully and see whether I cannot still discover in myself some other things which I have not hitherto perceived. I am certain that I am a thing which thinks; but do I not then likewise know what is requisite to render me certain of a truth? Certainly in this first knowledge there is nothing that assures me of its truth, excepting the clear and distinct perception of that which I state, which would not indeed suffice to assure me that what I say is true, if it could ever happen that a thing which I conceived so clearly and distinctly could be false; and accordingly it seems to me that already I can establish as a general rule that all things which I perceive very clearly and very distinctly are true.

At the same time I have before received and admitted many things to be very certain and manifest, which yet I afterwards recognised as being dubious. What then were these things? They were the earth, sky, stars and all other objects which I apprehended by means of the senses. But what did I clearly [and distinctly] perceive in them? Nothing more than that the ideas or thoughts of these things were presented to my mind. And not even now do I deny that these ideas are met with in me. But there was yet another thing which I affirmed, and which, owing to the habit which I had formed of believing it, I thought I perceived very clearly, although in truth I did not perceive it at all, to wit, that there were objects outside of me from which these ideas proceeded, and to which they were entirely similar. And it was in this that I erred, or, if perchance my judgment was correct, this was not due to any knowledge arising from my perception.

But when I took anything very simple and easy in the sphere of arithmetic or geometry into consideration, e.g. that two and three together made five, and other things of the sort, were not these present to my mind so clearly as to enable me to affirm that they were true? Certainly if I judged that since such matters could be doubted, this would not have been so for any other reason than that it came into my mind that perhaps a God might have endowed me with such a nature that I may have been deceived even concerning things which seemed to me most manifest. But every time that this preconceived opinion of the sovereign power of a God presents itself to my thought, I am constrained to confess that it is easy to Him, if He wishes it, to cause me to err, even in matters in which I believe myself to have the best evidence. And, on the other hand, always when I direct my attention to things which I believe myself to perceive very clearly, I am so persuaded of their truth that I let myself break out into words such as these: Let who will deceive me, He can never cause me to be nothing while I think that I am, or some day cause it to be true to say that I have never been, it being true now to say that I am, or that two and three make more or less than five, or any such thing in which I see a manifest contradiction. And, certainly, since I have no reason to believe that there is a God who is a deceiver, and as I have not yet satisfied myself that there is a God at all, the reason for doubt which depends on this opinion alone is very slight, and so to speak metaphysical. But in order to be able altogether to remove it, I must inquire whether there is a God as soon as the occasion presents itself; and if I find that there is a God, I must also inquire whether He may be a deceiver; for without a knowledge of these two truths I do not see that I can ever be certain of anything.

And in order that I may have an opportunity of inquiring into this in an orderly way [without interrupting the order of meditation which I have proposed to myself, and which is little by little to pass from the notions which I find first of all in my mind to those which I shall later on discover in it] it is requisite that I should here divide my thoughts into certain kinds, and that I should consider in which of these kinds there is, properly speaking, truth or error to be found. Of my thoughts some are, so to speak, images of the things, and to these alone is the title 'idea' properly applied; examples are my thought of a man or of a chimera, of heaven, of an angel, or [even] of God. But other thoughts possess other forms as well. For example in willing, fearing, approving, denying, though I always perceive something as the subject of the action of my mind, yet by this action I always add something else to the idea which I have of that thing; and of the thoughts of this kind some are called volitions or affections, and others judgments.

Now as to what concerns ideas, if we consider them only in themselves and do not relate them to anything else beyond themselves, they cannot properly speaking be false; for whether I imagine a goat or a chimera, it is not less true that I imagine the one than the other. We must not fear likewise that falsity can enter into will and into affections, for although I may desire evil things, or even things that never existed, it is not the less true that I desire them. Thus there remains no more than the judgments which we make, in which I must take the greatest care not to deceive myself. But the principal error and the commonest which we may meet with in them, consists in my judging that the ideas which are in me are similar or conformable to the things which are outside me; for without doubt if I considered the ideas only as certain modes of my thoughts, without trying to relate them to anything beyond, they could scarcely give me material for error.

But among these ideas, some appear to me to be innate, some adventitious, and others to be formed [or invented] by myself; for, as I have the power of understanding what is called a thing, or a truth, or a thought, it appears to me that I hold this power from no other source than my own nature. But if I now hear some sound, if I see the sun, or feel heat, I have hitherto judged that these sensations proceeded from certain things that exist outside of me; and finally it appears to me that sirens, hippogryphs, and the like, are formed out of my own mind. But again I may possibly persuade myself that all these ideas are of the nature of those which I term adventitious, or else that they are all innate, or all fictitious: for I have not yet clearly discovered their true origin.

And my principal task in this place is to consider, in respect to those ideas which appear to me to proceed from certain objects that are outside me, what are the reasons which cause me to think them similar to these objects. It seems indeed in the first place that I am taught this lesson by nature; and, secondly, I experience in myself that these ideas do not depend on my will nor therefore on myself – for they often present themselves to my mind in spite of my will. Just now, for instance, whether I will or whether I do not will, I feel heat, and thus I persuade myself that this feeling, or at least this idea of heat, is produced in me by something which is different from me, i.e. by the heat of the fire near which I sit. And nothing seems to me more obvious than to judge that this object imprints its likeness rather than anything else upon me.

Now I must discover whether these proofs are sufficiently strong and convincing. When I say that I am so instructed by nature, I merely mean a certain spontaneous inclination which impels me to believe in this connection, and not a natural light which makes me recognise that it is true. But these two things are very different; for I cannot doubt that which the natural light causes me to believe to be true, as, for example, it has shown me that I am from the fact that I doubt, or other facts of the same kind. And I possess no other faculty whereby to distinguish truth from falsehood, which can teach me that what this light shows me to be true is not really true, and no other faculty that is equally trustworthy. But as far as [apparently] natural impulses are concerned, I have frequently remarked, when I had to make active choice between virtue and vice, that they often enough led me to the part that was worse; and this is why I do not see any reason for following them in what regards truth and error.

And as to the other reason, which is that these ideas must proceed from objects outside me, since they do not depend on my will, I do not find it any the more convincing. For just as these impulses of which I have spoken are found in me, notwithstanding that they do not always concur with my will, so perhaps there is in me some faculty fitted to produce these ideas without the assistance of any external things, even though it is not yet known by me; just as, apparently, they have hitherto always been found in me during sleep without the aid of any external objects.

And finally, though they did proceed from objects different from myself, it is not a necessary consequence that they should resemble these. On the contrary, I have noticed that in many cases there was a great difference between the object and its idea. I find, for example, two completely diverse ideas of the sun in my mind; the one derives its origin from the senses, and should be placed in the category of adventitious ideas; according to this idea the sun seems to be extremely small; but the other is derived from astronomical reasonings, i.e. is elicited from certain notions that are innate in me, or else it is formed by me in some other manner; in accordance with it the sun appears to be several times greater than the earth. These two ideas cannot, indeed, both resemble the same sun, and reason makes me believe that the one which seems to have originated directly from the sun itself, is the one which is most dissimilar to it.

All this causes me to believe that until the present time it has not been by a judgment that was certain [or premeditated], but only by a sort of blind impulse that I believed that things existed outside of, and different from me, which, by the organs of my senses, or by some other method whatever it might be, conveyed these ideas or images to me [and imprinted on me their similitudes].

But there is yet another method of inquiring whether any of the objects of which I have ideas within me exist outside of me. If ideas are only taken as certain modes of thought, I recognise amongst them no difference or inequality, and all appear to proceed from me in the same manner; but when we consider them as images, one representing one thing and the other another, it is clear that they are very different one from the other. There is no doubt that those which represent to me substances are something more, and contain so to speak more objective reality within them [that is to say, by representation participate in a higher degree of being or perfection] than those that simply represent modes or accidents; and that idea again by which I understand a supreme God, eternal, infinite, [immutable], omniscient, omnipotent, and Creator of all things which are outside of Himself, has certainly more objective reality in itself than those ideas by which finite substances are represented.

Now it is manifest by the natural light that there must at least be as much reality in the efficient and total cause as in its effect. For, pray, whence can the effect derive its reality, if not from its cause? And in what way can this cause communicate this reality to it, unless it possessed it in itself? And from this it follows, not only that something cannot proceed from nothing, but likewise that what is more perfect – that is to say, which has more reality within itself – cannot proceed from the less perfect. And this is not only evidently true of those effects which possess actual or formal reality, but also of the ideas in which we consider merely what is termed objective reality. To take an example, the stone which has not yet existed not only cannot now commence to be unless it has been produced by something which possesses within itself, either formally or eminently, all that enters into the composition of the stone [i.e. it must possess the same things or other more excellent things than those which exist in the stone] and heat can only be produced in a subject in which it did not previously exist by a cause that is of an order [degree or kind] at least as perfect as heat, and so in all other cases. But further, the idea of heat, or of a stone, cannot exist in me unless it has been placed within me by some cause which possesses within it at least as much reality as that which I conceive to exist in the heat or the stone. For although this cause does not transmit anything of its actual or formal reality to my idea, we must not for that reason imagine that it is necessarily a less real cause; we must remember that [since every idea is a work of the mind] its nature is such that it demands of itself no other formal reality than that which it borrows from my thought, of which it is only a mode [i.e. a manner or way of thinking]. But in order that an idea should contain some one certain objective reality rather than another, it must without doubt derive it from some cause in which there is at least as much formal reality as this idea contains of objective reality. For if we imagine that something is found in an idea which is not found in the cause, it must then have been derived from nought; but however imperfect may be this mode of being by which a thing is objectively [or by representation] in the understanding by its idea, we cannot certainly say that this mode of being is nothing, nor, consequently, that the idea derives its origin from nothing.

Nor must I imagine that, since the reality that I consider in these ideas is only objective, it is not essential that this reality should be formally in the causes of my ideas, but that it is sufficient that it should be found objectively. For just as this mode of objective existence pertains to ideas by their proper nature, so does the mode of formal existence pertain to the causes of those ideas (this is at least true of the first and principal) by the nature peculiar to them. And although it may be the case that one idea gives birth to another idea, that cannot continue to be so indefinitely; for in the end we must reach an idea whose cause shall be so to speak an archetype, in which the whole reality [or perfection] which is so to speak objectively [or by representation] in these ideas is contained formally [and really]. Thus the light of nature causes me to know clearly that the ideas in me are like [pictures or] images which can, in truth, easily fall short of the perfection of the objects from which they have been derived, but which can never contain anything greater or more perfect.

And the longer and the more carefully that I investigate these matters, the more clearly and distinctly do I recognise their truth. But what am I to conclude from it all in the end? It is this, that if the objective reality of any one of my ideas is of such a nature as clearly to make me recognise that it is not in me either formally or eminently, and that consequently I cannot myself be the cause of it, it follows of necessity that I am not alone in the world, but that there is another being which exists, or which is the cause of this idea. On the other hand, had no such an idea existed in me, I should have had no sufficient argument to convince me of the existence of any being beyond myself; for I have made very careful investigation everywhere and up to the present time have been able to find no other ground.

But of my ideas, beyond that which represents me to myself, as to which there can here be no difficulty, there is another which represents a God, and there are others representing corporeal and inanimate things, others angels, others animals, and others again which represent to me men similar to myself.

As regards the ideas which represent to me other men or animals, or angels, I can however easily conceive that they might be formed by an admixture of the other ideas which I have of myself, of corporeal things, and of God, even although there were apart from me neither men nor animals, nor angels, in all the world.

And in regard to the ideas of corporeal objects, I do not recognise in them anything so great or so excellent that they might not have possibly proceeded from myself; for if I consider them more closely, and examine them individually, as I yesterday examined the idea of wax, I find that there is very little in them which I perceive clearly and distinctly. Magnitude or extension in length, breadth, or depth, I do so perceive; also figure which results from a termination of this extension, the situation which bodies of different figure preserve in relation to one another, and movement or change of situation; to which we may also add substance, duration and number. As to other things such as light, colours, sounds, scents, tastes, heat, cold and the other tactile qualities, they are thought by me with so much obscurity and confusion that I do not even know if they are true or false, i.e. whether the ideas which I form of these qualities are actually the ideas of real objects or not [or whether they only represent chimeras which cannot exist in fact]. For although I have before remarked that it is only in judgments that falsity, properly speaking, or formal falsity, can be met with, a certain material falsity may nevertheless be found in ideas, i.e. when these ideas represent what is nothing as though it were something. For example, the ideas which I have of cold and heat are so far from clear and distinct that by their means I cannot tell whether cold is merely a privation of heat, or heat a privation of cold, or whether both are real qualities, or are not such. And inasmuch as [since ideas resemble images] there cannot be any ideas which do not appear to represent some things, if it is correct to say that cold is merely a privation of heat, the idea which represents it to me as something real and positive will not be improperly termed false, and the same holds good of other similar ideas.

To these it is certainly not necessary that I should attribute any author other than myself. For if they are false, i.e. if they represent things which do not exist, the light of nature shows me that they issue from nought, that is to say, that they are only in me in so far as something is lacking to the perfection of my nature. But if they are true, nevertheless because they exhibit so little reality to me that I cannot even clearly distinguish the thing represented from non-being, I do not see any reason why they should not be produced by myself.

As to the clear and distinct idea which I have of corporeal things, some of them seem as though I might have derived them from the idea which I possess of myself, as those which I have of substance, duration, number, and such like. For [even] when I think that a stone is a substance, or at least a thing capable of existing of itself, and that I am a substance also, although I conceive that I am a thing that thinks and not one that is extended, and that the stone on the other hand is an extended thing which does not think, and that thus there is a notable difference between the two conceptions – they seem, nevertheless, to agree in this, that both represent substances. In the same way, when I perceive that I now exist and further recollect that I have in former times existed, and when I remember that I have various thoughts of which I can recognise the number, I acquire ideas of duration and number which I can afterwards transfer to any object that I please. But as to all the other qualities of which the ideas of corporeal things are composed, to wit, extension, figure, situation and motion, it is true that they are not formally in me, since I am only a thing that thinks; but because they are merely certain modes of substance [and so to speak the vestments under which corporeal substance appears to us] and because I myself am also a substance, it would seem that they might be contained in me eminently.

Hence there remains only the idea of God, concerning which we must consider whether it is something which cannot have proceeded from me myself. By the name God I understand a substance that is infinite [eternal, immutable], independent, all-knowing, all-powerful, and by which I myself and everything else, if anything else does exist, have been created. Now all these characteristics are such that the more diligently I attend to them, the less do they appear capable of proceeding from me alone; hence, from what has been already said, we must conclude that God necessarily exists.

For although the idea of substance is within me owing to the fact that I am substance, nevertheless I should not have the idea of an infinite substance – since I am finite – if it had not proceeded from some substance which was veritably infinite.

Nor should I imagine that I do not perceive the infinite by a true idea, but only by the negation of the finite, just as I perceive repose and darkness by the negation of movement and of light; for, on the contrary, I see that there is manifestly more reality in infinite substance than in finite, and therefore that in some way I have in me the notion of the infinite earlier than the finite – to wit, the notion of God before that of myself. For how would it be possible that I should know that I doubt and desire, that is to say, that something is lacking to me, and that I am not quite perfect, unless I had within me some idea of a Being more perfect than myself, in comparison with which I should recognise the deficiencies of my nature?

And we cannot say that this idea of God is perhaps materially false and that consequently I can derive it from nought [i.e. that possibly it exists in me because I am imperfect], as I have just said is the case with ideas of heat, cold and other such things; for, on the contrary, as this idea is very clear and distinct and contains within it more objective reality than any other, there can be none which is of itself more true, nor any in which there can be less suspicion of falsehood. The idea, I say, of this Being who is absolutely perfect and infinite, is entirely true; for although, perhaps, we can imagine that such a Being does not exist, we cannot nevertheless imagine that His idea represents nothing real to me, as I have said of the idea of cold. This idea is also very clear and distinct; since all that I conceive clearly and distinctly of the real and the true, and of what conveys some perfection, is in its entirety contained in this idea. And this does not cease to be true although I do not comprehend the infinite, or though in God there is an infinitude of things which I cannot comprehend, nor possibly even reach in any way by thought; for it is of the nature of the infinite that my nature, which is finite and limited, should not comprehend it; and it is sufficient that I should understand this, and that I should judge that all things which I clearly perceive and in which I know that there is some perfection, and possibly likewise an infinitude of properties of which I am ignorant, are in God formally or eminently, so that the idea which I have of Him may become the most true, most clear, and most distinct of all the ideas that are in my mind.

But possibly I am something more than I suppose myself to be, and perhaps all those perfections which I attribute to God are in some way potentially in me, although they do not yet disclose themselves, or issue in action. As a matter of fact I am already sensible that my knowledge increases [and perfects itself] little by little, and I see nothing which can prevent it from increasing more and more into infinitude; nor do I see, after it has thus been increased [or perfected], anything to prevent my being able to acquire by its means all the other perfections of the Divine nature; not finally why the power I have of acquiring these perfections, if it really exists in me, shall not suffice to produce the ideas of them.

At the same time I recognise that this cannot be. For, in the first place, although it were true that every day my knowledge acquired new degrees of perfection, and that there were in my nature many things potentially which are not yet there actually, nevertheless these excellences do not pertain to [or make the smallest approach to] the idea which I have of God in whom there is nothing merely potential [but in whom all is present really and actually]; for it is an infallible token of imperfection in my knowledge that it increases little by little. And further, although my knowledge grows more and more, nevertheless I do not for that reason believe that it can ever be actually infinite, since it can never reach a point so high that it will be unable to attain to any greater increase. But I understand God to be actually infinite, so that He can add nothing to His supreme perfection. And finally I perceive that the objective being of an idea cannot be produced by a being that exists potentially only, which properly speaking is nothing, but only by a being which is formal or actual.

To speak the truth, I see nothing in all that I have just said which by the light of nature is not manifest to anyone who desires to think attentively on the subject; but when I slightly relax my attention, my mind, finding its vision somewhat obscured and so to speak blinded by the images of sensible objects, I do not easily recollect the reason why the idea that I possess of a being more perfect than I, must necessarily have been placed in me by a being which is really more perfect; and this is why I wish here to go on to inquire whether I, who have this idea, can exist if no such being exists.

And I ask, from whom do I then derive my existence? Perhaps from myself or from my parents, or from some other source less perfect than God; for we can imagine nothing more perfect than God, or even as perfect as He is.

But [were I independent of every other and] were I myself the author of my being, I should doubt nothing and I should desire nothing, and finally no perfection would be lacking to me; for I should have bestowed on myself every perfection of which I possessed any idea and should thus be God. And it must not be imagined that those things that are lacking to me are perhaps more difficult of attainment than those which I already possess; for, on the contrary, it is quite evident that it was a matter of much greater difficulty to bring to pass that I, that is to say, a thing or a substance that thinks, should emerge out of nothing, than it would be to attain to the knowledge of many things of which I am ignorant, and which are only the accidents of this thinking substance. But it is clear that if I had of myself possessed this greater perfection of which I have just spoken [that is to say, if I had been the author of my own existence], I should not at least have denied myself the things which are the more easy to acquire [to wit, many branches of knowledge of which my nature is destitute]; nor should I have deprived myself of any of the things contained in the idea which I form of God, because there are none of them which seem to me specially difficult to acquire: and if there were any that were more difficult to acquire, they would certainly appear to me to be such (supposing I myself were the origin of the other things which I possess) since I should discover in them that my powers were limited.

But though I assume that perhaps I have always existed just as I am at present, neither can I escape the force of this reasoning, and imagine that the conclusion to be drawn from this is, that I need not seek for any author of my existence. For all the course of my life may be divided into an infinite number of parts, none of which is in any way dependent on the other; and thus from the fact that I was in existence a short time ago it does not follow that I must be in existence now, unless some cause at this instant, so to speak, produces me anew, that is to say, conserves me. It is as a matter of fact perfectly clear and evident to all those who consider with attention the nature of time, that, in order to be conserved in each moment in which it endures, a substance has need of the same power and action as would be necessary to produce and create it anew, supposing it did not yet exist, so that the light of nature shows us clearly that the distinction between creation and conservation is solely a distinction of the reason.

All that I thus require here is that I should interrogate myself, if I wish to know whether I possess a power which is capable of bringing it to pass that I who now am shall still be in the future; for since I am nothing but a thinking thing, or at least since thus far it is only this portion of myself which is precisely in question at present, if such a power did reside in me, I should certainly be conscious of it. But I am conscious of nothing of the kind, and by this I know clearly that I depend on some being different from myself.

Possibly, however, this being on which I depend is not that which I call God, and I am created either by my parents or by some other cause less perfect than God. This cannot be, because, as I have just said, it is perfectly evident that there must be at least as much reality in the cause as in the effect; and thus since I am a thinking thing, and possess an idea of God within me, whatever in the end be the cause assigned to my existence, it must be allowed that it is likewise a thinking thing and that it possesses in itself the idea of all the perfections which I attribute to God. We may again inquire whether this cause derives its origin from itself or from some other thing. For if from itself, it follows by the reasons before brought forward, that this cause must itself be God; for since it possesses the virtue of self-existence, it must also without doubt have the power of actually possessing all the perfections of which it has the idea, that is, all those which I conceive as existing in God. But if it derives its existence from some other cause than itself, we shall again ask, for the same reason, whether this second cause exists by itself or through another, until from one step to another, we finally arrive at an ultimate cause, which will be God.

And it is perfectly manifest that in this there can be no regression into infinity, since what is in question is not so much the cause which formerly created me, as that which conserves me at the present time.

Nor can we suppose that several causes may have concurred in my production, and that from one I have received the idea of one of the perfections which I attribute to God, and from another the idea of some other, so that all these perfections indeed exist somewhere in the universe, but not as complete in one unity which is God. On the contrary, the unity, the simplicity or the inseparability of all things which are in God is one of the principal perfections which I conceive to be in Him. And certainly the idea of this unity of all Divine perfections cannot have been placed in me by any cause from which I have not likewise received the ideas of all the other perfections; for this cause could not make me able to comprehend them as joined together in an inseparable unity without having at the same time caused me in some measure to know what they are [and in some way to recognise each one of them].

Finally, so far as my parents [from whom it appears I have sprung] are concerned, although all that I have ever been able to believe of them were true, that does not make it follow that it is they who conserve me, nor are they even the authors of my being in any sense, in so far as I am a thinking being; since what they did was merely to implant certain dispositions in that matter in which the self – i.e. the mind, which alone I at present identify with myself – is by me deemed to exist. And thus there can be no difficulty in their regard, but we must of necessity conclude from the fact alone that I exist, or that the idea of a Being supremely perfect – that is of God – is in me, that the proof of God's existence is grounded on the highest evidence.

It only remains to me to examine into the manner in which I have acquired this idea from God; for I have not received it through the senses, and it is never presented to me unexpectedly, as is usual with the ideas of sensible things when these things present themselves, or seem to present themselves, to the external organs of my senses; nor is it likewise a fiction of my mind, for it is not in my power to take from or to add anything to it; and consequently the only alternative is that it is innate in me, just as the idea of myself is innate in me.

And one certainly ought not to find it strange that God, in creating me, placed this idea within me to be like the mark of the workman imprinted on his work; and it is likewise not essential that the mark shall be something different from the work itself. For from the sole fact that God created me it is most probable that in some way he has placed his image and similitude upon me, and that I perceive this similitude (in which the idea of God is contained) by means of the same faculty by which I perceive myself – that is to say, when I reflect on myself I not only know that I am something [imperfect], incomplete and dependent on another, which incessantly aspires after something which is better and greater than myself, but I also know that He on whom I depend possesses in Himself all the great things towards which I aspire [and the ideas of which I find within myself], and that not indefinitely or potentially alone, but really, actually and infinitely; and that thus He is God. And the whole strength of the argument which I have here made use of to prove the existence of God consists in this, that I recognise that it is not possible that my nature should be what it is, and indeed that I should have in myself the idea of a God, if God did not veritably exist – a God, I say, whose idea is in me, i.e. who possesses all those supreme perfections of which our mind may indeed have some idea but without understanding them all, who is liable to no errors or defect [and who has none of all those marks which denote imperfection]. From this it is manifest that He cannot be a deceiver, since the light of nature teaches us that fraud and deception necessarily proceed from some defect.

But before I examine this matter with more care, and pass on to the consideration of other truths which may be derived from it, it seems to me right to pause for a while in order to contemplate God Himself, to ponder at leisure His marvellous attributes, to consider, and admire, and adore, the beauty of this light so resplendent, at least as far as the strength of my mind, which is in some measure dazzled by the sight, will allow me to do so. For just as faith teaches us that the supreme felicity of the other life consists only in this contemplation of the Divine Majesty, so we continue to learn by experience that a similar meditation, though incomparably less perfect, causes us to enjoy the greatest satisfaction of which we are capable in this life.

MEDITATION IV: *Of the True and the False*

I have been well accustomed these past days to detach my mind from my senses, and I have accurately observed that there are very few things that one knows with certainty respecting corporeal objects, that there are many more which are known to us respecting the human mind, and yet more still regarding God Himself; so that I shall now without any difficulty abstract my thoughts from the consideration of [sensible or] imaginable objects, and carry them to those which, being withdrawn from all contact with matter, are purely intelligible. And certainly the idea which I possess of the human mind inasmuch as it is a thinking thing, and not extended in length, width and depth, nor participating in anything pertaining to body, is incomparably more distinct than is the idea of any corporeal thing. And when I consider that I doubt, that is to say, that I am an incomplete and dependent being, the idea of a being that is complete and independent, that is of God, presents itself to my mind with so much distinctness and clearness – and from the fact alone that this idea is found in me, or that I who possess this idea exist, I conclude so certainly that God exists, and that my existence depends entirely on Him in every moment of my life – that I do not think that the human mind is capable of knowing anything with more evidence and certitude. And it seems to me that I now have before me a road which will lead us from the contemplation of the true God (in whom all the treasures of science and wisdom are contained) to the knowledge of the other objects of the universe.

For, first of all, I recognise it to be impossible that He should ever deceive me; for in all fraud and deception some imperfection is to be found, and although it may appear that the power of deception is a mark of subtility or power, yet the desire to deceive without doubt testifies to malice or feebleness, and accordingly cannot be found in God.

In the next place I experienced in myself a certain capacity for judging which I have doubtless received from God, like all the other things that I possess; and as He could not desire to deceive me, it is clear that He has not given me a faculty that will lead me to err if I use it aright.

And no doubt respecting this matter could remain, if it were not that the consequence would seem to follow that I can thus never be deceived; for if I hold all that I possess from God, and if He has not placed in me the capacity for error, it seems as though I could never fall into error. And it is true that when I think only of God [and direct my mind wholly to Him],[7] I discover [in myself] no cause of error, or falsity; yet directly afterwards, when recurring to myself, experience shows me that I am nevertheless subject to an infinitude of errors, as to which, when we come to investigate them more closely, I notice that not only is there a real and positive idea of God or of a Being of supreme perfection present to my mind, but also, so to speak, a certain negative idea of nothing, that is, of that which is infinitely removed from any kind of perfection; and that I am in a sense something intermediate between God and nought, i.e. placed in such a manner between the supreme Being and non-being, that there is in truth nothing in me that can lead to error in so far as a sovereign Being has formed me; but that, as I in some degree participate likewise in nought or in non-being, i.e. in so far as I am not myself the supreme Being, and as I find myself subject

7. Not in the French version.

to an infinitude of imperfections, I ought not to be astonished if I should fall into error. Thus do I recognise that error, in so far as it is such, is not a real thing depending on God, but simply a defect; and therefore, in order to fall into it, that I have no need to possess a special faculty given me by God for this very purpose, but that I fall into error from the fact that the power given me by God for the purpose of distinguishing truth from error is not infinite.

Nevertheless this does not quite satisfy me; for error is not a pure negation [i.e. is not the simple defect or want of some perfection which ought not to be mine], but it is a lack of some knowledge which it seems that I ought to possess. And on considering the nature of God it does not appear to me possible that He should have given me a faculty which is not perfect of its kind, that is, which is wanting in some perfection due to it. For if it is true that the more skilful the artisan, the more perfect is the work of his hands, what can have been produced by this supreme Creator of all things that is not in all its parts perfect? And certainly there is no doubt that God could have created me so that I could never have been subject to error; it is also certain that He ever wills what is best; is it then better that I should be subject to err than that I should not?

In considering this more attentively, it occurs to me in the first place that I should not be astonished if my intelligence is not capable of comprehending why God acts as He does; and that there is thus no reason to doubt of His existence from the fact that I may perhaps find many other things besides this as to which I am able to understand neither for what reason nor how God has produced them. For, in the first place, knowing that my nature is extremely feeble and limited, and that the nature of God is on the contrary immense, incomprehensible, and infinite, I have no further difficulty in recognising that there is an infinitude of matters in His power, the causes of which transcend my knowledge; and this reason suffices to convince me that the species of cause termed final, finds no useful employment in physical [or natural] things; for it does not appear to me that I can without temerity seek to investigate the [inscrutable] ends of God.

It further occurs to me that we should not consider one single creature separately, when we inquire as to whether the works of God are perfect, but should regard all his creations together. For the same thing which might possibly seem very imperfect with some semblance of reason if regarded by itself, is found to be very perfect if regarded as part of the whole universe; and although, since I resolved to doubt all things, I as yet have only known certainly my own existence and that of God, nevertheless since I have recognised the infinite power of God, I cannot deny that He may have produced many other things, or at least that He has the power of producing them, so that I may obtain a place as a part of a great universe.

Whereupon, regarding myself more closely, and considering what are my errors (for they alone testify to there being any imperfection in me), I answer that they depend on a combination of two causes, to wit, on the faculty of knowledge that rests in me, and on the power of choice or of free will – that is to say, of the understanding and at the same time of the will. For by the understanding alone I [neither assert nor deny anything, but] apprehend the ideas of things as to which I can form a judgment. But no error is properly speaking found in it, provided the word error is taken in its proper signification; and though there is possibly an infinitude of things in the world of which I have no idea in my understanding, we cannot for all that say that it is deprived of these ideas [as we might say of something which is required by its nature], but simply it does not possess these; because in truth there is no reason to prove that God should have given me a greater faculty of knowledge than He has given me; and however skilful a workman I represent Him to be, I should not for all that consider that He was bound to have placed in each of His works all the perfections which He may have been able to place in some. I likewise cannot complain that God has not given me a free choice or a will which is sufficient, ample and perfect, since as a matter of fact I am conscious of a will so extended as to be subject to no limits. And what seems to me very remarkable in this regard is that of all the qualities which I possess there is no one so perfcet and so comprehensive that I do not very clearly, recognise that it might be yet greater and more perfect. For, to take an example, if I consider the faculty of comprehension which I possess, I find that it is of very small extent and extremely limited, and at the same time I find the idea of another faculty much more ample and even infinite, and seeing that I can form the idea of it, I recognise from this very fact that it pertains to the nature of

God. If in the same way I examine the memory, the imagination, or some other faculty, I do not find any which is not small and circumscribed, while in God it is immense [or infinite]. It is free-will alone or liberty of choice which I find to be so great in me that I can conceive no other idea to be more great; it is indeed the case that it is for the most part this will that causes me to know that in some manner I bear the image and similitude of God. For although the power of will is incomparably greater in God than in me, both by reason of the knowledge and the power which, conjoined with it, render it stronger and more efficacious, and by reason of its object, inasmuch as in God it extends to a great many things; it nevertheless does not seem to me greater if I consider it formally and precisely in itself: for the faculty of will consists alone in our having the power of choosing to do a thing or choosing not to do it (that is, to affirm or deny, to pursue or to shun it), or rather it consists alone in the fact that in order to affirm or deny, pursue or shun those things placed before us by the understanding, we act so that we are unconscious that any outside force constrains us in doing so. For in order that I should be free it is not necessary that I should be indifferent as to the choice of one or the other of two contraries; but contrariwise the more I lean to the one – whether I recognise clearly that the reasons of the good and true are to be found in it, or whether God so disposes my inward thought – the more freely do I choose and embrace it. And undoubtedly both divine grace and natural knowledge, far from diminishing my liberty, rather increase it and strengthen it. Hence this indifference which I feel, when I am not swayed to one side rather than to the other by lack of reason, is the lowest grade of liberty, and rather evinces a lack or negation in knowledge than a perfection of will: for if I always recognised clearly what was true and good, I should never have trouble in deliberating as to what judgment or choice I should make, and then I should be entirely free without ever being indifferent.

From all this I recognise that the power of will which I have received from God is not of itself the source of my errors – for it is very ample and very perfect of its kind – any more than is the power of understanding; for since I understand nothing but by the power which God has given me for understanding, there is no doubt that all that I understand, I understand as I ought, and it is not possible that I err in this. Whence then come my errors? They come from the sole fact that since the will is much wider in its range and compass than the understanding, I do not restrain it within the same bounds, but extend it also to things which I do not understand: and as the will is of itself indifferent to these, it easily falls into error and sin, and chooses the evil for the good, or the false for the true.

For example, when I lately examined whether anything existed in the world, and found that from the very fact that I considered this question it followed very clearly that I myself existed, I could not prevent myself from believing that a thing I so clearly conceived was true: not that I found myself compelled to do so by some external cause, but simply because from great clearness in my mind there followed a great inclination of my will; and I believed this with so much the greater freedom or spontaneity as I possessed the less indifference towards it. Now, on the contrary, I not only know that I exist, inasmuch as I am a thinking thing, but a certain representation of corporeal nature is also presented to my mind; and it comes to pass that I doubt whether this thinking nature which is in me, or rather by which I am what I am, differs from this corporeal nature, or whether both are not simply the same thing; and I here suppose that I do not yet know any reason to persuade me to adopt the one belief rather than the other. From this it follows that I am entirely indifferent as to which of the two I affirm or deny, or even whether I abstain from forming any judgment in the matter.

And this indifference does not only extend to matters as to which the understanding has no knowledge, but also in general to all those which are not apprehended with perfect clearness at the moment when the will is deliberating upon them: for, however probable are the conjectures which render me disposed to form a judgment respecting anything, the simple knowledge that I have that those are conjectures alone and not certain and indubitable reasons, suffices to occasion me to judge the contrary. Of this I have had great experience of late when I set aside as false all that I had formerly held to be absolutely true, for the sole reason that I remarked that it might in some measure be doubted.

But if I abstain from giving my judgment on any thing when I do not perceive it with sufficient clearness and distinctness, it is plain that I act rightly and am not deceived. But if I determine to deny or affirm, I no longer make use as I should of my free will, and if I affirm what is not true, it is evident that I deceive myself; even though I judge according to truth, this comes about only by chance, and I do not escape the blame of misusing my freedom; for the light of nature teaches us that the knowledge of the understanding should always precede the determination of the will. And it is in the misuse of the free will that the privation which constitutes the characteristic nature of error is met with. Privation, I say, is found in the act, in so far as it proceeds from me, but it is not found in the faculty which I have received from God, nor even in the act in so far as it depends on Him.

For I have certainly no cause to complain that God has not given me an intelligence which is more powerful, or a natural light which is stronger than that which I have received from Him, since it is proper to the finite understanding not to comprehend a multitude of things, and it is proper to a created understanding to be finite; on the contrary, I have every reason to render thanks to God who owes me nothing and who has given me all the perfections I possess, and I should be far from charging Him with injustice, and with having deprived me of, or wrongfully withheld from me, these perfections which He has not bestowed upon me.

I have further no reason to complain that He has given me a will more ample than my understanding, for since the will consists only of one single element, and is so to speak indivisible, it appears that its nature is such that nothing can be abstracted from it [without destroying it]; and certainly the more comprehensive it is found to be, the more reason I have to render gratitude to the giver.

And, finally, I must also not complain that God concurs with me in forming the acts of the will, that is the judgment in which I go astray, because these acts are entirely true and good, inasmuch as they depend on God; and in a certain sense more perfection accrues to my nature from the fact that I can form them, than if I could not do so. As to the privation in which alone the formal reason of error or sin consists, it has no need of any concurrence from God, since it is not a thing [or an existence], and since it is not related to God as to a cause, but should be termed merely a negation [according to the significance given to these words in the Schools]. For in fact it is not an imperfection in God that He has given me the liberty to give or withhold my assent from certain things as to which He has not placed a clear and distinct knowledge in my understanding; but it is without doubt an imperfection in me not to make a good use of my freedom, and to give my judgment readily on matters which I only understand obscurely. I nevertheless perceive that God could easily have created me so that I never should err, although I still remained free, and endowed with a limited knowledge, viz. by giving to my understanding a clear and distinct intelligence of all things as to which I should ever have to deliberate: or simply by His engraving deeply in my memory the resolution never to form a judgment on anything without having a clear and distinct understanding of it, so that I could never forget it. And it is easy for me to understand that, in so far as I consider myself alone, and as if there were only myself in the world, I should have been much more perfect than I am, if God had created me so that I could never err. Nevertheless I cannot deny that in some sense it is a greater perfection in the whole universe that certain parts should not be exempt from error as others are than that all parts should be exactly similar. And I have no right to complain if God, having placed me in the world, has not called upon me to play a part that excels all others in distinction and perfection.

And further I have reason to be glad on the ground that if He has not given me the power of never going astray by the first means pointed out above, which depends on a clear and evident knowledge of all the things regarding which I can deliberate, He has at least left within my power the other means, which is firmly to adhere to the resolution never to give judgment on matters whose truth is not clearly known to me; for although I notice a certain weakness in my nature in that I cannot continually concentrate my mind on one single thought, I can yet, by attentive and frequently repeated meditation, impress it so forcibly on my memory that I shall never fail to recollect it whenever I have need of it, and thus acquire the habit of never going astray.

And inasmuch as it is in this that the greatest and principal perfection of man consists, it seems to me that I have not gained little by this day's Meditation, since I have discovered the source of falsity and error. And certainly there can be no other source than that which I have explained; for as often as I so restrain my will within the limits of my knowledge that it forms no judgment except on matters which are clearly and distinctly represented to it by the understanding, I can never be deceived; for every clear and distinct conception is without doubt something, and hence cannot derive its origin from what is nought, but must of necessity have God as its author – God, I say, who being supremely perfect, cannot be the cause of any error; and consequently we must conclude that such a conception [or such a judgment] is true. Nor have I only learned to-day what I should avoid in order that I may not err, but also how I should act in order to arrive at a knowledge of the truth; for without doubt I shall arrive at this end if I devote my attention sufficiently to those things which I perfectly understand; and if I separate from these that which I only understand confusedly and with obscurity. To these I shall henceforth diligently give heed.

MEDITATION V: *Of the essence of material things, and, again, of God, that He exists*

Many other matters respecting the attributes of God and my own nature or mind remain for consideration; but I shall possibly on another occasion resume the investigation of these. Now (after first noting what must be done or avoided, in order to arrive at a knowledge of the truth) my principal task is to endeavour to emerge from the state of doubt into which I have these last days fallen, and to see whether nothing certain can be known regarding material things.

But before examining whether any such objects as I conceive exist outside of me, I must consider the ideas of them in so far as they are in my thought, and see which of them are distinct and which confused.

In the first place, I am able distinctly to imagine that quantity which philosophers commonly call continuous, or the extension in length, breadth, or depth, that is in this quantity, or rather in the object to which it is attributed. Further I can number in it many different parts, and attribute to each of its parts many sorts of size, figure, situation and local movement, and, finally, I can assign to each of these movements all degrees of duration.

And not only do I know these things with distinctness when I consider them in general, but, likewise [however little I apply my attention to the matter], I discover an infinitude of particulars respecting numbers, figures, movements, and other such things, whose truth is so manifest, and so well accords with my nature, that when I begin to discover them, it seems to me that I learn nothing new, or recollect what I formerly knew – that is to say, that I for the first time perceive things which were already present to my mind, although I had not as yet applied my mind to them.

And what I here find to be most important is that I discover in myself an infinitude of ideas of certain things which cannot be esteemed as pure negations, although they may possibly have no existence outside of my thought, and which are not framed by me, although it is within my power either to think or not to think them, but which possess natures which are true and immutable. For example, when I imagine a triangle, although there may nowhere in the world be such a figure outside my thought, or ever have been, there is nevertheless in this figure a certain determinate nature, form, or essence, which is immutable and eternal, which I have not invented, and which in no wise depends on my mind, as appears from the fact that diverse properties of that triangle can be demonstrated, viz. that its three angles are equal to two right angles, that the greatest side is subtended by the greatest angle, and the like, which now, whether I wish it or do not wish it, I recognise very clearly as pertaining to it, although I never thought of the matter at all when I imagined a triangle for the first time, and which therefore cannot be said to have been invented by me.

Nor does the objection hold good that possibly this idea of a triangle has reached my mind through the medium of my senses, since I have sometimes seen bodies triangular in shape; because I can form in my mind an infinitude of other figures regarding which we cannot have the least conception of their ever having been objects of sense, and I can nevertheless demonstrate various properties pertaining to their nature as well as to that of the triangle, and these must certainly all be true since I conceive them clearly. Hence they are something, and not pure negation; for it is perfectly clear that all that is true is something, and I have already fully demonstrated that all that I know clearly is true. And even although I had not demonstrated this, the nature of my mind is such that I could not prevent myself from holding them to be true so long as I conceive them clearly;

and I recollect that even when I was still strongly attached to the objects of sense, I counted as the most certain those truths which I conceived clearly as regards figures, numbers, and the other matters which pertain to arithmetic and geometry, and, in general, to pure and abstract mathematics.

But now, if just because I can draw the idea of something from my thought, it follows that all which I know clearly and distinctly as pertaining to this object does really belong to it, may I not derive from this an argument demonstrating the existence of God? It is certain that I no less find the idea of God, that is to say, the idea of a supremely perfect Being, in me, than that of any figure or number whatever it is; and I do not know any less clearly and distinctly that an [actual and] eternal existence pertains to this nature than I know that all that which I am able to demonstrate of some figure or number truly pertains to the nature of this figure or number, and therefore, although all that I concluded in the preceding Meditations were found to be false, the existence of God would pass with me as at least as certain as I have ever held the truths of mathematics (which concern only numbers and figures) to be.

This indeed is not at first manifest, since it would seem to present some appearance of being a sophism. For being accustomed in all other things to make a distinction between existence and essence, I easily persuade myself that the existence can be separated from the essence of God, and that we can thus conceive God as not actually existing. But, nevertheless, when I think of it with more attention, I clearly see that existence can no more be separated from the essence of God than can its having its three angles equal to two right angles be separated from the essence of a [rectilinear] triangle, or the idea of a mountain from the idea of a valley; and so there is not any less repugnance to our conceiving a God (that is, a Being supremely perfect) to whom existence is lacking (that is to say, to whom a certain perfection is lacking), than to conceive of a mountain which has no valley.

But although I cannot really conceive of a God without existence any more than a mountain without a valley, still from the fact that I conceive of a mountain with a valley, it does not follow that there is such a mountain in the world; similarly although I conceive of God as possessing existence, it would seem that it does not follow that there is a God which exists;

for my thought does not impose any necessity upon things, and just as I may imagine a winged horse, although no horse with wings exists, so I could perhaps attribute existence to God, although no God existed.

But a sophism is concealed in this objection; for from the fact that I cannot conceive a mountain without a valley, it does not follow that there is any mountain or any valley in existence, but only that the mountain and the valley, whether they exist or do not exist, cannot in any way be separated one from the other. While from the fact that I cannot conceive God without existence, it follows that existence is inseparable from Him, and hence that He really exists; not that my thought can bring this to pass, or impose any necessity on things, but, on the contrary, because the necessity which lies in the thing itself, i.e. the necessity of the existence of God determines me to think in this way. For it is not within my power to think of God without existence (that is of a supremely perfect Being devoid of a supreme perfection) though it is in my power to imagine a horse either with wings or without wings.

And we must not here object that it is in truth necessary for me to assert that God exists after having presupposed that He possesses every sort of perfection, since existence is one of these, but that as a matter of fact my original supposition was not necessary, just as it is not necessary to consider that all quadrilateral figures can be inscribed in the circle; for supposing I thought this, I should be constrained to admit that the rhombus might be inscribed in the circle since it is a quadrilateral figure, which, however, is manifestly false. [We must not, I say, make any such allegations because] although it is not necessary that I should at any time entertain the notion of God, nevertheless whenever it happens that I think of a first and a sovereign Being, and, so to speak, derive the idea of Him from the storehouse of my mind, it is necessary that I should attribute to Him every sort of perfection, although I do not get so far as to enumerate them all, or to apply my mind to each one in particular. And this necessity suffices to make me conclude (after having recognised that existence is a perfection) that this first and sovereign Being really exists; just as though it is not necessary for me ever to imagine any triangle, yet, whenever I wish to consider a rectilinear figure composed only of three angles, it is absolutely essential that I should attribute to it all those properties which serve to bring about the conclusion that its three angles are not greater than two right angles, even although I may not then be considering this point in particular. But when I consider which figures are capable of being inscribed in the circle, it is in no wise necessary that I should think that all quadrilateral figures are of this number; on the contrary, I cannot even pretend that this is the case, so long as I do not desire to accept anything which I cannot conceive clearly and distinctly. And in consequence there is a great difference between the false suppositions such as this, and the true ideas born within me, the first and principal of which is that of God. For really I discern in many ways that this idea is not something factitious, and depending solely on my thought, but that it is the image of a true and immutable nature; first of all, because I cannot conceive anything but God himself to whose essence existence [necessarily] pertains; in the second place because it is not possible for me to conceive two or more Gods in this same position; and, granted that there is one such God who now exists, I see clearly that it is necessary that He should have existed from all eternity, and that He must exist eternally; and finally, because I know an infinitude of other properties in God, none of which I can either diminish or change.

For the rest, whatever proof or argument I avail myself of, we must always return to the point that it is only those things which we conceive clearly and distinctly that have the power of persuading me entirely. And although amongst the matters which I conceive of in this way, some indeed are manifestly obvious to all, while others only manifest themselves to those who consider them closely and examine them attentively; still, after they have once been discovered, the latter are not esteemed as any less certain than the former. For example, in the case of every right-angled triangle, although it does not so manifestly appear that the square of the base is equal to the squares of the two other sides as that this base is opposite to the greatest angle; still, when this has once been apprehended, we are just as certain of its truth as of the truth of the other. And as regards God, if my mind were not pre-occupied with prejudices, and if my thought did not find itself on all hands diverted by the continual pressure of sensible things, there would be nothing which I could know more immediately and more easily than Him. For is there anything more manifest than that there is a God, that is to say, a

Supreme Being, to whose essence alone existence pertains?

And although for a firm grasp of this truth I have need of a strenuous application of mind, at present I not only feel myself to be as assured of it as of all that I hold as most certain, but I also remark that the certainty of all other things depends on it so absolutely, that without this knowledge it is impossible ever to know anything perfectly.

For although I am of such a nature that as long as I understand anything very clearly and distinctly, I am naturally impelled to believe it to be true, yet because I am also of such a nature that I cannot have my mind constantly fixed on the same object in order to perceive it clearly, and as I often recollect having formed a past judgment without at the same time properly recollecting the reasons that led me to make it, it may happen meanwhile that other reasons present themselves to me, which would easily cause me to change my opinion, if I were ignorant of the facts of the existence of God, and thus I should have no true and certain knowledge, but only vague and vacillating opinions. Thus, for example, when I consider the nature of a [rectilinear] triangle, I who have some little knowledge of the principles of geometry recognise quite clearly that the three angles are equal to two right angles, and it is not possible for me not to believe this so long as I apply my mind to its demonstration; but so soon as I abstain from attending to the proof, although I still recollect having clearly comprehended it, it may easily occur that I come to doubt its truth, if I am ignorant of there being a God. For I can persuade myself of having been so constituted by nature that I can easily deceive myself even in those matters which I believe myself to apprehend with the greatest evidence and certainty, especially when I recollect that I have frequently judged matters to be true and certain which other reasons have afterwards impelled me to judge to be altogether false.

But after I have recognised that there is a God – because at the same time I have also recognised that all things depend upon Him, and that He is not a deceiver, and from that have inferred that what I perceive clearly and distinctly cannot fail to be true – although I no longer pay attention to the reasons for which I have judged this to be true, provided that I recollect having clearly and distinctly perceived it no contrary reason can be brought forward which could ever cause me to doubt of its truth;

and thus I have a true and certain knowledge of it. And this same knowledge extends likewise to all other things which I recollect having formerly demonstrated, such as the truths of geometry and the like; for what can be alleged against them to cause me to place them in doubt? Will it be said that my nature is such as to cause me to be frequently deceived? But I already know that I cannot be deceived in the judgment whose grounds I know clearly. Will it be said that I formerly held many things to be true and certain which I have afterwards recognised to be false? But I had not had any clear and distinct knowledge of these things, and not as yet knowing the rule whereby I assure myself of the truth, I had been impelled to give my assent from reasons which I have since recognised to be less strong than I had at the time imagined them to be. What further objection can then be raised? That possibly I am dreaming (an objection I myself made a little while ago), or that all the thoughts which I now have are no more true than the phantasies of my dreams? But even though I slept the case would be the same, for all that is clearly present to my mind is absolutely true.

And so I very clearly recognise that the certainty and truth of all knowledge depends alone on the knowledge of the true God, in so much that, before I knew Him, I could not have a perfect knowledge of any other thing. And now that I know Him I have the means of acquiring a perfect knowledge of an infinitude of things, not only of those which relate to God Himself and other intellectual matters, but also of those which pertain to corporeal nature in so far as it is the object of pure mathematics [which have no concern with whether it exists or not].

MEDITATION VI: *Of the Existence of Material Things, and of the real distinction between the Soul and Body of Man*

Nothing further now remains but to inquire whether material things exist. And certainly I at least know that these may exist in so far as they are considered as the objects of pure mathematics, since in this aspect I perceive them clearly and distinctly. For there is no doubt that God possesses the power to produce everything that I am capable of perceiving with distinctness, and I have never deemed that anything was impossible for Him, unless I found a contradiction in attempting to conceive it clearly. Further, the faculty of imagination which I possess, and of which, experience tells me, I make use when I apply myself to the consideration of material things, is capable of persuading me of their existence; for when I attentively consider what imagination is, I find that it is nothing but a certain application of the faculty of knowledge to the body which is immediately present to it, and which therefore exists.

And to render this quite clear, I remark in the first place the difference that exists between the imagination and pure intellection [or conception]. For example, when I imagine a triangle, I do not conceive it only as a figure comprehended by three lines, but I also apprehend these three lines as present by the power and inward vision of my mind, and this is what I call imagining. But if I desire to think of a chiliagon, I certainly conceive truly that it is a figure composed of a thousand sides, just as easily as I conceive of a triangle that it is a figure of three sides only; but I cannot in any way imagine the thousand sides of a chiliagon [as I do the three sides of a triangle], nor do I, so to speak, regard them as present [with the eyes of my mind]. And although in accordance with the habit I have formed of always employing the aid of my imagination when I think of corporeal things, it may happen that in imagining a chiliagon I confusedly represent to myself some figure, yet it is very evident that this figure is not a chiliagon, since it in no way differs from that which I represent to myself when I think of a myriagon or any other many-sided figure; nor does it serve my purpose in discovering the properties which go to form the distinction between a chiliagon and other polygons. But if the question turns upon a pentagon, it is quite true that I can conceive its figure as well as that of a chiliagon without the help of my imagination; but I can also imagine it by applying the attention of my mind to each of its five sides, and at the same time to the space which they enclose. And thus I clearly recognise that I have need of a particular effort of mind in order to effect the act of imagination, such as I do not require in order to understand, and this particular effort of mind clearly manifests the difference which exists between imagination and pure intellection.

I remark besides that this power of imagination which is in one, inasmuch as it differs from the power of understanding, is in no wise a necessary element in my nature, or in [my essence, that is so say, in] the essence of my mind; for although I did not possess it I should doubtless ever remain the same as I now am, from which it appears that we might conclude that it depends on something which differs from me. And I easily conceive that if some body exists with which my mind is conjoined and united in such a way that it can apply itself to consider it when it pleases, it may be that by this means it can imagine corporeal objects; so that this mode of thinking differs from pure intellection only inasmuch as mind in its intellectual activity in some manner turns on itself, and considers some of the ideas which it possesses in itself; while in imagining it turns towards the body, and there beholds in it something conformable to the idea which it has either conceived of itself or perceived by the senses. I easily understand, I say, that the imagination could be thus constituted if it is true that body exists; and because I can discover no other convenient mode of explaining it, I conjecture with probability that body does exist; but this is only with probability, and although I examine all things with care, I nevertheless do not find that from this distinct idea of corporeal nature, which I have in my imagination, I can derive any argument from which there will necessarily be deduced the existence of body.

But I am in the habit of imagining many other things besides this corporeal nature which is the object of pure mathematics, to wit, the colours, sounds, scents, pain, and other such things, although less distinctly. And inasmuch as I perceive these things much better through the senses, by the medium of which, and by the memory, they seem to have reached my imagination, I believe that, in order to examine them more conveniently, it is right that I should at the same time investigate the nature of sense perception, and that I should see if from the ideas which I apprehend by this mode of thought, which I call feeling, I cannot derive some certain proof of the existence of corporeal objects.

And first of all I shall recall to my memory those matters which I hitherto held to be true, as having perceived them through the senses, and the foundations on which my belief has rested; in the next place I shall examine the reasons which have since obliged me to place them in doubt; in the last place I shall consider which of them I must now believe.

First of all, then, I perceived that I had a head, hands, feet, and all other members of which this body – which I considered as a part, or possibly even as the whole, of myself – is composed. Further I was sensible that this body was placed amidst many others, from which it was capable of being affected in many different ways, beneficial and hurtful, and I remarked that a certain feeling of pleasure accompanied those that were beneficial, and pain those which were harmful. And in addition to this pleasure and pain, I also experienced hunger, thirst, and other similar appetites, as also certain corporeal inclinations towards joy, sadness, anger, and other similar passions. And outside myself, in addition to extension, figure, and motions of bodies, I remarked in them hardness, heat, and all other tactile qualities, and, further, light and colour, and scents and sounds, the variety of which gave me the means of distinguishing the sky, the earth, the sea, and generally all the other bodies, one from the other. And certainly, considered the ideas of all these qualities which presented themselves to my mind, and which alone I perceived properly or immediately, it was not without reason that I believed myself to perceive objects quite different from my thought, to wit, bodies from which those ideas proceeded; for I found by experience that these ideas presented themselves to me without my consent being requisite, so that I could not perceive any object, however desirous I might be, unless it were present to the organs of sense; and it was not in my power not to perceive it, when it was present. And because the ideas which I received through the senses were much more lively, more clear, and even, in their own way, more distinct than any of those which I could of myself frame in meditation, or than those I found impressed on my memory, it appeared as though they could not have proceeded from my mind, so that they must necessarily have been produced in me by some other things. And having no knowledge of those objects excepting the knowledge which the ideas themselves gave me, nothing was more likely to occur to my mind than that the objects were similar to the ideas which were caused. And because I likewise remembered that I had formerly made use of my senses rather than my reason, and recognised that the ideas which I formed of myself were not so distinct as those which I perceived through the senses, and that they were most frequently even composed of portions of these last, I persuaded myself easily that I had no idea in my mind which had not formerly come to me through the senses. Nor was it without some reason that I believed that this body (which by a certain special right I call my own) belonged to me more properly and more strictly than any other;

for in fact I could never be separated from it as from other bodies; I experienced in it and on account of it all my appetites and affections, and finally I was touched by the feeling of pain and the titillation of pleasure in its parts, and not in the parts of other bodies which were separated from it. But when I inquired, why, from some, I know not what, painful sensation, there follows sadness of mind, and from the pleasurable sensation there arises joy, or why this mysterious pinching of the stomach which I call hunger causes me to desire to eat, and dryness of throat causes a desire to drink, and so on, I could give no reason excepting that nature taught me so; for there is certainly no affinity (that I at least can understand) between the craving of the stomach and the desire to eat, any more than between the perceptions of whatever causes pain and the thought of sadness which arises from this perception. And in the same way it appeared to me that I had learned from nature all the other judgments which I formed regarding the objects of my senses, since I remarked that these judgments were formed in me before I had the leisure to weigh and consider any reasons which might oblige me to make them.

But afterwards many experiences little by little destroyed all the faith which I had rested in my senses; for I from time to time observed that those towers which from afar appeared to me to be round, more closely observed seemed square, and that colossal statues raised on the summit of these towers, appeared as quite tiny statues when viewed from the bottom; and so in an infinitude of other cases I found error in judgments founded on the external senses. And not only in those founded on the external senses, but even in those founded on the internal as well; for is there anything more intimate or more internal than pain? And yet I have learned from some persons whose arms or legs have been cut off, that they sometimes seemed to feel pain in the part which had been amputated, which made me think that I could not be quite certain that it was a certain member which pained me, even although I felt pain in it. And to those grounds of doubt I have lately added two others, which are very general; the first is that I never have believed myself to feel anything in waking moments which I cannot also sometimes believe myself to feel when I sleep, and as I do not think that these things which I seem to feel in sleep, proceed from objects outside of me, I do not see any reason why I should have this belief regarding objects which I seem to perceive while awake. The other was that being still ignorant, or rather supposing myself to be ignorant, of the author of my being, I saw nothing to prevent me from having been so constituted by nature that I might be deceived even in matters which seemed to me to be most certain. And as to the grounds on which I was formerly persuaded of the truth of sensible objects, I had not much trouble in replying to them. For since nature seemed to cause me to lean towards many things from which reason repelled me, I did not believe that I should trust much to the teachings of nature. And although the ideas which I receive by the senses do not depend on my will, I did not think that one should for that reason conclude that they proceeded from things different from myself, since possibly some faculty might be discovered in me – though hitherto unknown to me – which produced them.

But now that I begin to know myself better, and to discover more clearly the author of my being, I do not in truth think that I should rashly admit all the matters which the senses seem to teach us, but, on the other hand, I do not think that I should doubt them all universally.

And first of all, because I know that all things which I apprehend clearly and distinctly can be created by God as I apprehend them, it suffices that I am able to apprehend one thing apart from another clearly and distinctly in order to be certain that the one is different from the other, since they may be made to exist in separation at least by the omnipotence of God; and it does not signify by what power this separation is made in order to compel me to judge them to be different: and, therefore, just because I know certainly that I exist, and that meanwhile I do not remark that any other thing necessarily pertains to my nature or essence, excepting that I am a thinking thing, I rightly conclude that my essence consists solely in the fact that I am a thinking thing [or a substance whose whole essence or nature is to think]. And although possibly (or rather certainly, as I shall say in a moment) I possess a body with which I am very intimately conjoined, yet because, on the one side, I have a clear and distinct idea of myself inasmuch as I am only a thinking and unextended thing, and as, on the other, I possess a distinct idea of body, inasmuch as it is only an extended and unthinking thing, it is certain that this I [that is to say, my soul by which I am what I am], is entirely and absolutely distinct from my body, and can exist without it.

I further find in myself faculties employing modes of thinking peculiar to themselves, to wit, the faculties of imagination and feeling, without which I can easily conceive myself clearly and distinctly as a complete being; while, on the other hand, they cannot be so conceived apart from me, that is without an intelligent substance in which they reside, for [in the notion we have of these faculties, or, to use the language of the Schools] in their formal concept, some kind of intellection is comprised, from which I infer that they are distinct from me as its modes are from a thing. I observe also in me some other faculties such as that of change of position, the assumption of different figures and such like, which cannot be conceived, any more than can the preceding, apart from some substance to which they are attached, and consequently cannot exist without it; but it is very clear that these faculties, if it be true that they exist, must be attached to some corporeal or extended substance, and not to an intelligent substance, since in the clear and distinct conception of these there is some sort of extension found to be present, but no intellection at all. There is certainly further in me a certain passive faculty of perception, that is, of receiving and recognising the ideas of sensible things, but this would be useless to me [and I could in no way avail myself of it], if there were not either in me or in some other thing another active faculty capable of forming and producing these ideas. But this active faculty cannot exist in me [inasmuch as I am a thing that thinks] seeing that it does not presuppose thought, and also that those ideas are often produced in me without my contributing in any way to the same, and often even against my will; it is thus necessarily the case that the faculty resides in some substance different from me in which all the reality which is objectively in the ideas that are produced by this faculty is formally or eminently contained, as I remarked before. And this substance is either a body, that is, a corporeal nature in which there is contained formally [and really] all that which is objectively [and by representation] in those ideas, or it is God Himself, or some other creature more noble than body in which that same is contained eminently. But, since God is no deceiver, it is very manifest that He does not communicate to me these ideas immediately and by Himself, nor yet by the intervention of some creature in which their reality is not formally, but only eminently, contained. For since He has given me no faculty to recognise that this is the case, but, on the other hand, a very great inclination to believe [that they are sent to me or] that they are conveyed to me by corporeal objects, I do not see how He could be defended from the accusation of deceit if these ideas were produced by causes other than corporeal objects. Hence we must allow that corporeal things exist. However, they are perhaps not exactly what we perceive by the senses, since this comprehension by the senses is in many instances very obscure and confused; but we must at least admit that all things which I conceive in them clearly and distinctly, that is to say, all things which, speaking generally, are comprehended in the object of pure mathematics, are truly to be recognised as external objects.

As to other things, however, which are either particular only, as, for example, that the sun is of such and such a figure, etc., or which are less clearly and distinctly conceived, such as light, sound, pain and the like, it is certain that although they are very dubious and uncertain, yet on the sole ground that God is not a deceiver, and that consequently He has not permitted any falsity to exist in my opinion which He has not likewise given me the faculty of correcting, I may assuredly hope to conclude that I have within me the means of arriving at the truth even here. And first of all there is no doubt that in all things which nature teaches me there is some truth contained; for by nature, considered in general, I now understand no other thing than either God Himself or else the order and disposition which God has established in created things; and by my nature in particular I understand no other thing than the complexus of all the things which God has given me.

But there is nothing which this nature teaches me more expressly [nor more sensibly] than that I have a body which is adversely affected when I feel pain, which has need of food or drink when I experience the feelings of hunger and thirst, and so on; nor can I doubt there being some truth in all this.

Nature also teaches me by these sensations of pain, hunger, thirst, etc., that I am not only lodged in my body as a pilot in a vessel, but that I am very closely united to it, and so to speak so intermingled with it that I seem to compose with it one whole. For if that were not the case, when my body is hurt, I, who am merely a thinking thing, should not feel pain, for I should perceive this wound by the understanding only, just as the sailor perceives by sight when something is damaged in his vessel; and when my body has need of drink or food, I should clearly understand the fact without being warned of it by confused feelings of hunger and thirst. For all these sensations of hunger, thirst, pain, etc. are in truth none other than certain confused modes of thought which are produced by the union and apparent intermingling of mind and body.

Moreover, nature teaches me that many other bodies exist around mine, of which some are to be avoided, and others sought after. And certainly from the fact that I am sensible of different sorts of colours, sounds, scents, tastes, heat, hardness, etc., I very easily conclude that there are in the bodies from which all these diverse sense-perceptions proceed certain variations which answer to them, although possibly these are not really at all similar to them. And also from the fact that amongst these different sense-perceptions some are very agreeable to me and others disagreeable, it is quite certain that my body (or rather myself in my entirety, inasmuch as I am formed of body and soul) may receive different impressions agreeable and disagreeable from the other bodies which surround it.

But there are many other things which nature seems to have taught me, but which at the same time I have never really received from her, but which have been brought about in my mind by a certain habit which I have of forming inconsiderate judgments on things; and thus it may easily happen that these judgments contain some error. Take, for example, the opinion which I hold that all space in which there is nothing that affects [or makes an impression on] my senses is void; that in a body which is warm there is something entirely similar to the idea of heat which is in me; that in a white or green body there is the same whiteness or greenness that I perceive; that in a bitter or sweet body there is the same taste, and so on in other instances; that the stars, the towers, and all other distant bodies are of the same figure and size as they appear from far off to our eyes, etc. But in order that in this there should be nothing which I do not conceive distinctly, I should define exactly what I really understand when I say that I am taught somewhat by nature. For here I take nature in a more limited signification than when I term it the sum of all the things given me by God, since in this sum many things are comprehended which only pertain to mind (and to these I do not refer in speaking of nature) such as the notion which I have of the fact that what has once been done cannot ever be undone and an infinitude of such things which I know by the light of nature [without the help of the body]; and seeing that it comprehends many other matters besides which only pertain to body, and are no longer here contained under the name of nature, such as the quality of weight which it possesses and the like, with which I also do not deal; for in talking of nature I only treat of those things given by God to me as a being composed of mind and body. But the nature here described truly teaches me to flee from things which cause the sensation of pain, and seek after the things which communicate to me the sentiment of pleasure and so forth; but I do not see that beyond this it teaches me that from those diverse sense-perceptions we should ever form any conclusion regarding things outside of us, without having [carefully and maturely] mentally examined them beforehand. For it seems to me that it is mind alone, and not mind and body in conjunction, that is requisite to a knowledge of the truth in regard to such things. Thus, although a star makes no larger an impression on my eye than the flame of a little candle there is yet in me no real or positive propensity impelling me to believe that it is not greater than that flame; but I have judged it to be so from my earliest years, without any rational foundation. And although in approaching fire I feel heat, and in approaching it a little too near I even feel pain, there is at the same time no reason in this which could persuade me that there is in the fire something resembling this heat any more than there is in it something resembling the pain; all that I have any reason to believe from this is, that there is something in it, whatever it may be, which excites in me these sensations of heat or of pain. So also, although there are spaces in which I find nothing which excites my senses, I must not from that conclude that these spaces contain no body; for I see in this, as in other similar things, that I have been in the habit of perverting the order of nature, because these perceptions of sense having been placed within me by nature merely for the purpose of signifying to my mind what things are beneficial or hurtful to the composite whole of which it forms a part, and being up to that point sufficiently clear and distinct, I yet avail myself of them as though they were absolute rules by which I might immediately determine the essence of the bodies which are outside me, as to which, in fact, they can teach me nothing but what is most obscure and confused.

But I have already sufficiently considered how, notwithstanding the supreme goodness of God, falsity enters into the judgments I make. Only here a new difficulty is presented – one respecting those things the pursuit or avoidance of which is taught me by nature, and also respecting the internal sensations which I possess, and in which I seem to have sometimes detected error [and thus to be directly deceived by my own nature]. To take an example, the agreeable taste of some food in which poison has been intermingled may induce me to partake of the poison, and thus deceive me. It is true, at the same time, that in this case nature may be excused, for it only induces me to desire food in which I find a pleasant taste, and not to desire the poison which is unknown to it; and thus I can infer nothing from this fact, except that my nature is not omniscient, at which there is certainly no reason to be astonished, since man, being finite in nature, can only have knowledge the perfectness of which is limited.

But we not unfrequently deceive ourselves even in those things to which we are directly impelled by nature, as happens with those who when they are sick desire to drink or eat things hurtful to them. It will perhaps be said here that the cause of their deceptiveness is that their nature is corrupt, but that does not remove the difficulty, because a sick man is none the less truly God's creature than he who is in health; and it is therefore as repugnant to God's goodness for the one to have a deceitful nature as it is for the other. And as a clock composed of wheels and counter-weights no less exactly observes the laws of nature when it is badly made, and does not show the time properly, than when it entirely satisfies the wishes of its maker, and as, if I consider the body of a man as being a sort of machine so built up and composed of nerves, muscles, veins, blood and skin, that though there were no mind in it at all, it would not cease to have the same motions as at present, exception being made of those movements which are due to the direction of the will, and in consequence depend upon the mind [as opposed to those which operate by the disposition of its organs], I easily recognise that it would be as natural to this body, supposing it to be, for example, dropsical, to suffer the parchedness of the throat which usually signifies to the mind the feeling of thirst, and to be disposed by this parched feeling to move the nerves and other parts in the way requisite for drinking, and thus to augment its malady and do harm to itself, as it is natural to it, when it has no indisposition, to be impelled to drink for its good by a similar cause. And although, considering the use to which the clock has been destined by its maker, I may say that it deflects from the order of its nature when it does not indicate the hours correctly; and as, in the same way, considering the machine of the human body as having been formed by God in order to have in itself all the movements usually manifested there, I have reason for thinking that it does not follow the order of nature when, if the throat is dry, drinking does harm to the conservation of health, nevertheless I recognise at the same time that this last mode of explaining nature is very different from the other. For this is but a purely verbal characterisation depending entirely on my thought, which compares a sick man and a badly constructed clock with the idea which I have of a healthy man and a well made clock, and it is hence extrinsic to the things to which it is applied; but according to the other interpretation of the term nature I understand something which is truly found in things and which is therefore not without some truth.

But certainly although in regard to the dropsical body it is only so to speak to apply an extrinsic term when we say that its nature is corrupted, inasmuch as apart from the need to drink, the throat is parched; yet in regard to the composite whole, that is to say, to the mind or soul united to this body, it is not a purely verbal predicate, but a real error of nature, for it to have thirst when drinking would be hurtful to it. And thus it still remains to inquire how the goodness of God does not prevent the nature of man so regarded from being fallacious.

In order to begin this examination, then, I here say, in the first place, that there is a great difference between mind and body, inasmuch as body is by nature always divisible, and the mind is entirely indivisible. For, as a matter of fact, when I consider the mind, that is to say, myself inasmuch as I am only a thinking thing, I cannot distinguish in myself any parts, but apprehend myself to be clearly one and entire; and although the whole mind seems to be united to the whole body, yet if a foot, or an arm, or some other part, is separated from my body, I am aware that nothing has been taken away from my mind. And the faculties of willing, feeling, conceiving, etc. cannot be properly speaking said to be its parts, for it is one and the same mind which employs itself in willing and in feeling and understanding. But it is quite otherwise with corporeal or extended objects, for there is not one of these imaginable by me which my mind cannot easily divide into parts, and which consequently I do not recognise as being divisible; this would be sufficient to teach me that the mind or soul of man is entirely different from the body, if I had not already learned it from other sources.

I further notice that the mind does not receive the impressions from all parts of the body immediately, but only from the brain, or perhaps even from one of its smallest parts, to wit, from that in which the common sense is said to reside, which, whenever it is disposed in the same particular way, conveys the same thing to the mind, although meanwhile the other portions of the body may be differently disposed, as is testified by innumerable experiments which it is unnecessary here to recount.

I notice, also, that the nature of body is such that none of its parts can be moved by another part a little way off which cannot also be moved in the same way by each one of the parts which are between the two, although this more remote part does not act at all. As, for example, in the cord *ABCD* [which is in tension] if we pull the last part *D*, the first part *A* will not be moved in any way differently from what would be the case if one of the intervening parts *B* or *C* were pulled, and the last part *D* were to remain unmoved. And in the same way, when I feel pain in my foot, my knowledge of physics teaches me that this sensation is communicated by means of nerves dispersed through the foot, which, being extended like cords from there to the brain, when they are contracted in the foot, at the same time contract the inmost portions of the brain which is their extremity and place of origin, and then excite a certain movement which nature has established in order to cause the mind to be affected by a sensation of pain represented as existing in the foot. But because these nerves must pass through the tibia, the thigh, the loins, the back and the neck, in order to reach from the leg to the brain, it may happen that although their extremities which are in the foot are not affected, but only certain ones of their intervening parts [which pass by the loins or the neck], this action will excite the same movement in the brain that might have been excited there by a hurt received in the foot, in consequence of which the mind will necessarily feel in the foot the same pain as if it had received a hurt. And the same holds good of all the other perceptions of our senses.

I notice finally that since each of the movements which are in the portion of the brain by which the mind is immediately affected brings about one particular sensation only, we cannot under the circumstances imagine anything more likely than that this movement, amongst all the sensations which it is capable of impressing on it, causes mind to be affected by that one which is best fitted and most generally useful for the conservation of the human body when it is in health. But experience makes us aware that all the feelings with which nature inspires us are such as I have just spoken of; and there is therefore nothing in them which does not give testimony to the power and goodness of the God [who has produced them].[8] Thus, for example, when the nerves which are in the feet are violently or more than usually moved, their movement, passing through the medulla of the spine to the inmost parts of the brain, gives a sign to the mind which makes it feel somewhat, to wit, pain, as though in the foot, by which the mind is excited to do its utmost to remove the cause of the evil as dangerous and hurtful to the foot. It is true that God could have constituted the nature of man in such a way that this same movement in the brain would have conveyed something quite different to the mind; for example, it might have produced consciousness of itself either in so far as it is in the brain, or as it is in the foot, or as it is in some other place between the foot and the brain, or it might finally have produced consciousness of anything else whatsoever; but none of all this would have contributed so well to the conservation of the body. Similarly, when we desire to drink, a certain dryness of the throat is produced which moves its nerves, and by their means the internal portions of the brain; and this movement causes in the mind the sensation of thirst, because in this case there is nothing more useful to us than to become aware that we have need to drink for the conservation of our health; and the same holds good in other instances.

From this it is quite clear that, notwithstanding the supreme goodness of God, the nature of man, inasmuch as it is composed of mind and body, cannot be otherwise than sometimes a source of deception. For if there is any cause which excites, not in the foot but in some part of the nerves which are extended between

8. Latin version only.

the foot and the brain, or even in the brain itself, the same movement which usually is produced when the foot is detrimentally affected, pain will be experienced as though it were in the foot, and the sense will thus naturally be deceived; for since the same movement in the brain is capable of causing but one sensation in the mind, and this sensation is much more frequently excited by a cause which hurts the foot than by another existing in some other quarter, it is reasonable that it should convey to the mind pain in the foot rather than in any other part of the body. And although the parchedness of the throat does not always proceed, as it usually does, from the fact that drinking is necessary for the health of the body, but sometimes comes from quite a different cause, as is the case with dropsical patients, it is yet much better that it should mislead on this occasion than if, on the other hand, it were always to deceive us when the body is in good health; and so on in similar cases.

And certainly this consideration is of great service to me, not only in enabling me to recognise all the errors to which my nature is subject, but also in enabling me to avoid them or to correct them more easily. For knowing that all my senses more frequently indicate to me truth than falsehood respecting the things which concern that which is beneficial to the body, and being able almost always to avail myself of many of them in order to examine one particular thing, and, besides that, being able to make use of my memory in order to connect the present with the past, and of my understanding which already has discovered all the causes of my errors, I ought no longer to fear that falsity may be found in matters every day presented to me by my senses. And I ought to set aside all the doubts of these past days as hyperbolical and ridiculous, particularly that very common uncertainty respecting sleep, which I could not distinguish from the waking state; for at present I find a very notable difference between the two, inasmuch as our memory can never connect our dreams one with the other, or with the whole course of our lives, as it unites events which happen to us while we are awake. And, as a matter of fact, if someone, while I was awake, quite suddenly appeared to me and disappeared as fast as do the images which I see in sleep, so that I could not know from whence the form came nor whither it went, it would not be without reason that I should deem it a spectre or a phantom formed by my brain [and similar to those which I form in sleep], rather than a real man. But when I perceive things as to which I know distinctly both the place from which they proceed, and that in which they are, and the time at which they appeared to me; and when, without any interruption, I can connect the perceptions which I have of them with the whole course of my life, I am perfectly assured that these perceptions occur while I am waking and not during sleep. And I ought in no wise to doubt the truth of such matters, if, after having called up all my senses, my memory, and my understanding, to examine them, nothing is brought to evidence by any one of them which is repugnant to what is set forth by the others. For because God is in no wise a deceiver, it follows that I am not deceived in this. But because the exigencies of action often oblige us to make up our minds before having leisure to examine matters carefully, we must confess that the life of man is very frequently subject to error in respect to individual objects, and we must in the end acknowledge the infirmity of our nature.

Arguments demonstrating the Existence of God and the Distinction between Soul and Body, drawn up in Geometrical Fashion, 1641

DEFINITIONS

I. *Thought* is a word that covers everything that exists in us in such a way that we are immediately conscious of it. Thus all the operations of will, intellect, imagination, and of the senses are thoughts. But I have added *immediately*, for the purpose of excluding that which is a consequence of our thought; for example, voluntary movement, which, though indeed depending on thought as on a causal principle, is yet itself not thought.

II. *Idea* is a word by which I understand the form of any thought, that form by the immediate awareness of which I am conscious of that said thought; in such a way that, when understanding what I say, I can express nothing in words, without that very fact making it certain that I possess the idea of that which these words signify. And thus it is not only images depicted in the imagination that I call ideas; nay, to such images I here decidedly refuse the title of ideas, in so far as they are pictures in the corporeal imagination, i.e. in some part of the brain. They are ideas only in so far as they constitute the form of the mind itself that is directed towards that part of the brain.

III. By the *objective reality of an idea* I mean that in respect of which the thing represented in the idea is an entity, in so far as that exists in the idea; and in the same way we can talk of objective perfection, objective device, etc. For whatever we perceive as being as it were in the objects of our ideas, exists in the ideas themselves objectively.

IV. To exist *formally* is the term applied where the same thing exists in the object of an idea in such a manner that the way in which it exists in the object is exactly like what we know of it when aware of it; it exists *eminently* when, though not indeed of identical quality, it is yet of such amount as to be able to fulfil the function of an exact counterpart.

V. Everything in which there resides immediately, as in a subject, or by means of which there exists anything that we perceive, i.e. any property, quality, or attribute, of which we have a real idea, is called a *Substance*; neither do we have any other idea of substance itself, precisely taken, than that it is a thing in which this something that we perceive or which is present objectively in some of our ideas, exists formally or eminently. For by means of our natural light we know that a real attribute cannot be an attribute of nothing.

VI. That substance in which thought immediately resides, I call *Mind*. I use the term 'mind' here rather than 'spirit', as 'spirit' is equivocal and is frequently applied to what is corporeal.

VII. That substance, which is the immediate subject of extension in space and of the accidents that presuppose extension, e.g. figure, situation, movement in space, etc., is called *Body*. But we must postpone till later on the inquiry as to whether it is one and the same substance or whether there are two diverse substances to which the names Mind and Body apply.

VIII. That substance which we understand to be supremely perfect and in which we conceive absolutely nothing involving defect or limitation of its perfection, is called *God*.

IX. When we say that any attribute is contained in the nature or concept of anything, that is precisely the same as saying that it is true of that thing or can be affirmed of it.

X. Two substances are said to be really distinct, when each of them can exist apart from the other.

POSTULATES

The *First* request I press upon my readers is a recognition of the weakness of the reasons on account of which they have hitherto trusted their senses, and the insecurity of all the judgments they have based upon them. I beg them to revolve this in their minds so long and so frequently that at length they will acquire the habit of no longer reposing too much trust in them. For I deem that this is necessary in order to attain to a perception of the certainty of metaphysical truths (not dependent on the senses).

Secondly, I ask them to make an object of study of their own mind and all the attributes attaching to it, of which they find they cannot doubt, notwithstanding it be supposed that whatever they have at any time derived from their senses is false; and I beg them not to desist from attending to it, until they have acquired the habit of perceiving it distinctly and of believing that it can be more readily known than any corporeal thing.

Thirdly, I bid them carefully rehearse those propositions, intelligible *per se*, which they find they possess, e.g. *that the same thing cannot at the same time both be and not be; that nothing cannot be the efficient cause of anything*, and so forth; and thus employ in its purity, and in freedom from the interference of the senses, that clarity of understanding that nature has implanted in them, but which sensuous objects are wont to disturb and obscure. For by this means the truth of the following Axioms will easily become evident to them.

Fourthly, I postulate an examination of the ideas of those natures in which there is a complex of many coexistent attributes, such as e.g. the nature of the triangle or of the square, or of any other figure; and so too the nature of Mind, the nature of Body, and above all the nature of God, or of a supremely perfect entity. My readers must also notice that everything which we perceive to be contained in these natures can be truly predicated of the things themselves. For example, because the equality of its three angles to two right angles is contained in the idea of the Triangle, and divisibility is contained in the nature of Body or of extended thing (for we can conceive nothing that is extended as being so small as not to be capable of being divided in thought at least), we constantly assert that in every Triangle the angles are equal to two right angles, and that every Body is divisible.

Fifthly, I require my readers to dwell long and much in contemplation of the nature of the supremely perfect Being. Among other things they must reflect that while possible existence indeed attaches to the ideas of all other natures, in the case of the idea of God that existence is not possible but wholly necessary. For from this alone and without any train of reasoning they will learn that God exists, and it will be not less self evident to them than the fact that number two is even and number three odd, and similar truths. For there are certain truths evident to some people, without proof, that can be made intelligible to others only by a train of reasoning.

Sixthly, I ask people to go carefully over all the examples of clear and distinct perception, and likewise those that illustrate that which is obscure and confused, mentioned in my Meditations, and so accustom themselves to distinguish what is clearly known from what is obscure. For examples teach us better than rules how to do this; and I think that I have there either explained or at least to some extent touched upon all the instances of this subject.

Seventh and finally, I require them, in virtue of their consciousness that falsity has never been found in matters of clear perception, while, on the contrary, amidst what is only obscurely comprehended they have never come upon the truth, except accidentally, to consider it wholly irrational to regard as doubtful matters that are perceived clearly and distinctly by the understanding in its purity, on account of mere prejudices of the senses and hypotheses in which there is an element of the unknown. By doing so they will readily admit the truth and certainty of the following axioms. Yet I admit that several of them might have been much better explained and should have been brought forward as theorems if I had wished to be more exact.

AXIOMS OR COMMON PRINCIPLES

I. Nothing exists concerning which the question may not be raised – 'what is the cause of its existence?' For this question may be asked even concerning God. Not that He requires any cause in order to exist, but because in the very immensity of His being lies the cause or reason why He needs no cause in order to exist.

II. The present time has no causal dependence on the time immediately preceding it. Hence, in order to secure the continued existence of a thing, no less a cause is required than that needed to produce it at the first.

III. A thing, and likewise an actually existing perfection belonging to anything, can never have *nothing*, or a non-existent thing, as the cause of its existence.

IV. Whatever reality or perfection exists in a thing, exists formally or else eminently in its first and adequate cause.

V. Whence it follows also that the objective reality of our ideas requires a cause in which the same reality is contained not indeed objectively, but formally or else eminently. We have to note that the admission of this axiom is highly necessary for the reason that we must account for our knowledge all things, both of sensuous and of non-sensuous objects, and do so by means of it alone. For whence, e.g., comes our knowledge that there is a heaven? Because we behold it? But that vision does not reach the mind, except in so far as it is an idea, an idea, I say, inhering in the mind itself, and not an image depicted in the phantasy. But neither can we, in virtue of this idea, assert that there is a heaven, except because every idea needs to have some really existing cause of its objective reality; and this cause we judge to be the heaven itself, and so in other cases.

VI. There are diverse degrees of reality or (the quality of being an) entity. For substance has more reality than accident or mode; and infinite substance has more than finite substance. Hence there is more objective reality in the idea of substance than in that of accident; more in the idea of an infinite than in that of a finite substance.

VII. The will of a thinking being is borne, willingly indeed and freely (for that is of the essence of will), but none the less infallibly, towards the good that it clearly knows. Hence, if it knows certain perfections that it lacks, it will immediately give them to itself if they are in its power (for it will know that it is a greater good for it to possess them, than not to possess them).

VIII. That which can effect what is greater or more difficult, can also accomplish what is less.

IX. It is a greater thing to create or conserve substance than the attributes or properties of substance; it is not, moreover, a greater thing to create that than to conserve its existence, as I have already said.

x. Existence is contained in the idea or concept of everything, because we can conceive nothing except as existent, with this difference, that possible or contingent existence is contained in the concept of a limited thing, but necessary and perfect existence in the concept of a supremely perfect being.

PROPOSITION I: The Knowledge of the Existence of God Proceeds from the Mere Consideration of His Nature

Demonstration

To say that something is contained in the nature or concept of anything is the same as to say that it is true of that thing (Def. ix). But necessary existence is contained in the concept of God (Ax. x). Hence it is true to affirm of God that necessary existence exists in Him, or that God Himself exists.

And this is the syllogism of which I made use above, in replying to the sixth objection. Its conclusion is self-evident to those who are free from prejudices, as was said in the fifth postulate. But, because it is not easy to arrive at such clearness of mind, we seek to establish it by other methods.

PROPOSITION II: A Posteriori Demonstration of God's Existence from the Mere Fact that the Idea of God Exists in Us

Demonstration

The objective reality of any of our ideas must have a cause, in which the very same reality is contained, not merely objectively but formally, or else eminently (Ax. v). But we do possess the idea of God (Deff. ii and viii), and the objective reality of this idea is contained in us neither formally nor eminently (Ax. vi), nor can it be contained in anything other than God Himself (Def. viii). Hence this idea of God, which exists in us, must have God as its cause, and hence God exists (Ax. iii).

PROPOSITION III: The Existence of God is Proved by the Fact that We, Who Possess this Idea, Ourselves Exist

Demonstration

If I had the power of conserving my own existence, I should have had a proportionately greater power of giving myself the perfections that I lack (Axx. viii and ix); for they are only attributes of substances, whereas I am a substance. But I do not have the power of giving myself these perfections; otherwise I should already possess them (Ax. vii). Therefore I do not have the power of conserving myself.

Further, I cannot exist without being conserved, whilst I exist, either by myself, if I have that power, or by some other one who has that power (Axx. i and ii); yet, though I do exist, I have not the power of conserving myself; as has just been proved. Consequently it is another being that conserves my existence.

Besides, He to whom my conservation is due contains within Himself formally or eminently everything that is in me (Ax. iv). But there exists in me the perception of many perfections that I do not possess, as well as of the idea of God (Deff. ii and viii). Therefore the perception of the same perfections exists in Him by whom I am conserved.

Finally this Being cannot possess the perception of any perfections of which He is lacking, or which He does not possess within Himself either formally or eminently (Ax. vii). For, since He has the power of conserving me, as has been already said, He would have the power of bestowing these upon Himself, if He lacked them (Axx. viii and ix). But He possesses the perception of all those that I lack, and which I conceive can exist in God alone, as has been lately proved. Therefore He possesses those formally or eminently within Himself, and hence is God.

COROLLARY: God Has Created the Heaven and the Earth and All That in Them Is. Moreover He Can Bring to Pass Whatever We Clearly Conceive, Exactly As We Conceive It

Demonstration

This all follows from the previous proposition. For in it we prove that God exists, from the fact that someone must exist in whom are formally or eminently all the perfections of which we have any idea. But we possess the idea of a power so great that by Him and Him alone, in whom this power is found, must heaven and earth be created, and a power such that likewise whatever else is apprehended by me as possible must be created by Him too. Hence concurrently with God's existence we have proved all this likewise about him.

PROPOSITION IV: There is a Real Distinction Between Mind and Body

Demonstration

God can effect whatever we clearly perceive just as we perceive it (preceding Corollary). But we clearly perceive the mind, i.e. a thinking substance, apart from the body, i.e. apart from any extended substance (Post. ii); and *vice versa* we can (as all admit) perceive body apart from mind. Hence, at least through the instrumentality of the Divine power, mind can exist apart from body, and body apart from mind.

But now, substances that can exist apart from each other, are really distinct (Def. x). But mind and body are substances (Deff. v, vi and vii), that can exist apart from each other (just proved). Hence there is a real distinction between mind and body.

Here it must be noted that I employed the Divine power as a means, not because any extraordinary power was needed to effect the separation of mind and body, but because, treating as I did of God alone in what precedes, there was nothing else for me to use. But our knowledge of the real distinctness of two things is unaffected by any questions as to the power that disunites them.

Letters

FROM A LETTER TO MERSENNE, 15 April 1630

God and the Eternal Truths (1)

. . . Your question of theology is beyond my mental capacity, but it does not seem to me outside my province, since it has no concern with anything dependent on revelation, which is what I call theology in the strict sense; it is a metaphysical question which is to be examined by human reason. I think that all those to whom God has given the use of this reason have an obligation to employ it principally in the endeavour to know Him and to know themselves. That is the task with which I began my studies; and I can say that I would not have been able to discover the foundations of Physics if I had not looked for them along that road. It is the topic which I have studied more than anything and in which, thank God, I have not altogether wasted my time. At least I think that I have found how to prove metaphysical truths in a manner which is more evident that the proofs of geometry – in my own opinion, that is: I do not know if I shall be able to convince others of it. During my first nine months in this country I worked on nothing else. I think that you heard me speak once before of my plan to write something on the topic; but I do not think it opportune to do so before I have seen how my treatise of Physics is received. But if the book which you mention was very well written and fell into my hands I might perhaps feel obliged to reply to it immediately because if the report you heard is accurate it says things which are very dangerous and, I believe, very false. However in my treatise on Physics I shall discuss a number of metaphysical topics and especially the following. The mathematical truths which you call eternal have been laid down by God and depend on Him entirely no less than the rest of his creatures. Indeed to say that these truths are independent of God is to talk to Him as if He were Jupiter or Saturn and to subject Him to the Styx and the Fates. Please do not hesitate to assert and proclaim everywhere that it is God who has laid down these laws in nature just as a king lays down laws in his kingdom. There is no single one that we cannot understand if our mind turns to consider it. They are all *inborn in our minds*[9] just as a king would imprint his laws on the hearts of all his subjects if he had enough power to do so. The greatness of God, on the other hand, is something which we cannot comprehend even though we know it. But the very fact that we judge it incomprehensible makes us esteem it the more greatly; just as a king has more majesty when he is less familiarly known by his subjects, provided of course that they do not get the idea that they have no king – they must know him enough to be in no doubt about that.

It will be said that if God had established these truths He could change them as a king changes his laws. To this the answer is: 'Yes he can, if his will can change.' 'But I understand them to be eternal and unchangeable.' – 'I make the same judgment about God,' 'But His will is free.' – 'Yes, but his power is incomprehensible.' In general we can assert that God can do everything that we can comprehend but not that he cannot do what we cannot comprehend. It would be rash to think that our imagination reaches as far as His power.

I hope to put this in writing, within the next fortnight, in my

9. Italics represent Latin words in a French context.

treatise on Physics; but I do not want you to keep it secret. On the contrary I beg you to tell people as often as the occasion demands, provided that you do not mention my name. I should be glad to know the objection which can be made against this view; and I want people to get used to speaking of God in a manner worthier, I think, than the common and almost universal way of imagining him as a finite being.

FROM A LETTER TO MERSENNE, 6 May 1630

God and the Eternal Truths (2)

. . . As for the eternal truths, I say once more that *they are true or possible only because God knows them as true or possible. They are not known as true by God in any way which would imply that they are true independently of Him.* If men really understood the sense of their words they could never say without blasphemy that the truth of anything is prior to the knowledge which God has of it. In God willing and knowing are a single thing in such a way that *by the very fact of willing something he knows it and it is only for this reason that such a thing is true.* So we must not say that if God *did not exist nonetheless these truths would be true*; for the existence of God is the first and the most eternal of all possible truths and the one from which alone all others derive. It is easy to be mistaken about this because most men do not regard God as an infinite and incomprehensible being, the sole author on whom all things depend; they stick at the syllabus of His name and think it sufficient knowledge of Him to know that 'God' means what is meant by 'Deus' in Latin and what is adored by men. Those who have no higher thoughts than these can easily become atheists; and because they perfectly comprehend mathematical truths and do not perfectly comprehend the truth of God's existence, it is no wonder they do not think the former depend on the latter. But they should rather judge on the contrary, that since God is a cause whose power surpasses the bounds of human understanding, and since the necessity of these truths does not exceed our knowledge, they must be something less than, and subject to, the incomprehensible power of God. What you say about the production of the World[10] does not conflict, I think, with what I say; but I do not want to involve myself in theology, and I am already afraid that you will

10. The generation of the Second Person of the Trinity by the First.

think my philosophy too presumptuous for daring to express an opinion on such lofty matters.

FROM A LETTER TO MERSENNE, 27 May 1630

God and the Eternal Truths (3)

Reverend Father,

You ask me *by what kind of causality God established the eternal truths.* I reply: *by the same kind of causality* as he created all things, that is to say, is their *efficient and total cause.* For it is certain that he is no less the author of creatures' essence than he is of their existence; and this essence is nothing other than the eternal truths. I do not conceive them as emanating from God like rays from the sun; but I know that God is the author of everything and that these truths are something and consequently that he is their author. I say that I know this, not that I can conceive it or comprehend it; because it is possible to know that God is infinite and all-powerful although our soul, being finite, cannot comprehend or conceive Him. In the same way we can touch a mountain with our hands but we cannot put our arms around it as we could put them around a tree or something else not too large for them. To comprehend something is to embrace it in one's thought; to know something it is sufficient to touch it with one's thought.

You ask also what necessitated God to create these truths; and I reply that just as He was free not to create the world, so He was no less free to make it untrue that all the lines drawn from the centre of a circle to its circumference are equal. And it is certain that these truths are no more necessarily attached to his essence than other creatures are. You ask what God did in order to produce them. I reply that *from all eternity he willed and understood them to be, and by that very fact he created them.* Or, if you reserve the word *created* for the existence of things, then he *established them and made them.* In God, willing, understanding, and creating are all the same thing without one being prior to the other even *conceptually* . . .

FROM A LETTER TO RENERI FOR POLLOT, April 1638

Mind and Body (1)

. . . 3. When someone says, 'I am breathing, therefore I am,' if he wants to prove he exists from the fact that there cannot be breathing without existence, he proves nothing, because he would have to prove first that it is true that he is breathing, which is impossible unless he has also proved that he exists. But if he wants to prove his existence from the feeling or opinion that he has that he is breathing, so that he judges that even if the opinion was untrue he could not have it if he did not exist, then his proof is sound. For in such a case the thought of breathing is present to our mind before the thought of our existing, and we cannot doubt that we have it while we have it. To say 'I am breathing, therefore I am,' in this sense, is simply to say 'I am thinking, therefore I am'. You will find on examination that all the other propositions from which we can thus prove our existence reduce to the same one; so that one cannot prove from them the existence of the body, i.e. of a nature which occupies space, etc., but only that of the soul, i.e. of a nature which thinks. Of course one may wonder whether the nature which thinks may perhaps be the same as the nature which occupies space, so that there is one nature which is both intellectual and corporeal; but by the method which I suggested it is known only as intellectual.

4. From the very fact that we conceive clearly and distinctly the two natures of the body and the soul as different, we know that in reality they are different, and consequently that the soul can think without the body, even though, when it is joined to it, it can have its operation disturbed by the bad disposition of the bodily organs. . . .

FROM A LETTER TO REGIUS, January 1642

Mind and Body (2)

. . . We affirm that a human being is made up of body and soul, not by the mere presence or proximity of one to the other, but by a true substantial union. For this there is, indeed, required a natural disposition of the body and the appropriate configuration of its parts; but the union differs from position and shape and other purely corporeal modes, because it reaches the incorporea soul as well as the body. The idiom which we used was perhaps unusual, but we think it is sufficiently apt to express what we meant. When we said that a human being was an *ens per accidens* we meant this only in relation to its parts, the soul and the body; we meant that to each of these parts it was in a manner inessential to be joined to the other, because each could subsist apart, and what can be present or absent without its possessor ceasing to exist is called an accident. But if a human being is considered in himself as a whole, I say of course that he is a single *ens per se*, and not *per accidens*; because the union which joins a human body and soul to each other is not inessential to a human being, but essential, since a man without it is not a man. But many more people make the mistake of thinking that the soul is not really distinct from the body than make the mistake of admitting their distinction and denying their substantial union, and in order to refute those who believe souls to be mortal it is more important to teach the distinction of parts in man than to teach their union. And so I thought I would please the theologicians more by saying that a human being was an *ens per accidens*, in order to make the distinction, than if I said that he was an *ens per se*, in reference to the union of the parts.

FROM A LETTER TO MESLAND, 2 May 1644

Free Will (1)

. . . As to free will, I have not seen what Fr Petavius has written about it; but from what you say in explaining your opinion on the topic it does not appear that my views are very different. For first, I beg you to observe that I did not say that a man was indifferent only if he lacked knowledge; but rather, that he is more indifferent the less reasons he knows in favour of choosing one side rather than another; and this, I think, cannot be denied by anybody. I agree with you when you say that a man can suspend his judgement; but I tried to explain in what manner this can be done. For it seems to me certain that *a great light in the intellect is followed by a strong inclination in the will*; so that if we see very clearly that a thing is good for us it is very difficult – and, on my view, impossible, as long as one continues in the same thought – to stop the course of our desire. But the nature of the soul is such that it hardly attends for more than a moment to a single thing; and so, as soon as our attention turns from the reasons which show us that the thing is good for us, and we merely keep in our memory that it seemed desirable to us, we can call up before our mind some other reason to make us doubt of it, and so suspend our judgement, and perhaps even form a contrary judgement. And so, since you regard freedom not simply as indifference but rather as a real and positive power to determine oneself, and since I agree that the will has such a power, the difference between us is a merely verbal one. However, I do not see that it makes any difference to that power whether it is accompanied by indifference, which you agree is an imperfection, or whether it is not so accompanied, when there is nothing in the understanding except light, as in the case of the blessed who are confirmed in grace. And so I call free whatever is voluntary, whereas you wish to restrict the name to the power to determine oneself only if accompanied by indifference. But so far as concerns names, I wish above all to follow usage and precedent.

As for irrational animals, it is obvious that they are not free, since they do not have this positive power to determine themselves; what they have is a pure negation, namely, the not being forced or constrained.

The only thing which prevented me from speaking of the freedom which we have to follow good or evil was the fact that I wanted to avoid as far as possible all theological controversies and stay within the limits of natural philosophy. But I agree with you that wherever there is an occasion for sinning, there is indifference; and I do not think that in order to do wrong it is necessary to see clearly that what we are doing is evil. It is sufficient to see it confusedly, or without in any way seeing it or attending to the reasons which prove it simply to remember that one has hitherto judged it so. For if we saw it clearly it would be impossible to sin, as long as we saw it in that fashion; that is why they say that *whoever sins, does so in ignorance*. And a man may earn merit even though, seeing very clearly what he must do, he does it infallibly, and without any indifference, as Jesus Christ did during his earthly life. Since a man has the power not always to attend perfectly to what he ought to do, it is a good action to pay attention and thus to ensure that our will follows so promptly the light of our understanding that there is no longer in any way indifference. In any case, I did not write that grace entirely prevents indifference; but simply that it makes us incline to one side rather than to another, and so diminishes indifference without diminishing freedom; from which it follows, on my view, that this freedom does not consist in indifference.

I turn to the difficulty of conceiving how it was free and indifferent for God to make it not be true that the three angles of a triangle were equal to two right angles, or in general that contradictories could not be true together. It is easy to dispel this difficulty by considering that the power of God cannot have any limits, and that our mind is finite and so created as to be able to conceive as possible things which God has wished to be in fact possible, but not to be able to conceive as possible things which God could have made possible, but which he has in fact wished to make impossible. The first consideration shows us that God cannot have been determined to make it true that contradictions cannot be true together, and therefore that he could have done the opposite. The second consideration shows us that even if this be true, we should not try to comprehend it since our nature is incapable of doing so. And even if God has willed that some truths should be necessary, this does not mean that he willed them necessarily; for it is one thing to will that they be necessary, and quite another to will them necessarily, or to be necessitated to will them. I agree that there are contradictions which are so evident, that we cannot put them before our minds without judging them entirely impossible, like the one which you suggest: *that God might have made creatures independent of him*. But if we would know the immensity of his power we should not put these thoughts before our minds, nor should we conceive any precedence or priority between his understanding and his will; for the idea which we have of God teaches us that there is in him only a single activity, entirely simple and entirely pure. This is well expressed by the words of St Augustine: *They are so because you see them to be so*;[11] because in God *seeing and willing* are one and the same thing . . .

FROM A LETTER TO PRINCESS ELIZABETH, January 1646

Free Will (2)

I turn to your Highness' problem about free will. I will try to give an illustration to explain how this is both dependent and free. Suppose that a King has forbidden duels, and knows with certainty that two gentlemen of his kingdom who live in different towns have a quarrel, and are so hostile to each other that if they meet nothing will stop them from fighting. If this King orders

11. *Confessions* xiii. 30.

one of them to go on a certain day to the town where the other lives, and orders the other to go on the same day to the place where the first is, he knows with certainty that they will meet, and fight, and thus disobey his prohibition; but none the less he does not compel them, and his knowledge, and even his will to make them act thus, does not prevent their fighting when they meet being as voluntary and as free as if they had met on some other occasion and he had known nothing about it. And they can be no less justly punished for disobeying the prohibition. Now what a King can do in such a case, concerning certain free actions of his subjects, God, with His infinite foresight and power does infallibly in regard to all the free actions of all men. Before He sent us into the world He knew exactly what all the inclinations of our will would be; it is He who gave us them, it is He who has disposed all the other things outside us so that such and such objects would present themselves to our senses as such and such times, on the occasion of which he knew that our freewill would determine us to such or such an action; and He so willed, but without using any compulsion. In the King of my story it is possible to distinguish two different types of volition, one according to which he willed that these gentlemen should fight, since he caused them to meet; and the other according to which he willed that they should not, since he forbade duels. In the same way the theologicians make a distinction in God's willing: He has an absolute and independent will, according to which He wills all things to come about as they do, and another relative will which concerns the merit and demerit of men, according to which He wants them to obey His laws . . .

3. Reason is the Pace

Thomas Hobbes, 1588–1679

Hobbes is best known for his peerless *Leviathan* (published 1651), in which a mechanical model of man is used to reveal how commonwealths are to be made and maintained. But political philosophy was only one of his interests, which included logic, methodology, optics, psychology, ethics, law, theology and attempts to square the circle. Together with Machiavelli and Spinoza, he belonged to a trinity of arch-devils incarnate, whose works were burnt, denounced and suppressed. He was notorious as an atheist and materialist, whose sins were not redeemed by a mordant prose. Who, for instance, could forget his description of the papacy as 'no other than the ghost of the deceased Roman Empire, sitting crowned upon the grave thereof'?

Whether he can rightly be convicted of atheism and materialism calls for judgement. But he certainly issued a licence to theorise without reference to God and he insisted very strictly that nature was mechanical. It was not that Reason was hostile to religion – indeed he wanted to see Reason 'employed in the purchase of justice, peace and true religion' – but that it rendered religion otiose. If the scientific study of minerals, mice and men can in principle reveal all we want to know in physics, politics and ethics, then thoughts of God need not detain the enquirer. Consequently Hobbes was as embarrassing to Rationalists as Spinoza. He threatened to make explicit a threat to belief in God (and in human freewill) which Descartes and Leibniz swore was not even implicit.

He is included here for his reflections on method. He held that all scientific truths could be deduced from a basic theory of motion, resting on concepts like 'motion' and 'extension', which cannot be further analysed. The model was Galilean mechanics and the method its mixture of analysis and synthesis. Men being mechanical creatures, political behaviour would turn out as a case of the impact of body on body, according to laws of cause and effect, ('Conceptions and apparitions are nothing really but motions in some internal substance of the head.' (*Elements of Law*)). His place in a Rationalist anthology may surprise those who know him as a cross between an empiricist and a modern analytical philosopher. It is true enough that he held no brief for 'essences' and insisted that truth and falsity are attributes not of things but of speech. This however signals his contempt for Aristotelians and scholastics and can be offset by his scorn for inductivism and mere generalisation from experience. His own view is uncompromisingly that wisdom is the product of Reason, which alone gives us 'general, eternal and immutable truths' and that, as in geometry, 'the only way to know is by definition'.

Chapter 6 of *De Corpore* (1665) gives a rationalist account of the true method of philosophy, with a useful distinction between the analytical and synthetical (neither of which corresponds to what we would now call synthetic, since both are *a priori* methods).[1] *My Opinion about Liberty and Necessity* is taken from a letter to the Marquis of Newcastle, showing how freedom and determinism can perhaps be reconciled. The strategy has since become classic in British philosophy but few others have dared to try it for 'hard', as opposed to 'soft', determinism.

From *De Corpore*, 1665

CHAPTER 6: *Of Method*

1. Method and science defined. For the understanding of *method*, it will be necessary for me to repeat the definition of philosophy, delivered above (Chap. 1, art. 2) in this manner, *Philosophy is the knowledge we acquire, by true ratiocination, of appearances, or apparent effects, from the knowledge we have of some possible production or generation of the same; and of such production, as has been or may be, from the knowledge we have of the effects*. METHOD, therefore, in the study of philosophy, *is the shortest way of finding out effects by their known causes, or of causes by their known effects.* But we are then said to know any effect, when we know *that there be causes of the same*, and *in what subject those causes are*, and *in*

1. From *English Works*, vol. I, Molesworth edition 1839. *My Opinion about Liberty and Necessity* is from vol. IV, pp. 272–8.

what subject they produce that effect, and *in what manner they work the same*. And this is the science of causes, or, as they call it, of the διότι. All other science, which is called ὅτι, is either perception by sense, or the imagination, or memory remaining after such perception.

The first beginnings, therefore, of knowledge, are the phantasms of sense and imagination; and that there be such phantasms we know well enough by nature; but to know why they be, or from what causes they proceed, is the work of ratiocination; which consists (as is said above, in the 1st Chapter, art. 2) in *composition* and *division* or *resolution*. There is therefore no method, by which we find out the causes of things, but is either *compositive* or *resolutive*, or *partly compositive*, and *partly resolutive*. And the resolutive is commonly called *analytical* method, as the compositive is called *synthetical*.

2. It is easier known concerning singular than universal things, that they are; and contrarily it is easier known concerning universal than singular things, why they are, or what are their causes. It is common to all sorts of method, to proceed from known things to unknown; and this is manifest from the cited definition of philosophy. But in knowledge by sense, the whole object is more known, than any part thereof; as when we see a man, the conception or whole idea of that man is first or more known, than the particular ideas of his being *figurate*, *animate*, and *rational*; that is, we first see the whole man, and take notice of his being, before we observe in him those other particulars. And therefore in any knowledge of the ὅτι, or that any thing *is*, the beginning of our search is from the whole idea; and contrarily, in our knowledge of the διότι, or of the causes of anything, that is in the sciences, we have more knowledge of the causes of the parts than of the whole. For the cause of the whole is compounded of the causes of the parts; but it is necessary that we know the things that are to be compounded, before we can know the whole compound. Now, by parts, I do not here mean parts of the thing itself, but parts of its nature; as, by the parts of man, I do not understand his head, his shoulders, his arms, &c., but his figure, quantity, motion, sense, reason, and the like; which accidents being compounded or put together, constitute the whole nature of man, but not the man himself. And this is the meaning of that common saying, namely, that some things are more known to us, others more known to nature; for I do not

think that they, which so distinguish, mean that something is known to nature, which is known to no man; and therefore, by those things, that are more known to us, we are to understand things we take notice of by our senses and, by more known to nature, those we acquire the knowledge of by reason; for in this sense it is, that the *whole*, that is, those things that have universal names, (which, for brevity's sake, I call *universal*) are more known to us than the *parts*, that is, such things as have names less universal, (which I therefore call *singular*); and the causes of the parts are more known to nature than the cause of the whole; that is, universals than singulars.

3. What it is philosophers seek to know. In the study of philosophy, men search after science either simply or indefinitely; that is, to know as much as they can, without propounding to themselves any limited question; or they inquire into the cause of some determined appearance, or endeavour to find out the certainty of something in question, as what is the cause of *light*, of *heat*, of *gravity*, of a *figure* propounded, and the like; or in what *subject* any propounded *accident* is inherent; or what may conduce most to the *generation* of some propounded *effect* from many *accidents*; or in what manner particular causes ought to be compounded for the production of some certain effect. Now, according to this variety of things in question, sometimes the *analytical method* is to be used, and sometimes the *synthetical*.

4. The first part, by which principles are discovered, is purely analytical. But to those that search after science indefinitely, which consists in the knowledge of the causes of all things, as far forth as it may be attained, (and the causes of singular things are compounded of the causes of universal or simple things) it is necessary that they know the causes of universal things, or of such accidents as are common to all bodies, that is, to all matter, before they can know the causes of singular things, that is, of those accidents by which one thing is distinguished from another. And, again, they must know their causes. Moreover, seeing universal things are contained in the nature of singular things, the knowledge of them is to be acquired by reason, that is, by resolution. For example, if there be propounded a conception or *idea* of some singular thing, as of a *square*, this square is to be resolved *into a plane, terminated with a certain number of equal and straight lines and right angles*. For by this resolution we have

these things universal or agreeable to all matter, namely, *line*, *plane*, (which contains *superficies*) *terminated*, *angle*, *straightness*, *rectitude*, and equality; and if we can find out the causes of these, we may compound them altogether into the causes of a square. Again, if any man propound to himself the conception of *gold*, he may, by resolving, come to the ideas of *solid*, *visible*, *heavy*, (that is, tending to the centre of the earth, or downwards) and many other more universal than gold itself; and these he may resolve again, till he come to such things as are most universal. And in this manner, by resolving continually, we may come to know what those things are, whose causes being known first severally, and afterwards compounded, bring us to the knowledge of singular things. I conclude, therefore, that the method of attaining to the universal knowledge of things, is purely *analytical*.

5. The highest causes, and most universal in every kind, are known by themselves. But the causes of universal things (of those, at least, that have any cause) are manifest of themselves, or (as they say commonly) known to nature; so that they need no method at all; for they have all but one universal cause, which is motion. For the variety of all figures arises out of the variety of those motions by which they are made; and motion cannot be understood to have any other cause besides motion; nor has the variety of those things we perceive by sense, as of colours, sounds, savours, &c., any other cause than motion, residing partly in the objects that work upon our senses, and partly in ourselves, in such manner, as that it is manifestly some kind of motion, though we cannot without ratiocination, come to know what kind. For though many cannot understand till it be in some sort demonstrated to them, that all mutation consists in motion; yet this happens not from any obscurity in the thing itself (for it is not intelligible that anything can depart either from rest, or from the motion it has, except by motion), but either by having their natural discourse corrupted with former opinions received from their masters, or else for this, that they do not at all bend their mind to the inquiring out of truth.

6. Method from principles found out, tending to science simply, what it is. By the knowledge therefore of universals, and of their causes (which are the first principles by which we know the διότι of things) we have in the first place their definitions (which are nothing but the explication of our simple conceptions).

For example, he that has a true conception of *place*, cannot be ignorant of this definition, *place is that space which is possessed or filled adequately by some body*; and so, he that conceives *motion* aright, cannot but know that *motion is the privation of one place, and the acquisition of another*. In the next place, we have their generations or descriptions; as (for example) that *a line is made by the motion of a point*, *superficies by the motion of a line*, and *one motion by another motion*, &c. It remains, that we inquire what motion begets such and such effects; as, what motion makes a straight line, and what a circular; what motion thrusts, what draws, and by what way; what makes a thing which is seen or heard, to be seen or heard sometimes in one manner, sometimes in another. Now the method of this kind of inquiry, is *compositive*. For first we are to observe what effect a body moved produceth, when we consider nothing in it besides its motion; and we see presently that this makes a line, or length; next what the motion of a long body produces, which we find to be superficies; and so forwards, till we see what the effects of simple motion are; and then, in like manner we are to observe what proceeds from the addition, multiplication, subtraction, and division, of these motions, and what effects, what figures, and what properties, they produce; from which kind of contemplation sprung that part of philosophy which is called *geometry*.

From this consideration of what is produced by simple motion, we are to pass to the consideration of what effects one body moved worketh upon another; and because there may be motion in all the several parts of a body, yet so as that the whole body remain still in the same place, we must inquire first, what motion causeth such and such motion in the whole, that is, when one body invades another body which is either at rest or in motion, what way, and with what swiftness, the invaded body shall move; and, again, what motion this second body will generate in a third, and so forwards. From which contemplation shall be drawn that part of philosophy which treats of motion.

In the third place we must proceed to the inquiry of such effects as are made by the motion of the parts of any body, as, how it comes to pass, that things when they are the same, yet seem not to be the same, but changed. And here the things we search after are sensible qualities, such as *light*, *colour*, *transparency*, *opacity*, *sound*, *odour*, *savour*, *heat*, *cold*, and the like; which because they cannot be known till we know the causes of sense itself, therefore the consideration of the causes of *seeing*, *hearing*, *smelling*, *tasting*, and *touching*, belongs to this third place; and all those qualities and changes, above mentioned, are to be referred to the fourth place; which two considerations comprehend that part of philosophy which is called *physics*. And in these four parts is contained whatsoever in natural philosophy may be explicated by demonstration, properly so called. For if a cause were to be rendered of natural appearances in special, as, what are the motions and influences of the heavenly bodies, and of their parts, the reason hereof must either be drawn from the parts of the sciences above mentioned, or no reason at all will be given, but all left to uncertain conjecture.

After *physics* we must come to *moral philosophy*; in which we are to consider the motions of the mind, namely, *appetite*, *aversion*, *love*, *benevolence*, *hope*, *fear*, *anger*, *emulation*, *envy*, *&c.*; what causes they have, and of what they be causes. And the reason why these are to be considered after *physics* is, that they have their causes in sense and imagination, which are the subject of *physical* contemplation. Also the reason, why all these things are to be searched after in the order above-said, is, that physics cannot be understood, except we know first what motions are in the smallest parts of bodies; nor such motion of parts, till we know what it is that makes another body move; nor this, till we know what simple motion will effect. And because all appearance of things to sense is determined, and made to be of such and such quality and quantity by compounded motions, every one of which has a certain degree of velocity, and a certain and determined way; therefore, in the first place, we are to search out the ways of motion simply (in which geometry consists); next the ways of such generated motions as are manifest; and, lastly, the ways of internal and invisible motions (which is the inquiry of natural philosophers). And, therefore, they that study natural philosophy, study in vain, except they begin at geometry; and such writers or disputers thereof, as are ignorant of geometry, do but make their readers and hearers lose their time.

7. That method of civil and natural science, proceeding from sense to principles, is analytical; and again, that which begins at principles is synthetical. *Civil* and *moral philosophy* do not so adhere to one another, but that they may be severed. For the causes of the motions of the mind are known, not only by ratiocination, but also by the experience of every man that takes

the pains to observe those motions within himself. And, therefore, not only they that have attained the knowledge of the passions and perturbations of the mind, by the *synthetical method*, and from the very first principles of philosophy, may by proceeding in the same way, come to the causes and necessity of constituting commonwealths, and to get the knowledge of what is natural right, and what are civil duties; and, in every kind of government, what are the rights of the commonwealth, and all other knowledge appertaining to civil philosophy; for this reason, that the principles of the politics consist in the knowledge of the motions of the mind, and the knowledge of these motions from the knowledge of sense and imagination; but even they also that have not learned the first part of philosophy, namely, *geometry* and *physics*, may, notwithstanding, attain the principles of civil philosophy, by the *analytical method*. For if a question be propounded, as, *whether such an action be just or unjust*; if that *unjust* be resolved into *fact against law*, and that notion *law* into the *command* of him or them that have *coercive power*; and that *power* be derived from the *wills* of men that constitute such power, to the end they may live in peace, they may at last come to this, that the appetites of men and the passions of their minds are such, that, unless they be restrained by some power, they will always be making war upon one another; which may be known to be so by any man's experience, that will but examine his own mind. And, therefore, from hence he may proceed, by compounding, to the determination of the justice or injustice of any propounded action. So that it is manifest, by what has been said, that the method of philosophy, to such as seek science simply, without propounding to themselves the solution of any particular question, is partly analytical, and partly synthetical; namely, that which proceeds from sense to the invention of principles, analytical; and the rest synthetical.

8. The method of searching out, whether anything propounded be matter or accident. To those that seek the cause of some certain and propounded appearance or effect, it happens, sometimes, that they know not whether the thing, whose cause is sought after, be matter or body, or some accident of a body. For though in geometry, when the cause is sought of magnitude, or proportion, or figure, it be certainly known that these things, namely magnitude, proportion, and figure, are accidents; yet in natural philosophy, where all questions are concerning the causes

of the phantasms of sensible things, it is not so easy to discern between the things themselves, from which those phantasms proceed, and the appearances of those things to the sense; which have deceived many, especially when the phantasms have been made by light. For example, a man that looks upon the sun, has a certain shining idea of the magnitude of about a foot over, and this he calls the sun, though he know the sun to be truly a great deal bigger; and, in like manner, the phantasm of the same thing appears sometimes round, by being seen afar off, and sometimes square, by being nearer. Whereupon it may well be doubted, whether that phantasm be matter, or some body natural, or only some accident of a body; in the examination of which doubt we may use this method. The properties of matter and accidents already found out by us, by the synthetical method, from their definitions, are to be compared with the idea we have before us; and if it agree with the properties of matter or body, then it is a body; otherwise it is an accident. Seeing, therefore, matter cannot by any endeavour of ours be either made or destroyed, or increased, or diminished, or moved out of its place, whereas that idea appears, vanishes, is increased and diminished, and moved hither and thither at pleasure; we may certainly conclude that it is not a body, but an accident only. And this method is *synthetical*.

9. The method of seeking whether any accident be in this or in that subject. But if there be a doubt made concerning the subject of any known accident (for this may be doubted sometimes, as in the precedent example, doubt may be made in what subject that splendour and apparent magnitude of the sun is), then our inquiry must proceed in this manner. First, matter in general must be divided into parts, as, into object, medium, and the sentient itself, or such other parts as seem most conformable to the thing propounded. Next, these parts are severally to be examined how they agree with the definition of the subject; and such of them as are not capable of that accident are to be rejected. For example, if by any true ratiocination the sun be found to be greater than its apparent magnitude, then that magnitude is not in the sun; if the sun be in one determined straight line, and one determined distance, and the magnitude and splendour be seen in more lines and distances than one, as it is in reflection, or refraction, then neither that splendour nor apparent magnitude are in the sun itself, and, therefore, the body of the sun cannot be

the subject of that splendour and magnitude. And for the same reasons the air and other parts will be rejected, till at last nothing remain which can be the subject of that splendour and magnitude but the sentient itself. And this method, in regard the subject is divided into parts, is analytical; and in regard the properties, both of the subject and accident, are compared with the accident whose subject the inquiry is made, it is synthetical.

10. Method of searching for the cause of any effect, propounded. But when we seek after the cause of any propounded effect, we must in the first place get into our mind an exact notion or idea of that which we call cause, namely, that *a cause is the sum or aggregate of all such accidents, both in the agents and the patient, as concur to the producing of the effect propounded; all which existing together, it cannot be understood but that the effect existeth with them; or that it can possibly exist if any one of them be absent.* This being known, in the next place we must examine singly every accident that accompanies or precedes the effect, as far forth as it seems to conclude in any manner to the production of the same, and see whether the propounded effect may be conceived to exist, without the existence of any of those accidents; and by this means separate such accidents, as do not concur, from such as concur to produce the said effect; which being done, we are to put together the concurring accidents, and consider whether we can possibly conceive, that when these are all present, the effect propounded will not follow; and if it be evident that the effect will follow, then that aggregate of accidents is the entire cause, otherwise not; but we must still search out and put together other accidents. For example, if the cause of light be propounded to be sought out; first, we examine things without us, and find that whensoever light appears, there is some principal object, as it were the fountain of light, without which we cannot have any perception of light; and, therefore, the concurrence of that object is necessary to the generation of light. Next we consider the medium, and find, that unless it be disposed in a certain manner, namely, that it be transparent, though the object remain the same, yet the effect will not follow; and, therefore, the concurrence of transparency is also necessary to the generation of light. Thirdly, we observe our own body, and find that by the indisposition of the eyes, the brain, the nerves, and the heart, that is, by obstructions, stupidity, and debility, we are deprived of light, so that a fitting disposition of the organs to

receive impressions from without is likewise a necessary part of the cause of light. Again, of all the accidents inherent in the object, there is none that can conduce to the effecting of light, but only action (or a certain motion), which cannot be conceived to be wanting, whensoever the effect is present; for, that anything may shine, it is not requisite that it be of such or such magnitude or figure, or that the whole body of it be moved out of the place it is in (unless it may perhaps be said, that in the sun, or other body, that which causes light is the light it hath in itself; which yet is but a trifling exception, seeing nothing is meant thereby but the cause of light; as if any man should say that the cause of light is that in the sun which produceth it); it remains, therefore, that the action, by which light is generated, is motion only in the parts of the object. Which being understood, we may easily conceive what it is the medium contributes, namely, the continuation of that motion to the eye; and, lastly, what the eye and the rest of the organs of the sentient contribute, namely, the continuation of the same motion to the last organ of sense, the heart. And in this manner the cause of light may be made up of motion continued from the original of the same motion, to the original of vital motion, light being nothing but the alteration of vital motion, made by the impression upon it of motion continued from the object. But I give this only for an example, for I shall shall speak more at large of light, and the generation of it, in its proper place. In the mean time it is manifest, that in the searching out of causes, there is need partly of the analytical, and partly of the synthetical method; of the analytical, to conceive how circumstances conduce severally to the production of effects; and of the synthetical, for the adding together and compounding of what they can effect singly by themselves. And thus much may serve for the method of invention. It remains that I speak of the method of teaching, that is, of demonstration, and of the means by which we demonstrate.

11. Words serve to invention as marks; to demonstration as signs. In the method of invention, the use of words consists in this, that they may serve for marks, by which, whatsoever we have found out may be recalled to memory; for without this all our inventions perish, nor will it be possible for us to go on from principles beyond a syllogism or two, by reason of the weakness of memory. For example, if any man, by considering a triangle set before him, should find that all its angles together taken are

equal to two right angles, and that by thinking of the same tacitly, without any use of words either understood or expressed; and it should happen afterwards that another triangle, unlike the former, or the same in different situation, should be offered to his consideration, he would not know readily whether the same property were in this last or no, but would be forced, as often as a different triangle were brought before him (and the difference of triangles is infinite) to begin his contemplation anew; which he would have no need to do if he had the use of names, for every universal name denotes the conceptions we have of infinite singular things. Nevertheless, as I have said above, they serve as *marks* for the help of our memory, whereby we register to ourselves our own inventions; but not as *signs* by which we declare the same to others; so that a man may be a philosopher alone to himself, without any master; Adam had this capacity. But to teach, that is, to demonstrate, supposes two at the least, and syllogistical speech.

12. The method of demonstration is synthetical. And seeing teaching is nothing but leading the mind of him we teach, to the knowledge of our inventions, in that track by which we attained the same with our own mind; therefore, the same method that served for our invention, will serve also for demonstration to others, saving that we omit the first part of method which proceeded from the sense of things to universal principles, which, because they are principles, cannot be demonstrated; and seeing they are known by nature, (as was said in the 5th article) they need no demonstration, though they need explication. The whole method, therefore, of demonstration, is *synthetical*, consisting of that order of speech which begins from primary or most universal propositions, which are manifest of themselves, and proceeds by a perpetual composition of propositions into syllogisms, till at last the learner understand the truth of the conclusion sought after.

13. Definitions only are primary, & universal propositions. Now, such principles are nothing but definitions, whereof there are two sorts; one of names, that signifies such things as have some conceivable cause, and another of such names as signify things of which we can conceive no cause at all. Names of the former kind are, *body*, or *matter*, *quantity*, or *extension*, *motion*, and whatsoever is common to all matter. Of the second kind, are *such a body*, *such and so great motion*, *so great magnitude*, *such*

figure, and whatsoever we can distinguish one body from another by. And names of the former kind are well enough defined, when, by speech as short as may be, we raise in the mind of the hearer perfect and clear ideas or conceptions of the things named, as when we define motion to be *the leaving of one place, and the acquiring of another continually*; for though no thing moved, nor any cause of motion be in that definition, yet, at the hearing of that speech, there will come into the mind of the hearer an *idea* of motion clear enough. But definitions of things, which may be understood to have some cause, must consist of such names as express the cause or manner of their generation, as when we define a circle to be a figure made by the circumduction of a straight line in a plane, &c. Besides definitions, there is no other proposition that ought to be called primary, or (according to severe truth) be received into the number of principles. For those *axioms of Euclid*, seeing they may be demonstrated, are no principles of demonstration, though they have by the consent of all men gotten the authority of principles, because they need not be demonstrated. Also, those *petitions*, or *postulata* (as they call them) though they be principles, yet they are not principles of demonstration, but of construction only; that is, not of science, but of power; or (which is all one) not of *theorems*, which are speculations, but of *problems*, which belong to practice, or the doing of something. But as for those common received opinions, *Nature abhors vacuity*, *Nature doth nothing in vain*, and the like, which are neither evident in themselves, nor at all to be demonstrated, and which are oftener false than true, they are much less to be acknowledged for principles.

To return, therefore, to definitions; the reason why I say that the cause and generation of such things, as have any cause or generation, ought to enter into their definitions, is this. The end of science is the demonstration of the causes and generations of things; which if they be not in the definitions, they cannot be found in the conclusion of the first syllogism, that is made from those definitions; and if they be not in the first conclusion, they will not be found in any further conclusion deduced from that; and, therefore, by proceding in this manner, we shall never come to science; which is against the scope and intention of demonstration.

14. The nature & definition of a definition. Now, seeing definitions (as I have said) are principles, or primary propositions,

they are therefore speeches; and seeing they are used for the raising of an *idea* of some thing in the mind of the learner, whensoever that thing has a name, the definition of it can be nothing but the explication of that name by speech; and if that name be given it for some compounded conception, the definition is nothing but a resolution of that name into its most universal parts. As when we define man, saying *man is a body animated, sentient, rational,* those names, *body animated, &c.* are parts of that whole name *man*; so that definitions of this kind always consist of *genus* and *difference*; the former names being all, till the last, *general*; and the last of all, *difference.* But if any name be the most universal in its kind, then the definition of it cannot consist of *genus* and *difference,* but is to be made by such circumlocution, as best explicateth the force of that name. Again, it is possible, and happens often, that the *genus* and *difference* are put together, and yet make no definition; as these words, *a straight line,* contain both the *genus* and *difference,* but are not a definition, unless we should think a straight line may be thus defined, *a straight line is a straight line*: and yet if there were added another name, consisting of different words, but signifying the same thing which these signify, then these might be the definition of that name. From what has been said, it may be understood how a definition ought to be defined, namely, *that it is a proposition, whose predicate resolves the subject, when it may; and when it may not, it exemplifies the same.*

15. Properties of a definition. The properties of a definition are:

First, that it takes away equivocation, as also all that multitude of distinctions, which are used by such as think they may learn philosophy by disputation. For the nature of a definition is to define, that is, to determine the signification of the defined name, and to pare from it all other signification besides what is contained in the definition itself; and therefore one definition does as much, as all the distinctions (how many soever) that can be used about the name defined.

Secondly, that it gives a universal notion of the thing defined, representing a certain universal picture thereof, not to the eye, but to the mind. For as when one paints a man, he paints the image of some man; so he, that defines the name man, makes a representation of some man to the mind.

Thirdly, that it is not necessary to dispute whether definitions are to be admitted or no. For when a master is instructing his scholar, if the scholar understand all the parts of the thing defined, which are resolved in the definition, and yet will not admit of the definition, there needs no further controversy betwixt them, it being all one as if he refused to be taught. But if he understand nothing, then certainly the definition is faulty; for the nature of a definition consists in this, that it exhibit a clear idea of the thing defined; and principles are either known by themselves, or else they are not principles.

Fourthly, that, in philosophy, definitions are before defined names. For in teaching philosophy, the first beginning is from definitions; and all progression in the same, till we come to the knowledge of the thing compounded is compositive. Seeing, therefore, definition is the explication of a compounded name by resolution, and the progression is from the parts to the compound, definitions must be understood before compounded names; nay, when the names of the parts of any speech be explicated, it is not necessary that the definitions should be a name compounded of them. For example, when these names *equilateral*, *quadrilateral*, *right-angled*, are sufficiently understood, it is not necessary in geometry that there should be at all such a name as *square*; or defined names are received in philosophy for brevity's sake only.

Fifthly, that compounded names, which are defined one way in some one part of philosophy, may in another part of the same be otherwise defined; as a *parabola* and a *hyperbole* have one definition in geometry, and another in rhetoric; for definitions are instituted and serve for the understanding of the doctrine which is treated of. And, therefore, as in one part of philosophy, a definition may have in it some one fit name for the more brief explanation of some proposition in geometry; so it may have the same liberty in other parts of philosophy; for the use of names is particular (even where many agree to the settling of them) and arbitrary.

Sixthly, that no name can be defined by any one word; because no one word is sufficient for the resolving of one or more words.

Seventhly, that a defined name ought not to be repeated in the definition. For a defined name is the whole compound, and a definition is the resolution of that compound into parts; but no total can be part of itself.

16. Nature of a demonstration. Any two definitions, that may

be compounded into a syllogism, produce a conclusion; which, because it is derived from principles, that is, from definitions, is said to be demonstrated; and the derivation or composition itself is called a demonstration. In like manner, if a syllogism be made of two propositions, whereof one is a definition, the other a demonstrated conclusion, or neither of them is a definition, but both formerly demonstrated, that syllogism is also called a demonstration, and so successively. The definition therefore of a demonstration is this, *a demonstration is a syllogism, or series of syllogisms, derived and continued, from the definitions of names, to the last conclusion*. And from hence it may be understood, that all true ratiocination, which taketh its beginning from true principles, produceth science, and is true demonstration. For as for the original of the name, although that, which the Greeks called ἀπόδειξις, and the Latins *demonstratio*, was understood by them for that sort only of ratiocination, in which, by the describing of certain lines and figures, they placed the thing they were to prove, as it were before men's eyes, which is properly ἀποδεικνύειν, or to *show* by the figure; yet they seem to have done it for this reason, that unless it were in geometry, (in which only there is place for such figures) there was no ratiocination certain, and ending in science, their doctrines concerning all other things being nothing but controversy and clamour; which, nevertheless, happened, not because the truth to which they pretended could not be made evident without figures, but because they wanted true principles, from which they might derive their ratiocination; and, therefore, there is no reason but that if true definitions were premised in all sorts of doctrines, the demonstration also would be true.

17. Properties of a demonstration, and order of things to be demonstrated. It is proper to methodical demonstrations:

First, that there be a true succession of one reason to another, according to the rules of syllogizing delivered above.

Secondly, that the premises of all syllogisms be demonstrated from the first definitions.

Thirdly, that after definitions, he that teaches or demonstrates any thing, proceed in the same method by which he found it out; namely that in the first place those things be demonstrated, which immediately succeed to universal definitions (in which is contained that part of philosophy which is called *philosophia prima*). Next, those things which may be demonstrated by simple motion (in which geometry consists). After geometry, such things as may be taught or showed by manifest action, that is, by thrusting from, or pulling towards. And after these, the motion or mutation of the invisible parts of things, and the doctrine of sense and imaginations, and of the internal passions, especially those of men, in which are comprehended the grounds of civil duties, or civil philosophy; which takes up the last place. And that this method ought to be kept in all sorts of philosophy, is evident from hence, that such things as I have said are to be taught last, cannot be demonstrated, till such as are propounded to be first treated of, be fully understood. Of which method no other example can be given, but that treatise of the elements of philosophy, which I shall begin in the next chapter, and continue to the end of the work.

18. Faults of a demonstration. Besides those *paralogisms*, whose fault lies either in the falsity of the premises, or the want of true composition, of which I have spoken in the precedent chapter, there are two more, which are frequent in demonstration; one whereof is commonly called *petitio principii*; the other is the supposing of a *false cause*; and these do not only deceive unskilful learners, but sometimes masters themselves, by making them take that for well demonstrated, which is not demonstrated at all. *Petitio principii* is, when the conclusion to be proved is disguised in other words, and put for the definition or principle from whence it is to be demonstrated; and thus, by putting for the cause of the thing sought, either the thing itself or some effect of it, they make a circle in their demonstration. As for example, he that would demonstrate that the earth stands still in the centre of the world, and should suppose the earth's gravity to be the cause thereof, and define gravity to be a quality by which every heavy body tends towards the centre of the world, would lose his labour; for the question is, what is the cause of that quality in the earth? and, therefore, he that supposes gravity to be the cause, puts the thing itself for its own cause.

Of a *false cause* I find this example in a certain treatise where the thing to be demonstrated is the motion of the earth. He begins therefore, with this, that seeing the earth and the sun are not always in the same situation, it must needs be that one of them be locally moved, which is true; next, he affirms that the vapours, which the sun raises from the earth and sea, are, by reason of this motion, necessarily moved, which also is true; from whence he infers the winds are made, and this may pass for granted; and by these winds he says, the waters of the sea are moved, and by their motion the bottom of the sea, as if it were beaten forwards, moves round; and let this also be granted; wherefore, he concludes, the earth is moved; which is, nevertheless, a paralogism. For, if that wind were the cause why the earth was, from the beginning, moved round, and the motion either of the sun or the earth were the cause of that wind, then the motion of the sun or the earth was before the wind itself; and if the earth were moved, before the wind was made, then the wind could not be the cause of the earth's revolution; but, if the sun were moved, and the earth stand still, then it is manifest the earth might remain unmoved, notwithstanding that wind; and therefore that motion was not made by the cause which he allegeth. But paralogisms of this kind are very frequent among the writers of *physics*, though none can be more elaborate than this in the example given.

19. Why the analytical method of geometricans cannot be treated of in this place. It may to some men seem pertinent to treat in this place of that art of the geometricians, which they call *logistica*, that is, the art, by which, from supposing the thing in question to be true, they proceed by ratiocination, till either they come to something known, by which they may demonstrate the truth of the thing sought for; or to something which is impossible, from whence they collect that to be false, which they supposed true. But this art cannot be explicated here, for this reason, that the method of it can neither be practiced, nor understood, unless by such as are well versed in geometry; and among geometricians themselves, they, that have most theorems in readiness, are the most ready in the use of this *logistica*; so that, indeed, it is not a distinct thing from geometry itself; for there are, in the method of it, three parts; the first whereof consists in the finding out of equality betwixt known and unknown things, which they call equation; and this equation cannot be found out, but by such as know perfectly the nature, properties, and transpositions of proportion, as also the addition, subtraction, multiplication, and division of lines and superficies, and the extraction of roots; which are the parts of no mean geometrician. The second is, when an equation is found, to be able to judge whether the truth or falsity of the question may be deduced from it, or no; which yet requires greater knowledge. And the third is, when such an equation is found, as is fit for the solution of the question, to

know how to resolve the same in such manner, that the truth or falsity may thereby manifestly appear; which, in hard questions, cannot be done without the knowledge of the nature of crooked-lined figures; but he that understands readily the nature and properties of these, is a complete geometrician. It happens besides, that for the finding out of equations, there is no certain method, but he is best able to do it, that has the best natural wit.

My Opinion about Liberty and Necessity

First I conceive, that when it cometh into a man's mind to do or not to do some certain action, if he have no time to *deliberate*, the doing it or abstaining *necessarily* follow the *present* thought he hath of the *good* or *evil* consequence thereof to himself. As for example, in sudden *anger*, the *action* shall follow the thought of *revenge*; in sudden *fear*, the thought of *escape*. Also when a man hath time to *deliberate*, but deliberates not, because never anything appeared that could make him doubt of the consequence, the *action* follows his opinion of the *goodness* or *harm* of it. These actions I call VOLUNTARY, my Lord, if I understand him aright that calls them SPONTANEOUS. I call them *voluntary*, because those *actions* that follow immediately the *last* appetite, are *voluntary*, and here where is one only appetite, that one is the last. Besides, I see it is reasonable to punish a *rash* action, which could not be justly done by man to man, unless the same were *voluntary*. For no *action* of a man can be said to be without *deliberation*, though never so sudden, because it is supposed he had time to *deliberate* all the precedent time of his life, whether he should do that kind of action or not. And hence it is, that he that killeth in a sudden passion of *anger*, shall nevertheless be justly put to *death*, because all the time, wherein he was able to consider whether to kill were good or evil, shall be held for one continual *deliberation*, and consequently the killing shall be judged to proceed from *election*.

Secondly, I conceive when a man *deliberates* whether he shall do a thing or not do it, that he does nothing else but consider whether it be better for himself to do it or not to do it. And to *consider* an action, is to imagine the *consequences* of it, both *good* and *evil*. From whence is to be inferred that *deliberation* is nothing else but *alternate* imagination of the *good* and *evil* sequels of an *action*, or, which is the same thing, alternate *hope* and *fear*, or alternate *appetite* to do or quit the action of which he *deliberateth*.

Thirdly, I conceive that in all *deliberations*, that is to say, in all alternate *succession* of contrary *appetites*, the last is that which we call the WILL, and is immediately next before the doing of the action, or next before the doing of it become impossible. All other *appetites* to do, and to quit, that come upon a man during his deliberations, are called *intentions* and *inclinations*, but not *wills* there being but one *will*, which also in this case may be called the *last will*, though the *intentions* change often.

Fourthly, I conceive that those *actions*, which a man is said to do upon *deliberation*, are said to be *voluntary*, and done upon *choice* and *election*, so that *voluntary* action, and action proceeding from *election* is the same thing; and that of a *voluntary agent*, it is all one to say, he is *free*, and to say, he hath not made an end of *deliberating*.

Fifthly, I conceive *liberty* to be rightly defined in this manner: *Liberty is the absence of all the impediments to action that are not contained in the nature and intrinsical quality of the agent*. As for example, the water is said to descend *freely*, or to have *liberty* to descend by the channel of the river, because there is no impediment that way, but not across, because the banks are impediments. And though the water cannot ascend, yet men never say it wants the *liberty* to ascend, but the *faculty* or *power*, because the impediment is in the nature of the water, and intrinsical. So also we say, he that is tied, wants the *liberty* to go, because the impediment is not in him, but in his hands; whereas we say not so of him that is sick or lame, because the impediment is in himself.

Sixthly, I conceive that nothing taketh beginning from *itself*, but from the *action* of some other immediate *agent* without itself. And that therefore, when first a man hath an *appetite* or *will* to something, to which immediately before he had no appetite nor will, the *cause* of his *will*, is not the *will* itself, but *something* else not in his own disposing. So that whereas it is out of controversy, that of *voluntary* actions the *will* is the *necessary* cause, and by this which is said, the *will* is also *caused* by other things whereof it disposeth not, it followeth, that *voluntary* actions have all of them *necessary* causes, and therefore are *necessitated*.

Seventhly, I hold that to be a *sufficient cause*, to which nothing is wanting that is needful to the producing of the *effect*. The same also is a *necessary* cause. For if it be possible that a *sufficient* cause shall not bring forth the *effect*, then there wanteth somewhat which was needful to the producing of it, and so the *cause* was not *sufficient*; but if it be impossible that a *sufficient* cause should not produce the *effect*, then is a *sufficient* cause a *necessary* cause, for that is said to produce an effect *necessarily* that cannot but produce it. Hence it is manifest, that whatsoever is produced, is produced *necessarily*; for whatsoever is produced hath had a *sufficient* cause to produce it, or else it had not been; and therefore also *voluntary* actions are *necessitated*.

Lastly, that ordinary *definition* of a *free agent*, namely, *that a* free agent *is that, which, when all things are present which are needful to produce the* effect, *can nevertheless not produce it*, implies a contradiction, and is nonsense; being as much as to say, the cause may be *sufficient*, that is to say, *necessary*, and yet the effect shall not follow.

MY REASONS

For the first five points, wherein it is explicated I, what *spontaneity* is; II, what *deliberation* is; III, what *will*, *propension* and *appetite* are; IV, what a *free agent* is; V, what *liberty* is; there can no other proof be offered but every man's own experience, by reflection on himself, and remembering what he useth in his mind, that is, what he himself meaneth when he saith an action is *spontaneous*, a man *deliberates*; such is his *will*, that *agent* or that *action* is *free*. Now he that reflecteth so on himself, cannot but be satisfied, that *deliberation* is the *consideration of the good and evil sequels of an action to come*; that by *spontaneity* is meant *inconsiderate action*, or else nothing is meant by it; that *will* is the *last act of our deliberation*; that a *free agent* is he *that can do if he will*, and *forbear if he will*; and that *liberty* is *the absence of external impediments*. But to those that out of custom speak not what they conceive, but what they hear, and are not able, or will not take the pains to consider what they think when they hear such words, no argument can be sufficient, because *experience* and *matter of fact* are not verified by other men's arguments, but by every man's own *sense* and *memory*. For example, how can it be proved that to *love* a thing and to think it *good* is all one, to a man that doth not mark his own meaning by those words? Or how can it be proved that *eternity* is not *nunc stans* to a man that says those words by custom, and never considers how he can conceive the thing in his mind?

Also the sixth point, that a man cannot imagine anything to begin *without a cause*, can no other way be made known, but by trying how he can imagine it; but if he try, he shall find as much reason, if there be no cause of the thing, to conceive it should begin at one time as another, that he hath equal reason to think it should begin at all times, which is impossible, and therefore he must think there was some special cause why it began then, rather than sooner or later; or else that it began never, but was *eternal*.

For the seventh point, which is, that all *events* have *necessary* causes, it is there proved, in that they have *sufficient* causes. Further let us in this place also suppose any event never so casual, as the throwing, for example, *ames ace* upon a pair of dice, and see, if it must not have been *necessary* before it was thrown. For seeing it was thrown, it had a *beginning*, and consequently a *sufficient* cause to produce it, consisting partly in the *dice*, partly in outward things, as the posture of the parts of the *hand*, the measure of *force* applied by the caster, the posture of the parts of the *table*, and the like. In sum, there was nothing wanting which was necessarily requisite to the producing of that particular cast, and consequently the cast was necessarily thrown; for if it had not been thrown, there had wanted somewhat requisite to the throwing of it, and so the cause had not been *sufficient*. In the like manner it may be proved that every other accident, how *contingent* soever it seem, or how *voluntary* soever it be, is produced *necessarily*, which is that that my Lord Bishop disputes against. The same may be proved also in this manner. Let the case be put, for example, of the weather. *It is necessary that tomorrow it shall rain or not rain.* If therefore it be not *necessary* it shall rain, it is *necessary* it shall not rain, otherwise there is no necessity that the proposition, *it shall rain or not rain*, should be true. I know there be some that say, it may necessarily be true that one of the two shall come to pass, but not, singly that it shall rain, or that it shall not rain, which is as much to say, *one* of them is *necessary*, yet neither of them is *necessary*; and therefore to seem to avoid that absurdity, they make a distinction, that neither of them is true *determinate*, but *indeterminate*; which distinction either signifies no more but this, one of them is true, but we know not which, and so the necessity remains, though we know it not; or if the meaning of the distinction be not that, it hath no meaning, and they might as well have said, one of them is true *Titirice*, but neither of them, *Tu patulice*.

The last thing, in which also consisteth the whole controversy, namely that there is no such thing as an agent, *which when all things requisite to action are present, can nevertheless forbear to produce it*; or, which is all one, that there is no such thing as *freedom from necessity*, is easily inferred from that which hath been before alleged. For if it be an *agent*, it can *work*; and if it *work*, there is nothing wanting of what is requisite to produce the *action*, and consequently the cause of the action is *sufficient*; and if *sufficient*, then also *necessary*, as hath been proved before.

And thus you see how the *inconveniences*, which his Lordship objecteth must follow upon the holding of *necessity*, are avoided, and the *necessity* itself *demonstratively* proved. To which I could add, if I thought it good logic, the *inconvenience* of denying *necessity*, as that it destroyeth both the *decrees* and the *prescience* of God Almighty; for whatsoever God hath *purposed* to bring to pass by *man*, as an instrument, or foreseeth shall come to pass; a man, if he have *liberty*, such as his Lordship affirmeth, from *necessitation*, might frustrate, and make not to come to pass, and God should either not *foreknow* it, and not *decree* it, or he should *foreknow* such things shall be, as shall never be, and *decree* that which shall never *come to pass*.

This is all that hath come into my mind touching this question since I last considered it. And I humbly beseech your Lordship to communicate it only to my Lord Bishop. And so praying God to prosper your Lordship in all your designs, I take leave, and am,

My most noble and most obliging Lord,
Your most humble servant,
THOMAS HOBBES

Rouen, August 20, 1652.[2]

2. In the first edition of 1654 this date is 1646.

4. The True Philosophy

Benedict Spinoza, 1632–77

Spinoza wrote with the serene majesty of an unclouded Intellect. Nothing was conceded to Imagination. No place was left for mystery, contingency or accident in a world where everything must be as it is. The universe was a complete, self-contained system, to be regarded from one point of view as God and from another as Nature. God was immanent and impersonal. He did not create the world and had no plans for it, being but the active and, in a sense, spiritual aspect of whatever there is. (To suppose otherwise would be anthropomorphic and would illustrate the dangers of trying to Imagine what could only be Understood.) Nature was the physical aspect of this same totality. All its states could be explained from within by showing the place of each in an inexorable causal series. Human minds and bodies were neither more nor less parts of the system than anything else. There was no freedom of the will but a man, who understood why things had to be as they were and lived with his passions subordinate to his reason, would be a man whose actions sprang from his true nature and so a free man.

This ambitious scheme is set out in the *Ethics*, using the Geometrical Method in its purest form. The root question is, in effect, what we must suppose, if the universe is to be wholly intelligible to Reason. To answer it, Spinoza in part I interdefines Substance, Cause, Attribute, Freedom and Necessity and then, taking the definitions as the only coherent and true ones possible, explains God-or-Nature in terms of them. Since there has been space in this anthology only for part I, the reader may wish for an outline of the rest. Part II deals with mind and body and their relation, arguing that they are a case of the wholly general truth that 'the order and connection of ideas is the same as the order and connection of things'. Part III treats of the emotions in a spirit instructively put thus in the second paragraph:

> Nothing comes to pass in nature, which can be set down to a flaw therein; for nature is always the same, and everywhere one and the same in her efficacy and power of action; that is, nature's laws and ordinances, whereby all things come to pass and change from one form to another, are everywhere and always the same; so that there should be one and the same method of understanding the nature of all things whatsoever, namely, through nature's universal laws and rules. Thus the passions of hatred, anger, envy, and so on, considered in themselves, follow from this same necessity and efficacy of nature; they answer to certain definite causes, through which they are understood, and possess certain properties as worthy of being known as the properties of anything else, whereof the contemplation in itself affords us delight. I shall, therefore, treat of the nature and strength of the emotions according to the same method, as I employed heretofore in my investigations concerning God and the mind. I shall consider human actions and desires in exactly the same manner, as though I were concerned with lines, planes, and solids.

Part IV is entitled 'Of Human Bondage or the Strength of the Emotions' and ends with a famous appendix on the Right Way of Life. Part V movingly presents the life of the free man and culminates with reflections on the Intellectual Love of God. The work is a masterpiece by any standard and would take pride of place in any complete Rationalist corpus. However, as space did not permit, it seemed better here to make room for some letters and most of *On the Improvement of the Understanding*.[1] This piece is a prolegomenon to a much larger work which was never written but it is interesting in its own right and important for understanding Rationalist epistemology. (Nor does it lack popularity: it is still sometimes sold from slot machines on American railroad stations under the title *Improve Your Mind.*)

To set the tone for an encounter with Spinoza, we might note a remark in one of his letters: 'I do not presume to have discovered the best philosophy but I know that I understand the true one. I know it in the same way as you know that the angles of a triangle are equal to two right angles.' (Ep. 76)

1. The extracts used here are all from the translation by R. H. M. Elwes, Bohn, 1884. The notes are mostly Spinoza's own.

On the Improvement of the Understanding, 1662

After experience had taught me that all the usual surroundings of social life are vain and futile; seeing that none of the objects of my fears contained in themselves anything either good or bad, except in so far as the mind is affected by them, I finally resolved to inquire whether there might be some real good having power to communicate itself, which would affect the mind singly, to the exclusion of all else: whether, in fact, there might be anything of which the discovery and attainment would enable me to enjoy continuous, supreme, and unending happiness. I say 'I *finally* resolved,' for at first sight it seemed unwise willingly to lose hold on what was sure for the sake of something then uncertain. I could see the benefits which are acquired through fame and riches, and that I should be obliged to abandon the quest of such objects, if I seriously devoted myself to the search for something different and new. I perceived that if true happiness chanced to be placed in the former I should necessarily miss it; while if, on the other hand, it were not so placed, and I gave them my whole attention, I should equally fail.

I therefore debated whether it would not be possible to arrive at the new principle, or at any rate at a certainty concerning its existence, without changing the conduct and usual plan of my life; with this end in view I made many efforts, but in vain. For the ordinary surroundings of life which are esteemed by men (as their actions testify) to be the highest good, may be classed under the three heads – Riches, Fame, and the Pleasures of Sense: with these three the mind is so absorbed that it has little power to reflect on any different good. By sensual pleasure the mind is enthralled to the extent of quiescence, as if the supreme good were actually attained, so that is is quite incapable of thinking of any other object; when such pleasure has been gratified it is followed by extreme melancholy, whereby the mind, though not enthralled, is disturbed and dulled.

The pursuit of honours and riches is likewise very absorbing, especially if such objects be sought simply for their own sake,[2]

2. *The pursuit of honours and riches is likewise very absorbing, especially if such objects be sought simply for their own sake.* This might be explained more at large and more clearly: I mean, by distinguishing riches according as they are pursued for their own sake, or in furtherance of fame, or sensual pleasure,

inasmuch as they are then supposed to constitute the highest good. In the case of fame the mind is still more absorbed, for fame is conceived as always good for its own sake, and as the ultimate end to which all actions are directed. Further, the attainment of riches and fame is not followed as in the case of sensual pleasures by repentance, but, the more we acquire, the greater is our delight, and, consequently, the more are we incited to increase both the one and the other; on the other hand, if our hopes happen to be frustrated we are plunged into the deepest sadness. Fame has the further drawback that it compels its votaries to order their lives according to the opinions of their fellow-men, shunning what they usually shun, and seeking what they usually seek.

When I saw that all these ordinary objects of desire would be obstacles in the way of a search for something different and new – nay, that they were so opposed thereto, that either they or it would have to be abandoned, I was forced to inquire which would prove the most useful to me: for, as I say, I seemed to be willingly losing hold on a sure good for the sake of something uncertain. However, after I had reflected on the matter, I came in the first place to the conclusion that by abandoning the ordinary objects of pursuit, and betaking myself to a new quest, I should be leaving a good, uncertain by reason of its own nature, as may be gathered from what has been said, for the sake of a good not uncertain in its nature (for I sought for a fixed good), but only in the possibility of its attainment.

Further reflection convinced me, that if I could really get to the root of the matter I should be leaving certain evils for a certain good. I thus perceived that I was in a state of great peril, and I compelled myself to seek with all my strength for a remedy however uncertain it might be; as a sick man struggling with a deadly disease, when he sees that death will surely be upon him unless a remedy be found, is compelled to seek such a remedy with all his strength, inasmuch as his whole hope lies therein. All the objects pursued by the multitude not only bring no remedy that tends to preserve our being, but even act as hindrances, causing the death not seldom of those who possess them, and always of those who are possessed by them.[3] There are many

---

or the advancement of science and art. But this subject is reserved to its own place, for it is not here proper to investigate the matter more accurately.

3. These considerations should be set forth more precisely.

examples of men who have suffered persecution even to death for the sake of their riches, and of men who in pursuit of wealth have exposed themselves to so many dangers, that they have paid away their life as a penalty for their folly. Examples are no less numerous of men, who have endured the utmost wretchedness for the sake of gaining or preserving their reputation. Lastly, there are innumerable cases of men, who have hastened their death through over-indulgence in sensual pleasure. All these evils seem to have arisen from the fact, that happiness or unhappiness is made wholly to depend on the quality of the object which we love. When a thing is not loved, no quarrels will arise concerning it – no sadness will be felt if it perishes – no envy if it is possessed by another – no fear, no hatred, in short no disturbances of the mind. All these arise from the love of what is perishable, such as the objects already mentioned. But love towards a thing eternal and infinite feeds the mind wholly with joy, and is itself unmingled with any sadness, wherefore it is greatly to be desired and sought for with all our strength. Yet it was not at random that I used the words, 'If I could go to the root of the matter,' for, though what I have urged was perfectly clear to my mind, I could not forthwith lay aside all love of riches, sensual enjoyment, and fame. One thing was evident, namely, that while my mind was employed with these thoughts it turned away from its former objects of desire, and seriously considered the search for a new principle; this state of things was a great comfort to me, for I perceived that the evils were not such as to resist all remedies. Although these intervals were at first rare, and of very short duration, yet afterwards, as the true good became more and more discernible to me, they became more frequent and more lasting; especially after I had recognized that the acquisition of wealth, sensual pleasure, or fame, is only a hindrance, so long as they are sought as ends not as means; if they be sought as means, they will be under restraint, and, far from being hindrances, will further not a little the end for which they are sought, as I will show in due time.

I will here only briefly state what I mean by true good, and also what is the nature of the highest good. In order that this may be rightly understood, we must bear in mind that the terms good and evil are only applied relatively, so that the same thing may be called both good and bad, according to the relations in view, in the same way as it may be called perfect or imperfect.

Nothing regarded in its own nature can be called perfect or imperfect; especially when we are aware that all things which come to pass, come to pass according to the eternal order and fixed laws of nature. However, human weakness cannot attain to this order in its own thoughts, but meanwhile man conceives a human character much more stable than his own, and sees that there is no reason why he should not himself acquire such a character. Thus he is led to seek for means which will bring him to this pitch of perfection, and calls everything which will serve as such means a true good. The chief good is that he should arrive, together with other individuals if possible, at the possession of the aforesaid character. What that character is we shall show in due time, namely, that it is the knowledge of the union existing between the mind and the whole of nature.[4] This, then, is the end for which I strive, to attain to such a character myself, and to endeavour that many should attain to it with me. In other words, it is part of my happiness to lend a helping hand, that many others may understand even as I do so that their understanding and desire may entirely agree with my own. In order to bring this about, it is necessary to understand as much of nature as will enable us to attain to the aforesaid character, and also to form a social order such as is most conducive to the attainment of this character by the greatest number with the least difficulty and danger. We must seek the assistance of Moral Philosophy[5] and the Theory of Education; further, as health is no insignificant means for attaining our end, we must also include the whole science of Medicine, and, as many difficult things are by contrivance rendered easy, and we can in this way gain much time and convenience, the science of Mechanics must in no way be despised. But, before all things, a means must be devised for improving the understanding and purifying it, as far as may be at the outset, so that it may apprehend things without error, and in the best possible way.

Thus it is apparent to everyone that I wish to direct all sciences to one end and aim,[6] so that we may attain to the supreme human perfection which we have named; and, therefore, whatsoever in

4. These matters are explained more at length elsewhere.

5. N.B. I do no more here than enumerate the sciences necessary for our purpose; I lay no stress on their order.

6. There is for the sciences but one end, to which they should all be directed.

the sciences does not serve to promote our object will have to be rejected as useless. To sum up the matter in a word, all our actions and thoughts must be directed to this one end. Yet, as it is necessary that while we are endeavouring to attain our purpose, and bring the understanding into the right path, we should carry on our life, we are compelled first of all to lay down certain rules of life as provisionally good, to wit the following:

I. To speak in a manner intelligible to the multitude, and to comply with every general custom that does not hinder the attainment of our purpose. For we can gain from the multitude no small advantages, provided that we strive to accommodate ourselves to its understanding as far as possible: moreover, we shall in this way gain a friendly audience for the reception of the truth.

II. To indulge ourselves with pleasures only in so far as they are necessary for preserving health.

III. Lastly, to endeavour to obtain only sufficient money or other commodities to enable us to preserve our life and health, and to follow such general customs as are consistent with our purpose.

Having laid down these preliminary rules, I will betake myself to the first and most important task, namely, the amendment of the understanding, and the rendering it capable of understanding things in the manner necessary for attaining our end.

In order to bring this about, the natural order demands that I should here recapitulate all the modes of perception, which I have hitherto employed for affirming or denying anything with certainty, so that I may choose the best, and at the same time begin to know my own powers and the nature which I wish to perfect.

Reflection shows that all modes of perception or knowledge may be reduced to four:

I. Perception arising from hearsay or from some sign which everyone may name as he pleases.

II. Perception arising from mere experience – that is, from experience not yet classified by the intellect, and only so called because the given event has happened to take place, and we have no contradictory fact to set against it, so that it therefore remains unassailed in our mind.

III. Perception arising when the essence of one thing is inferred from another thing, but not adequately; this comes [7] when

7. In this case we do not understand anything of the cause from the con-

from some effect we gather its cause, or when it is inferred from some general proposition that some property is always present.

IV. Lastly, there is the perception arising when a thing is perceived solely through its essence, or through the knowledge of its proximate cause.

All these kinds of perception I will illustrate by examples. By hearsay I know the day of my birth, my parentage, and other matters about which I have never felt any doubt. By mere experience I know that I shall die, for this I can affirm from having seen that others like myself have died, though all did not live for the same period, or die by the same disease. I know by mere experience that oil has the property of feeding fire, and water of extinguishing it. In the same way I know that a dog is a barking animal, man a rational animal, and in fact nearly all the practical knowledge of life.

We deduce one thing from another as follows: when we clearly perceive that we feel a certain body and no other, we thence clearly infer that the mind is united to the body,[8] and that their union is the cause of the given sensation; but we cannot thence absolutely understand the nature of the sensation and the union.[9] Or, after I have become acquainted with the nature of vision, and know that it has the property of making one and the same thing appear smaller when far off than when near, I can infer that the sun is larger than it appears, and can draw other conclusions of the same kind.

---

sideration of it in the effect. This is sufficiently evident from the fact that the cause is only spoken of in very general terms, such as – there exists then something; there exists then some power, &c.; or from the fact that we only express it in a negative manner – it is not this or that, &c. In the second case something is ascribed to the cause because of the effect, as we shall show in an example, but only a property, never the essence.

8. From this example may be clearly seen what I have just drawn attention to. For through this union we understand nothing beyond the sensation, the effect, to wit, from which we inferred the cause of which we understand nothing.

9. A conclusion of this sort, though it be certain, is yet not to be relied on without great caution; for unless we are exceedingly careful we shall forthwith fall into error. When things are conceived thus abstractedly, and not through their true essence, they are apt to be confused by the imagination. For that which is in itself one, men imagine to be multiplex. To those things which are conceived abstractedly, apart, and confusedly, terms are applied which are apt to become wrested from their strict meaning, and bestowed on things more familiar; whence it results that these latter are imagined in the same way as the former to which the terms were originally given.

Lastly, a thing may be perceived solely through its essence; when, from the fact of knowing something, I know what it is to know that thing, or when, from knowing the essence of the mind, I know that it is united to the body. By the same kind of knowledge we know that two and three make five, or that two lines each parallel to a third, are parallel to one another, &c. The things which I have been able to know by this kind of knowledge are as yet very few.

In order that the whole matter may be put in a clearer light, I will make use of a single illustration as follows. Three numbers are given – it is required to find a fourth, which shall be to the third as the second is to the first. Tradesmen will at once tell us that they know what is required to find the fourth number, for they have not yet forgotten the rule which was given to them arbitrarily without proof by their masters; others construct a universal axiom from their experience with simple numbers, where the fourth number is self-evident, as in the case of 2, 4, 3, 6; here it is evident that if the second number be multiplied by the third, and the product divided by the first, the quotient is 6; when they see that by this process the number is produced which they knew beforehand to be the proportional, they infer that the process always holds good for finding a fourth number proportional. Mathematicians, however, know by the proof of the nineteenth proposition of the seventh book of Euclid, what numbers are proportionals, namely, from the nature and property of proportion it follows that the product of the first and fourth will be equal to the product of the second and third: still they do not see the adequate proportionality of the given numbers, or, if they do see it, they see it not by virtue of Euclid's proposition, but intuitively, without going through any process.

In order that from these modes of perception the best may be selected, it is well that we should briefly enumerate the means necessary for attaining our end.

I. To have an exact knowledge of our nature which we desire to perfect, and to know as much as is needful of nature in general.

II. To collect in this way the differences, the agreements, and the oppositions of things.

III. To learn thus exactly how far they can or cannot be modified.

IV. To compare this result with the nature and power of man. We shall thus discern the highest degree of perfection to which man is capable of attaining. We shall then be in a position to see which mode of perception we ought to choose.

As to the first mode, it is evident that from hearsay our knowledge must always be uncertain, and, moreover, can give us no insight into the essence of a thing, as is manifest in our illustration; now one can only arrive at knowledge of a thing through knowledge of its essence, as will hereafter appear. We may, therefore, clearly conclude that the certainty arising from hearsay cannot be scientific in its character. For simple hearsay cannot affect anyone whose understanding does not, so to speak, meet it half way.

The second mode of perception[10] cannot be said to give us the idea of the proportion of which we are in search. Moreover its results are very uncertain and indefinite, for we shall never discover anything in natural phenomena by its means, except accidental properties, which are never clearly understood, unless the essence of the things in question be known first. Wherefore this mode also must be rejected.

Of the third mode of perception we may say in a manner that it gives us the idea of the thing sought, and that it enables us to draw conclusions without risk of error; yet it is not by itself sufficient to put us in possession of the perfection we aim at.

The fourth mode alone apprehends the adequate essence of a thing without danger of error. This mode, therefore, must be the one which we chiefly employ. How, then, should we avail ourselves of it so as to gain the fourth kind of knowledge with the least delay concerning things previously unknown? I will proceed to explain.

Now that we know what kind of knowledge is necessary for us, we must indicate the way and the method whereby we may gain the said knowledge concerning the things needful to be known. In order to accomplish this, we must first take care not to commit ourselves to a search, going back to infinity – that is, in order to discover the best method for finding out the truth, there is no need of another method to discover such method; nor of a third method for discovering the second, and so on to infinity. By such proceedings, we should never arrive at the knowledge of the truth, or, indeed, at any knowledge at all. The matter stands on

10. I shall here treat a little more in detail of experience, and shall examine the method adopted by the Empirics, and by recent philosophers.

the same footing as the making of material tools, which might be argued about in a similar way. For, in order to work iron, a hammer is needed, and the hammer cannot be forthcoming unless it has been made; but, in order to make it, there was need of another hammer and other tools, and so on to infinity. We might thus vainly endeavour to prove that men have no power of working iron. But as men at first made use of the instruments supplied by nature to accomplish very easy pieces of workmanship, laboriously and imperfectly, and then, when these were finished, wrought other things more difficult with less labour and greater perfection; and so gradually mounted from the simplest operations to the making of tools, and from the making of tools to the making of more complex tools, and fresh feats of workmanship, till they arrived at making, with small expenditure of labour, the vast number of complicated mechanisms which they now possess. So, in like manner, the intellect, by its native strength,[11] makes for itself intellectual instruments, whereby it acquires strength for performing other intellectual operations,[12] and from these operations gets again fresh instruments, or the power of pushing its investigations further, and thus gradually proceeds till it reaches the summit of wisdom.

That this is the path pursued by the understanding may be readily seen, when we understand the nature of the method for finding out the truth, and of the natural instruments so necessary for the construction of more complex instruments, and for the progress of investigation. I thus proceed with my demonstration.

A true idea[13] (for we possess a true idea) is something different from its correlate (*ideatum*); thus a circle is different from the idea of a circle. The idea of a circle is not something having a circumference and a centre, as a circle has; nor is the idea of a body that body itself. Now, as it is something different from its correlate, it is capable of being understood through itself; in other words, the idea, in so far as its actual essence (*essentia formalis*) is concerned, may be the subject of another subjective

11. By native strength, I mean that bestowed on us by external causes, as I shall afterwards explain in my philosophy.

12. I here term them operations: I shall explain their nature in my philosophy.

13. I shall take care not only to demonstrate what I have just advanced, but also that we have hitherto proceeded rightly, and other things needful to be known.

essence (*essentia objectiva*).[14] And, again, this second subjective essence will, regarded in itself, be something real, and capable of being understood; and so on, indefinitely. For instance, the man Peter is something real; the true idea of Peter is the reality of Peter represented subjectively, and is in itself something real, and quite distinct from the actual Peter. Now, as this true idea of Peter is in itself something real, and has its own individual existence, it will also be capable of being understood – that is, of being the subject of another idea, which will contain by representation (*objective*) all that the idea of Peter contains actually (*formaliter*). And, again, this idea of the idea of Peter has its own individuality, which may become the subject of yet another idea; and so on, indefinitely. This everyone may make trial of for himself, by reflecting that he knows what Peter is, and also knows that he knows, and further knows that he knows that he knows, &c. Hence it is plain that, in order to understand the actual Peter, it is not necessary first to understand the idea of Peter, and still less the idea of the idea of Peter. This is the same as saying that, in order to know, there is no need to know that we know, much less to know that we know that we know. This is no more necessary than to know the nature of a circle before knowing the nature of a triangle.[15] But, with these ideas, the contrary is the case: for, in order to know that I know, I must first know. Hence it is clear that certainty is nothing else than the subjective essence of a thing: in other words, the mode in which we perceive an actual reality is certainty. Further, it is also evident that, for the certitude of truth, no further sign is necessary beyond the possession of a true idea: for, as I have shown, it is not necessary to know that we know that we know. Hence, again, it is clear that no one can know the nature of the highest certainty, unless he possesses an adequate idea, or the subjective essence of a thing: for certainty is identical with such subjective essence. Thus, as the truth needs no sign – it being sufficient to possess the subjective essence of things, or, in other words, the ideas of them, in order that all doubts may be removed – it

14. In modern language, 'the idea may become the subject of another representation.' *Objectivus* generally corresponds to the modern 'subjective', *formalis* to the modern 'objective'. – [Tr.]

15. Observe that we are not here inquiring how this first subjective essence is innate to us. This belongs to an investigation into nature, where all these matters are amply explained, and it is shown that without ideas neither affirmation, nor negation, nor volition are possible.

follows that the true method does not consist in seeking for the signs of truth after the acquisition of the idea, but that the true method teaches us the order in which we should seek for truth itself,[16] or the subjective essences of things, or ideas, for all these expressions are synonymous. Again, method must necessarily be concerned with reasoning or understanding – I mean, method is not identical with reasoning in the search for causes, still less is it the comprehension of the causes of things: it is the discernment of a true idea, by distinguishing it from other perceptions, and by investigating its nature, in order that we may thus know our power of understanding, and may so train our mind that it may, by a given standard, comprehend whatsoever is intelligible, by laying down certain rules as aids, and by avoiding useless mental exertion.

Whence we may gather that method is nothing else than reflective knowledge, or the idea of an idea; and that as there can be no idea of an idea – unless an idea exists previously, – there can be no method without a pre-existent idea. Therefore, that will be a good method which shows us how the mind should be directed, according to the standard of the given true idea.

Again, seeing that the ratio existing between two ideas is the same as the ratio between the actual realities corresponding to those ideas, it follows that the reflective knowledge which has for its object the most perfect being is more excellent than reflective knowledge concerning other objects – in other words, that method will be most perfect which affords the standard of the given idea of the most perfect being whereby we may direct our mind. We thus easily understand how, in proportion as it acquires new ideas, the mind simultaneously acquires fresh instruments for pursuing its inquiries further. For we may gather from what has been said, that a true idea must necessarily first of all exist in us as a natural instrument; and that when this idea is apprehended by the mind, it enables us to understand the difference existing between itself and all other perceptions. In this, one part of the method consists.

Now it is clear that the mind apprehends itself better in proportion as it understands a greater number of natural objects; it follows, therefore, that this portion of the method will be more perfect in proportion as the mind attains to the comprehension of a greater number of objects, and that it will be absolutely perfect

16. The nature of mental search is explained in my philosophy.

when the mind gains a knowledge of the absolutely perfect being, or becomes conscious thereof. Again, the more things the mind knows, the better does it understand its own strength and the order of nature; by increased self-knowledge, it can direct itself more easily, and lay down rules for its own guidance; and, by increased knowledge of nature, it can more easily avoid what is useless.

And this is the sum total of method, as we have already stated. We may add that the idea in the world of thought is in the same case as its correlate in the world of reality. If, therefore, there be anything in nature which is without connection[17] with any other thing, and if we assign to it a subjective essence, which would in every way correspond to the objective reality, the subjective essence would have no connection with any other ideas – in other words, we could not draw any conclusion with regard to it. On the other hand, those things which are connected with others – as all things that exist in nature – will be understood by the mind, and their subjective essences will maintain the same mutual relations as their objective realities – that is to say, we shall infer from these ideas other ideas, which will in turn be connected with others, and thus our instruments for proceeding with our investigation will increase. This is what we were endeavouring to prove. Further, from what has just been said – namely, that an idea must, in all respects, correspond to its correlate in the world of reality, – it is evident that, in order to reproduce in every respect the faithful image of nature, our mind must deduce all its ideas from the idea which represents the origin and source of the whole of nature, so that it may itself become the source of other ideas.

It may, perhaps, provoke astonishment that, after having said that the good method is that which teaches us to direct our mind according to the standard of the given true idea, we should prove our point by reasoning, which would seem to indicate that it is not self-evident. We may, therefore, be questioned as to the validity of our reasoning. If our reasoning be sound, we must take as a starting-point a true idea. Now, to be certain that our starting-point is really a true idea, we need a proof. This first course of reasoning must be supported by a second, the second by a third, and so on to infinity. To this I make answer that, if by

17. To be connected with other things is to be produced by them, or to produce them.

some happy chance anyone had adopted this method in his investigations of nature – that is, if he had acquired new ideas in the proper order, according to the standard of the original true idea, he would never have doubted of the truth of his knowledge,[18] inasmuch as truth, as we have shown, makes itself manifest, and all things would flow, as it were, spontaneously towards him. But as this never, or rarely, happens, I have been forced so to arrange my proceedings, that we may acquire by reflection and forethought what we cannot acquire by chance, and that it may at the same time appear that, for proving the truth, and for valid reasoning, we need no other means than the truth and valid reasoning themselves: for by valid reasoning I have established valid reasoning, and, in like measure, I seek still to establish it. Moreover, this is the order of thinking adopted by men in their inward meditations. The reasons for its rare employment in investigations of nature are to be found in current misconceptions, whereof we shall examine the causes hereafter in our philosophy. Moreover, it demands, as we shall show, a keen and accurate discernment. Lastly, it is hindered by the conditions of human life, which are, as we have already pointed out, extremely changeable. There are also other obstacles, which we will not here inquire into.

If anyone asks why I have not at the starting-point set forth all the truths of nature in their due order, inasmuch as truth is self-evident, I reply by warning him not to reject as false any paradoxes he may find here, but to take the trouble to reflect on the chain of reasoning by which they are supported; he will then be no longer in doubt that we have attained to the truth. This is why I have begun as above.

If there yet remains some sceptic, who doubts of our primary truth, and of all deductions we make, taking such truth as our standard, he must either be arguing in bad faith, or we must confess that there are men in complete mental blindness, either innate or due to misconceptions – that is, to some external influence.

Such persons are not conscious of themselves. If they affirm or doubt anything, they know not that they affirm or doubt: they say that they know nothing, and they say that they are ignorant of the very fact of their knowing nothing. Even this they

18. In the same way as we have here no doubt of the truth of our knowledge.

do not affirm absolutely, they are afraid of confessing that they exist, so long as they know nothing; in fact, they ought to remain dumb, for fear of haply supposing something which should smack of truth. Lastly, with such persons, one should not speak of sciences: for, in what relates to life and conduct, they are compelled by necessity to suppose that they exist, and seek their own advantage, and often affirm and deny, even with an oath. If they deny, grant, or gainsay, they know not that they deny, grant or gainsay, so that they ought to be regarded as automata, utterly devoid of intelligence.

Let us now return to our proposition. Up to the present, we have, first, defined the end to which we desire to direct all our thoughts; secondly, we have determined the mode of perception best adapted to aid us in attaining our perfection; thirdly, we have discovered the way which our mind should take, in order to make a good beginning – namely, that it should use every true idea as a standard in pursuing its inquiries according to fixed rules. Now, in order that it may thus proceed, our method must furnish us, first, with a means of distinguishing a true idea from all other perceptions, and enabling the mind to avoid the latter; secondly, with rules for perceiving unknown things according to the standard of the true idea; thirdly, with an order which enables us to avoid useless labour. When we became acquainted with this method, we saw that, fourthly, it would be perfect when we had attained to the idea of the absolutely perfect Being. This is an observation which should be made at the outset, in order that we may arrive at the knowledge of such a being more quickly.

* * *

There follows a section on 'the first part of the method', which is 'to distinguish and separate the true idea from other perceptions, and to keep the mind from confusing with true ideas those which are false, fictitious and doubtful.' Two remarks in it are especially noteworthy. 'As regards that which constitutes the reality of truth, it is certain that a true idea is distinguished from a false one, not so much by its extrinsic object as by its intrinsic nature.' 'Thus falsity *consists only in this, that something is affirmed of a thing, which is not contained in the conception we have formed of that thing.'*]

* * *

Now, in order at length to pass on to the second part of this method,[19] I shall first set forth the object aimed at, and next the means for its attainment. The object aimed at is the acquisition of clear and distinct ideas, such as are produced by the pure intellect, and not by chance physical motions. In order that all ideas may be reduced to unity, we shall endeavour so to associate and arrange them that our mind may, as far as possible, reflect subjectively the reality of nature, both as a whole and as parts.

As for the first point, it is necessary (as we have said) for our purpose that everything should be conceived, either *solely through its essence*, or *through its proximate cause*. If the thing be self-existent, or, as is commonly said, the cause of itself, it must be understood through its essence only; if it be not self-existent, but requires a cause for its existence, it must be understood through its proximate cause. For, in reality, the knowledge of an effect is nothing else than the acquisition of more perfect knowledge of its cause.[20] Therefore, we may never, while we are concerned with inquiries into actual things, draw any conclusion from abstractions; we shall be extremely careful not to confound that which is only in the understanding with that which is in the thing itself. The best basis for drawing a conclusion will be either some particular affirmative essence, or a true and legitimate definition. For the understanding cannot descend from universal axioms by themselves to particular things, since axioms are of infinite extent, and do not determine the understanding to contemplate one particular thing more than another. Thus the true method of discovery is to form thoughts from some given definition. This process will be the more fruitful and easy in proportion as the thing given be better defined. Wherefore, the cardinal point of all this second part of method consists in the knowledge of the conditions of good definition, and the means of finding them. I will first treat of the conditions of definition.

A definition, if it is to be called perfect, must explain the inmost essence of a thing, and must take care not to substitute for this any of its properties. In order to illustrate my meaning,

19. The chief rule of this part is, as appears from the first part, to review all the ideas coming to us through pure intellect, so as to distinguish them from such as we imagine: the distinction will be shown through the properties of each, namely, of the imagination and of the understanding.

20. Observe that it is hereby manifest that we cannot understand anything of nature without at the same time increasing our knowledge of the first cause, or God.

without taking an example which would seem to show a desire to expose other people's errors, I will choose the case of something abstract, the definition of which is of little moment. Such is a circle. If a circle be defined as a figure, such that all straight lines drawn from the centre to the circumference are equal, every one can see that such a definition does not in the least explain the essence of a circle, but solely one of its properties. Though, as I have said, this is of no importance in the case of figures and other abstractions, it is of great importance in the case of physical beings and realities: for the properties of things are not understood so long as their essences are unknown. If the latter be passed over, there is necessarily a perversion of the succession of ideas which should reflect the succession of nature, and we go far astray from our object.

In order to be free from this fault, the following rules should be observed in definition:

I. If the thing in question be created, the definition must (as we have said) comprehend the proximate cause. For instance, a circle should, according to this rule, be defined as follows: the figure described by any line whereof one end is fixed and the other free. This definition clearly comprehends the proximate cause.

II. A conception or definition of a thing should be such that all the properties of that thing, in so far as it is considered by itself, and not in conjunction with other things, can be deduced from it, as may be seen in the definition given of a circle: for from that it clearly follows that all straight lines drawn from the centre to the circumference are equal. That this is a necessary characteristic of a definition is so clear to anyone, who reflects on the matter, that there is no need to spend time in proving it, or in showing that, owing to this second condition, every definition should be affirmative. I speak of intellectual affirmation, giving little thought to verbal affirmations which, owing to the poverty of language, must sometimes, perhaps, be expressed negatively, though the idea contained is affirmative.

The rules for the definition of an uncreated thing are as follows:

I. The exclusion of all idea of cause – that is, the thing must not need explanation by anything outside itself.

II. When the definition of the thing has been given, there must be no room for doubt as to whether the thing exists or not.

III. It must contain, as far as the mind is concerned, no substantives which could be put into an adjectival form; in other words, the object defined must not be explained through abstractions.

IV. Lastly, though this is not absolutely necessary, it should be possible to deduce from the definition all the properties of the thing defined.

All these rules become obvious to anyone giving strict attention to the matter.

I have also stated that the best basis for drawing a conclusion is a particular affirmative essence. The more specialized the idea is, the more is it distinct, and therefore clear. Wherefore a knowledge of particular things should be sought for as diligently as possible.

As regards the order of our perceptions, and the manner in which they should be arranged and united, it is necessary that, as soon as is possible and rational, we should inquire whether there be any being (and, if so, what being), that is the cause of all things, so that its essence, represented in thought, may be the cause of all our ideas, and then our mind will to the utmost possible extent reflect nature. For it will possess, subjectively, nature's essence, order, and union. Thus we can see that it is before all things necessary for us to deduce all our ideas from physical things – that is, from real entities, proceeding, as far as may be, according to the series of causes, from one real entity to another real entity, never passing to universals and abstractions, either for the purpose of deducing some real entity from them, or deducing them from some real entity. Either of these processes interrupts the true progress of the understanding. But it must be observed that, by the series of causes and real entities, I do not here mean the series of particular and mutable things, but only the series of fixed and eternal things. It would be impossible for human infirmity to follow up the series of particular mutable things, both on account of their multitude, surpassing all calculation, and on account of the infinitely diverse circumstances surrounding one and the same thing, any one of which may be the cause for its existence or non-existence. Indeed, their existence has no connection with their essence, or (as we have said already) is not an eternal truth. Neither is there any need that we should understand their series, for the essences of particular mutable things are not to be gathered from their series or order of existence, which would furnish us with nothing beyond their extrinsic denominations, their relations, or, at most, their circumstances, all of which are very different from their inmost essence. This inmost essence must be sought solely from fixed and eternal things, and from the laws, inscribed (so to speak) in those things as in their true codes, according to which all particular things take place and are arranged; nay, these mutable particular things depend so intimately and essentially (so to phrase it) upon the fixed things, that they cannot either be or be conceived without them.

Whence these fixed and eternal things, though they are themselves particular, will nevertheless, owing to their presence and power everywhere, be to us as universals, or genera of definitions of particular mutable things, and as the proximate causes of all things.

But, though this be so, there seems to be no small difficulty in arriving at the knowledge of these particular things, for to conceive them all at once would far surpass the powers of the human understanding. The arrangement whereby one thing is understood before another, as we have stated, should not be sought from their series of existence, nor from eternal things. For the latter are all by nature simultaneous. Other aids are therefore needed besides those employed for understanding eternal things and their laws; however, this is not the place to recount such aids, nor is there any need to do so, until we have acquired a sufficient knowledge of eternal things and their infallible laws, and until the nature of our senses has become plain to us.

Before betaking ourselves to seek knowledge of particular things, it will be seasonable to speak of such aids, as all tend to teach us the mode of employing our senses, and to make certain experiments under fixed rules and arrangement which may suffice to determine the object of our inquiry, so that we may therefrom infer what laws of eternal things it has been produced under, and may gain an insight into its inmost nature, as I will duly show. Here, to return to my purpose, I will only endeavour to set forth what seems necessary for enabling us to attain to knowledge of eternal things, and to define them under the conditions laid down above.

With this end, we must bear in mind what has already been stated, namely, that when the mind devotes itself to any thought, so as to examine it, and to deduce therefrom in due order all the legitimate conclusions possible, any falsehood which may lurk in the thought will be detected; but if the thought be true, the mind will readily proceed without interruption to deduce truths from it. This, I say, is necessary for our purpose, for our thoughts may be brought to a close by the absence of a foundation. If, therefore, we wish to investigate the first thing of all, it will be necessary to supply some foundation which may direct our thoughts thither. Further, since method is reflective knowledge, the foundation which must direct our thoughts can be nothing else than the knowledge of that which constitutes the reality of truth, and the knowledge of the understanding, its properties, and powers. When this has been acquired we shall possess a foundation wherefrom we can deduce our thoughts, and a path whereby the intellect, according to its capacity, may attain the knowledge of eternal things, allowance being made for the extent of the intellectual powers.

If, as I stated in the first part, it belongs to the nature of thought to form true ideas, we must here inquire what is meant by the faculties and power of the understanding. The chief part of our method is to understand as well as possible the powers of the intellect, and its nature; we are, therefore, compelled (by the considerations advanced in the second part of the method) necessarily to draw these conclusions from the definition itself of thought and understanding. But, so far, we have not got any rules for finding definitions, and, as we cannot set forth such rules without a previous knowledge of nature, that is without a definition of the understanding and its power, it follows either that the definition of the understanding must be clear in itself or that we can understand nothing. Nevertheless this definition is not absolutely clear in itself; however, since its properties, like all things that we possess through the understanding, cannot be known clearly and distinctly, unless its nature be known previously, the definition of the understanding makes itself manifest, if we pay attention to its properties, which we know clearly and distinctly. Let us, then, enumerate here the properties of the understanding, let us examine them, and begin by discussing the instruments for research which we find innate in us.

The properties of the understanding which I have chiefly remarked, and which I clearly understand, are the following:

1. It involves certainty – in other words, it knows that a thing exists in reality as it is reflected subjectively.

II. That it perceives certain things, or forms some ideas absolutely, some ideas from others. Thus it forms the idea of quantity absolutely, without reference to any other thoughts; but ideas of motion it only forms after taking into consideration the idea of quantity.

III. Those ideas which the understanding forms absolutely express infinity; determinate ideas are derived from other ideas. Thus in the idea of quantity, perceived by means of a cause, the quantity is determined, as when a body is perceived to be formed by the motion of a plane, a plane by the motion of a line, or, again, a line by the motion of a point. All these are perceptions which do not serve towards understanding quantity, but only towards determining it. This is proved by the fact that we conceive them as formed as it were by motion, yet this motion is not perceived unless the quantity be perceived also; we can even prolong the motion so as to form an infinite line, which we certainly could not do unless we had an idea of infinite quantity.

IV. The understanding forms positive ideas before forming negative ideas.

V. It perceives things not so much under the condition of duration as under a certain form of eternity, and in an infinite number; or rather in perceiving things it does not consider either their number or duration, whereas, in imagining them, it perceives them in a determinate number, duration, and quantity.

VI. The ideas which we form as clear and distinct, seem so to follow from the sole necessity of our nature, that they appear to depend absolutely on our sole power; with confused ideas the contrary is the case. They are often formed against our will.

VII. The mind can determine in many ways the ideas of things, which the understanding forms from other ideas: thus, for instance, in order to define the plane of an ellipse, it supposes a point adhering to a cord to be moved round two centres, or, again, it conceives an infinity of points, always in the same fixed relation to a given straight line, or a cone cut in an oblique plane, so that the angle of inclination is greater than the angle of the vertex of the cone, or in an infinity of other ways.

VIII. The more ideas express perfection of any object, the more perfect are they themselves; for we do not admire the architect who has planned a chapel so much as the architect who has planned a splendid temple.

I do not stop to consider the rest of what is referred to thought, such as love, joy, &c. They are nothing to our present purpose, and cannot even be conceived unless the understanding be perceived previously. When perception is removed, all these go with it.

False and fictitious ideas have nothing positive about them (as we have abundantly shown), which causes them to be called false or fictitious; they are only considered as such through the defectiveness of knowledge. Therefore, false and fictitious ideas as such can teach us nothing concerning the essence of thought; this must be sought from the positive properties just enumerated; in other words, we must lay down some common basis from which these properties necessarily follow, so that when this is given, the properties are necessarily given also, and when it is removed, they too vanish with it.

The rest of the treatise is wanting.

The Ethics, 1677

PART I CONCERNING GOD

Definitions

I. By that which is *self-caused*, I mean that of which the essence involves existence, or that of which the nature is only conceivable as existent.

II. A thing is called *finite after its kind*, when it can be limited by another thing of the same nature; for instance, a body is called finite because we always conceive another greater body. So, also, a thought is limited by another thought, but a body is not limited by thought, nor a thought by body.

III. By *substance*, I mean that which is in itself, and is conceived through itself: in other words, that of which a conception can be formed independently of any other conception.

IV. By *attribute*, I mean that which the intellect perceives as constituting the essence of substance.

V. By *mode*, I mean the modifications[21] of substance, or that which exists in, and is conceived through, something other than itself.

VI. By *God*, I mean a being absolutely infinite – that is, a substance consisting in infinite attributes, of which each

21. '*Affectiones*.'

expresses eternal and infinite essentiality.

Explanation. I say absolutely infinite, not infinite after its kind: for, of a thing infinite only after its kind, infinite attributes may be denied; but that which is absolutely infinite, contains in its essence whatever expresses reality, and involves no negation.

VII. That thing is called free, which exists solely by the necessity of its own nature, and of which the action is determined by itself alone. On the other hand, that thing is necessary, or rather constrained, which is determined by something external to itself to a fixed and definite method of existence or action.

VIII. By *eternity*, I mean existence itself, in so far as it is conceived necessarily to follow solely from the definition of that which is eternal.

Explanation. Existence of this kind is conceived as an eternal truth, like the essence of a thing, and, therefore, cannot be explained by means of continuance or time, though continuance may be conceived without a beginning or end.

Axioms

I. Everything which exists, exists either in itself or in something else.

II. That which cannot be conceived through anything else must be conceived through itself.

III. From a given definite cause an effect necessarily follows; and, on the other hand, if no definite cause be granted, it is impossible that an effect can follow.

IV. The knowledge of an effect depends on and involves the knowledge of a cause.

V. Things which have nothing in common cannot be understood, the one by means of the other; the conception of one does not involve the conception of the other.

VI. A true idea must correspond with its ideate or object.

VII. If a thing can be conceived as non-existing, its essence does not involve existence.

Propositions

PROP. I. *Substance is by nature prior to its modifications.*

Proof. This is clear from Deff. iii and v.

PROP. II. *Two substances, whose attributes are different, have nothing in common.*

Proof. Also evident from Def. iii. For each must exist in itself, and be conceived through itself; in other words, the conception of one does not imply the conception of the other.

PROP. III. *Things which have nothing in common cannot be one the cause of the other.*

Proof. If they have nothing in common, it follows that one cannot be apprehended by means of the other (Ax. v), and, therefore, one cannot be the cause of the other (Ax. iv). *Q.E.D.*

PROP. IV. *Two or more distinct things are distinguished one from the other, either by the difference of the attributes of the substances, or by the difference of their modifications.*

Proof. Everything which exists, exists either in itself or in something else (Ax. i), that is (by Deff. iii and v), nothing is granted in addition to the understanding, except substance and its modifications. Nothing is, therefore, given besides the understanding, by which several things may be distinguished one from the other, except the substances, or, in other words (see Ax. iv), their attributes and modifications. *Q.E.D.*

PROP. V. *There cannot exist in the universe two or more substances having the same nature or attribute.*

Proof. If several distinct substances be granted, they must be distinguished one from the other, either by the difference of their attributes, or by the difference of their modifications (Prop. iv). If only by the difference of their attributes, it will be granted that there cannot be more than one with an identical attribute. If by the difference of their modifications – as substance is naturally prior to its modifications (Prop. i), – it follows that setting the modifications aside, and considering substance in itself, that is truly, (Deff. iii and vi), there cannot be conceived one substance different from another, – that is (by Prop. iv), there cannot be granted several substances, but one substance only. *Q.E.D.*

PROP. VI. *One substance cannot be produced by another substance.*

Proof. It is impossible that there should be in the universe two substances with an identical attribute, *i.e.* which have anything common to them both (Prop. ii), and, therefore (Prop. iii), one cannot be the cause of another, neither can one be produced by the other. *Q.E.D.*

Corollary. Hence it follows that a substance cannot be produced by anything external to itself. For in the universe nothing is granted, save substances and their modifications (as appears from Ax. i and Deff. iii and v). Now (by the last Prop.) substance cannot be produced by another substance, therefore it cannot be produced by anything external to itself. *Q.E.D.* This is shown still more readily by the absurdity of the contradictory. For, if substance be produced by an external cause, the knowledge of it would depend on the knowledge of its cause (Ax. iv), and (by Def. iii) it would itself not be substance.

PROP. VII. *Existence belongs to the nature of substance.*

Proof. Substance cannot be produced by anything external (Corollary, Prop. vi), it must, therefore, be its own cause – that is, its essence necessarily involves existence, or existence belongs to its nature.

PROP. VIII. *Every substance is necessarily infinite.*

Proof. There can only be one substance with an identical attribute, and existence follows from its nature (Prop. vii); its nature, therefore, involves existence, either as finite or infinite. It does not exist as finite, for (by Def. ii) it would then be limited by something else of the same kind, which would also necessarily exist (Prop. vii); and there would be two substances with an identical attribute, which is absurd (Prop. v). It therefore exists as infinite. *Q.E.D.*

Note I. As finite existence involves a partial negation, and infinite existence is the absolute affirmation of the given nature, it follows (solely from Prop. vii) that every substance is necessarily infinite.

Note II. No doubt it will be difficult for those who think about things loosely, and have not been accustomed to know them by their primary causes, to comprehend the demonstration of Prop. vii: for such persons make no distinction between the modifications of substances and the substances themselves, and are ignorant of the manner in which things are produced; hence they attribute to substances the beginning which they observe in natural objects. Those who are ignorant of true causes, make complete confusion – think that trees might talk just as well as men – that men might be formed from stones as well as from seed; and imagine that any form might be changed into any other. So, also, those who confuse the two natures, divine and human, readily attribute human passions to the deity, especially so long as they do not know how passions originate in the mind. But, if people would consider the nature of substance, they would have no doubt about the truth of Prop. vii. In fact, this proposition would be a universal axiom, and accounted a truism. For, by substance, would be understood that which is in itself, and is conceived through itself – that is, something of which the conception requires not the conception of anything else; whereas modifications exist in something external to themselves, and a conception of them is formed by means of a conception of the thing in which they exist. Therefore, we may have true ideas of non-existent modifications; for, although they may have no *actual* existence apart from the conceiving intellect, yet their essence is so involved in something external to themselves that they may through it be conceived. Whereas the only truth substances can have, external to the intellect, must consist in their existence, because they are conceived through themselves. Therefore, for a person to say that he has a clear and distinct – that is, a true – idea of a substance, but that he is not sure whether such substance exists, would be the same as if he said that he had a true idea, but was not sure whether or no it was false (a little consideration will make this plain); or if anyone affirmed that substance is created, it would be the same as saying that a false idea was true – in short, the height of absurdity. It must, then, necessarily be admitted that the existence of substance as its essence is an eternal truth. And we can hence conclude by another process of reasoning – that there is but one such substance. I think that this may profitably be done at once; and, in order to proceed regularly with the demonstration, we must premise:

1. The true definition of a thing neither involves nor expresses anything beyond the nature of the thing defined. From this it follows that –

2. No definition implies or expresses a certain number of individuals, inasmuch as it expresses nothing beyond the nature of the thing defined. For instance, the definition of a triangle expresses nothing beyond the actual nature of a triangle: it does not imply any fixed number of triangles.

3. There is necessarily for each individual existent thing a cause why it should exist.

4. This cause of existence must either be contained in the nature and definition of the thing defined, or must be postulated apart from such definition.

It therefore follows that, if a given number of individual things exist in nature, there must be some cause for the existence of exactly that number, neither more nor less. For example, if twenty men exist in the universe (for simplicity's sake, I will suppose them existing simultaneously, and to have had no predecessors), and we want to account for the existence of these twenty men, it will not be enough to show the cause of human existence in general; we must also show why there are exactly twenty men, neither more nor less: for a cause must be assigned for the existence of each individual. Now this cause cannot be contained in the actual nature of man, for the true definition of man does not involve any consideration of the number twenty. Consequently, the cause for the existence of these twenty men, and, consequently, of each of them, must necessarily be sought externally to each individual. Hence we may lay down the absolute rule, that everything which may consist of several individuals must have an external cause. And, as it has been shown already that existence appertains to the nature of substance, existence must necessarily be included in its definition; and from its definition alone existence must be deducible. But from its definition (as we have shown, Notes ii, iii), we cannot infer the existence of several substances; therefore it follows that there is only one substance of the same nature. *Q.E.D.*

PROP. IX. *The more reality or being a thing has the greater the number of its attributes* (Def. iv).

PROP. X. *Each particular attribute of the one substance must be conceived through itself.*

Proof. An attribute is that which the intellect perceives of substance, as constituting its essence (Def. iv), and, therefore, must be conceived through itself (Def. iii). *Q.E.D.*

Note. It is thus evident that, though two attributes are, in fact, conceived as distinct – that is, one without the help of the other – yet we cannot, therefore, conclude that they constitute two entities, or two different substances. For it is the nature of substance that each of its attributes is conceived through itself, inasmuch as all the attributes it has have always existed simultaneously in it, and none could be produced by any other; but each expresses the reality or being of substance. It is, then, far from an absurdity to ascribe several attributes to one substance: for nothing in nature is more clear than that each and every entity must be conceived under some attribute, and that its reality or being is in proportion to the number of its attributes expressing necessity or eternity and infinity. Consequently it is abundantly clear, that an absolutely infinite being must necessarily be defined as consisting in infinite attributes, each of which expresses a certain eternal and infinite essence.

If anyone now ask, by what sign shall he be able to distinguish different substances, let him read the following propositions, which show that there is but one substance in the universe, and that it is absolutely infinite, wherefore such a sign would be sought for in vain.

PROP. XI. *God, or substance, consisting of infinite attributes, of which each expresses eternal and infinite essentiality, necessarily exists.*

Proof. If this be denied, conceive, if possible, that God does not exist: then his essence does not involve existence. But this (by Prop. vii) is absurd. Therefore God necessarily exists.

Another proof. Of everything whatsoever a cause or reason must be assigned, either for its existence, or for its non-existence – *e.g.* if a triangle exist, a reason or cause must be granted for its existence; if, on the contrary, it does not exist, a cause must also be granted, which prevents it from existing, or annuls its existence. This reason or cause must either be contained in the nature of the thing in question, or be external to it. For instance, the reason for the non-existence of a square circle is indicated in its nature, namely, because it would involve a contradiction. On the other hand, the existence of substance follows also solely from its nature, inasmuch as its nature involves existence. (See Prop. vii.)

But the reason for the existence of a triangle or a circle does not follow from the nature of those figures, but from the order of universal nature in extension. From the latter it must follow, either that a triangle necessarily exists, or that it is impossible that it should exist. So much is self-evident. It follows therefrom that a thing necessarily exists, if no cause or reason be granted which prevents its existence.

If, then, no cause or reason can be given, which prevents the existence of God, or which destroys his existence, we must certainly conclude that he necessarily does exist. If such a reason or cause should be given, it must either be drawn from the very nature of God, or be external to him – that is, drawn from another substance of another nature. For if it were of the same nature, God, by that very fact, would be admitted to exist. But substance of another nature could have nothing in common with God (by Prop. ii), and therefore would be unable either to cause or to destroy his existence.

As, then, a reason or cause which would annul the divine existence cannot be drawn from anything external to the divine nature, such cause must perforce, if God does not exist, be drawn from God's own nature, which would involve a contradiction. To make such an affirmation about a being absolutely infinite and supremely perfect, is absurd; therefore, neither in the nature of God, nor externally to his nature, can a cause or reason be assigned which would annul his existence. Therefore, God necessarily exists. *Q.E.D.*

Another proof. The potentiality of non-existence is a negation of power, and contrariwise the potentiality of existence is a power, as is obvious. If, then, that which necessarily exists is nothing but finite beings, such finite beings are more powerful than a being absolutely infinite, which is obviously absurd; therefore, either nothing exists, or else a being absolutely infinite necessarily exists also. Now we exist either in ourselves, or in something else which necessarily exists (see Axiom i and Prop. vii). Therefore a being absolutely infinite – in other words, God (Def. vi) – necessarily exists. *Q.E.D.*

Note. In this last proof, I have purposely shown God's existence *à posteriori*, so that the proof might be more easily followed, not because, from the same premises, God's existence does not follow *à priori*. For, as the potentiality of existence is a power, it follows that, in proportion as reality increases in the nature of a thing, so also will it increase its strength for existence. Therefore a being absolutely infinite, such as God, has from himself an absolutely infinite power of existence, and hence he does absolutely exist. Perhaps there will be many who will be unable to see the force of this proof, inasmuch as they are accustomed only to consider those things which flow from external causes. Of such things, they see that those which quickly come to pass – that is, quickly come into existence – quickly also disappear; whereas they regard as more difficult of accomplishment – that is, not so easily brought into existence – those things which they conceive as more complicated.

However, to do away with this misconception, I need not here show the measure of truth in the proverb, 'What comes quickly, goes quickly,' nor discuss whether, from the point of view of universal nature, all things are equally easy, or otherwise: I need only remark, that I am not here speaking of things, which come to pass through causes external to themselves, but only of substances which (by Prop. vi) cannot be produced by any external cause. Things which are produced by external causes, whether they consist of many parts or few, owe whatsoever perfection or reality they possess solely to the efficacy of their external cause, and therefore their existence arises solely from the perfection of their external cause, not from their own. Contrariwise, whatsoever perfection is possessed by substance is due to no external cause; wherefore the existence of substance must arise solely from its own nature, which is nothing else but its essence. Thus, the perfection of a thing does not annul its existence, but, on the contrary, asserts it. Imperfection, on the other hand, does annul it; therefore we cannot be more certain of the existence of anything, than of the existence of a being absolutely infinite or perfect – that is, of God. For inasmuch as his essence excludes all imperfection, and involves absolute perfection, all cause for doubt concerning his existence is done away, and the utmost certainty on the question is given. This, I think, will be evident to every moderately attentive reader.

PROP. XII. *No attribute of substance can be conceived from which it would follow that substance can be divided.*

Proof. The parts into which substance as thus conceived would be divided, either will retain the nature of substance, or they will not. If the former, then (by Prop. viii) each part will necessarily be infinite, and (by Prop. vi) self-caused, and (by Prop. v) will perforce consist of a different attribute, so that, in that case, several substances could be formed out of one substance, which (by Prop. vi) is absurd. Moreover, the parts (by Prop. ii) would have nothing in common with their whole, and the whole (by Def. iv and Prop. x) could both exist and be conceived without its parts, which everyone will admit to be absurd. If we adopt the second alternative – namely, that the parts will not retain the nature of substance – then, if the whole substance were divided into equal parts, it would lose the nature of substance, and would cease to exist, which (by Prop. vii) is absurd.

PROP. XIII. *Substance absolutely infinite is indivisible.*

Proof. If it could be divided, the parts into which it was divided would either retain the nature of absolutely infinite substance, or they would not. If the former, we should have several substances of the same nature, which (by Prop. v) is absurd. If the latter, then (by Prop. vii) substance absolutely infinite could cease to exist, which (by Prop. xi) is also absurd.

Corollary. It follows, that no substance, and consequently no extended substance, in so far as it is substance, is divisible.

Note. The indivisibility of substance may be more easily understood as follows. The nature of substance can only be conceived as infinite, and by a part of substance, nothing else can be understood than finite substance, which (by Prop. viii) involves a manifest contradiction.

PROP. XIV. *Besides God no substance can be granted or conceived.*

Proof. As God is a being absolutely infinite, of whom no attribute that expresses the essence of substance can be denied (by Def. vi), and he necessarily exists (by Prop. xi); if any substance besides God were granted, it would have to be explained by some attribute of God, and thus two substances with the same attribute would exist, which (by Prop. v) is absurd; therefore, besides God no substance can be granted, or, consequently, be conceived. If it could be conceived, it would necessarily have to be conceived as existent; but this (by the first part of this proof) is absurd. Therefore, besides God no substance can be granted or conceived. *Q.E.D.*

Corollary I. Clearly, therefore: 1. God is one, that is (by Def. vi) only one substance can be granted in the universe, and that substance is absolutely infinite, as we have already indicated (in the note to Prop. x).

Corollary II. It follows: 2. That extension and thought are either attributes of God or (by Ax. i) accidents (*affectiones*) of the attributes of God.

PROP. XV. *Whatsoever is, is in God, and without God nothing can be, or be conceived.*

Proof. Besides God, no substance is granted or can be conceived (by Prop. XIV), that is (by Def. iii) nothing which is in itself and is conceived through itself. But modes (by Def. v) can neither be, nor be conceived without substance; wherefore they can only be in the divine nature, and can only through it be conceived. But substances and modes form the sum total of existence (by Ax. i), therefore, without God nothing can be, or be conceived. *Q.E.D.*

Note. Some assert that God, like a man, consists of body and mind, and is susceptible of passions. How far such persons have strayed from the truth is sufficiently evident from what has been said. But these I pass over. For all who have in anywise reflected on the divine nature deny that God has a body. Of this they find excellent proof in the fact that we understand by body a definite quantity, so long, so broad, so deep, bounded by a certain shape, and it is the height of absurdity to predicate such a thing of God, a being absolutely infinite. But meanwhile by the other reasons with which they try to prove their point, they show that they think corporeal or extended substance wholly apart from the divine nature, and say it was created by God. Wherefrom the divine nature can have been created, they are wholly ignorant; thus they clearly show, that they do not know the meaning of their own words. I myself have proved sufficiently clearly, at any rate in my own judgment (Corroll. Prop. vi, and Note 2, Prop. viii), that no substance can be produced or created by anything other than itself. Further, I showed (in Prop. xiv), that besides God no substance can be granted or conceived. Hence we drew the conclusion that extended substance is one of the infinite attributes of God. However, in order to explain more fully, I will refute the arguments of my adversaries, which all start from the following points:

Extended substance, in so far as it is substance, consists, as they think, in parts, wherefore they deny that it can be infinite, or, consequently, that it can appertain to God. This they illustrate with many examples, of which I will take one or two. If extended substance, they say, is infinite, let it be conceived to be divided into two parts; each part will then be either finite or infinite. If the former, then infinite substance is composed of two finite parts, which is absurd. If the latter, then one infinite will be twice as large as another infinite, which is also absurd.

Further, if an infinite line be measured out in foot lengths, it will consist of an infinite number of such parts; it would equally consist of an infinite number of parts, if each part measured only an inch: therefore, one infinity would be twelve times as great as the other.

Lastly, if from a single point there be conceived to be drawn two diverging lines which at first are at a definite distance apart, but are produced to infinity, it is certain that the distance between the two lines will be continually increased, until at length it changes from definite to indefinable. As these absurdities follow, it is said, from considering quantity as infinite, the conclusion is drawn, that extended substance must necessarily be finite, and, consequently, cannot appertain to the nature of God.

The second argument is also drawn from God's supreme perfection. God, it is said, inasmuch as he is a supremely perfect being, cannot be passive; but extended substance, in so far as it is divisible, is passive. It follows, therefore, that extended substance does not appertain to the essence of God.

Such are the arguments I find on the subject in writers, who by them try to prove that extended substance is unworthy of the divine nature, and cannot possibly appertain thereto. However, I think an attentive reader will see that I have already answered their propositions; for all their arguments are founded on the hypothesis that extended substance is composed of parts, and such a hypothesis I have shown (Prop. xii, and Coroll. Prop. xiii) to be absurd. Moreover, anyone who reflects will see that all these absurdities (if absurdities they be, which I am not now discussing), from which it is sought to extract the conclusion that extended substance is finite, do not at all follow from the notion of an infinite quantity, but merely from the notion that an infinite quantity is measurable, and composed of finite parts: therefore, the only fair conclusion to be drawn is that infinite quantity is not measurable, and cannot be composed of finite parts. This is exactly what we have already proved (in Prop. xii). Wherefore the weapon which they aimed at us has in reality recoiled upon themselves. If, from this absurdity of theirs, they persist in drawing the conclusion that extended substance must be finite, they will in good sooth be acting like a man who asserts that circles have the properties of squares, and, finding himself thereby landed in absurdities, proceeds to deny that circles have any centre, from which all lines drawn to the circumference are equal. For, taking extended substance, which can only be conceived as infinite, one, and indivisible (Props. viii, v, xii) they assert, in order to prove that it is finite, that it is composed of finite parts, and that it can be multiplied and divided.

So, also, others, after asserting that a line is composed of points, can produce many arguments to prove that a line cannot be infinitely divided. Assuredly it is not less absurd to assert that extended substance is made up of bodies or parts, than it would be to assert that a solid is made up of surfaces, a surface of lines, and a line of points. This must be admitted by all who know clear reason to be infallible, and most of all by those who deny the possibility of a vacuum. For if extended substance could be so divided that its parts were really separate, why should not one part admit of being destroyed, the others remaining joined together as before? And why should all be so fitted into one another as to leave no vacuum? Surely in the case of things, which are really distinct one from the other, one can exist without the other, and can remain in its original condition. As, then, there does not exist a vacuum in nature (of which anon), but all parts are bound to come together to prevent it, it follows from this also that the parts cannot be really distinguished, and that extended substance in so far as it is substance cannot be divided.

If anyone asks me the further question, Why are we naturally so prone to divide quantity? I answer, that quantity is conceived by us in two ways; in the abstract and superficially, as we imagine it; or as substance, as we conceive it solely by the intellect. If, then, we regard quantity as it is represented in our imagination, which we often and more easily do, we shall find that it is finite, divisible, and compounded of parts; but if we regard it as it is represented in our intellect, and conceive it as substance, which it is very difficult to do, we shall then, as I have sufficiently proved, find that it is infinite, one, and indivisible. This will be plain enough to all, who make a distinction between the intellect and the imagination, especially if it be remembered, that matter is everywhere the same, that its parts are not distinguishable, except in so far as we conceive matter as diversely modified, whence its parts are distinguished, not really, but modally. For instance, water, in so far as it is water, we conceive to be divided, and its parts to be separated one from the other; but not in so far as it is extended substance; from this point of view it is neither separated nor divisible. Further, water, in so far as it is water, is produced and corrupted; but, in so far as it is substance, it is neither produced nor corrupted.

I think I have now answered the second argument; it is, in fact, founded on the same assumption as the first – namely, that matter, in so far as it is substance, is divisible, and composed of parts. Even if it were so, I do not know why it should be considered unworthy of the divine nature, inasmuch as besides God (by Prop. xiv) no substance can be granted, wherefrom it could receive its modifications. All things, I repeat, are in God, and all things which come to pass, come to pass solely through the laws of the infinite nature of God, and follow (as I will shortly show) from the necessity of his essence. Wherefore it can in nowise be said, that God is passive in respect to anything other than himself, or that extended substance is unworthy of the Divine nature, even if it be supposed divisible, so long as it is granted to be infinite and eternal. But enough of this for the present.

PROP. XVI. *From the necessity of the divine nature must follow an infinite number of things in infinite ways – that is, all things which can fall within the sphere of infinite intellect.*

Proof. This proposition will be clear to everyone, who remembers that from the given definition of any thing the intellect infers several properties, which really necessarily follow therefrom (that is, from the actual essence of the thing defined); and it infers more properties in proportion as the definition of the thing expresses more reality, that is, in proportion as the essence of the thing defined involves more reality. Now, as the divine nature has absolutely infinite attributes (by Def. vi), of which each expresses infinite essence after its kind, it follows that from the necessity of its nature an infinite number of things (that is, everything which can fall within the sphere of an infinite intellect) must necessarily follow. *Q.E.D.*

Corollary I. Hence it follows, that God is the efficient cause of all that can fall within the sphere of an infinite intellect.

Corollary II. It also follows that God is a cause in himself, and not through an accident of his nature.

Corollary III. It follows, thirdly, that God is the absolutely first cause.

PROP. XVII. *God acts solely by the laws of his own nature, and is not constrained by anyone.*

Proof. We have just shown (in Prop. xvi), that solely from the necessity of the divine nature, or, what is the same thing, solely from the laws of his nature, an infinite number of things absolutely follow in an infinite number of ways; and we proved (in Prop. xv), that without God nothing can be nor be conceived; but that all things are in God. Wherefore nothing can exist outside himself, whereby he can be conditioned or constrained to act. Wherefore God acts solely by the laws of his own nature, and is not constrained by anyone. *Q.E.D.*

Corollary I. It follows: 1. That there can be no cause which, either extrinsically or intrinsically, besides the perfection of his own nature, moves God to act.

Corollary II. It follows: 2. That God is the sole free cause. For God alone exists by the sole necessity of his nature (by Prop. xi and Prop. xiv, Coroll. i), and acts by the sole necessity of his nature, wherefore God is (by Def. vii) the sole free cause. *Q.E.D.*

Note. Others think that God is a free cause, because he can, as they think, bring it about, that those things which we have said follow from his nature – that is, which are in his power, should not come to pass, or should not be produced by him. But this is the same as if they said, that God could bring it about, that it should not follow from the nature of a triangle, that its three interior angles should not be equal to two right angles; or that from a given cause no effect should follow, which is absurd.

Moreover, I will show below, without the aid of this proposition, that neither intellect nor will appertain to God's nature. I know that there are many who think that they can show, that supreme intellect and free will do appertain to God's nature; for they say they know of nothing more perfect, which they can attribute to God, than that which is the highest perfection in ourselves. Further, although they conceive God as actually supremely intelligent, they yet do not believe, that he can bring into existence everything which he actually understands, for they think that they would thus destroy God's power. If, they contend, God had created everything which is in his intellect, he would not be able to create anything more, and this, they think, would clash with God's omnipotence; therefore, they prefer to assert that God is indifferent to all things, and that he creates nothing except that which he has decided, by some absolute exercise of will, to create. However, I think I have shown sufficiently clearly (by Prop. xvi), that from God's supreme power, or infinite nature, an infinite number of things – that is, all things have necessarily flowed forth in an infinite number of ways, or always follow from the same necessity; in the same way as from the nature of a triangle it follows from eternity and for eternity, that its three interior angles are equal to two right angles. Wherefore the omnipotence of God has been displayed from all eternity, and will for all eternity remain in the same state of activity. This manner of treating the question attributes to God an omnipotence, in my opinion, far more perfect. For, otherwise, we are compelled to confess that God understands an infinite number of creatable things, which he will never be able to create, for, if he created all that he understands, he would, according to this showing, exhaust his omnipotence, and render himself imperfect. Wherefore, in order to establish that God is perfect, we should be reduced to establishing at the same time, that he cannot bring to pass everything over which his power extends; this seems to be a hypothesis most absurd, and most repugnant to God's omnipotence.

Further (to say a word here concerning the intellect and the will which we attribute to God), if intellect and will appertain to the eternal essence of God, we must take these words in some significations quite different from those they usually bear. For intellect and will, which should constitute the essence of God, would perforce be as far apart as the poles from the human intellect and will, in fact, would have nothing in common with them but the name; there would be about as much correspondence between the two as there is between the Dog, the heavenly constellation, and a dog, an animal that barks. This I will prove as follows. If intellect belongs to the divine nature, it cannot be in nature, as ours is generally thought to be, posterior to, or simultaneous with the things understood, inasmuch as God is prior to all things by reason of his causality (Prop. xvi, Coroll. i). On the contrary, the truth and formal essence of things is as it is, because it exists by representation as such in the intellect of God. Wherefore the intellect of God, in so far as it is conceived to constitute God's essence, is, in reality, the cause of things, both of their essence and of their existence. This seems to have been recognised by those who have asserted, that God's intellect, God's will, and God's power, are one and the same. As, therefore, God's intellect is the sole cause of things, namely, both of their essence and existence, it must necessarily differ from them in respect to its essence, and in respect to its existence. For a cause differs from a thing it causes, precisely in the quality which the latter gains from the former.

For example, a man is the cause of another man's existence, but not of his essence (for the latter is an eternal truth), and, therefore, the two men may be entirely similar in essence, but must be different in existence; and hence if the existence of one of them cease, the existence of the other will not necessarily cease also; but if the essence of one could be destroyed, and be made false, the essence of the other would be destroyed also. Wherefore, a thing which is the cause both of the essence and of the existence of a given effect, must differ from such effect both in respect to its essence, and also in respect to its existence. Now the intellect of God is the cause of both the essence and the existence of our intellect; therefore, the intellect of God in so far as it is conceived to constitute the divine essence, differs from our intellect both in respect to essence and in respect to existence, nor can it in anywise agree therewith save in name, as we said before. The reasoning would be identical in the case of the will, as anyone can easily see.

PROP. XVIII. *God is the indwelling and not the transient cause of all things.*

Proof. All things which are, are in God, and must be conceived through God (by Prop. xv), therefore (by Prop. xvi, Coroll. i) God is the cause of those things which are in him. This is our first point. Further, besides God there can be no substance (by Prop. xiv), that is nothing in itself external to God. This is our second point. God, therefore, is the indwelling and not the transient cause of all things. *Q.E.D.*

PROP. XIX. *God, and all the attributes of God, are eternal.*

Proof. God (by Def. vi) is substance, which (by Prop. xi) necessarily exists, that is (by Prop. vii) existence appertains to its nature, or (what is the same thing) follows from its definition; therefore, God is eternal (by Def. viii). Further, by the attributes of God we must understand that which (by Def. iv) expresses the essence of the divine substance – in other words, that which appertains to substance: that, I say, should be involved in the attributes of substance. Now eternity appertains to the nature of substance (as I have already shown in Prop. vii); therefore, eternity must appertain to each of the attributes, and thus all are eternal. *Q.E.D.*

Note. This proposition is also evident from the manner in which (in Prop. xi) I demonstrated the existence of God: it is evident, I repeat, from that proof, that the existence of God, like his essence, is an eternal truth. Further (in Prop. xix of my 'Principles of the Cartesian Philosophy'), I have proved the eternity of God, in another manner, which I need not here repeat.

PROP. XX. *The existence of God and his essence are one and the same.*

Proof. God (by the last Prop.) and all his attributes are eternal, that is (by Def. viii) each of his attributes expresses existence. Therefore the same attributes of God which explain his eternal essence, explain at the same time his eternal existence – in other words, that which constitutes God's essence constitutes at the same time his existence. Wherefore God's existence and God's essence are one and the same. *Q.E.D.*

Corollary I. Hence it follows that God's existence, like His essence, is an eternal truth.

Corollary II. Secondly, it follows that God, and all the attributes of God, are unchangeable. For if they could be changed in respect to existence, they must also be able to be changed in respect to essence – that is, obviously, be changed from true to false, which is absurd.

PROP. XXI. *All things which follow from the absolute nature of any attribute of God must always exist and be infinite, or, in other words, are eternal and infinite through the said attribute.*

Proof. Conceive, if it be possible (supposing the proposition to be denied), that something in some attribute of God can follow from the absolute nature of the said attribute, and that at the same time it is finite, and has a conditioned existence or duration; for instance, the idea of God expressed in the attribute thought. Now thought, in so far as it is supposed to be an attribute of God, is necessarily (by Prop. xi) in its nature infinite. But, in so far as it possesses the idea of God, it is supposed finite. It cannot, however, be conceived as finite, unless it be limited by thought (by Def. ii); but it is not limited by thought itself, in so far as it has constituted the idea of God (for so far it is supposed to be finite); therefore, it is limited by thought, in so far as it has not constituted the idea of God, which nevertheless (by Prop. xi) must necessarily exist.

We have now granted, therefore, thought not constituting the idea of God, and, accordingly, the idea of God does not naturally follow from its nature in so far as it is absolute thought (for it is conceived as constituting, and also as not constituting, the idea of God), which is against our hypothesis. Wherefore, if the idea of God expressed in the attribute thought, or, indeed, anything else in any attribute of God (for we may take any example, as the proof is of universal application) follows from the necessity of the absolute nature of the said attribute, the said thing must necessarily be infinite, which was our first point.

Furthermore, a thing which thus follows from the necessity of the nature of any attribute cannot have a limited duration. For if it can, suppose a thing, which follows from the necessity of the nature of some attribute, to exist in some attribute of God, for instance, the idea of God expressed in the attribute thought, and let it be supposed at some time not to have existed, or to be about not to exist.

Now thought being an attribute of God, must necessarily exist unchanged (by Prop. xi, and Prop. xx, Coroll. ii); and beyond the limits of the duration of the idea of God (supposing the latter at some time not to have existed, or not to be going to exist) thought would perforce have existed without the idea of God, which is contrary to our hypothesis, for we supposed that, thought being given, the idea of God necessarily flowed therefrom. Therefore the idea of God expressed in thought, or anything which necessarily follows from the absolute nature of some attribute of God, cannot have a limited duration, but through the said attribute is eternal, which is our second point. Bear in mind that the same proposition may be affirmed of anything, which in any attribute necessarily follows from God's absolute nature.

PROP. XXII. *Whatsoever follows from any attribute of God, in so far as it is modified by a modification, which exists necessarily and as infinite, through the said attribute, must also exist necessarily and as infinite.*

Proof. The proof of this proposition is similar to that of the preceding one.

PROP. XXIII. *Every mode, which exists both necessarily and as infinite, must necessarily follow either from the absolute nature of some attribute of God, or from an attribute modified by a modification which exists necessarily, and as infinite.*

Proof. A mode exists in something else, through which it must be conceived (Def. v), that is (Prop. xv), it exists solely in God, and solely through God can be conceived. If therefore a mode is conceived as necessarily existing and infinite, it must necessarily be inferred or perceived through some attribute of God, in so far as such attribute is conceived as expressing the infinity and necessity of existence, in other words (Def. viii) eternity; that is, in so far as it is considered absolutely. A mode, therefore, which necessarily exists as infinite, must follow from the absolute nature of some attribute of God, either immediately (Prop. xxi) or through the means of some modification, which follows from the absolute nature of the said attribute; that is (by Prop. xxii), which exists necessarily and as infinite.

PROP. XXIV. *The essence of things produced by God does not involve existence.*

Proof. This proposition is evident from Def. i. For that of which the nature (considered in itself) involves existence is self-caused, and exists by the sole necessity of its own nature.

Corollary. Hence it follows that God is not only the cause of things coming into existence, but also of their continuing in existence, that is, in scholastic phraseology, God is cause of the being of things (*essendi rerum*). For whether things exist, or do not exist, whenever we contemplate their essence, we see that it involves neither existence nor duration; consequently, it cannot be the cause of either the one or the other. God must be the sole cause, inasmuch as to him alone does existence appertain. (Prop. xiv, Coroll. i.) *Q.E.D.*

PROP. XXV. *God is the efficient cause not only of the existence of things, but also of their essence.*

Proof. If this be denied, then God is not the cause of the essence of things; and therefore the essence of things can (by Ax. iv) be conceived without God. This (by Prop. xv) is absurd. Therefore, God is the cause of the essence of things. *Q.E.D.*

Note. This proposition follows more clearly from Prop. xvi. For it is evident thereby that, given the divine nature, the essence of things must be inferred from it, no less than their existence – in a word, God must be called the cause of all things, in the same sense as he is called the cause of himself. This will be made still clearer by the following corollary.

Corollary. Individual things are nothing but modifications of the attributes of God, or modes by which the attributes of God are expressed in a fixed and definite manner. The proof appears from Prop. xv and Def. v.

PROP. XXVI. *A thing which is conditioned to act in a particular manner, has necessarily been thus conditioned by God; and that which has not been conditioned by God cannot condition itself to act.*

Proof. That by which things are said to be conditioned to act in a particular manner is necessarily something positive (this is obvious); therefore both of its essence and of its existence God by the necessity of his nature is the efficient cause (Props. xxv and xvi); this is our first point. Our second point is plainly to be inferred therefrom. For if a thing, which has not been conditioned by God, could condition itself, the first part of our proof would be false, and this, as we have shown, is absurd.

PROP. XXVII. *A thing, which has been conditioned by God to act in a particular way, cannot render itself unconditioned.*

Proof. This proposition is evident from the third axiom.

PROP. XXVIII. *Every individual thing, or everything which is finite and has a conditioned existence, cannot exist or be conditioned to act, unless it be conditioned for existence and action by a cause other than itself, which also is finite, and has a conditioned existence; and likewise this cause cannot in its turn exist, or be conditioned to act, unless it be conditioned for existence and action by another cause, which also is finite, and has a conditioned existence, and so on to infinity.*

Proof. Whatsoever is conditioned to exist and act, has been thus conditioned by God (by Prop. xxvi and Prop. xxiv, Coroll.).

But that which is finite, and has a conditioned existence, cannot be produced by the absolute nature of any attribute of God; for whatsoever follows from the absolute nature of any attribute of God is infinite and eternal (by Prop. xxi). It must, therefore, follow from some attribute of God, in so far as the said attribute is considered as in some way modified; for substance and modes make up the sum total of existence (by Ax. i and Def. iii, v), while modes are merely modifications of the attributes of God. But from God, or from any of his attributes, in so far as the latter is modified by a modification infinite and eternal, a conditioned thing cannot follow. Wherefore it must follow from, or be conditioned for, existence and action by God or one of his attributes, in so far as the latter are modified by some modification which is finite, and has a conditioned existence. This is our first point. Again, this cause or this modification (for the reason by which we established the first part of this proof) must in its turn be conditioned by another cause, which also is finite, and has a conditioned existence, and, again, this last by another (for the same reason); and so on (for the same reason) to infinity. *Q.E.D.*

Note. As certain things must be produced immediately by God, namely those things which necessarily follow from his absolute nature, through the means of these primary attributes, which, nevertheless, can neither exist nor be conceived without God, it follows: 1. That God is absolutely the proximate cause of these things immediately produced by him. I say absolutely, not after his kind, as is usually stated. For the effects of God cannot either exist or be conceived without a cause (Prop. xv and Prop. xxiv, Coroll.). 2. That God cannot properly be styled the remote cause of individual things, except for the sake of distinguishing these from what he immediately produces, or rather from what follows from his absolute nature. For, by a remote cause, we understand a cause which is in no way conjoined to the effect. But all things which are, are in God, and so depend on God, that without him they can neither be nor be conceived.

PROP. XXIX. *Nothing in the universe is contingent, but all things are conditioned to exist and operate in a particular manner by the necessity of the divine nature.*

Proof. Whatsoever is, is in God (Prop. xv). But God cannot be called a thing contingent. For (by Prop. xi) he exists necessarily, and not contingently. Further, the modes of the divine nature follow therefrom necessarily, and not contingently (Prop. xvi); and they thus follow, whether we consider the divine nature absolutely, or whether we consider it as in any way conditioned to act (Prop. xxvii). Further, God is not only the cause of these modes, in so far as they simply exist (by Prop. xxiv, Coroll.), but also in so far as they are considered as conditioned for operating in a particular manner (Prop. xxvi). If they be not conditioned by God (Prop. xxvi), it is impossible, and not contingent, that they should condition themselves; contrariwise, if they be conditioned by God, it is impossible, and not contingent, that they should render themselves unconditioned. Wherefore all things are conditioned by the necessity of the divine nature, not only to exist, but also to exist and operate in a particular manner, and there is nothing that is contingent. *Q.E.D.*

Note. Before going any further, I wish here to explain, what we should understand by nature viewed as active (*natura naturans*), and nature viewed as passive (*natura naturata*). I say to explain, or rather call attention to it, for I think that, from what has been said, it is sufficiently clear, that by nature viewed as active we should understand that which is in itself, and is conceived through itself, or those attributes of substance, which express eternal and infinite essence, in other words (Prop. xiv, Coroll. i, and Prop. xvii, Coroll. ii) God in so far as he is considered as a free cause.

By nature viewed as passive I understand all that which follows from the necessity of the nature of God, or of any of the attributes of God, that is, all the modes of the attributes of God, in so far as they are considered as things which are in God, and which without God cannot exist or be conceived.

PROP. XXX. *Intellect, in function* (*actu*) *finite, or in function infinite, must comprehend the attributes of God and the modifications of God, and nothing else.*

Proof. A true idea must agree with its object (Ax. vi); in other words (obviously), that which is contained in the intellect in representation must necessarily be granted in nature. But in nature (by Prop. xiv, Coroll. i) there is no substance save God, nor any modifications save those (Prop. xv) which are in God, and cannot without God either be or be conceived. Therefore the intellect, in function finite, or in function infinite, must comprehend the attributes of God and the modifications of God, and nothing else. *Q.E.D.*

PROP. XXXI. *The intellect in function, whether finite or infinite, as will, desire, love, &c., should be referred to passive nature and not to active nature.*

Proof. By the intellect we do not (obviously) mean absolute thought, but only a certain mode of thinking, differing from other modes, such as love, desire, &c., and therefore (Def. v) requiring to be conceived through absolute thought. It must (by Prop. xv and Def. vi), through some attribute of God which expresses the eternal and infinite essence of thought, be so conceived, that without such attribute it could neither be nor be conceived. It must therefore be referred to nature passive rather than to nature active, as must also the other modes of thinking. *Q.E.D.*

Note. I do not here, by speaking of intellect in function, admit that there is such a thing as intellect in potentiality: but, wishing to avoid all confusion, I desire to speak only of what is most clearly perceived by us, namely, of the very act of understanding, than which nothing is more clearly perceived. For we cannot perceive anything without adding to our knowledge of the act of understanding.

PROP. XXXII. *Will cannot be called a free cause, but only a necessary cause.*

Proof. Will is only a particular mode of thinking, like intellect; therefore (by Prop. xxviii) no volition can exist, nor be conditioned to act, unless it be conditioned by some cause other than itself, which cause is conditioned by a third cause, and so on to infinity. But if will be supposed infinite, it must also be conditioned to exist and act by God, not by virtue of his being substance absolutely infinite, but by virtue of his possessing an attribute which expresses the infinite and eternal essence of thought (by Prop. xxiii). Thus, however it be conceived, whether as finite or infinite, it requires a cause by which it should be conditioned to exist and act. Thus (Def. vii) it cannot be called a free cause, but only a necessary or constrained cause. *Q.E.D.*

Corollary I. Hence it follows, first, that God does not act according to freedom of the will.

Corollary II. It follows, secondly, that will and intellect stand in the same relation to the nature of God as do motion, and rest, and absolutely all natural phenomena, which must be conditioned by God (Prop. xxix) to exist and act in a particular manner. For will, like the rest, stands in need of a cause, by which it is conditioned to exist and act in a particular manner. And although, when will or intellect be granted, an infinite number of results may follow, yet God cannot on that account be said to act from freedom of the will, any more than the infinite number of results from motion and rest would justify us in saying that motion and rest act by free will. Wherefore will no more appertains to God than does anything else in nature, but stands in the same relation to him as motion, rest, and the like, which we have shown to follow from the necessity of the divine nature, and to be conditioned by it to exist and act in a particular manner.

PROP. XXXIII. *Things could not have been brought into being by God in any manner or in any order different from that which has in fact obtained.*

Proof. All things necessarily follow from the nature of God (Prop. xvi), and by the nature of God are conditioned to exist and act in a particular way (Prop. xxix). If things, therefore, could have been of a different nature, or have been conditioned to act in a different way, so that the order of nature would have been different, God's nature would also have been able to be different from what it now is; and therefore (by Prop. xi) that different nature also would have perforce existed, and consequently there would have been able to be two or more Gods. This (by Prop. xiv, Coroll. i) is absurd. Therefore things could not have been brought into being by God in any other manner, &c. *Q.E.D.*

Note I. As I have thus shown, more clearly than the sun at noonday, that there is nothing to justify us in calling things contingent, I wish to explain briefly what meaning we shall attach to the word contingent; but I will first explain the words necessary and impossible.

A thing is called necessary either in respect to its essence or in respect to its cause; for the existence of a thing necessarily follows, either from its essence and definition, or from a given efficient cause. For similar reasons a thing is said to be impossible; namely, inasmuch as its essence or definition involves a contradiction, or because no external cause is granted, which is conditioned to produce such an effect; but a thing can in no respect be called contingent, save in relation to the imperfection of our knowledge.

A thing of which we do not know whether the essence does or does not involve a contradiction, or of which, knowing that it does not involve a contradiction, we are still in doubt concerning the existence, because the order of causes escapes us, – such a thing, I say, cannot appear to us either necessary or impossible. Wherefore we call it contingent or possible.

Note II. It clearly follows from what we have said, that things have been brought into being by God in the highest perfection, inasmuch as they have necessarily followed from a most perfect nature. Nor does this prove any imperfection in God, for it has compelled us to affirm his perfection. From its contrary proposition, we should clearly gather (as I have just shown), that God is not supremely perfect, for if things had been brought into being in any other way, we should have to assign to God a nature different from that, which we are bound to attribute to him from the consideration of an absolutely perfect being.

I do not doubt, that many will scout this idea as absurd, and will refuse to give their minds up to contemplating it, simply because they are accustomed to assign to God a freedom very different from that which we (Def. vii) have deduced. They assign to him, in short, absolute free will. However, I am also convinced that if such persons reflect on the matter, and duly weigh in their minds our series of propositions, they will reject such freedom as they now attribute to God, not only as nugatory, but also as a great impediment to organized knowledge. There is no need for me to repeat what I said in the note to Prop. xvii. But, for the sake of my opponents, I will show further, that although it be granted that will appertains to the essence of God, it nevertheless follows from his perfection, that things could not have been by him created other than they are, or in a different order; this is easily proved, if we reflect on what our opponents themselves concede, namely, that it depends solely on the degree and will of God, that each thing is what it is. If it were otherwise,

God would not be the cause of all things. Further, that all the decrees of God have been ratified from all eternity by God himself. If it were otherwise, God would be convicted of imperfection or change. But in eternity there is no such thing as when, before, or after; hence it follows solely from the perfection of God, that God never can decree, or never could have decreed anything but what is; that God did not exist before his decrees, and would not exist without them. But, it is said, supposing that God had made a different universe, or had ordained other decrees from all eternity concerning nature and her order, we could not therefore conclude any imperfection in God. But persons who say this must admit that God can change his decrees. For if God had ordained any decrees concerning nature and her order, different from those which he has ordained – in other words, if he had willed and conceived something different concerning nature – he would perforce have had a different intellect from that which he has, and also a different will. But if it were allowable to assign to God a different intellect and a different will, without any change in his essence or his perfection, what would there be to prevent him changing the decrees which he has made concerning created things, and nevertheless remaining perfect? For his intellect and will concerning things created and their order are the same, in respect to his essence and perfection, however they be conceived.

Further, all the philosophers whom I have read admit that God's intellect is entirely actual, and not at all potential; as they also admit that God's intellect, and God's will, and God's essence are identical, it follows that, if God had had a different actual intellect and a different will, his essence would also have been different; and thus, as I concluded at first, if things had been brought into being by God in a different way from that which has obtained, God's intellect and will, that is (as is admitted) his essence would perforce have been different, which is absurd.

As these things could not have been brought into being by God in any but the actual way and order which has obtained; and as the truth of this proposition follows from the supreme perfection of God; we can have no sound reason for persuading ourselves to believe that God did not wish to create all the things which were in his intellect, and to create them in the same perfection as he had understood them.

But, it will be said, there is in things no perfection nor imperfection; that which is in them, and which causes them to be called perfect or imperfect, good or bad, depends solely on the will of God. If God had so willed, he might have brought it about that what is now perfection should be extreme imperfection, and *vice versâ*. What is such an assertion, but an open declaration that God, who necessarily understands that which he wishes, might bring it about by his will, that he should understand things differently from the way in which he does understand them? This (as we have just shown) is the height of absurdity. Wherefore, I may turn the argument against its employers, as follows: All things depend on the power of God. In order that things should be different from what they are, God's will would necessarily have to be different. But God's will cannot be different (as we have just most clearly demonstrated) from God's perfection. Therefore neither can things be different. I confess, that the theory which subjects all things to the will of an indifferent deity, and asserts that they are all dependent on his fiat, is less far from the truth than the theory of those, who maintain that God acts in all things with a view of promoting what is good. For these latter persons seem to set up something beyond God, which does not depend on God, but which God in acting looks to as an exemplar, or which he aims at as a definite goal. This is only another name for subjecting God to the dominion of destiny, an utter absurdity in respect to God, whom we have shown to be the first and only free cause of the essence of all things and also of their existence. I need, therefore, spend no time in refuting such wild theories

PROP. XXXIV. *God's power is identical with his essence.*

Proof. From the sole necessity of the essence of God it follows that God is the cause of himself (Prop. xi) and of all things (Prop. xvi and Coroll.). Wherefore the power of God, by which he and all things are and act, is identical with his essence. *Q.E.D.*

PROP. XXXV. *Whatsoever we conceive to be in the power of God, necessarily exists.*

Proof. Whatsoever is in God's power, must (by the last Prop.) be comprehended in his essence in such a manner, that it necessarily follows therefrom, and therefore necessarily exists. *Q.E.D.*

PROP. XXXVI. *There is no cause from whose nature some effect does not follow.*

Proof. Whatsoever exists expresses God's nature or essence in a given conditioned manner (by Prop. xxv, Coroll.); that is (by Prop. xxxiv), whatsoever exists, expresses in a given conditioned manner God's power, which is the cause of all things, therefore an effect must (by Prop. xvi) necessarily follow. *Q.E.D.*

Appendix. In the foregoing I have explained the nature and properties of God. I have shown that he necessarily exists, that he is one: that he is, and acts solely by the necessity of his own nature; that he is the free cause of all things, and how he is so; that all things are in God, and so depend on him, that without him they could neither exist nor be conceived; lastly, that all things are predetermined by God, not through his free will or absolute fiat, but from the very nature of God or infinite power. I have further, where occasion offered, taken care to remove the prejudices, which might impede the comprehension of my demonstrations. Yet there still remain misconceptions not a few, which might and may prove very grave hindrances to the understanding of the concatenation of things, as I have explained it above. I have therefore thought it worth while to bring these misconceptions before the bar of reason.

All such opinions spring from the notion commonly entertained, that all things in nature act as men themselves act, namely, with an end in view. It is accepted as certain, that God himself directs all things to a definite goal (for it is said that God made all things for man, and man that he might worship him). I will, therefore, consider this opinion, asking first, why it obtains general credence, and why all men are naturally so prone to adopt it? secondly, I will point out its falsity; and, lastly, I will show how it has given rise to prejudices about good and bad, right and wrong, praise and blame, order and confusion, beauty and ugliness, and the like. However, this is not the place to deduce these misconceptions from the nature of the human mind: it will be sufficient here, if I assume as a starting point, what ought to be universally admitted, namely, that all men are born ignorant of the causes of things, that all have the desire to seek for what is useful to them, and that they are conscious of such desire. Herefrom it follows, first, that men think themselves free inasmuch as they are conscious of their volitions and desires, and never even dream, in their ignorance, of the causes which have disposed them so to wish and desire. Secondly, that men do all things for an end, namely, for that which is useful to them, and which they seek. Thus it comes to pass that they only look for a knowledge of the final causes of events, and when these are learned, they are content, as having no cause for further doubt. If they cannot learn such causes from external sources, they are compelled to turn to considering themselves, and reflecting what end would have induced them personally to bring about the given event, and thus they necessarily judge other natures by their own. Further, as they find in themselves and outside themselves many means which assist them not a little in their search for what is useful, for instance, eyes for seeing, teeth for chewing, herbs and animals for yielding food, the sun for giving light, the sea for breeding fish, &c., they come to look on the whole of nature as a means for obtaining such conveniences. Now as they are aware, that they found these conveniences and did not make them, they think they have cause for believing, that some other being has made them for their use. As they look upon things as means, they cannot believe them to be self-created; but, judging from the means which they are accustomed to prepare for themselves, they are bound to believe in some ruler or rulers of the universe endowed with human freedom, who have arranged and adapted everything for human use. They are bound to estimate the nature of such rulers (having no information on the subject) in accordance with their own nature, and therefore they assert that the gods ordained everything for the use of man, in order to bind man to themselves and obtain from him the highest honour. Hence also it follows, that everyone thought out for himself, according to his abilities, a different way of worshipping God, so that God might love him more than his fellows, and direct the whole course of nature for the satisfaction of his blind cupidity and insatiable avarice. Thus the prejudice developed into superstition, and took deep root in the human mind; and for this reason everyone strove most zealously to understand and explain the final causes of things; but in their endeavour to show that nature does nothing in vain, *i.e.*, nothing which is useless to man, they only seem to have demonstrated that nature, the gods, and men are all mad together. Consider, I pray you, the result: among the many helps of nature they were bound to find some hindrances, such as storms, earthquakes, diseases, &c.: so they declared that such things happen, because the gods are angry at some wrong done them by men, or at some fault committed in their worship. Experience day by day protested and showed by infinite examples, that good and evil fortunes fall to the lot of pious and impious alike; still they would not abandon their inveterate prejudice, for it was more easy for them to class such contradictions among other unknown things of whose use they were ignorant, and thus to retain their actual and innate condition of ignorance, than to destroy the whole fabric of their reasoning and start afresh. They therefore laid down as an axiom, that God's judgments far transcend human understanding. Such a doctrine might well have sufficed to conceal the truth from the human race for all eternity, if mathematics had not furnished another standard of verity in considering solely the essence and properties of figures without regard to their final causes. There are other reasons (which I need not mention here) besides mathematics, which might have caused men's minds to be directed to these general prejudices, and have led them to the knowledge of the truth.

I have now sufficiently explained my first point. There is no need to show at length, that nature has no particular goal in view, and that final causes are mere human figments. This, I think, is already evident enough, both from the causes and foundations on which I have shown such prejudice to be based, and also from Prop. xvi, and the Corollary of Prop. xxxii, and, in fact, all those propositions in which I have shown, that everything in nature proceeds from a sort of necessity, and with the utmost perfection. However, I will add a few remarks, in order to overthrow this doctrine of a final cause utterly. That which is really a cause it considers as an effect, and *vice versâ*: it makes that which is by nature first to be last, and that which is highest and most perfect to be most imperfect. Passing over the questions of cause and priority as self-evident, it is plain from Props. xxi, xxii, xxiii that that effect is most perfect which is produced immediately by God; the effect which requires for its production several intermediate causes is, in that respect, more imperfect. But if those things which were made immediately by God were made to enable him to attain his end, then the things which come after, for the sake of which the first were made, are necessarily the most excellent of all.

Further, this doctrine does away with the perfection of God: for, if God acts for an object, he necessarily desires something which he lacks. Certainly, theologians and metaphysicians draw a distinction between the object of want and the object of assimilation; still they confess that God made all things for the sake of himself, not for the sake of creation. They are unable to point to anything prior to creation, except God himself, as an object for which God should act, and are therefore driven to admit (as they clearly must), that God lacked those things for whose attainment he created means, and further that he desired them.

We must not omit to notice that the followers of this doctrine, anxious to display their talent in assigning final causes, have imported a new method of argument in proof of their theory – namely, a reduction, not to the impossible, but to ignorance; thus showing that they have no other method of exhibiting their doctrine. For example, if a stone falls from a roof on to someone's head, and kills him, they will demonstrate by their new method, that the stone fell in order to kill the man; for, if it had not by God's will fallen with that object, how could so many circumstances (and there are often many concurrent circumstances) have all happened together by chance? Perhaps you will answer that the event is due to the facts that the wind was blowing, and the man was walking that way. 'But why,' they will insist, 'was the wind blowing, and why was the man at that very time walking that way?' If you again answer, that the wind had then sprung up because the sea had begun to be agitated the day before, the weather being previously calm, and that the man had been invited by a friend, they will again insist: 'But why was the sea agitated, and why was the man invited at that time?' So they will pursue their questions from cause to cause, till at last you take refuge in the will of God – in other words, the sanctuary of ignorance. So, again, when they survey the frame of the human body, they are amazed; and being ignorant of the causes of so great a work of art, conclude that it has been fashioned, not mechanically, but by divine and supernatural skill, and has been so put together that one part shall not hurt another.

Hence anyone who seeks for the true causes of miracles, and strives to understand natural phenomena as an intelligent being, and not to gaze at them like a fool, is set down and denounced as an impious heretic by those, whom the masses adore as the interpreters of nature and the gods. Such persons know that, with the removal of ignorance, the wonder which forms their only available means for proving and preserving their authority would vanish also. But I now quit this subject, and pass on to my third point.

After men persuaded themselves, that everything which is created is created for their sake, they were bound to consider as the chief quality in everything that which is most useful to themselves, and to account those things the best of all which have the most beneficial effect on mankind. Further, they were bound to form abstract notions for the explanation of the nature of things, such as *goodness*, *badness*, *order*, *confusion*, *warmth*, *cold*, *beauty*, *deformity*, and so on; and from the belief that they are free agents arose the further notions *praise* and *blame*, *sin* and *merit*.

I will speak of these latter hereafter, when I treat of human nature; the former I will briefly explain here.

Everything which conduces to health and the worship of God they have called *good*, everything which hinders these objects they have styled *bad*; and inasmuch as those who do not understand the nature of things do not verify phenomena in any way, but merely imagine them after a fashion, and mistake their imagination for understanding, such persons firmly believe that there is an *order* in things, being really ignorant both of things and their own nature. When phenomena are of such a kind, that the impression they make on our senses requires little effort of imagination, and can consequently be easily remembered, we say that they are *well-ordered*; if the contrary, that they are *ill-ordered* or *confused*. Further, as things which are easily imagined are more pleasing to us, men prefer order to confusion – as though there were any order in nature, except in relation to our imagination – and say that God has created all things in order; thus, without knowing it, attributing imagination to God, unless, indeed, they would have it that God foresaw human imagination, and arranged everything, so that it should be most easily imagined. If this be their theory, they would not, perhaps, be daunted by the fact that we find an infinite number of phenomena, far surpassing our imagination, and very many others which confound its weakness. But enough has been said on this subject. The other abstract notions are nothing but modes of imagining, in which the imagination is differently affected, though they are considered by the ignorant as the chief attributes of things, inasmuch as they believe that everything was created for the sake of themselves; and, according as they are affected by it, style it good or bad, healthy or rotten and corrupt. For instance, if the motion which objects we see communicate to our nerves be conducive to health, the objects causing it are styled *beautiful*; if a contrary motion be excited, they are styled *ugly*.

Things which are perceived through our sense of smell are styled fragrant or fetid; if through our taste, sweet or bitter, full-flavoured or insipid; if through our touch, hard or soft, rough or smooth, &c.

Whatsoever affects our ears is said to give rise to noise, sound, or harmony. In this last case, there are men lunatic enough to believe, that even God himself takes pleasure in harmony; and philosophers are not lacking who have persuaded themselves, that the motion of the heavenly bodies gives rise to harmony – all of which instances sufficiently show that everyone judges of things according to the state of his brain, or rather mistakes for things the forms of his imagination. We need no longer wonder that there have arisen all the controversies we have witnessed, and finally scepticism: for, although human bodies in many respects agree, yet in very many others they differ; so that what seems good to one seems bad to another; what seems well ordered to one seems confused to another; what is pleasing to one displeases another, and so on. I need not further enumerate, because this is not the place to treat the subject at length, and also because the fact is sufficiently well known. It is commonly said: 'So many men, so many minds; everyone is wise in his own way; brains differ as completely as palates.' All of which proverbs show, that men judge of things according to their mental disposition, and rather imagine than understand: for, if they understood phenomena, they would, as mathematics attest, be convinced, if not attracted, by what I have urged.

We have now perceived, that all the explanations commonly given of nature are mere modes of imagining, and do not indicate the true nature of anything, but only the constitution of the imagination; and, although they have names, as though they were entities, existing externally to the imagination, I call them entities imaginary rather than real; and, therefore, all arguments against us drawn from such abstractions are easily rebutted.

Many argue in this way. If all things follow from a necessity of the absolutely perfect nature of God, why are there so many imperfections in nature? such, for instance, as things corrupt to the point of putridity, loathsome deformity, confusion, evil, sin, &c. But these reasoners are, as I have said, easily confuted, for the perfection of things is to be reckoned only from their own nature and power; things are not more or less perfect, according as they delight or offend human senses, or according as they are serviceable or repugnant to mankind. To those who ask why God did not so create all men, that they should be governed only by reason, I give no answer but this: because matter was not lacking to him for the creation of every degree of perfection from highest to lowest; or, more strictly, because the laws of his nature are so vast, as to suffice for the production of everything conceivable by an infinite intelligence, as I have shown in Prop. xvi.

Such are the misconceptions I have undertaken to note; if there are any more of the same sort, everyone may easily dissipate them for himself with the aid of a little reflection.

Letters

LETTER 9 (27)[22] TO SIMON DE VRIES, March 1663

Concepts and Definitions

Respected Friend,

I have received[23] your long wished-for letter, for which, and for your affection towards me, I heartily thank you. Your long absence has been no less grievous to me than to you; yet in the meantime I rejoice that my trifling studies are of profit to you and our friends. For thus while you[24] are away, I in my absence speak to you.[24] You need not envy my fellow-lodger. There is no one who is more displeasing to me, nor against whom I have been more anxiously on my guard; and therefore I would have you and all my acquaintance warned not to communicate my opinions to him, except when he has come to maturer years. So far he is too childish and inconstant, and is fonder of novelty than of truth. But I hope, that in a few years he will amend these childish faults. Indeed I am almost sure of it, as far as I can judge from his nature. And so his temperament bids me like him.

22. The first number given is that in van Vloten's edition, which is now standard. The number in brackets is the older number, which is still to be found, for instance in the Elwes' translation used here.

23. The whole beginning of this letter, till after the mention of the club, is omitted in the editions before van Vloten's Supplementum, to make the letter agree with the altered version of Letter 26, to which it is the answer.

24. 'You' in these two places is plural, and refers to the club; so also the second 'your' on the next page; elsewhere 'you' and 'your' refer to De Vries only.

As for the questions propounded in your club, which is wisely enough ordered, I see that your[25] difficulties arise from not distinguishing between kinds of definition: that is, between a definition serving to explain a thing, of which the essence only is sought and in question, and a definition which is put forward only for purposes of inquiry. The former having a definite object ought to be true, the latter need not. For instance, if someone asks me for a description of Solomon's temple, I am bound to give him a true description, unless I want to talk nonsense with him. But if I have constructed, in my mind, a temple which I desire to build, and infer from the description of it that I must buy such and such a site and so many thousand stones and other materials, will any sane person tell me that I have drawn a wrong conclusion because my definition is possibly untrue? or will anyone ask me to prove my definition? Such a person would simply be telling me, that I had not conceived that which I had conceived, or by requiring me to prove, that I had conceived that which I had conceived; in fact, evidently trifling. Hence a definition either explains a thing, in so far as it is external to the intellect, in which case it ought to be true and only to differ from a proposition or an axiom in being concerned merely with the essences of things, or the modifications of things, whereas the latter has a wider scope and extends also to eternal truths. Or else it explains a thing, as it is conceived or can be conceived by us; and then it differs from an axiom or proposition, inasmuch as it only requires to be conceived absolutely, and not like an axiom as true. Hence a bad definition is one which is not conceived. To explain my meaning, I will take Borel's example – a man saying that two straight lines enclosing a space shall be called 'figurals'. If the man means by a straight line the same as the rest of the world means by a curved line, his definition is good (for by the definition would be meant some such figure as ( ), or the like); so long as he does not afterwards mean a square or other kind of figure. But, if he attaches the ordinary meaning to the words straight line, the thing is evidently inconceivable, and therefore there is no definition. These considerations are plainly confused by Borel, to whose opinion you incline. I give another example, the one you cite at the end of your letter. If I say that each substance has only one attribute, this is an unsupported statement and needs proof. But, if I say that I mean by substance

25. See note 24.

that which consists in only one attribute, the definition will be good, so long as entities consisting of several attributes are afterwards styled by some name other than substance. When you say that I do not prove, that substance (or being) may have several attributes, you do not perhaps pay attention to the proofs given. I adduced two: First, 'that nothing is plainer to us, than that every being may be conceived by us under some attribute, and that the more reality or essence a given being has, the more attributes may be attributed to it. Hence a being absolutely infinite must be defined, &c.' Secondly, and I think this is the stronger proof of the two, 'the more attributes I assign to any being, the more am I compelled to assign to it existence'; in other words, the more I conceive it as true. The contrary would evidently result if I were feigning a chimera or some such being.

Your remark, that you cannot conceive thought except as consisting in ideas, because, when ideas are removed, thought is annihilated, springs, I think, from the fact that while you, a thinking thing, do as you say, you abstract all your thoughts and conceptions. It is no marvel that, when you have abstracted all your thoughts and conceptions, you have nothing left for thinking with. On the general subject I think I have shown sufficiently clearly and plainly, that the intellect, although infinite, belongs to nature regarded as passive rather than nature regarded as active (*ad naturam naturatam, non vero ad naturam naturantem*).

However, I do not see how this helps towards understanding the third definition, not what difficulty the latter presents. It runs, if I mistake not, as follows: 'By substance I mean that, which is in itself and is conceived through itself; that is, of which the conception does not involve the conception of anything else. By attribute I mean the same thing, except that it is called attribute with respect to the understanding, which attributes to substance the particular nature aforesaid.' This definition, I repeat, explains with sufficient clearness what I wish to signify by substance or attribute. You desire, though there is no need, that I should illustrate by an example, how one and the same thing can be stamped with two names. In order not to seem miserly, I will give you two. First, I say that by Israel is meant the third patriarch; I mean the same by Jacob, the name Jacob being given, because the patriarch in question had caught hold of the heel of his brother. Secondly, by a colourless surface I mean a surface, which reflects all rays of light without altering them.

I mean the same by a white surface, with this difference, that a surface is called white in reference to a man looking at it, &c.

LETTER 32 (15) TO OLDENBURG, 20 November 1665

Mind and Body

Distinguished Sir,

For the encouragement to pursue my speculations given me by yourself and the distinguished R. Boyle, I return you my best thanks. I proceed as far as my slender abilities will allow me, with full confidence in your aid and kindness. When you ask me my opinion on the question raised concerning our knowledge of the means, whereby each part of nature agrees with its whole, and the manner in which it is associated with the remaining parts, I presume you are asking for the reasons which induce us to believe, that each part of nature agrees with its whole, and is associated with the remaining parts. For as to the means whereby the parts are really associated, and each part agrees with its whole, I told you in my former letter that I am in ignorance. To answer such a question we should have to know the whole of nature and its several parts. I will therefore endeavour to show the reason, which led me to make the statement; but I will premise that I do not attribute to nature either beauty or deformity, order or confusion. Only in relation to our imagination can things be called beautiful or deformed, ordered or confused.

By the association of parts, then, I merely mean that the laws of nature of one part adapt themselves to the laws of nature of another part, so as to cause the least possible inconsistency. As to the whole and the parts, I mean that a given number of things are parts of a whole, in so far as the nature of each of them is adapted to the nature of the rest, so that they all, as far as possible, agree together. On the other hand, in so far as they do not agree, each of them forms, in our mind, a separate idea, and is to that extent considered as a whole, not as a part. For instance, when the parts of lymph, chyle, &c., combine, according to the proportion of the figure and size of each, so as to evidently unite, and form one fluid, the chyle, lymph, &c., considered under this aspect, are part of the blood; but, in so far as we consider the particles of lymph as differing in figure and size from the particles of chyle, we shall consider each of the two as a whole, not as a part.

Let us imagine with your permission, a little worm, living in the blood, able to distinguish by sight the particles of blood, lymph, &c., and to reflect on the manner in which each particle, on meeting with another particle, either is repulsed, or communicates a portion of its own motion. This little worm would live in the blood, in the same way as we live in a part of the universe, and would consider each particle of blood, not as a part, but as a whole. He would be unable to determine, how all the parts are modified by the general nature of blood, and are compelled by it to adapt themselves, so as to stand in a fixed relation to one another. For, if we imagine that there are no causes external to the blood, which could communicate fresh movements to it, nor any space beyond the blood, nor any bodies whereto the particles of blood could communicate their motion, it is certain that the blood would always remain in the same state, and its particles would undergo no modifications, save those which may be conceived as arising from the relations of motion existing between the lymph, the chyle, &c. The blood would then always have to be considered as a whole, not as a part. But, as there exist, as a matter of fact, very many causes which modify, in a given manner, the nature of the blood, and are, in turn, modified thereby, it follows that other motions and other relations arise in the blood, springing not from the mutual relations of its parts only, but from the mutual relations between the blood as a whole and external causes. Thus the blood comes to be regarded as a part, not as a whole. So much for the whole and the part.

All natural bodies can and ought to be considered in the same way as we have here considered the blood, for all bodies are surrounded by others, and are mutually determined to exist and operate in a fixed and definite proportion, while the relations between motion and rest in the sum total of them, that is, in the whole universe, remain unchanged. Hence it follows that each body, in so far as it exists as modified in a particular manner, must be considered as a part of the whole universe, as agreeing with the whole, and associated with the remaining parts. As the nature of the universe is not limited, like the nature of blood, but is absolutely infinite, its parts are by this nature of infinite power infinitely modified, and compelled to undergo infinite variations.

But, in respect to substance, I conceive that each part has a more close union with its whole. For, as I said in my first letter (addressed to you while I was still at Rhijnsburg), substance being infinite in its nature, it follows, as I endeavoured to show, that each part belongs to the nature of substance, and, without it, can neither be nor be conceived.

You see, therefore, how and why I think that the human body is a part of nature. As regards the human mind, I believe that it also is a part of nature; for I maintain that there exists in nature an infinite power of thinking, which, in so far as it is infinite, contains subjectively the whole of nature, and its thoughts proceed in the same manner as nature – that is, in the sphere of ideas. Further, I take the human mind to be identical with this said power, not in so far as it is infinite, and perceives the whole of nature, but in so far as it is finite, and perceives only the human body; in this manner, I maintain that the human mind is a part of an infinite understanding.

But to explain, and accurately prove, all these and kindred questions, would take too long; and I do not think you expect as much of me at present. I am afraid that I may have mistaken your meaning, and given an answer to a different question from that which you asked. Please inform me on this point.

You write in your last letter, that I hinted that nearly all the Cartesian laws of motion are false. What I said was, if I remember rightly, that Huyghens thinks so; I myself do not impeach any of the laws except the sixth, concerning which I think Huyghens is also in error. I asked you at the same time to communicate to me the experiment made according to that hypothesis in your Royal Society; as you have not replied, I infer that you are not at liberty to do so. The above-mentioned Huyghens is entirely occupied in polishing lenses. He has fitted up for the purpose a handsome workshop, in which he can also construct moulds. What will be the result I know not, nor, to speak the truth, do I greatly care. Experience has sufficiently taught me, that the free hand is better and more sure than any machine for polishing spherical moulds. I can tell you nothing certain as yet about the success of the clocks or the date of Huyghens' journey to France.

LETTER 34 (39) TO JOHN HUDDE,[26] 7 January 1666

The Unity of God (*1*)

Distinguished Sir,

The demonstration of the unity of God, on the ground that His nature involves necessary existence, which you asked for, and I took note of, I have been prevented by various business from sending to you before. In order to accomplish my purpose, I will premise –

I. That the true definition of anything includes nothing except the simple nature of the thing defined. From this it follows –

II. That no definition can involve or express a multitude or a given number of individuals, inasmuch as it involves and expresses nothing except the nature of the thing as it is in itself. For instance, the definition of a triangle includes nothing beyond the simple nature of a triangle; it does not include any given number of triangles. In like manner, the definition of the mind as a thinking thing, or the definition of God as a perfect Being, includes nothing beyond the natures of the mind and of God, not a given number of minds or gods.

III. That for everything that exists there must necessarily be a positive cause, through which it exists.

IV. This cause may be situate either in the nature and definition of the thing itself (to wit, because existence belongs to its nature or necessarily includes it), or externally to the thing.

From these premisses it follows, that if any given number of individuals exists in nature, there must be one or more causes, which have been able to produce exactly that number of individuals, neither more nor less. If, for instance, there existed in nature twenty men (in order to avoid all confusion, I will assume that these all exist together as primary entities), it is not enough to investigate the cause of human nature in general, in order to account for the existence of these twenty; we must also inquire into the reason, why there exist exactly twenty men, neither more nor less. For (by our third hypothesis) for each man a reason and a cause must be forthcoming, why he should exist. But this cause (by our second and third hypothesis) cannot be contained in the nature of man himself; for the true definition of man does not involve the number of twenty men. Hence (by our fourth hypothesis) the cause for the existence of each of them,

26. Elwes gives the addressee as Christian Huyghens.

must exist externally to them. We may thus absolutely conclude, that all things, which are conceived to exist in the plural number, must necessarily be produced by external causes and not by the force of their own nature. But since (by our second hypothesis) necessary existence appertains to the nature of God, His true definition must necessarily include necessary existence: therefore from His true definition His necessary existence must be inferred. But from His true definition (as I have already demonstrated from our second and third hypotheses) the necessary existence of many gods cannot be inferred. Therefore there only follows the existence of a single God. Which was to be proved.

This, distinguished Sir, has now seemed to me the best method for demonstrating the proposition. I have also proved it differently by means of the distinction between essence and existence; but bearing in mind the object you mentioned to me, I have preferred to send you the demonstration given above. I hope it will satisfy you, and I will await your reply, meanwhile remaining, &c.

LETTER 35 (40) TO JOHN HUDDE,[27] 10 April 1666

The Unity of God (2)

Distinguished Sir,

In your last letter, written on March 30th, you have excellently elucidated the point, which was somewhat obscure to me in your letter of February 10th. As I now know your opinion, I will set forth the state of the question as you conceive it; whether there be only a single Being who subsists by his own sufficiency or force? I not only affirm this to be so, but also undertake to prove it from the fact, that the nature of such a Being necessarily involves existence; perhaps it may also be readily proved from the understanding of God (as I set forth, 'Principles of Cartesian Philosophy,' I. Prop. i), or from others of His attributes. Before treating of the subject I will briefly show, as preliminaries, what properties must be possessed by a Being including necessary existence. To wit:

I. It must be eternal. For if a definite duration be assigned to it, it would beyond that definite duration be conceived as non-existent, or as not involving necessary existence, which would be contrary to its definition.

27. Elwes gives the addressee as Christian Huyghens.

II. It must be simple, not made up of parts. For parts must in nature and knowledge be prior to the whole they compose: this could not be the case with regard to that which is eternal.

III. It cannot be conceived as determinate, but only as infinite. For, if the nature of the said Being were determinate, and conceived as determinate, that nature would beyond the said limits be conceived as non-existant, which again is contrary to its definition.

IV. It is indivisible. For if it were divisible, it could be divided into parts, either of the same or of different nature. If the latter, it could be destroyed and so not exist, which is contrary to its definition. Thus we see that, in attempting to ascribe to such a Being any imperfection, we straightway fall into contradictions. For, whether the imperfection which we wish to assign to the said Being be situate in any defect, or in limitations possessed by its nature, or in any change which it might, through deficiency of power, undergo from external causes, we are always brought back to the contradiction, that a nature which involves necessary existence, does not exist, or does not necessarily exist. I conclude, therefore –

V. That everything, which includes necessary existence, cannot have in itself any imperfection, but must express pure perfection.

VI. Further, since only from perfection can it come about, that any Being should exist by its own sufficiency and force, it follows that, if we assume a Being to exist by its own nature, but not to express all perfections, we must further suppose that another Being exists, which does comprehend in itself all perfections. For, if the less powerful Being exists by its own sufficiency, how much more must the more powerful so exist?

Lastly, to deal with the question, I affirm that there can only be a single Being, of which the existence belongs to its nature; such a Being possesses in itself all perfections I will call God. If there be any Being to whose nature existence belongs, such a Being can contain in itself no imperfection, but must (by my fifth premiss) express every perfection; therefore, the nature of such a Being seems to belong to God (whose existence we are bound to affirm by Premiss VI), inasmuch as He has in Himself all perfections and no imperfections. Nor can it exist externally to God. For if, externally to God, there existed one and the same nature involving necessary existence, such nature would be twofold; but this, by what we have just shown, is absurd. Therefore there is nothing save God, but there is a single God, that involves necessary existence, which was to be proved.

Such, distinguished Sir, are the arguments I can now produce for demonstrating this question. I hope I may also demonstrate to you, that I am, &c.

LETTER 54 (58) TO HUGO BOXEL, September 1674

The World Was Not Made By Chance

Dear Sir,

I will rely on what you said in your letter of the 21st of last month, that friends may disagree on indifferent questions, without injury to their friendship, and will frankly tell you my opinion on the reasons and stories whereon you base your conclusion, that *there are ghosts of every kind, but perhaps none of the female sex.* The reason for my not replying sooner is that the books you quoted are not at hand, in fact I have not found any except Pliny and Suetonius. However, these two have saved me the trouble of consulting any other, for I am persuaded that they all talk in the same strain and hanker after extraordinary tales, which rouse men's astonishment and compel their wonder. I confess that I am not a little amazed, not at the stories, but at those who narrate them. I wonder, that men of talent and judgment should so employ their readiness of speech, and abuse it in endeavouring to convince us of such trifles.

However, let us dismiss the writers, and turn to the question itself. In the first place, we will reason a little about your conclusion. Let us see whether I, who deny that there are spectres or spirits, am on that account less able to understand the authors, who have written on the subject; or whether you, who assert that such beings exist, do not give to the aforesaid writers more credit than they deserve. The distinction you drew, in admitting without hesitation spirits of the male sex, but doubting whether any female spirits exist, seems to me more like a fancy than a genuine doubt. If it were really your opinion, it would resemble the common imagination, that God is masculine, not feminine. I wonder that those, who have seen naked ghosts, have not cast their eyes on those parts of the person, which would remove all doubt; perhaps they were timid, or did not know of this distinction. You would say that this is ridicule, not reasoning: and hence I see, that your reasons appear to you so strong and well founded, that no one can (at least in your judgment) contradict them, unless he be some perverse fellow, who thinks the world has been made by chance. This impels me, before going into your reasons, to set forth briefly my opinion on the question, *whether the world was made by chance*. But I answer, that as it is clear that chance and necessity are two contraries, so is it also clear, that he, who asserts the world to be a necessary effect of the divine nature, must utterly deny that the world has been made by chance; whereas, he who affirms, that God need not have made the world, confirms, though in different language, the doctrine that it has been made by chance; inasmuch as he maintains that it proceeds from a wish, which might never have been formed. However, as this opinion and theory is on the face of it absurd, it is commonly very unanimously admitted, that God's will is eternal, and has never been indifferent; hence it must necessarily be also admitted, you will observe, that the world is a necessary effect of the divine nature. Let them call it will, understanding, or any name they like, they come at last to the same conclusion, that under different names they are expressing one and the same thing. If you ask them, whether the divine will does not differ from the human, they answer, that the former has nothing in common with the latter except its name; especially as they generally admit that God's will, understanding, intellect, essence, and nature are all identical; so I, myself, lest I should confound the divine nature with the human, do not assign to God human attributes, such as will, understanding, attention, hearing, &c. I therefore say, as I have said already, *that the world is a necessary effect of the divine nature, and that it has not been made by chance*. I think this is enough to persuade you, that the opinion of those (if such there be), who say that the world has been made by chance, is entirely contrary to mine; and, relying on this hypothesis, I proceed to examine those reasons which lead you to infer the existence of all kinds of ghosts. I should like to say of these reasons generally, that they seem rather conjectures than reasons, and I can with difficulty believe, that you take them for guiding reasons. However, be they conjectures or be they reasons, let us see whether we can take them for foundations.

Your first reason is, that the existence of ghosts is needful for the beauty and perfection of the universe. Beauty, my dear Sir, is not so much a quality of the object beheld as an effect in him who beholds it. If our sight were longer or shorter, or if our constitution were different, what now appears beautiful to us would seem misshapen, and what we now think misshapen we should regard as beautiful. The most beautiful hand seen through the microscope will appear horrible. Some things are beautiful at a distance, but ugly near; thus things regarded in themselves, and in relation to God, and neither ugly nor beautiful. Therefore, he who says that God has created the world, so that it might be beautiful, is bound to adopt one of the two alternatives, either that God created the world for the sake of men's pleasure and eyesight, or else that He created men's pleasure and eyesight for the sake of the world. Now, whether we adopt the former or the latter of these views, how God could have furthered His object by the creation of ghosts, I cannot see. Perfection and imperfection are names, which do not differ much from the names beauty and ugliness. I only ask, therefore (not to be tedious), which would contribute most to the perfect adornment of the world, ghosts, or a quantity of monsters, such as centaurs, hydras, harpies, satyrs, gryphons, arguses, and other similar inventions? Truly the world would be handsomely bedecked, if God had adorned and embellished it, in obedience to our fancy, with beings, which anyone may readily imagine and dream of, but no one can understand.

Your second reason is, that because spirits express God's image more than embodied creatures, it is probable that He has created them. I frankly confess, that I am as yet in ignorance, how spirits more than other creatures express God. This I know, that between finite and infinite there is no comparison; so that the difference between God and the greatest and most excellent created thing is no less than the difference between God and the least created thing. This argument, therefore, is beside the mark. If I had as clear an idea of ghosts, as I have of a triangle or a circle, I should not in the least hesitate to affirm that they had been created by God; but as the idea I possess of them is just like the ideas, which my imagination forms of harpies, gryphons, hydras, &c., I cannot consider them as anything but dreams, which differ from God as totally, as that which is not differs from that which is.

Your third reason (that as body exists without soul, so soul should exist without body) seems to me equally absurd. Pray tell me, is it not also likely, that memory, hearing, sight, &c., exist without bodies, because bodies exist without memory, hearing, sight, &c., or that a sphere exists without a circle, because a circle exists without a sphere?

Your fourth, and last reason, is the same as your first, and I refer you to my answer given above. I will only observe here, that I do not know which are the highest or which the lowest places, which you conceive as existing in infinite matter, unless you take the earth as the centre of the universe. For if the sun or Saturn be the centre of the universe, the sun, or Saturn, not the earth, will be the lowest.

Thus, passing by this argument and what remains, I conclude, that these and similar reasons will convince no one of the existence of all kinds of ghosts and spectres, unless it be those persons, who shut their ears to the understanding, and allow themselves to be led away by superstition. This last is so hostile to right reason, that she lends willing credence to old wives' tales for the sake of discrediting philosophers.

As regards the stories, I have already said in my first letter, that I do not deny them altogether, but only the conclusion drawn from them. To this I may add, that I do not believe them so thoroughly, as not to doubt many of the details, which are generally added rather for ornament than for bringing out the truth of the story or the conclusion drawn from it. I had hoped, that out of so many stories you would at least have produced one or two, which could hardly be questioned, and which would clearly show that ghosts or spectres exist. The case you relate of the burgomaster, who wanted to infer their existence, because he heard spectral brewers working in his mother's brewhouse at night, and making the same noises as he was accustomed to hear by day, seems to me laughable. In like manner it would be tedious here to examine all the stories of people, who have written on these trifles. To be brief, I cite the instance of Julius Caesar, who, as Suetonius testifies, laughed at such things and yet was happy, if we may trust what Suetonius says in the 59th chapter of his life of that leader. And so should all, who reflect on the human imagination, and the effects of the emotions, laugh at such notions; whatever Lavater and others, who have gone dreaming with him in the matter, may produce to the contrary.

5. Real Definitions

Antoine Arnauld, 1611–1694

Arnauld's clear, firm and judicious tones were often heard amid the controversies of the seventeenth century. He is perhaps best known now for the Fourth Objections to Descartes' *Meditations* and, in particular for his statement of one of the 'Cartesian circles':

> We can be sure that God exists only because we clearly and evidently perceive that; therefore prior to being certain that God exists, we should be certain that whatever we clearly and distinctly perceive is true.

Descartes' reply was unconvincing. Nevertheless the *Meditations* found favour with Arnauld, who later saved their author from suspicion of heresy. Arnauld also crossed swords with Leibniz in an interesting correspondence on the nature of substances and with Malebranche, whose *Traité de la Nature et de la Grace* provoked the *Traité des Vraies et Fausses Idées* in rebuttal.

For modern purposes, however, *The Art of Thinking*, written jointly by Arnauld and Nicole and also known as the *Port Royal Logic*, is the most useful. It appeared anonymously in 1662, when Arnauld and the other inhabitants of the Cistercian abbey of Port Royal du Champs near Paris were up to their ears in theological and political controversy and is, in effect, a plea for reasoned debate. Written in a robust and plain prose and full of scientific and homely examples, it stands between scholastic and recent logics. It contains, for instance, a perceptive treatment of probability which finds echoes in Hume. It contains also lucid accounts of notions like substance, accident, mode, category, sign, cause and definition, which give trouble to the modern reader of seventeenth-century texts.

The passage which follows is entitled in full 'A remedy for confusion introduced by ambiguity; the need and usefulness of definition; real and nominal definition.'[1] The topic is important for grasping what rationalists took to lie at the roots of the tree of knowledge. A logical argument only transmits truth, in the sense that it guarantees only that, *if* its premisses are true, then its conclusions are true. There must therefore be truths to act as the ultimate premisses of all arguments, if the rationalist method is to deliver any truths at all. There must be real as well as nominal definitions.

From *The Art of Thinking*, part I, 1662

CHAPTER 12: *Nominal and Real Definitions*

Our best method of avoiding the confusion born of the ambiguity of words in ordinary language is to construct a new language with new words to which we join only those ideas we want the words to express. For our new language we need not invent new sounds; those already in existence may be used provided that we regard them as mere sounds expressing no meaning. Then, using simple unambiguous words, we specify the meaning to be joined to each such sound. Suppose, for instance, that I wish to prove that the soul is immortal. Since the word 'soul' is ambiguous, as shown in the preceding chapter, its use in my proof will easily give rise to confusion. To avoid this confusion I employ a simple expedient: I regard the sound linked to the word 'soul' as having no meaning whatsoever; and then I assign to this sound – and thus to the word to which the sound is linked – the meaning the word will have throughout my proof, saying, 'In the following discourse let the word 'soul' mean that which is the principle of thought in us.'

I have just given an example of a nominal definition, a type of definition which geometers use. We must now make clear the distinction between nominal and real definitions.

In a real definition we do not arbitrarily join an idea to a word being defined; instead we allow the idea that is ordinarily joined to the word to remain while attempting to discover what other ideas are contained in the idea the word ordinarily expresses. For example, we give a real definition of 'man' when we say that man is a rational animal, for our examination of the idea ex-

1. From the translation by James Dickoff and Patricia James, Bobbs-Merrill, 1964.

pressed by 'man' reveals that another idea is contained therein – in particular, the idea of rational animal. Similarly, when we say that time is the measure of motion, we give a real definition of the word 'time'. Real definitions are in marked contrast to nominal definitions since in nominal definitions we arbitarily assign to a given sound any idea we please by means of words we already understand.

The expression 'nominal definition' is itself ambiguous. We caution the reader not to confuse our use of 'nominal definition' with the use some philosophers make of the expression when they say that a nominal definition is an explication of what a word expresses according either to ordinary usage or to etymology. Of their use of 'nominal definition' we shall speak subsequently. But at the moment we are concerned only that the reader understand that a nominal definition is a writer's arbitrary assigning of a meaning to a word without concern for common usage in order that his discourse might be understood.

Some conclusions may be drawn from what we have said so far concerning nominal and real definitions. First of all, nominal definitions are arbitrary but real definitions are not. Since any sound is intrinsically capable of expressing any idea whatsoever, I am permitted for my own use to choose a certain sound to express one precise idea, provided that I make my usage known to my readers. But the case is completely different with real definitions, for the relations which obtain among ideas independent of man's will. If in attempting to define a word we relate to the idea expressed by the word another idea not contained in the former idea, we necessarily fall into error.

Let me illustrate my first conclusion by an example. Suppose I strip the word 'parallelogram' of all meaning. I can then let the word refer to a triangle without committing error, provided that I understand the word 'parallelogram' only in the sense mentioned. I shall be able to say now that a parallelogram has three angles whose sum is that of two right angles. But suppose I allow 'parallelogram' to keep its ordinary meaning – in short, to be used to refer to a figure whose sides are parallel. Then if I offered as a definition the statement that a parallelogram was a three-sided figure. I would have formed a real definition; but this real definition would be false, since it is impossible that a three-sided figure have parallel sides.

Secondly, we may conclude that nominal definitions cannot

be questioned, for they are arbitrary. Once a man has told us that he has assigned a certain meaning to a given sound, we cannot contest this assignment nor deny that the sound has this meaning in the use he makes of the sound. We may, however, question real definitions, since they can be false as shown above.

Thirdly, it follows that a nominal definition, because it cannot be questioned, may be taken at face value as an 'assumption'. Since a statement of a real definition can be denied by anyone who finds in it some obscurity, the real definition must be proved and cannot be assumed – at least, not unless it is as self-evident as an axiom.

What we have just said – that nominal definitions can be taken as assumptions – requires some explanation. Nominal definitions can be so taken only because we cannot dispute that a certain cited idea can be assigned as the meaning of a given word. But from such an assignment nothing further can be concluded. Nor can we say that, simply because an idea has been assigned to a word, the referent of the word is an existent thing. For example, I can define the word 'chimera' as follows: I call a chimera that which implies a contradiction. Yet, it does not follow from this definition that a chimera is any existent thing. Similarly, if a philosopher says to me, 'I shall call heaviness the internal principle that makes a stone fall without anything having pushed it', I shall not contest his definition. On the contrary, I shall receive it willingly because it enables me to understand what he wishes to say. I shall deny, however, that what he understands by this word 'heaviness' is any existent thing; for there is no such principle in stones.

I have expounded this third point somewhat at length, because there are two major abuses which are current on this subject in philosophy. The first is to confuse real definitions with nominal definitions and to ascribe to the former what belongs only to the latter. Philosophers offer many real definitions but claim for them the unassailability of nominal definitions, even though the proposed definitions be false, capturing neither our natural ideas or things nor the true natures of things. If one is bold enough to reject these very assailable definitions, he is claimed to be unworthy even of refutation.

The second abuse is the practice of leaving ideas in confusion, a practice which results from a failure to join given words to certain clearly cited ideas by means of nominal definitions.

Consequently, many disputes in philosophy are really only verbal. In his 'proofs' a philosopher often makes use of what is clear and true in a confused idea in order to establish something that is false and obscure – a deception which would be easily recognized had he defined the words he was using. For example, philosophers commonly believe that there is nothing in the world clearer than that fire is hot and that a stone is heavy; to deny this, they say, would be sheer folly. As long as the philosopher does not define his words, no one will dispute him. Once the words are defined, the truth or falsity of the philosopher's contention will be easily ascertained.

For in defining words, the philosopher must tell us what he understands by the word 'hot' and the word 'heavy'. If he takes 'heat' to mean that which causes in us the feeling of heat and takes 'heaviness' to mean that which causes things to fall when unsupported, then the philosopher is quite right in maintaining that to deny that fire is hot or that a stone is heavy is unreasonable. If, however, the philosopher means by 'heat' that which has in itself a quality similar to what we imagine when we sense heat and means by 'heavy' that which is itself impelled by some inner principle toward the earth's centre without being pushed by anything, then the philosopher's position is untenable. To deny that fire is hot or that a stone is heavy in the senses of 'hot' and 'heavy' just explained is to deny not a clear statement but a very obscure one.

The great utility of nominal definitions lies in their enabling us to understand what is the point at issue. Once a nominal definition is made, we avoid those endless disputes – so common in ordinary conversation – which arise from a word's ambiguity.

There is still another advantage in using nominal definitions. Although often a great many words are required to express an idea distinctly, repeating such a string of words is a cumbersome nuisance, especially in scientific treatises. So, having once explained an idea by an expression consisting of many words, we then adopt the convention of allowing a single word to express that idea. For example, having understood that there are some numbers which are exactly divisible by two, we use a single word to refer to this characteristic: We say that any number which is exactly divisible by two is to be called an even number. Clearly, then, every time we use the defined word we must mentally substitute the definition if we are to understand the discourse.

We must, so to speak, have the definition at our fingertips so that as soon as the defined word is used – say 'even number' – we immediately call to mind the definition, 'a number which is exactly divisible by two'. People – for example, the geometers – who define their terms with such care hope by these definitions to shorten their explanations. (For, as St Augustine says, repeated circumlocutions make a word very tiresome.) But when a definition is used there is no intention of abridging the ideas to be expressed. The claim is that wherever the defined word is used the mind supplies the complete idea which is more explicitly, though more clumsily, expressed by the definition than by the defined word.

6. The Best of All Possible Worlds

Gottfried Wilhelm Leibniz, 1646–1714

Spinoza's notion of substance required that each item in a complete system was fully explicable in terms of the whole. This meant, among other things, that free will as commonly conceived was impossible. But there seemed to be no escaping Spinozist conclusions, given the Rationalist account of human knowledge and scientific explanation. Spinoza's remedy for the muddles of Descartes' dualism threatened to be the only one.

So the only move open to Leibniz was to replace Spinoza's single, total substance with infinitely many independent ones. In the *Monadology* he depicted the universe as an infinite set of Monads, each expressing all the others from its own point of view. This difficult conception is variously put but the following remark (from a letter to Arnauld) is as helpful as any:

> In consulting the notion which I have of every true proposition, I find that every predicate, necessary or contingent, past or present or future, is comprised in the notion of the subject, and I ask no more . . . The proposition in question is of great importance, and deserves to be well established, for it follows that every soul is as a world apart, independent of everything else except God; that it is not only immortal and so to speak impassible, but that it keeps in its substance traces of all that happens to it.

Monads, being substances, cannot interact but there can and, in a rationally ordered world, must be correlations among the predicates true of each. God allowed for the desires of the monads when choosing which of the possible worlds to create, rather as a perfect author might plot the perfect novel by looking simultaneously through the eyes of all the characters. There is a determinate rational harmony but not a determinate necessity about the history of the universe.

The stuff of Leibniz' universe is ultimately living force or vital energy (*vis viva*), which in its active aspect is to be taken as consciousness. A monad is a sort of locus of energy, a notional point, which would be an infinitely small atom, were space a set of real positions and not, as Leibniz held, a scheme of relations. Again, the conception is a hugely difficult one and the reader will find further problems as he proceeds.

Epistemologically 'our reasonings are founded on two great principles, that of Contradiction, in virtue of which we judge that to be false which involves contradiction and that true which is opposed or contradictory to the false; and that of Sufficient Reason, in virtue of which we hold that no fact can be real or existent, no statement true, unless there be a sufficient reason why it is so and not otherwise, although most often these reasons cannot be known to us' (*Monadology* 31, 32). The former principle defines the set of all possible worlds; the latter determines which of the possible worlds we actually live in. 'God has chosen that world which is the most perfect, that is to say, which is at the same time the simplest in its laws and the richest in its phenomena' (*Discourse on Metaphysics* sec. 6). It can be argued that the upshot is a determinism as complete as Spinoza's. (According to Russell, for instance, the Law of Non-contradiction states that all analytic propositions are true and the Principle of Sufficient Reason that all true propositions are analytic.) Leibniz never accepted this, however, insisting that some truths were genuinely contingent, that reasons incline without necessitating and, in general, that there is a basic distinction between what is morally necessary (because God is good) and what is metaphysically necessary (because absolutely true for all possible worlds). The viability of Leibniz' Rationalist distinction between necessary and contingent remains perhaps the major crux in Rationalist scholarship.

There are also other principles in Leibniz' work, which can plausibly be treated as applications of the Principles of Sufficient Reason. Leibniz held that every event has a cause (or 'reason'); that God always acts for the best (for instance, in creating a world which embodies the best solution to the problem of evil); that no two monads have all their properties in common (the Identity of Indiscernibles); that the history of each monad accords with the history of all others (the Preestablished Harmony). The number and relation of these principles is a further topic of dispute.

Leibniz is a clever, mercurial and ambitious thinker, whose huge and flamboyant output was halted only by his death in the midst of a splenetic correspondence with Samuel Clarke. His contributions to mathematics, jurisprudence, ethics and theology were important and distinguished and his careers as diplomat, inventor and man of affairs are noteworthy. The selections here[1] are followed by two brief excerpts from Locke's *Essay Concerning the Human Understanding* set against remarks from Leibniz' *New Essays*.[2] The subject is Locke's celebrated assault on Innate Ideas. Leibniz is able to show that rationalism is not so easily demolished but students of Locke will appreciate that Leibniz is not simply teasing, when he remarks, 'I am led to believe that at bottom his opinion is not different from mine, or rather from the common opinion, inasmuch as he recognises two sources of our knowledge, the Senses and Reflection.'[3]

Discourse on Metaphysics, 1686

I. *Concerning the divine perfection and that God does everything in the most desirable way.*

The conception of God which is the most common and the most full of meaning is expressed well enough in the words: God is an absolutely perfect being. The implications, however, of these words fail to receive sufficient consideration. For instance, there are many different kinds of perfection, all of which God possesses, and each one of them pertains to him in the highest degree.

We must also know what perfection is. One thing which can surely be affirmed about it is that those forms or natures which are not susceptible of it to the highest degree, say the nature of numbers or of figures, do not permit of perfection. This is because the number which is the greatest of all (that is, the sum of all the numbers), and likewise the greatest of all figures, imply contradictions. The greatest knowledge, however, and omnipotence contain no impossibility. Consequently power and

1. From *Leibniz Selections*, edited by Philip Wiener, Scribners, 1951.
2. From the translation by A. G. Langley, New York, Macmillan, 1896.
3. c.f. p. 364 below.

knowledge do admit of perfection, and in so far as they pertain to God they have no limits.

Whence it follows that God who possesses supreme and infinite wisdom acts in the most perfect manner not only metaphysically, but also from the moral standpoint. And with respect to ourselves it can be said that the more we are enlightened and informed in regard to the works of God the more will we be disposed to find them excellent and conforming entirely to that which we might desire.

II. *Against those who hold that there is in the works of God no goodness, or that the principles of goodness and beauty are arbitrary.*

Therefore I am far removed from the opinion of those who maintain that there are no principles of goodness or perfection in the nature of things, or in the ideas which God has about them, and who say that the works of God are good only through the formal reason that God has made them. If this position were true, God, knowing that he is the author of things, would not have to regard them afterwards and find them good, as the Holy Scripture witnesses. Such anthropological expressions are used only to let us know that excellence is recognized in regarding the works themselves, even if we do not consider their evident dependence on their author. This is confirmed by the fact that it is in reflecting upon the works that we are able to discover the one who wrought. They must therefore bear in themselves his character. I confess that the contrary opinion seems to me extremely dangerous and closely approaches that of recent innovators who hold that the beauty of the universe and the goodness which we attribute to the works of God are chimeras of human beings who think of God in human terms In saying, therefore, that things are not good according to any standard of goodness, but simply by the will of God, it seems to me that one destroys, without realizing it, all the love of God and all his glory; for why praise him for what he has done, if he would be equally praiseworthy in doing the contrary? Where will be his justice and his wisdom if he has only a certain despotic power, if arbitrary will takes the place of reasonableness, and if in accord with the definition of tyrants, justice consists in that which is pleasing to the most powerful? Besides it seems that every act of willing supposes some reason for the willing and this reason, of course, must precede the act. This is why, accordingly, I find so strange those expressions of certain philosophers who say that the eternal truths of metaphysics and Geometry, and consequently the principles of goodness, of justice, and of perfection are effects only of the will of God. To me it seems that all these follow from his understanding, which does not depend upon his will any more than does his essence.

III. *Against those who think that God might have made things better than he has.*

Neither am I able to approve of the opinion of certain modern writers who boldly maintain that that which God has made is not perfect in the highest degree, and that he might have done better. It seems to me that the consequences of such an opinion are wholly inconsistent with the glory of God. *Uti minus malum habet rationem boni, ita minus bonum habet rationem mali.* I think that one acts imperfectly if he acts with less perfection than he is capable of. To show that an architect could have done better is to find fault with his work. Furthermore this opinion is contrary to the Holy Scriptures when they assure us of the goodness of God's work. For if comparative perfection were sufficient, then in whatever way God had accomplished his work, since there is an infinitude of possible imperfections, it would always have been good in comparison with the less perfect; but a thing is little praiseworthy when it can be praised only in this way.

I believe that a great many passages from the divine writings and from the holy fathers will be found favoring my position, while hardly any will be found in favor of that of these modern thinkers. Their opinion is, in my judgment, foreign to the writers of antiquity and is a deduction based upon the too slight acquaintance which we have with the general harmony of the universe and with the hidden reasons for God's conduct. In our ignorance, therefore, we are tempted to decide audaciously that many things might have been done better.

These modern thinkers insist upon certain hardly tenable subtleties, for they imagine that nothing is so perfect that there might not have been something more perfect. This is an error. They think, indeed, that they are thus safeguarding the liberty of God. As if it were not the highest liberty to act in perfection according to the sovereign reason. For to think that God acts in anything without having any reason for his willing, even if we overlook the fact that such action seems impossible, is an opinion which conforms little to God's glory. For example, let us suppose that God chooses between A and B, and that he takes A without any reason for preferring it to B. I say that this action on the part of God is at least not praiseworthy, for all praise ought to be founded upon reason which *ex hypothesei* is not present here. My opinion is that God does nothing for which he does not deserve to be glorified.

IV. *That love for God demands on our part complete satisfaction with and acquiescence in that which he has done.*

The general knowledge of this great truth that God acts always in the most perfect and most desirable manner possible, is in my opinion the basis of the love which we owe to God in all things; for he who loves seeks his satisfaction in the felicity or perfection of the subject loved and in the perfection of his actions. *Idem velle et idem nolle vera amicitia est.* I believe that it is difficult to love God truly when one, having the power to change his disposition, is not disposed to wish for that which God desires. In fact those who are not satisfied with what God does seem to me like dissatisfied subjects whose attitude is not very different from that of rebels. I hold, therefore, that on these principles, to act conformably to the love of God is it not sufficient to force oneself to be patient, we must be really satisfied with all that comes to us according to his will. I mean this acquiescence in regard to the past; for as regards the future one should not be a quietist with the arms folded, open to ridicule, awaiting that which God will do; according to the sophism which the ancients called λόγον ἄεργον, the lazy reason. It is necessary to act conformably to the presumptive will of God as far as we are able to judge of it, trying with all our might to contribute to the general welfare and particularly to the ornamentation and the perfection of that which touches us, or of that which is nigh and so to speak at our hand. For if the future shall perhaps show that God has not wished our good intention to have its way, it does not follow that he has not wished us to act as we have; on the contrary, since he is the best of all masters, he ever demands only the right intentions, and it is for him to know the hour and the proper place to let good designs succeed.

V. *In what the principles of the divine perfection consist, and that the simplicity of the means counterbalances the richness of the effects.*

It is sufficient, therefore, to have this confidence in God, that he has done everything for the best and that nothing will be able to injure those who love him. To know in particular, however, the reasons which have moved him to choose this order of the universe, to permit sin, to dispense his salutary grace in a certain manner – this passes the capacity of a finite mind, above all when such a mind has not come into the joy of the vision of God. Yet it is possible to make some general remarks touching the course of providence in the government of things. One is able to say, therefore, that he who acts perfectly is like an excellent Geometer who knows how to find the best construction for a problem; like a good architect who utilizes his location and the funds destined for the building in the most advantageous manner, leaving nothing which shocks or which does not display that beauty of which it is capable; like a good householder who employs his property in such a way that there shall be nothing uncultivated or sterile; like a clever machinist who makes his production in the least difficult way possible; and like an intelligent author who encloses the most of reality in the least possible compass.

Of all beings those which are the most perfect and occupy the least possible space, that is to say those which interfere with one another the least, are the spirits whose perfections are the virtues. That is why we may not doubt that the felicity of the spirits is the principal aim of God and that he puts this purpose into execution, as far as the general harmony will permit. We will recur to this subject again.

When the simplicity of God's way is spoken of, reference is specially made to the means which he employs, and on the other hand when the variety, richness and abundance are referred to, the ends or effects are had in mind. Thus one ought to be proportioned to the other, just as the cost of a building should balance the beauty and grandeur which is expected. It is true that nothing costs God anything, just as there is no cost for a philosopher who makes hypotheses in constructing his imaginary world, because God has only to make decrees in order that a real world come into being; but in matters of wisdom the decrees or hypotheses meet the expenditure in proportion as they are more independent of one another. Reason wishes to avoid multiplicity in hypotheses or principles very much as the simplest system is preferred in Astronomy.

VI. *That God does nothing which is not orderly, and that it is not even possible to conceive of events which are not regular.*

The activities or the acts of will of God are commonly divided into ordinary and extraordinary. But it is well to bear in mind that God does nothing out of order. Therefore, that which passes for extraordinary is so only with regard to a particular order established among the created things, for as regards the universal order, everything conforms to it. This is so true that not only does nothing occur in this world which is absolutely irregular, but it is even impossible to conceive of such an occurrence. Because, let us suppose for example that some one jots down a quantity of points upon a sheet of paper helter skelter, as do those who exercise the ridiculous art of Geomancy; now I say that it is possible to find a geometrical line whose concept shall be uniform and constant, that is, in accordance with a certain formula, and which line at the same time shall pass through all of those points, and in the same order in which the hand jotted them down; also if a continuous line be traced, which is now straight, now circular, and now of any other description, it is possible to find a mental equivalent, a formula or an equation common to all the points of this line by virtue of which formula the changes in the direction of the line must occur. There is no instance of a face whose contour does not form part of a geometric line and which can not be traced entire by a certain mathematical motion. But when the formula is very complex, that which conforms to it passes for irregular. Thus we may say that in whatever manner God might have created the world, it would always have been regular and in a certain order. God, however, has chosen the most perfect, that is to say the one which is at the same time the simplest in hypotheses and the richest in phenomena, as might be the case with a geometric line, whose construction was easy, but whose properties and effects were extremely remarkable and of great significance. I use these comparisons to picture a certain imperfect resemblance to the divine wisdom, and to point out that which may at least raise our minds to conceive in some sort what cannot otherwise be expressed. I do not pretend at all to explain thus the great mystery upon which the whole universe depends.

VII. *That miracles conform to the regular order although they go against the subordinate regulations; concerning that which God desires or permits and concerning general and particular intentions.*

Now since nothing is done which is not orderly, we may say that miracles are quite within the order of natural operations. We use the term natural of these operations because they conform to certain subordinate regulations which we call the nature of things. For it can be said that this nature is only a custom of God's which he can change on the occasion of a stronger reason than that which moved him to use these regulations. As regards general and particular intentions, according to the way in which we understand the matter, it may be said on the one hand that everything is in accordance with his most general intention, or that which best conforms to the most perfect order he has chosen; on the other hand, however, it is also possible to say that he has particular intentions which are exceptions to the subordinate regulations above mentioned. Of God's laws, however, the most universal, i.e., that which rules the whole course of the universe, is without exceptions.

It is possible to say that God desires everything which is an object of his particular intention. When we consider the objects of his general intentions, however, such as are the modes of activities of created things and especially of the reasoning creatures with whom God wishes to co-operate, we must make a distinction; for if the action is good in itself, we may say that God wishes it and at times commands it, even though it does not take place; but if it is bad in itself and becomes good only by accident through the course of events and especially after chastisement and satisfaction have corrected its malignity and rewarded the ill with interest in such a way that more perfection results in the whole train of circumstances than would have come if that ill had not occurred, – if all this takes place we must say that God permits the evil, and not that he desired it, although he has co-operated by means of the laws of nature which he has established. He knows how to produce the greatest good from them.

VIII. *In order to distinguish between the activities of God and the activities of created things we must explain the conception of an individual substance.*

It is quite difficult to distinguish God's actions from those of his creatures. Some think that God does everything; others imagine that he only conserves the force that he has given to created things. How far can we say either of these opinions is right?

In the first place since activity and passivity pertain properly to individual substances (*actiones sunt suppositorum*) it will be necessary to explain what such a substance is. It is indeed true that when several predicates are attributes of a single subject and this subject is not an attribute of another, we speak of it as an individual substance, but this is not enough, and such an explanation is merely nominal. We must therefore inquire what it is to be an attribute in reality of a certain subject. Now it is evident that every true predication has some basis in the nature of things, and even when a proposition is not identical, that is, when the predicate is not expressly contained in the subject, it is still necessary that it be virtually contained in it, and this is what the philosophers call *in-esse*, saying thereby that the predicate is in the subject. Thus the content of the subject must always include that of the predicate in such a way that if one understands perfectly the concept of the subject, he will know that the predicate appertains to it also. This being so, we are able to say that this is the nature of an individual substance or of a complete being, namely, to afford a conception so complete that the concept shall be sufficient for the understanding of it and for the deduction of all the predicates of which the substance is or may become the subject. Thus the quality of king, which belonged to Alexander the Great, an abstraction from the subject, is not sufficiently determined to constitute an individual, and does not contain the other qualities of the same subject, nor everything which the idea of this prince includes. God, however, seeing the individual concept, or hæcceity, of Alexander, sees there at the same time the basis and the reason of all the predicates which can be truly uttered regarding him; for instance that he will conquer Darius and Porus, even to the point of knowing *a priori* (and not by experience) whether he died a natural death or by poison, – facts which we can learn only through history. When we carefully consider the connection of things we see also the possibility of saying that there was always in the soul of Alexander marks of all that had happened to him and evidences of all that would happen to him and traces even of everything which occurs in the universe, although God alone could recognize them all.

IX. *That every individual substance expresses the whole universe in its own manner and that in its full concept are included all its experiences together with all the attendant circumstances and the whole sequence of exterior events.*

There follow from these considerations several noticeable paradoxes; among others that it is not true that two substances may be exactly alike and differ only numerically, *solo numero*, and that what St Thomas says on this point regarding angels and intelligences (*quod ibi omne individuum sit species infima*) is true of all substances, provided that the specific difference is understood as Geometers understand it in the case of figures; again that a substance will be able to commence only through creation and perish only through annihilation; that a substance cannot be divided into two nor can one be made out of two, and that thus the number of substances neither augments nor diminishes through natural means, although they are frequently transformed. Furthermore every substance is like an entire world and like a mirror of God, or indeed of the whole world which it portrays, each one in its own fashion; almost as the same city is variously represented according to the various viewpoints from which it is regarded. Thus the universe is multiplied in some sort as many times as there are substances, and the glory of God is multiplied in the same way by as many wholly different representations of his works. It can indeed be said that every substance bears in some sort the character of God's infinite wisdom and omnipotence, and imitates him as much as it is able to; for it expresses, although confusedly, all that happens in the universe, past, present and future, deriving thus a certain resemblance to an infinite perception or power of knowing. And since all other substances express this particular substance and accommodate themselves to it, we can say that it exerts its power upon all the others in imitation of the omnipotence of the creator.

X. *That the belief in substantial forms has a certain basis in fact, but that these forms effect no changes in the phenomena and must not be employed for the explanation of particular events.*

It seems that the ancients, able men, who were accustomed to profound meditations and taught theology and philosophy for several centuries and some of whom recommend themselves to us on account of their piety, had some knowledge of that which we have just said and this is why they introduced and maintained the substantial forms so much decried to-day. But they were not so far from the truth nor so open to ridicule as the common run of our new philosophers imagine. I grant that the consideration of these forms is of no service in the details of physics and ought not to be employed in the explanation of particular phenomena. In regard to this last point, the schoolmen were at fault, as were also the physicists of times past who followed their example, thinking they had given the reason for the properties of a body in mentioning the forms and qualities without going to the trouble of examining the manner of operation; as if one should be content to say that a clock had a certain amount of clockness derived from its form, and should not inquire in what that clockness consisted. This is indeed enough for the man who buys it, provided he surrenders the care of it to someone else. The fact, however, that there was this misunderstanding and misuse of the substantial forms should not bring us to throw away something whose recognition is so necessary in metaphysics. Since without these we will not be able, I hold, to know the ultimate principles nor to lift our minds to the knowledge of the incorporeal natures and of the marvels of God. Yet as the geometer does not need to encumber his mind with the famous puzzle of the composition of the continuum, and as no moralist, and still less a jurist or a statesman has need to trouble himself with the great difficulties which arise in conciliating free will with the providential activity of God (since the geometer is able to make all his demonstrations and the statesman can complete all his deliberations without entering into these discussions which are so necessary and important in Philosophy and Theology), so in the same way the physicist can explain his experiments, now using simpler experiments already made, now employing geometrical and mechanical demonstrations without any need of the general considerations which belong to another sphere, and if he employs the co-operation of God, or perhaps of some soul or animating force, or something else of a similar nature, he goes out of his path quite as much as that man who, when facing an important practical question, would wish to enter into profound argumentations regarding the nature of destiny and of our liberty; a fault which men quite frequently commit without realizing it when they cumber their minds with considerations regarding fate, and thus they are even sometimes turned from a good resolution or from some necessary provision.

XI. *That the opinions of the theologians and of the so-called scholastic philosophers are not to be wholly despised.*

I know that I am advancing a great paradox in pretending to resuscitate in some sort the ancient philosophy, and to recall *postliminio* the substantial forms almost banished from our modern thought. But perhaps I will not be condemned lightly when it is known that I have long meditated over the modern philosophy and that I have devoted much time to experiments in physics and to the demonstrations of geometry and that I, too, for a long time was persuaded of the baselessness of those 'beings' which, however, I was finally obliged to take up again in spite of myself and as though by force. The many investigations which I carried on compelled me to recognize that our moderns do not do sufficient justice to Saint Thomas and to the other great men of that period and that there is in the theories of the scholastic philosophers and theologians far more solidity than is imagined, provided that these theories are employed *à propos* and in their place. I am persuaded that if some careful and meditative mind were to take the trouble to clarify and direct their thoughts in the manner of analytic geometers, he would find a great treasure of very important truths, wholly demonstrable.

XII. *That the conception of the extension of a body is in a way imaginary and does not constitute the substance of the body.*

But to resume the thread of our discussion, I believe that he who will meditate upon the nature of substance, as I have explained it above, will find that the whole nature of bodies is not exhausted in their extension, that is to say, in their size, figure and motion, but that we must recognize something which corresponds to soul, something which is commonly called substantial form, although these forms effect no change in the phenomena, any more than do the souls of beasts, that is if they have souls. It is even possible to demonstrate that the ideas of size, figure and motion are not so distinctive as is imagined, and that they stand for something imaginary relative to our perceptions as do, although to a greater extent, the ideas of color, heat, and the other similar qualities in regard to which we may doubt whether they are actually to be found in the nature of the things outside of us. This is why these latter qualities are unable to constitute 'substance' and if there is no other principle of identity in bodies than that which has just been referred to a body would not subsist more than for a moment.

The souls and the substance-forms of other bodies are entirely different from intelligent souls which alone know their actions, and not only do not perish through natural means but indeed always retain the knowledge of what they are; a fact which makes them alone open to chastisement or recompense, and makes them citizens of the republic of the universe whose monarch is God. Hence it follows that all the other creatures should serve them, a point which we shall discuss more amply later.

XIII. *As the individual concept of each person includes once for all everything which can ever happen to him, in it can be seen the* a priori *evidences or the reasons for the reality of each event, and why one happened sooner than the other. But these events, however certain, are nevertheless contingent, being based on the free choice of God and of his creatures. It is true that their choices always have their reasons, but they incline to the choices under no compulsion of necessity.*

But before going further it is necessary to meet a difficulty which may arise regarding the principles which we have set forth in the preceding. We have said that the concept of an individual substance includes once for all everything which can ever happen to it and that in considering this concept one will be able to see everything which can truly be said concerning the individual, just as we are able to see in the nature of a circle all the properties which can be derived from it. But does it not seem that in this way the difference between contingent and necessary truths will be destroyed, that there will be no place for human liberty, and that an absolute fatality will rule as well over all our actions as over all the rest of the events of the world? To this I reply that a distinction must be made between that which is certain and that which is necessary. Every one grants that future contingencies are assured since God foresees them, but we do not say just because of that that they are necessary. But it will be objected, that if any conclusion can be deduced infallibly from some definition or concept, it is necessary; and now since we have maintained that everything which is to happen to anyone is already virtually included in his nature or concept, as all the properties are contained in the definition of a circle, therefore, the difficulty still remains. In order to meet the objection completely, I say that the connection or sequence is of two kinds: the one, absolutely necessary, whose contrary implies contradiction, occurs in the eternal verities like the truths of geometry; the other is necessary only *ex hypothesei*, and so to speak by accident, and in itself it is contingent since the contrary is not implied. This latter sequence is not founded upon ideas wholly pure and upon the pure understanding of God, but upon his free decrees and upon the processes of the universe. Let us give an example. Since Julius Caesar will become perpetual Dictator and master of the Republic and will overthrow the liberty of Rome, this action is contained in his concept, for we have supposed that it is the nature of such a perfect concept of a subject to involve everything, in fact so that the predicate may be included in the subject *ut possit inesse subjecto*. We may say that it is not in virtue of this concept or idea that he is obliged to perform this action, since it pertains to him only because God knows everything. But it will be insisted in reply that his nature or form responds to this concept, and since God imposes upon him this personality, he is compelled henceforth to live up to it. I could reply by instancing the similar case of the future contingencies which as yet have no reality save in the understanding and will of God, and which, because God has given them in advance this form, must needs correspond to it. But I prefer to overcome a difficulty rather than to excuse it by instancing other difficulties, and what I am about to say will serve to clear up the one as well as the other. It is here that must be applied the distinction in the kind of relation, and I say that that which happens conformably to these decrees is assured, but that it is not therefore necessary, and if anyone did the contrary, he would do nothing impossible in itself, although it is impossible *ex hypothesei* that that other happen. For if anyone were capable of carrying out a complete demonstration by virtue of which he could prove this connection of the subject, which is Caesar, with the predicate, which is his successful enterprise, he would bring us to see in fact that the future dictatorship of Caesar had its basis in his concept or nature, so that one would see there a reason why he resolved to cross the Rubicon rather than to stop, and why he gained instead of losing the day at Pharsalus, and that it was reasonable and by consequence assured that this would occur, but one would not prove that it was necessary in itself, nor that the contrary implied a contradiction, almost in the same way in which it is reasonable and assured that God will always do what is best although that which is less perfect is not thereby implied. For it would be found that this demonstration of this predicate as belonging to Caesar is not as absolute as are those of numbers or of geometry, but that this predicate supposes a sequence of things which God has shown by his free will. This sequence is based on the first free decree of God which was to do always that which is the most perfect and upon the decree which God made following the first one, regarding human nature, which is that men should always do, although freely, that which appears to be the best. Now every truth which is founded upon this kind of decree is contingent, although certain, for the decrees of God do not change the possibilities of things and, as I have already said, although God assuredly chooses the best, this does not prevent that which is less perfect from being possible in itself. Although it will never happen, it is not its impossibility but its imperfection which causes him to reject it. Now nothing is necessitated whose opposite is possible. One will then be in a position to satisfy these kinds of difficulties, however great they may appear (and in fact they have not been less vexing to all other thinkers who have ever treated this matter), provided that he considers well that all contingent propositions have reasons why they are thus, rather than otherwise, or indeed (what is the same thing) that they have proof *a priori* of their truth, which render them certain and show that the connection of the subject and predicate in these propositions has its basis in the nature of the one and of the other, but he must further remember that such contingent propositions have not the demonstrations of necessity, since their reasons are founded only on the principle of contingency or of the existence of things, that is to say, upon that which is, or which appears to be the best among several things equally possible. Necessary truths, on the other hand, are founded upon the principle of contradiction, and upon the possibility or impossibility of the essences themselves, without regard here to the free will of God or of creatures.

XIV. *God produces different substances according to the different views which he has of the world, and by the intervention of God, the appropriate nature of each substance brings it about that what happens to one corresponds to what happens to all the others, without, however, their acting upon one another directly.*

After having seen, to a certain extent, in what the nature of substances consists, we must try to explain the dependence they have upon one another and their actions and passions. Now it is first of all very evident that created substances depend upon God who preserves them and can produce them continually by a kind of emanation just as we produce our thoughts, for when God turns, so to say, on all sides and in all fashions, the general system of phenomena which he finds it good to produce for the sake of manifesting his glory, and when he regards all the aspects of the world in all possible manners, since there is no relation which escapes his omniscience, the result of each view of the universe as seen from a different position is a substance which expresses the universe conformably to this view, provided God sees fit to render his thought effective and to produce the substance, and since God's vision is always true, our perceptions are always true and that which deceives us are our judgments, which are of us. Now we have said before, and it follows from what we have just said that each substance is a world by itself, independent of everything else excepting God; therefore, all our phenomena that is all things which are ever able to happen to us, are only consequences of our being. Now as the phenomena maintain a certain order conformably to our nature, or so to speak to the world which is in us (from whence it follows that we can, for the regulation of our conduct, make useful observations which are justified by the outcome of the future phenomena) and as we are thus able often to judge the future by the past without deceiving ourselves, we have sufficient grounds for saying that these phenomena are true and we will not be put to the task of inquiring whether they are outside of us, and whether others perceive them also.

Nevertheless it is most true that the perceptions and expressions of all substances intercorrespond, so that each one following independently certain reasons or laws which he has noticed meets others which are doing the same, as when several have agreed to meet together in a certain place on a set day, they are able to carry out the plan if they wish. Now although all express the same phenomena, this does not bring it about that their expressions are exactly alike. It is sufficient if they are proportional. As when several spectators think they see the same thing and are agreed about it, although each one sees or speaks according to the measure of his vision. It is God alone (from whom all individuals emanate continually, and who sees the universe not only as they see it, but besides in a very different way from them) who is the cause of this correspondence in their phenomena and who brings it about that that which is particular to one, is also common to all, otherwise there would be no relation. In a way, then, we might properly say, although it seems strange, that a particular substance never acts upon another particular substance nor is it acted upon by it. That which happens to each one is only the consequence of its complete idea or concept, since this idea already includes all the predicates and expresses the whole universe. In fact nothing can happen to us except thoughts and perceptions, and all our thoughts and perceptions are but the consequence, contingent it is true, of our precedent thoughts and perceptions, in such a way that were I able to consider directly all that happens or appears to me at the present time, I should be able to see all that will happen to me or that will ever appear to me. This future will not fail me, and will surely appear to me even if all that which is outside of me were destroyed, save only that God and myself were left.

Since, however, we ordinarily attribute to other things an action upon us which brings us to perceive things in a certain manner, it is necessary to consider the basis of this judgment and to inquire what there is of truth in it.

XV. *The action of one finite substance upon another consists only in the increase in the degrees of the expression of the first combined with a decrease in that of the second, in so far as God has in advance fashioned them so that they shall act in accord.*

Without entering into a long discussion it is sufficient for reconciling the language of metaphysics with that of practical life to remark that we preferably attribute to ourselves, and with reason, the phenomena which we express the most perfectly, and that we attribute to other substances these phenomena which each one expresses the best. Thus a substance, which is of an infinite extension in so far as it expresses all, becomes limited in proportion to its more or less perfect manner of expression. It is thus then that we may conceive of substances as interfering with and limiting one another, and hence we are able to say that in this sense they act upon one another, and that they, so to speak, accommodate themselves to one another. For it can happen that a single change which augments the expression of the one may diminish that of the other. Now the virtue of a particular substance is to express well the glory of God, and the better it expresses it, the less is it limited. Everything when it expresses its virtue or power, that is to say, when it acts, changes to better, and expands just in so far as it acts. When therefore a change occurs by which several substances are affected (in fact every change affects them all) I think we may say that those substances, which by this change pass immediately to a greater degree of perfection, or to a more perfect expression, exert power and act, while those which pass to a lesser degree disclose their weakness and suffer. I also hold that every activity of a substance which has perception implies some pleasure, and every passion some pain, except that it may very well happen that a present advantage will be eventually destroyed by a greater evil, whence it comes that one may sin in acting or exerting his power and in finding pleasure.

XVI. *The extraordinary intervention of God is not excluded in that which our particular essences express, because their expression includes everything. Such intervention, however, goes beyond the power of our natural being or of our distinct expression, because these are finite, and follow certain subordinate regulations.*

There remains for us at present only to explain how it is possible that God has influence at times upon men or upon other substances by an extraordinary or miraculous intervention, since it seems that nothing is able to happen which is extraordinary or supernatural in as much as all the events which occur to the other substances are only the consequences of their natures. We must recall what was said above in regard to the miracles in the universe. These always conform to the universal law of the general order, although they may contravene the subordinate regulations, and since every person or substance is like a little world which expresses the great world, we can say that this extraordinary action of God upon this substance is nevertheless miraculous, although it is comprised in the general order of the universe in so far as it is expressed by the individual essence or concept of this substance. This is why, if we understand in our natures all that they express, nothing is supernatural in them, because they reach out to everything, an effect always expressing its cause, and God being the veritable cause of the substances. But as that which our natures express the most perfectly pertains to them in a particular manner, that being their special power, and since they are limited, as I have just explained, many things there are which surpass the powers of our natures and even of all limited natures. As a consequence, to speak more clearly, I say that the miracles and the extraordinary interventions of God have this peculiarity that they cannot be foreseen by any created mind however enlightened. This is because the distinct comprehension of the fundamental order surpasses them all, while on the other hand, that which is called natural depends upon less fundamental regulations which the creatures are able to understand. In order then that my words may be as irreprehensible as the meaning I am trying to convey, it will be well to associate certain words with certain significations. We may call that which includes everything that we express and which expresses our union with God himself, nothing going beyond it, our essence. But that which is limited in us may be designated as our nature or our power, and in accordance with this terminology that which goes beyond the natures of all created substances is supernatural.

XVII. *An example of a subordinate regulation in the law of nature which demonstrates that God always preserves the same amount of force but not the same quantity of motion: against the Cartesians and many others.*

I have frequently spoken of subordinate regulations, or of the laws of nature, and it seems that it will be well to give an example. Our new philosophers are unanimous in employing that famous law that God always preserves the same amount of motion in the universe. In fact it is a very plausible law, and in times past I held it as indubitable. But since then I have learned in what its fault consists. Monsieur Descartes and many other clever mathematicians have thought that the quantity of motion, that is to say the velocity multiplied by the bulk of the moving body, is exactly equivalent to the moving force, or to speak in mathematical terms that the force varies as the velocity multiplied by the bulk. Now it is reasonable that the same force is always preserved in the universe. So also, looking to phenomena, it will be readily seen that a mechanical perpetual motion is impossible, because the force in such a machine, being always diminished a little by friction and so ultimately destined to be entirely spent, would necessarily have to recoup its losses, and consequently would keep on increasing of itself without any new impulsion from without; and we see furthermore that the force of a body is diminished only in proportion as it gives up force, either to a contiguous body or to its own parts, in so far as they have a separate movement. The mathematicians to whom I have referred think that what can be said of force can be said of the quantity of motion. In order, however, to show the difference I make two suppositions: in the first place, that a body falling from a certain height acquires a force enabling it to remount to the same height, provided that its direction is turned that way, or provided that there are no hindrances. For instance, a pendulum will rise exactly to the height from which it has fallen, provided the resistance of the air and of certain other small particles do not diminish a little its acquired force.

I suppose in the second place that it will take as much force to lift a body *A* weighing one pound to the height *CD*, four feet, as to raise a body *B* weighing four pounds to the height *EF*, one

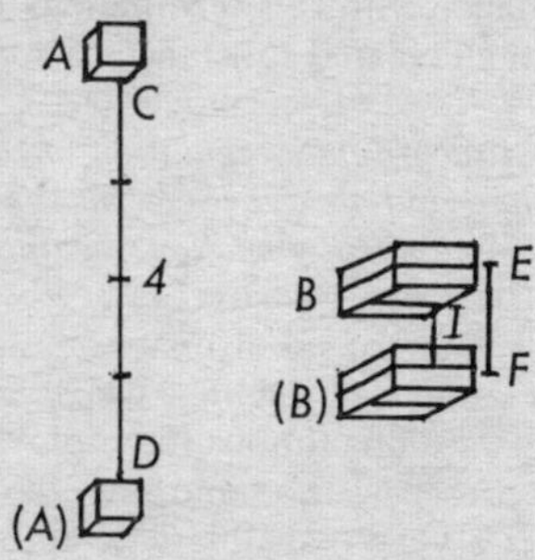

foot. These two suppositions are granted by our new philosophers. It is therefore manifest that the body *A* falling from the height *CD* acquires exactly as much force as the body *B* falling from the height *EF*, for the body *B* at *F*, having by the first supposition sufficient force to return to *E*, has therefore the force to carry a body of four pounds to the distance of one foot, *EF*. And likewise the body *A* at *D*, having the force to return to *C*, has also the force required to carry a body weighing one pound, its own weight, back to *C*, a distance of four feet. Now by the second supposition the force of these two bodies is equal. Let us now see if the quantity of motion is the same in each case. It is here that we will be surprised to find a very great difference, for it has been proved by Galileo that the velocity acquired by the fall *CD* is double the velocity acquired by the fall *EF*, although the height is four times as great. Multiplying, therfore, the body

A, whose bulk is 1, by its velocity, which is 2, the product or the quantity of movement will be 2, and on the other hand, if we multiply the body *B*, whose bulk is 4, by its velocity, which is 1, the product or quantity of motion will be 4. Hence the quantity of the motion of the body *A* at the point *D* is half the quantity of motion of the body *B* at the point *F*, yet their forces are equal, and there is therefore a great difference between the quantity of motion and the force. This is what we set out to show. We can see therefore how the force ought to be estimated by the quantity of the effect which it is able to produce, for example by the height to which a body of certain weight can be raised. This is a very different thing from the velocity which can be imparted to it, and in order to impart to it double the velocity we must have double the force. Nothing is simpler than this proof and Monsieur Descartes has fallen into error here, only because he trusted too much to his thoughts even when they had not been ripened by reflection. But it astonishes me that his disciples have not noticed this error, and I am afraid that they are beginning to imitate little by little certain Peripatetics whom they ridicule, and that they are accustoming themselves to consult rather the books of their master, than reason or nature.

XVIII. *The distinction between force and the quantity of motion is, among other reasons, important as showing that we must have recourse to metaphysical considerations in addition to discussions of extension if we wish to explain the phenomena of matter.*

This consideration of the force, distinguished from the quantity of motion, is of importance, not only in physics and mechanics for finding the real laws of nature and the principles of motion, and even for correcting many practical errors which have crept into the writings of certain able mathematicians, but also in metaphysics it is of importance for the better understanding of principles. Because motion, if we regard only its exact and formal meaning, that is, change of place, is not something really absolute, and when several bodies change their places reciprocally, it is not possible to determine by considering the bodies alone to which among them movement or repose is to be attributed, as I could demonstrate geometrically, if I wished to stop for it now. But the force, or the proximate cause of these changes in something more real, and there are sufficient grounds for attributing it to one body rather than to another, and it is only through this latter investigation that we can determine to which one the movement must appertain. Now this force is something different from size, from form or from motion and it can be seen from this consideration that the whole meaning of a body is not exhausted in its extension together with its modifications as our moderns persuade themselves. We are therefore obliged to restore certain beings or forms which they have banished. It appears more and more clear that although all the particular phenomena of nature can be explained mathematically or mechanically by those who understand them, yet nevertheless, the general principles of corporeal nature and even of mechanics are metaphysical rather than geometric, and belong rather to certain indivisible forms or natures as the causes of the appearances, than to the corporeal mass or to extension. In this way we are able to reconcile the mechanical philosophy of the moderns with the circumspection of those intelligent and well-meaning persons who, with a certain justice, fear that we are becoming too far removed from immaterial beings and that we are thus prejudicing piety.

XIX. *The utility of final causes in Physics.*

As I do not wish to judge people in ill part I bring no accusation against our new philosophers who pretend to banish final causes from physics, but I am nevertheless obliged to avow that the consequences of such a banishment appear to me dangerous, especially when joined to that position which I refuted at the beginning of this treatise. That position seemed to go the length of discarding final causes entirely as though God proposed no end and no good in his activity, or as if good were not to be the object of his will. I hold on the contrary that it is just in this that the principle of all existences and of the laws of nature must be sought, hence God always proposes the best and most perfect. I am quite willing to grant that we are liable to err when we wish to determine the purposes or councils of God, but this is the case only when we try to limit them to some particular design, thinking that he has had in view only a single thing, while in fact he regards everything at once. As for instance, if we think that God has made the world only for us, it is a great blunder, although it may be quite true that he has made it entirely for us, and that there is nothing in the universe which does not touch us and which does not accommodate itself to the regard which he has for us according to the principle laid down above. Therefore when we see some good effect or some perfection which happens or which follows from the works of God we are able to say assuredly that God has purposed it, for he does nothing by chance, and is not like us who sometimes fail to do well. Therefore, far from being able to fall into error in this respect as do the extreme statesmen who postulate too much foresight in the designs of Princes, or as do commentators who seek for too much erudition in their authors, it will be impossible to attribute too much reflection to God's infinite wisdom, and there is no matter in which error is less to be feared provided we confine ourselves to affirmations and provided we avoid negative statements which limit the designs of God. All those who see the admirable structure of animals find themselves led to recognize the wisdom of the author of things and I advise those who have any sentiment of piety and indeed of true philosophy to hold aloof from the expressions of certain pretentious minds who instead of saying that eyes were made for seeing, say that we see because we find ourselves having eyes. When one seriously holds such opinions which hand everything over to material necessity or to a kind of chance (although either alternative ought to appear ridiculous to those who understand what we have explained above) it is difficult to recognize an intelligent author of nature. The effect should correspond to its cause and indeed it is best known through the recognition of its cause, so that it is reasonable to introduce a sovereign intelligence ordering things, and in place of making use of the wisdom of this sovereign being, to employ only the properties of matter to explain phenomena. As if in order to account for the capture of an important place by a prince, the historian should say it was because the particles of powder in the cannon having been touched by a spark of fire expanded with a rapidity capable of pushing a hard solid body against the walls of the place, while the little particles which composed the brass of the cannon were so well interlaced that they did not separate under this impact, – as if he should account for it in this way instead of making us see how the foresight of the conqueror brought him to choose the time and the proper means and how his ability surmounted all obstacles.

XX. *A noteworthy disquisition in Plato's Phaedo against the philosophers who were too materialistic.*

This reminds me of a fine disquisition by Socrates in Plato's Phaedo, which agrees perfectly with my opinion on this subject and seems to have been uttered expressly for our too materialistic philosophers. This agreement has led me to a desire to translate it although it is a little long. Perhaps this example will give some of us an incentive to share in many of the other beautiful and well balanced thoughts which are found in the writings of this famous author.

XXI. *If the mechanical laws depended upon Geometry alone without metaphysical influences, the phenomena would be very different from what they are.*

Now since the wisdom of God has always been recognized in the details of the mechanical structures of certain particular bodies, it should also be shown in the general economy of the world and in the constitution of the laws of nature. This is so true that even in the laws of motion in general, the plans of this wisdom have been noticed. For if bodies were only extended masses, and motion were only a change of place, and if everything ought to be and could be deduced by geometric necessity from these two definitions alone, it would follow, as I have shown elsewhere, that the smallest body on contact with a very large one at rest would impart to it its own velocity, yet without losing any of the velocity that it had. A quantity of other rules wholly contrary to the formation of a system would also have to be admitted. But the decree of the divine wisdom in preserving always the same force and the same total direction has provided for a system. I find indeed that many of the effects of nature can be accounted for in a twofold way, that is to say by a consideration of efficient causes, and again independently by a consideration of final causes. An example of the latter is God's decree always to carry out his plan by the easiest and most determined way. I have shown this elsewhere in accounting for the catoptric and dioptric laws, and I will speak more at length about it in what follows.

XXII. *Reconciliation of the two methods of explanation, the one using final causes, and the other efficient causes, thus satisfying both those who explain nature mechanically and those who have recourse to incorporeal natures.*

It is worth while to make the preceding remark in order to reconcile those who hope to explain mechanically the formation of the first tissue of an animal and all the interrelation of the parts, with those who account for the same structure by referring to final causes. Both explanations are good; both are useful not only for the admiring of the work of a great artificer, but also for the discovery of useful facts in physics and medicine. And writers who take these diverse routes should not speak ill of each other. For I see that those who attempt to explain beauty by the divine anatomy ridicule those who imagine that the apparently fortuitous flow of certain liquids has been able to produce such a beautiful variety and that they regard them as overbold and irreverent. These others on the contrary treat the former as simple and superstitious, and compare them to those ancients who regarded the physicists as impious when they maintained that not Jupiter thundered but some material which is found in the clouds. The best plan would be to join the two ways of thinking. To use a practical comparison, we recognize and praise the ability of a workman not only when we show what designs he had in making the parts of his machine, but also when we explain the instruments which he employed in making each part, especially if these instruments are simple and ingeniously contrived. God is also a workman able enough to produce a machine still a thousand times more ingenious than is our body, by employing only certain quite simple liquids purposely composed in such a way that ordinary laws of nature alone are required to develop them so as to produce such a marvellous effect. But it is also true that this development would not take place if God were not the author of nature. Yet I find that the method of efficient causes, which goes much deeper and is in a measure more immediate and *a priori*, is also more difficult when we come to details, and I think that our philosophers are still very frequently far removed from making the most of this method. The method of final causes, however, is easier and can be frequently employed to find out important and useful truths which we should have to seek for a long time, if we were confined to that other more physical method of which anatomy is able to furnish many examples. It seems to me that Snellius, who was the first discoverer of the laws of refraction, would have waited a long time before finding them if he had wished to seek out first how light was formed. But he apparently followed that method which the ancients employed for Catoptrics, that is, the method of final causes. Because, while seeking for the easiest way in which to conduct a ray of light from one given point to another given point by reflection from a given plane (supposing that that was the design of nature) they discovered the equality of the angles of incidence and reflection, as can be seen from a little treatise by Heliodorus of Larissa and also elsewhere. This principle Mons. Snellius, I believe, and afterwards independently of him, M. Fermat, applied most ingeniously to refraction. For since the rays while in the same media always maintain the same proportion of sines, which in turn corresponds to the resistance of the media, it appears that they follow the easiest way, or at least that way which is the most determinate for passing from a given point in one medium to a given point in another medium. That demonstration of this same theorem which M. Descartes has given, using efficient causes, is much less satisfactory. At least we have grounds to think that he would never have found the principle by that means if he had not learned in Holland of the discovery of Snellius.

XXIII. *Returning to immaterial substances we explain how God acts upon the understanding of spirits and ask whether one always keeps the idea of what he thinks about.*

I have thought it well to insist a little upon final causes, upon incorporeal natures and upon an intelligent cause with respect to bodies so as to show the use of these conceptions in physics and in mathematics. This for two reasons, first to purge from mechanical philosophy the impiety that is imputed to it, second, to elevate to nobler lines of thought the thinking of our philosophers who incline to materialistic considerations alone. Now, however, it will be well to return from corporeal substances to the consideration of immaterial natures and particularly of spirits, and to speak of the methods which God uses to enlighten them and to act upon them. Although we must not forget that there are here at the same time certain laws of nature in regard to which I can speak more amply elsewhere. It will be enough for now to touch upon ideas and to inquire if we see everything in God and how God is our light. First of all it will be in place to remark that the wrong use of ideas occasions many errors. For when one reasons in regard to anything, he imagines that he has an idea of it and this is the foundation upon which certain philosophers, ancient and modern, have constructed a demonstration of God that is extremely imperfect. It must be, they say, that I have an idea of God, or of a perfect being, since I think of him and we cannot think without having ideas; now the idea of this being includes all perfections and since existence is one of these perfections, it follows that he exists. But I reply, inasmuch as we often think of impossible chimeras, for example of the highest degree of swiftness, of the greatest number, of the meeting of the conchoid with its base or determinant, such reasoning is not sufficient. It is therefore in this sense that we can say that there are true and false ideas according as the thing which is in question is possible or not. And it is when he is assured of the possibility of a thing, that one can boast of having an idea of it. Therefore, the aforesaid argument proves that God exists, if he is possible. This is in fact an excellent privilege of the divine nature, to have need only of a possibility or an essence in order to actually exist, and it is just this which is called self-sufficient being, *ens a se*.

XXIV. *What clear and obscure, distinct and confused, adequate and inadequate, intuitive and assumed knowledge is, and the definition of nominal, real, causal and essential.*

In order to understand better the nature of ideas it is necessary to touch somewhat upon the various kinds of knowledge. When I am able to recognize a thing among others, without being able to say in what its differences or characteristics consist, the knowledge is confused. Sometimes indeed we may know clearly, that is without being in the slightest doubt, that a poem or a picture is well or badly done because there is in it an 'I know not what' which satisfies or shocks us. Such knowledge is not yet distinct. It is when I am able to explain the peculiarities which a thing has, that the knowledge is called distinct. Such is the knowledge of an assayer who discerns the true gold from the false by means of certain tests or marks which make up the definition of gold. But distinct knowledge has degrees, because ordinarily the conceptions which enter into the definitions will themselves be in need of definition, and are only known confusedly. When at length everything which enters into a definition or into distinct knowledge is known distinctly, even back to the primitive conception, I call that knowledge adequate. When my mind understands at once and distinctly all the primitive ingredients of a conception, then we have intuitive knowledge. This is extremely rare as most human knowledge is only confused or indeed assumed. It is well also to distinguish nominal from real definition. I call a definition nominal when there is doubt whether an exact conception of it is possible; as for instance, when I say that an endless screw is a line in three dimensional space whose parts are congruent or fall one upon another. Now although this is one of the reciprocal properties of an endless screw, he who did not know by other means what an endless screw was could doubt if such a line were possible, because the other lines whose ends are congruent (there are only two: the circumference of a circle and the straight line) are plane figures, that is to say they can be described *in plano*. This instance enables us to see that any reciprocal property can serve as a nominal definition, but when the property brings us to see the possibility of a thing it makes the definition real, and as long as one has only a nominal definition he cannot be sure of the consequences which he draws, because if it conceals a contradiction or an impossibility he would be able to draw the opposite conclusions. That is why truths do not depend upon names and are not arbitrary, as some of our new philosophers think. There is also a considerable difference among real definitions, for when the possibility proves itself only by experience, as in the definition of quicksilver, whose possibility we know because such a body, which is both an extremely heavy fluid and quite volatile, actually exists, the definition is merely real and nothing more. If, however, the proof of the possibility is *a priori*, the definition is not only real but also causal as for instance when it contains the possible generation of a thing. Finally, when the definition, without assuming anything which requires a proof *a priori* of its possibility, carries the analysis clear of the primitive conception, the definition is perfect or essential.

XXV. *In what cases knowledge is added to mere contemplation of the idea.*

Now it is manifest that we have no idea of a conception when it is impossible. And in case the knowledge, where we have the idea of it, is only assumed, we do not visualize it because such a conception is known only in like manner as conceptions internally impossible. And if it be in fact possible, it is not by this kind of knowledge that we learn its possibility. For instance when I am thinking of a thousand or of a chiliagon, I frequently do it without contemplating the idea. Even if I say a thousand is ten times a hundred, I frequently do not trouble to think what ten and a hundred are, because I assume that I know, and I do not consider it necessary to stop just at present to conceive of them. Therefore it may well happen, as it in fact does happen often enough, that I am mistaken in regard to a conception which I assume that I understand, although it is an impossible truth or at least is incompatible with others with which I join it, and whether I am mistaken or not, this way of assuming our knowledge remains the same. It is, then, only when our knowledge is clear in regard to confused conceptions, and when it is intuitive in regard to those which are distinct, that we see its entire idea.

XXVI. *Ideas are all stored up within us. Plato's doctrine of reminiscence.*

In order to see clearly what an idea is, we must guard ourselves against a misunderstanding. Many regard the idea as the form or the differentiation of our thinking, and according to this opinion we have the idea in our mind, in so far as we are thinking of it, and each separate time that we think of it anew we have another idea although similar to the preceding one. Some, however, take the idea as the immediate object of thought, or as a permanent form which remains even when we are no longer contemplating it. As a matter of fact our soul has the power of representing to itself any form or nature whenever the occasion comes for thinking about it, and I think that this activity of our soul is, so far as it expresses some nature, form or essence, properly the idea of the thing. This is in us, and is always in us, whether we are thinking of it or no. (Our soul expresses God and the universe and all essences as well as all existences.) This position is in accord with my principles that naturally nothing enters into our minds from outside.

It is a bad habit we have of thinking as though our minds receive certain messengers, as it were, or as if they had doors or windows. We have in our minds all those forms for all periods of time because the mind at every moment expresses all its future thoughts and already thinks confusedly of all that of which it will ever think distinctly. Nothing can be taught us of which we have not already in our minds the idea. This idea is as it were the material out of which the thought will form itself. This is what

Plato has excellently brought out in his doctrine of reminiscence, a doctrine which contains a great deal of truth, provided that it is properly understood and purged of the error of pre-existence, and provided that one does not conceive of the soul as having already known and thought at some other time what it learns and thinks now. Plato has also confirmed his position by a beautiful experiment. He introduces [*Meno*] a boy, whom he leads by short steps, to extremely difficult truths of geometry bearing on incommensurables, all this without teaching the boy anything, merely drawing out replies by a well arranged series of questions. This shows that the soul virtually knows those things, and needs only to be reminded (animadverted) to recognize the truths. Consequently it possesses at least the idea upon which those truths depend. We may say even that it already possesses those truths, if we consider them as the relations of the ideas.

XXVII. *In what respect our souls can be compared to blank tablets and how conceptions are derived from the senses.*

Aristotle preferred to compare our souls to blank tablets prepared for writing, and he maintained that nothing is in the understanding which does not come through the senses. This position is in accord with the popular conceptions, as Aristotle's approach usually is. Plato thinks more profoundly. Such tenets or practicologies are nevertheless allowable in ordinary use somewhat in the same way as those who accept the Copernican theory still continue to speak of the rising and setting of the sun. I find indeed that these usages can be given a real meaning containing no error, quite in the same way as I have already pointed out that we may truly say particular substances act upon one another. In this same sense we may say that knowledge is received from without through the medium of the senses because certain exterior things contain or express more particularly the causes which determine us to certain thoughts. Because in the ordinary uses of life we attribute to the soul only that which belongs to it most manifestly and particularly, and there is no advantage in going further. When, however, we are dealing with the exactness of metaphysical truths, it is important to recognize the powers and independence of the soul which extend infinitely further than is commonly supposed. In order, therefore, to avoid misunderstandings it would be well to choose separate terms for the two. These expressions which are in the soul whether one is conceiving of them or not may be called ideas, while those which one conceives of or constructs may be called conceptions, *conceptus*. But whatever terms are used, it is always false to say that all our conceptions come from the so-called external senses, because these conceptions which I have of myself and of my thoughts, and consequently of being, of substance, of action, of identity, and of many others come from an inner experience.

XXVIII. *The only immediate object of our perceptions which exists outside of us is God, and in him alone is our light.*

In the strictly metaphysical sense no external cause acts upon us excepting God alone, and he is in immediate relation with us only by virtue of our continual dependence upon him. Whence it follows that there is absolutely no other external object which comes into contact with our souls and directly excites perceptions in us. We have in our souls ideas of everything, only because of the continual action of God upon us, that is to say, because every effect expresses its cause and therefore the essences of our souls are certain expressions, imitations or images of the divine essence, divine thought and divine will, including all the ideas which are there contained. We may say, therefore, that God is for us the only immediate external object, and that we see things through him. For example, when we see the sun or the stars, it is God who gives to us and preserves in us the ideas and whenever our senses are affected according to his own laws in a certain manner, it is he, who by his continual concurrence, determines our thinking. God is the sun and the light of souls, *lumen illuminans omnem hominen venientem in hunc mundum*, although this is not the current conception. I think I have already remarked that during the scholastic period many believed God to be the light of the soul, *intellectus agens animæ rationalis*, following in this the Holy Scriptures and the fathers who were always more Platonic than Aristotelian in their mode of thinking. The Averroists misused this conception, but others, among whom were several mystic theologians, and William of Saint Amour also, I think, understood this conception in a manner which assured the dignity of God and was able to raise the soul to a knowledge of its welfare.

XXIX. *Yet we think directly by means of our own ideas and not through God's.*

Nevertheless I cannot approve of the position of certain able philosophers who seem to hold that our ideas themselves are in God and not at all in us. I think that in taking this position they have neither sufficiently considered the nature of substance, which we have just explained, nor the complete purview and independence of the soul which includes all that happens to it, and expresses God, and with him all possible and actual beings in the same way that an effect expresses its cause. It is indeed inconceivable that the soul should think using the ideas of something else. The soul when it thinks of anything must be affected dynamically in a certain manner, and it must needs have in itself in advance not only the passive capacity of being thus affected, a capacity already wholly determined, but it must have besides an active power by virtue of which it has always had in its nature the marks of the future production of this thought, and the disposition to produce it at its proper time. All of this shows that the soul already includes the idea which is comprised in any particular thought.

XXX. *How God inclines our souls without necessitating them; that there are no grounds for complaint; that we must not ask why Judas sinned because this free act is contained in his concept, the only question being why Judas the sinner is admitted to existence, preferably to other possible persons; concerning the original imperfection or limitation before the fall and concerning the different degrees of grace.*

Regarding the action of God upon the human will there are many quite different considerations which it would take too long to investigate here. Nevertheless the following is what can be said in general. God in co-operating with ordinary actions only follows the laws which he has established, that is to say, he continually preserves and produces our being so that the ideas come to us spontaneously or with freedom in that order which the concept of our individual substance carries with itself. In this concept they can be foreseen for all eternity. Furthermore, by virtue of the decree which God has made that the will shall always seek the apparent good in certain particular respects (in regard to which this apparent good always has in it something of reality expressing or imitating God's will), he, without at all necessitating our choice, determines it by that which appears most desirable. For absolutely speaking, our will as contrasted with necessity, is in a state of indifference, being able to act otherwise, or wholly to suspend its action, either alternative being and remaining possible. It therefore devolves upon the soul to be on guard against appearances, by means of a firm will, to reflect and to refuse to act or decide in certain circumstances, except after mature deliberation. It is, however, true and has been assured from all eternity that certain souls will not employ their power upon certain occasions.

But who could do more than God has done, and can such a soul complain of anything except itself? All these complaints after the deed are unjust, inasmuch as they would have been unjust before the deed. Would this soul shortly before committing the sin have had the right to complain of God as though he had determined the sin? Since the determinations of God in these matters cannot be foreseen, how would the soul know that it was pre-ordained to sin unless it had already committed the sin? It is merely a question of wishing to or not wishing to, and God could not have set an easier or juster condition. Therefore all judges without asking the reasons which have disposed a man to have an evil will, consider only how far this will is wrong. But, you object, perhaps it is ordained from all eternity that I will sin. Find your own answer. Perhaps it has not been. Now then, without asking for what you are unable to know and in regard to which you can have no light, act according to your duty and your knowledge. But, some one will object; whence comes it then that this man will assuredly do this sin? The reply is easy. It is that otherwise he would not be a man. For God foresees from all time that there will be a certain Judas, and in the concept or idea of him which God has, is contained this future free act. The only question, therefore, which remains is why this certain Judas, the betrayer who is possible only because of the idea of God, actually exists. To this question, however, we can expect no answer here on earth excepting to say in general that it is because God has found it good that he should exist notwithstanding that sin which he foresaw. This evil will be more than overbalanced. God will derive a greater good from it, and it will finally turn out that this series of events in which is included the existence of this sinner, is the most perfect among all the possible series of events. An explanation in every case of the admirable economy of this choice cannot be given while we are sojourners on earth. It is enough to known the excellence without understanding it. It is here that we must recognize the unfathomable depth of the divine wisdom, without hesitating at a detail which involves an infinite number of considerations. It is clear, however, that God is not the cause of ill. For not only after the loss of innocence by men, has original sin possessed the soul, but even before that there was an original limitation or imperfection in the very nature of all creatures, which rendered them open to sin and able to fall. There is, therefore, no more difficulty in the supralapsarian view than there is in the other views of sin. To this also, it seems to me, can be reduced the opinion of Saint Augustine and of other authors: that the root of evil is in the privation, that is to say, in the lack or limitation of creatures which God graciously remedies by whatever degree of perfection it pleases him to give. This grace of God, whether ordinary or extraordinary, has its degrees and its measures. It is always efficacious in itself to produce a certain proportionate effect and furthermore it is always sufficient not only to keep one from sin but even to effect his salvation, provided that the man co-operates with that which is in him. It has not always, however, sufficient power to overcome the inclination, for, if it did, it would no longer be limited in any way, and this superiority to limitations is reserved to that unique grace which is absolutely efficacious. This grace is always victorious whether through its own self or through the congruity of circumstances.

XXXI. *Concerning the motives of election; concerning faith foreseen and the absolute decree and that it all reduces to the question why God has chosen and resolved to admit to existence just such a possible person, whose concept includes just such a sequence of free acts and of free gifts of grace. This at once puts an end to all difficulties.*

Finally, the grace of God is wholly unprejudiced and creatures have no claim upon it. Just as it is not sufficient in accounting for God's choice in his dispensations of grace to refer to his absolute or conditional prevision of men's future actions, so it is also wrong to imagine his decrees as absolute with no reasonable motive. As concerns foreseen faith and good works, it is very true that God has elected none but those whose faith and charity he foresees, *quos se fide donaturum praescivit*. The same question, however, arises again as to why God gives to some rather than to others the grace of faith or of good works. As concerns God's ability to foresee not only the faith and good deeds, but also their content and predisposition, or that which a man on his part contributes to them (since there are as truly diversities on the part of men as on the part of grace, and a man although he needs to be aroused to good and needs to become converted, yet acts in accordance with his temperament) – as regards his ability to foresee there are many who say that God, knowing what a particular man will do without grace, that is without his extraordinary assistance, or knowing at least what will be the human contribution, resolves to give grace to those whose natural dispositions are the best, or at any rate are the least imperfect and evil. But if this were the case then the natural dispositions in so far as they were good would be like gifts of grace, since God would have given advantages to some over others; and therefore, since he would well know that the natural advantages which he had given would serve as motives for his grace or for his extraordinary assistance, would not everything be reduced to his mercy? I think, therefore, that since we do not know how much and in what way God regards natural dispositions in the dispensations of his grace, it would be safest and most exact to say, in accordance with our principles and as I have already remarked, that there must needs be among possible beings the person Peter or John whose concept or idea contains all that particular sequence of ordinary and extraordinary manifestations of grace together with the rest of the accompanying events and circumstances, and that it has pleased God to choose him among an infinite number of persons equally possible for actual existence. When we have said this there seems nothing left to ask, and all difficulties vanish. For in regard to that great and ultimate question why it has pleased God to choose him among so great a number of possible persons, it is surely unreasonable to demand more than the general reasons which we have given. The reasons in detail surpass our ken. Therefore, instead of postulating an absolute decree, which being without reason would be unreasonable, and instead of postulating reasons which do not succeed in solving the difficulties and in turn have need themselves of reasons, it will be best to say with St Paul that there are for God's choice certain great reasons of wisdom and congruity which he follows, which reasons, however, are unknown to mortals and are founded upon the general order, whose goal is the greatest perfection of the world. This is what is meant when the motives of

God's glory and of the manifestation of his justice are spoken of, as well as when men speak of his mercy, and his perfection in general; that immense vastness of wealth, in fine, with which the soul of the same St Paul was to be thrilled.

XXXII. *Usefulness of these principles in matters of piety and of religion.*

In addition it seems that the thoughts which we have just explained and particularly the great principle of the perfection of God's operations and the concept of substance which includes all its changes with all its accompanying circumstances, far from injuring, serve rather to confirm religion, serve to dissipate great difficulties, to inflame souls with a divine love and to raise the mind to a knowledge of incorporeal substances much more than the present-day hypotheses. For it appears clearly that all other substances depend upon God just as our thoughts emanate from our own substances; that God is all in all and that he is intimately united to all created things, in proportion however to their perfection; that it is he alone who determines them from without by his influence, and if to act is to determine directly, it may be said in metaphysical language that God alone acts upon me and he alone causes me to do good or ill, other substances contributing only because of his determinations; because God, who takes all things into consideration, distributes his bounties and compels created beings to accommodate themselves to one another. Thus God alone constitutes the relation or communication between substances. It is through him that the phenomena of the one meet and accord with the phenomena of the others, so that there may be a reality in our perceptions. In common parlance, however, an action is attributed to particular causes in the sense that I have explained above because it is not necessary to make continual mention of the universal cause when speaking of particular cases. It can be seen also that every substance has a perfect spontaneity (which becomes liberty with intelligent substances). Everything which happens to it is a consequence of its idea or its being and nothing determines it except God only. It is for this reason that a person of exalted mind and revered saintliness may say that the soul ought often to think as if there were only God and itself in the world. Nothing can make us hold to immortality more firmly than this independence and vastness of the soul which protects it completely against exterior things, since it alone constitutes our universe and together with God is sufficient for itself. It is as impossible for it to perish save through annihilation as it is impossible for the universe to destroy itself, the universe whose animate and perpetual expression it is. Furthermore, the changes in this extended mass which is called our body cannot possibly affect the soul nor can the dissipation of the body destroy that which is indivisible.

XXXIII. *Explanation of the relation between the soul and the body, a matter which has been regarded as inexplicable or else as miraculous; concerning the origin of confused perceptions.*

We can also see the explanation of that great mystery 'the union of the soul and the body,' that is to say how it comes about that the passions and actions of the one are accompanied by the actions and passions or else the appropriate phenomena of the other. For it is not possible to conceive how one can have an influence upon the other and it is unreasonable to have recourse at once to the extraordinary intervention of the universal cause in an ordinary and particular case. The following, however, is the true explanation. We have said that everything which happens to a soul or to any substance is a consequence of its concept; hence the idea itself or the essence of the soul brings it about that all of its appearances or perceptions should be born out of its nature and precisely in such a way that they correspond of themselves to that which happens in the universe at large, but more particularly and more perfectly to that which happens in the body associated with it, because it is in a particular way and only for a certain time according to the relation of other bodies to its own body that the soul expresses the state of the universe. This last fact enables us to see how our body belongs to us, without, however, being attached to our essence. I believe that those who are careful thinkers will decide favorably for our principles because of this single reason, viz., that they are able to see in what consists the relation between the soul and the body, a parallelism which appears inexplicable in any other way. We can also see that the perceptions of our senses even when they are clear must necessarily contain certain confused elements, for as all the bodies in the universe are in sympathy, ours receives the impressions of all the others, and while our senses respond to everything, our soul cannot pay attention to every particular. That is why our confused sensations are the result of a variety of perceptions. This variety is infinite. It is almost like the confused murmuring which is heard by those who approach the shore of a sea. It comes from the continual beatings of innumerable waves. If now, out of many perceptions which do not at all fit together to make one, no particular one perception surpasses the others, and if they make impressions about equally strong or equally capable of holding the attention of the soul, they can be perceived only confusedly.

XXXIV. *Concerning the difference between spirits and other substances, souls or substantial forms; that the immortality which men desire includes memory.*

Supposing that the bodies which constitute a *unum per se*, as human bodies, are substances, and have substantial forms, and supposing that animals have souls, we are obliged to grant that these souls and these substantial forms cannot entirely perish, any more than can the atoms or the ultimate elements of matter, according to the position of other philosophers; for no substance perishes, although it may become very different. Such substances also express the whole universe, although more imperfectly than do spirits. The principal difference, however, is that they do not know that they are, nor what they are. Consequently, not being able to reason, they are unable to discover necessary and universal truths. It is also because they do not reflect regarding themselves that they have no moral qualities, whence it follows that they undergo myriad transformations – as we see a caterpillar change into a butterfly; the result from a moral or practical standpoint is the same as if we said that they perished in each case, and we can indeed say it from the physical standpoint in the same way that we say bodies perish in their dissolution. But the intelligent soul, knowing that it exists, having the ability to say that word 'I' so full of meaning, not only continues and exists, metaphysically far more certainly than do the others, but it remains the same from the moral standpoint, and constitutes the same personality, for it is its memory or knowledge of this ego which renders it open to punishment and reward. Also the immortality which is required in morals and in religion does not consist merely in this perpetual existence, which pertains to all substances, for if in addition there were no remembrance of what one had been, immortality would not be at all desirable. Suppose that some individual could suddenly become

King of China on condition, however, of forgetting what he had been, as though being born again, would it not amount to the same practically, or as far as the effects could be perceived, as if the individual were annihilated, and a king of China were the same instant created in his place? The individual would have no reason to desire this.

XXXV. *The excellence of spirits; that God considers them preferable to other creatures; that the spirits express God rather than the world, while other simple substances express the world rather than God.*

In order, however, to prove by natural reasons that God will preserve forever not only our substance, but also our personality, that is to say the recollection and knowledge of what we are (although the distinct knowledge is sometimes suspended during sleep and in swoons) it is necessary to join to metaphysics moral considerations. God must be considered not only as the principle and the cause of all substances and of all existing things, but also as the chief of all persons or intelligent substances, as the absolute monarch of the most perfect city or republic, such as is constituted by all the spirits together in the universe, God being the most complete of all spirits at the same time that he is greatest of all beings. For assuredly the spirits are the most perfect of substances and best express the divinity. Since all the nature, purpose, virtue and function of substances is, as has been sufficiently explained, to express God and the universe, there is no room for doubting that those substances which give the expression, knowing what they are doing and which are able to understand the great truths about God and the universe, do express God and the universe incomparably better than do those natures which are either brutish and incapable of recognizing truths, or are wholly destitute of sensation and knowledge. The difference between intelligent substances and those which are not intelligent is quite as great as between a mirror and one who sees. As God is himself the greatest and wisest of spirits it is easy to understand that the spirits with which he can, so to speak, enter into conversation and even into social relations by communicating to them in particular ways his feelings and his will so that they are able to know and love their benefactor, must be much nearer to him than the rest of created things which may be regarded as the instruments of spirits. In the same way we see that all wise persons consider far more the condition of a man than of anything else however precious it may be; and it seems that the greatest satisfaction which a soul, satisfied in other respects, can have is to see itself loved by others. However, with respect to God there is this difference that his glory and our worship can add nothing to his satisfaction, the recognition of creatures being nothing but a consequence of his sovereign and perfect felicity and being far from contributing to it or from causing it even in part. Nevertheless, that which is reasonable in finite spirits is found eminently in him and as we praise a king who prefers to preserve the life of a man before that of the most precious and rare of his animals, we should not doubt that the most enlightened and most just of all monarchs has the same preference.

XXXVI. *God is the monarch of the most perfect republic composed of all the spirits, and the happiness of this city of God is his principal purpose.*

Spirits are of all substances the most capable of perfection and their perfections are different in this that they interfere with one another the least, or rather they aid one another the most, for only the most virtuous can be the most perfect friends. Hence it follows that God who in all things has the greatest perfection will have the greatest care for spirits and will give not only to all of them in general, but even to each one in particular the highest perfection which the universal harmony will permit. We can even say that it is because he is a spirit that God is the originator of existences, for if he had lacked the power of will to choose what is best, there would have been no reason why one possible being should exist rather than any other. Therefore God's being a spirit himself dominates all the consideration which he may have toward created things. Spirits alone are made in his image, being as it were of his blood or as children in the family, since they alone are able to serve him of free will and to act consciously imitating the divine nature. A single spirit is worth a whole world, because it not only expresses the whole world, but it also knows it and governs itself as does God. In this way we may say that though every substance expresses the whole universe, yet the other substances express the world rather than God, while spirits express God rather than the world. This nature of spirits, so noble that it enables them to approach divinity as much as is possible for created things, has as a result that God derives infinitely more glory from them than from the other beings, or rather the other beings furnish to spirits the material for glorifying him. This moral quality of God which constitutes him Lord and Monarch of spirits influences him so to speak personally and in a unique way. It is through this that he humanizes himself, that he is willing to suffer anthropologies, and that he enters into social relations with us; and this consideration is so dear to him that the happy and prosperous condition of his empire which consists in the greatest possible felicity of its inhabitants, becomes supreme among his laws. Happiness is to persons what perfection is to beings. And if the dominant principle in the existence of the physical world is the decree to give it the greatest possible perfection, the primary purpose in the moral world or in the city of God which constitutes the noblest part of the universe ought to be to extend the greatest happiness possible. We must not therefore doubt that God has so ordained everything that spirits not only shall live forever, because this is unavoidable, but that they shall also preserve forever their moral quality, so that his city may never lose a person, quite in the same way that the world never loses a substance. Consequently they will always be conscious of their being, otherwise they would be open to neither reward nor punishment, a condition which is the essence of a republic, and above all of the most perfect republic where nothing can be neglected. In fine, God being at the same time the most just and the most debonaire of monarchs, and requiring only a good will on the part of men, provided that it be sincere and intentional, his subjects cannot desire a better condition. To render them perfectly happy he desires only that they love him.

XXXVII. *Jesus Christ has revealed to men the mystery and the admirable laws of the kingdom of heaven, and the greatness of the supreme happiness which God has prepared for those who love him.*

The ancient philosophers knew very little of these important truths. Jesus Christ alone has expressed them divinely well, and in a way so clear and simple that the dullest minds have understood them. His gospel has entirely changed the face of human affairs. It has brought us to know the kingdom of heaven, or that perfect republic of spirits which deserves to be called the city of God. He it is who has discovered to us its wonderful laws. He alone has made us see how much God loves us and with what care everything that concerns us has been provided for; how God, inasmuch as he cares for the sparrows, will not neglect reasoning beings, who are infinitely more dear to him; how all the hairs of our heads are numbered; how heaven and earth may pass away but the word of God and that which belongs to the means of our salvation will not pass away; how God has more regard for the least one among intelligent souls than for the whole machinery of the world; how we ought not to fear those who are able to destroy the body but are unable to destroy the soul, since God alone can render the soul happy or unhappy; and how the souls of the righteous are protected by his hand against all the upheavals of the universe, since God alone is able to act upon them; how none of our acts are forgotten; how everything is to be accounted for; even careless words and even a spoonful of water which is well used; in fact how everything must result in the greatest welfare of the good, for then shall the righteous become like suns and neither our sense nor our minds have ever tasted of anything approaching the joys which God has laid up for those that love him.

New System of Nature and of the Communication of Substances, as well as of the Union of Soul and Body, 1695

[*Journal des Savans*, June 27, 1695]

1. Several years ago I conceived this system and communicated with some learned men about it, especially with one of the greatest theologians and philosophers of our time [Mons. Arnauld] who, having learnt some of my thoughts through a person of the highest quality, had found them quite paradoxical. But after receiving my elucidations, he changed his attitude in the most generous and edifying way in the world; and having approved a part of my propositions, he withdrew his censure regarding the rest of them with which he had still remained in disagreement. Since then I have on occasions continued my meditations in order to give the public only well examined opinions, and I have tried thus to satisfy objections made against my Essays on Dynamics (*Act. Erudit.*, April 1695) connected with this one. Now, at last, since important persons have desired to see my thoughts elucidated more, I have hazarded these meditations, though they are in no way popular nor appropriately served to

any kind of mind. I have brought myself to do it mainly in order to profit by the judgments of those who are enlightened in these matters; for it would be too embarrassing to seek and summon in particular all those who would be disposed to give me instructions, which I shall always be very glad to receive, provided the love of truth appears in them rather than a passion for prejudiced opinions.

2. Although I am one of those who have worked hard on mathematics, I have not ceased meditating on philosophy since my youth, for it always seemed to me there was a means to establish in philosophy something solid through clear demonstrations. I had penetrated far into the land of the scholastics when mathematics and the modern authors made me emerge from it while I was still young. I was charmed by their beautiful ways of explaining Nature mechanically, and I despised with reason the method of those who use only forms or faculties from which nothing is learnt. But since, having tried to lay the foundations of the very principles of mechanics in order to give a rational account of the laws of nature known to us by experiment, I realized that the sole consideration of an extended mass did not suffice, and that we must again employ the notion of force which is very intelligible despite its springing from metaphysics. It seemed to me also that the opinion of those who transform or degrade animals into pure machines, though a possible one apparently, is against appearances, and even against the order of things.

3. In the beginning when I had freed myself from the yoke of Aristotle, I had taken to the void and the atoms, for they best fill the imagination; but on recovering from that, after many reflections, I realized that it is impossible to find the principles of *a true unity* in matter alone or in that which is only passive, since everything in it is only a collection or mass of parts to infinity. Now multitude can only get its reality from *true unities* which come from elsewhere and are quite different from points (it is known that the continuum cannot be composed of points). Therefore to find these *real unities* I was compelled to have recourse to a formal atom, since a material being cannot be both material and perfectly indivisible or endowed with a true unity. It was necessary, hence, to recall and, so to speak, rehabilitate the *substantial forms* so decried today, but in a way which would make them intelligible and which would separate the use we

should make of them from the abuse that has been made of them. I thence found that their nature consists in force, and that from that there ensues something analogous to feeling and appetite; and that accordingly they must be conceived in imitation of the idea we have of Souls. But as the soul should never be used to explain any detail of the economy of the animal's body, I judged likewise that these forms must not be used to explain the particular problems of nature though they are necessary to establish true general principles. Aristotle calls them *first Entelechies*. I call them perhaps more intelligibly, *primitive Forces* which do not contain only the *act* or the complement of possibility, but further an *original activity*.

4. I saw that these forms and these souls should be indivisible, as our mind is, remembering indeed that that was the thought of Saint Thomas regarding the souls of animals. But this truth renewed the great difficulties of the origin and duration of souls and forms. For every substance, being a true unity and not capable of beginning or ceasing to exist without a miracle, it follows that they can only begin by creation and end only by annihilation. Thus, except the souls that God wishes still to create expressly, I was obliged to recognize that it is necessary that the forms constitutive of substances should have been created with the world and that they should subsist forever. Thus a few scholastics like Albert the Great and John Bacon had glimpsed a part of the truth about their origin. And that should not appear extraordinary, since we are only giving to forms the duration which the Gassendists give to their atoms.

5. I judged, however, that we must not be indifferent to the different grades of minds or reasonable souls, the higher orders being incomparably more perfect than those forms buried in matter, being like little Gods by contrast with the latter, and are made in the image of God, having in them some ray of the light of Divinity. That is why God governs minds as a Prince governs his subjects, and even as a father cares for his children, whereas he disposes of other substances as an engineer manipulates his machines. Thus minds have particular laws which put them above the revolutions of matter; and we may say that everything else is made only for them, these very revolutions being accommodated for the happiness of the good and the punishment of the wicked.

6. Nevertheless, giving back to ordinary forms or *material*

souls that duration which must be attributed to them in the place of what had been attributed to atoms, might arouse the suspicion that they go from one body to another, which would be *metempsychosis*, almost as some philosophers have believed in the propagation of motion and that of species. But this is a piece of imagination far removed from the nature of things. There is no such passage; and this is where the 'metamorphoses' of Messrs Swammerdam, Malpighi, and Leeuwenhoeck, who are excellent observers in our day, have come to my aid, and have made me admit more confidently that the animal as every other organized substance has no beginning, though we think so, and that its apparent generation is only a development and a kind of augmentation. Thus I have noticed that the author of the *Recherche de la Vérité* [Malebranche], Mr Regis, Mr Hartsoeker, and other able men, have not been very far from having this thought.

7. But there still remained the biggest question, what becomes of these souls or forms after the death of the animal or the destruction of the individual with organized substance? And that is a most embarrassing problem; in so far as it scarcely seems reasonable for souls to remain uselessly in a chaos of confused matter. That made me finally judge that there was only one single reasonable line to take, and that is the conservation not only of the soul but also of the animal itself and its organic machine even though the destruction of the gross parts may have reduced it to a smallness which is as much beyond our senses as it was before being born. Thus nobody can really observe the true time of death; the latter may pass a long time for a simple suspension of noticeable actions, and at bottom is never anything else in simple animals: witness the resuscitations of drowned flies buried under pulverized chalk, and several other similar examples which make us sufficiently aware that there would be many other resuscitations, and even more than that, if men were able to restore the machine. And there is some evidence apparently that something of that sort was discussed by the great Democritus, atomist that he was, though Pliny makes fun of him. It is, hence, natural that the animal having always been alive and organized (as some persons of great penetration are beginning to recognize), he remains so always. And since there is no first birth nor entirely new generation of the animal, it follows that there will not be any final extinction, nor any complete death taken in a strict meta-

physical sense. Consequently, instead of the transmigration of souls, there is only a transformation of the same animal, according to the different ways the organs are unfolded and more or less developed.

8. However, reasonable souls follow much higher laws and are exempt from anything which might make them lose the quality of being citizens of the society of spirits. God has so well seen to it that no changes of matter can make them lose the moral qualities of their personality. And we may say that everything tends to the perfection, not solely of the universe in general, but also of those creatures in particular who are destined to such a degree of happiness that the Universe finds itself interested by virtue of the divine goodness which is communicated to each one as much as the sovereign Wisdom may permit.

9. Concerning the ordinary course of animals and other corporeal substances whose complete extinction has been accepted until now, and whose changes depend on mechanical rather than on moral laws, I noticed with pleasure that the ancient author of the book *On Diet*, attributed to Hippocrates, had glimpsed something of the truth when he said explicitly that animals are not born and do not die, and that the things believed to begin and to perish only appear and disappear. That is the thought also of Parmenides and of Melissus, according to Aristotle. For these ancients were more solid than people believe.

10. I am the most readily disposed person in the world to do justice to the moderns; however, I find they have carried reform too far. Among other things, they confuse natural with artificial things for lack of insufficiently broad ideas about the majesty of nature. They conceive the difference existing between her machines and ours to be only one of size, Nature's being larger. This view has recently led a very able man (Fontenelle), the author of *Entretiens sur la pluralité des Mondes* (*Dialogues on the plurality of worlds*), to say that on looking closely at Nature, we find her less admirable than we had thought, and more like the shop of a working man. I believe that that view does not give us a worthy idea of her. Only in my system is one able to realize at last the true and immense distance between the smallest productions and mechanisms of divine wisdom and the greatest masterpieces of art of a limited mind, this difference being not simply one of degree but of very kind. We must then know that

Nature's machines have a truly infinite number of organs, and are so well supplied and resistant to all accidents that it is impossible to destroy them. A natural machine still remains a machine in its least parts, and furthermore, it remains forever the same machine that it has been, being only transformed by the different habits it takes on, at one time expansive, at another restrictive and concentrated, when believed to be lost.

11. Besides, by means of the soul or form, there is a true unity which answers to what is called the Ego in us. This cannot take place in the machines of art, nor in the simple mass of matter no matter how organized it is. Matter can only be considered like an army or herd, or like a pond full of fish, or like a watch made up of springs and wheels. However, if there were no true substantial unities, there would be nothing substantial or real in the collection. That was what forced Mr Cordemoi to abandon Descartes and embrace the Democritean doctrine of atoms in order to find a true unity. But *material atoms* are contrary to reason, apart from the fact that they are still composed of parts, since the invincible attachment of one part to the other (if one could conceive or suppose it with reason) would not destroy their multitude. There are only *substantial atoms*, that is to say, real unities, absolutely destitute of parts, which are the sources of actions; they are the first absolute principles of the composition of things, and like the last elements of the analysis of substances. They might be called *metaphysical points*: they have *something vital* and a kind of perception; *mathematical points* are their *point of view* for expressing the Universe. But when corporeal substances are close together, all their organs together make only one *physical point* relatively to us. Thus physical points are indivisible only in appearance; mathematical points are exact, but they are only modalities; only metaphysical or substantial points (constituted by forms or souls) are exact *and* real; without them there would be nothing real, since without true unities there would be no multitude.

12. After establishing these things, I thought I had arrived in port; but when I began to meditate on the union of the soul with the body, I was cast back, as it were, into the open sea. For I found no way of explaining how the body causes something to happen in the soul, or *vice versa*; nor how a substance can communicate with another created substance. Descartes had given up the game on that point, so far as we can know from his

writings; but his disciples seeing that the common opinion is inconceivable judged that we feel the qualities of bodies because God causes thoughts to arise in the soul on the occasion of the movements of matter, and when our soul wishes in its turn to move the body they judged that it is God who moves it for the soul. And as the communication of the movements appeared to them inconceivable again, they believed that God gives movement to a body on the occasion of the movement of another body. That is what they call the *System of Occasional Causes*, which has been made very fashionable through the beautiful reflections of the author of the *Recherche de la Vérité*.

13. It must be admitted that by noting what cannot be the case concerning the soul and body, the Cartesians have at least penetrated to the difficulty, but it has not been alleviated by simply describing what in fact happens. In strict metaphysical language, there is very truly no real influence of one created substance on another, all things with all their realities being continually produced by the power of God; but in order to solve problems it is not enough to employ the general cause and to invoke what is called *Deus ex machinâ*. For when that is done without any other explanation drawn from the order of secondary causes, recourse is being taken to miracle, properly speaking. In philosophy we must try to give reasons by showing in what way things are brought about by divine wisdom in conformity with the notion of the subject under investigation.

14. Therefore, though I was obliged to agree that it is impossible for the soul, or any other true substance, to receive any influence from the outside except through divine omnipotence, I was gradually led to a thought which surprised me but seems to me inevitable and indeed has very great advantages and a very considerable attraction. That is, we must say that God has from the first created the soul or any other real unity in such a way that everything arises in it from its own internal nature through a perfect *spontaneity* relatively to itself, and yet with a perfect *conformity* to external things. Thus our internal thoughts, that is, those in the soul itself and not in the brain nor in the subtle parts of the body (which are only phenomena following on external beings, or else, true appearances, like well ordered dreams), these perceptions internal to the soul itself, must happen to it through its own original constitution, that is to say, through its representative nature (capable of expressing beings

outside itself by the mediation of its organs) given to it since its creation and constituting its individual character. And that is what makes each one of these substances represent, each exactly in its own way, the whole universe from a certain point of view. The perceptions or expressions of external things occur in the soul at a fixed moment by virtue of its own laws, as in a world apart and as if there existed nothing but God and itself (to use a manner of speaking employed by a certain person [Mons. Foucher] of great spiritual elevation and famous for his holiness). There will be a perfect harmony among all these substances which produces the same effect that would be noticed if they communicated mutually through that propagation of species or of qualities imagined by the common run of philosophers. Moreover, the organized mass in which the point of view of the soul lies, is expressed more proximately and finds itself in turn ready to act itself by obeying the laws of the bodily machine at the moment the soul wishes to act, without disturbing the laws of nature, the spirits and blood then having exactly the motions they need to correspond to the soul's passions and perceptions. It is this mutual relationship regulated in advance in each substance of the universe which produces what we call their communication, and which alone causes *the union of soul and body*.

15. This hypothesis is indeed possible. For why could not God first give to substance a nature or internal force which could produce in it, in an orderly way, everything which will happen to it (as in a *spiritual or formal automaton* but *free* in that it has a share of reason), that is, all the appearances or expressions it will have, and that, without the aid of any creature? All the more so since the nature of substance requires necessarily and conceals a progression or change without which it would not have the force to act. And this nature of the soul being representative of the universe in a very exact though more or less distinct manner, the series of representations produced in the soul will correspond naturally to the series of changes in the Universe itself: as, conversely, the body has also been accommodated to the soul in those transactions in which the soul is conceived as acting on external things. This is all the more reasonable in so far as bodies are made only for minds capable of entering into society with God and to appreciate his glory. Thus, as soon as one sees the possibility of this hypothesis of harmonies, it is seen as most

reasonable both for giving a marvelous idea of the harmony of the Universe and of the perfection of God's works.

16. There is to be discovered in it also this great advantage that instead of saying that we are free only in appearance in a way sufficient for practical life, as several intelligent persons have believed, we should rather say that we are determined only in appearance but that in strict metaphysical language we are perfectly independent relatively to the influence of all other creatures. This again puts in a marvelous light the immortality of our soul and the constantly uniform conservation of our individuality, perfectly well regulated by its own nature, protected from all external accidents, notwithstanding any appearance to the contrary. Never has a system put our elevation in greater evidence. Every mind being like a world apart, sufficient unto itself, independent of any other creature, containing the infinite, expressing the universe, is as enduring, as subsistent, and as absolute as the very universe of creatures. Thus one should judge that he ought to behave in the most proper way to contribute to the perfection of the society of all the minds which make their moral union in the City of God. We also have in our system a new and surprisingly clear proof of God's existence. For this perfect harmony of so many substances which have no mutual communication can only come from the common cause.

17. Besides all these advantages recommending this hypothesis, we may say that it is something more than a hypothesis, since it scarcely seems possible to explain the thing in any other intelligible way, and since several big difficulties which have until now worried minds seem to disappear by themselves when we have understood the system. Ordinary ways of speaking are still preserved quite well. For we can say that the substance whose disposition gives a reason for change in an intelligible way (so that we can judge that other substances have been harmonized with it on that point from the beginning, according to the order of God's decree), such a substance may be conceived in that respect as *acting* consequently on the others. Thus the action of one substance on another is not the emission or transplantation of an entity, as is commonly conceived, and cannot be taken reasonably except in the way I have just mentioned. It is true that in matter we conceive very well both emissions and receptions of parts through which many are right in explaining all the phenomena of Physics mechanically; but as the material

mass is not a substance itself, it cannot be other than what I have just indicated.

18. These considerations, however metaphysical they may appear, still have a marvelous use in Physics for establishing the laws of motion, as our *Dynamics* will enable us to show. For we can say that in the collision of bodies each one suffers only through its own elasticity, because of the movement already in it. And as to absolute motion, nothing can determine it mathematically, since everything terminates in relations: which makes for the perfect equivalence of hypotheses, e.g., in Astronomy; so that whatever number of bodies we take, we may arbitrarily assign rest or any degree of velocity we choose without being refuted by the phenomena of rectilinear, circular, or composite motion. However, it is reasonable to attribute to bodies true movements following the supposition which gives a reason for phenomena in the most intelligible manner, this denomination of movement being in conformity with the notion of action which we have just established.

SECOND EXPLANATION OF THE SYSTEM OF THE COMMUNICATION OF SUBSTANCES

(*Histoire des Ouvrages des Savans,* Feb. 1696)

You do not understand, you say, how I could prove what I have proposed concerning the *Communication* or *Harmony* of two *Substances* as different as the *soul* is from the *body*. It is true that I believe I have found the way, and here is how I intend to satisfy you.

Imagine two clocks or watches in perfect agreement. That can happen in three ways:

(1) The first consists in a mutual influence.

(2) The second is to have a skillful worker continually adjust them and keep them in agreement.

(3) The third is to manufacture these two time-pieces with so much art and accuracy that their agreement is guaranteed thereafter.

Now substitute the *soul* and *body* for these two time-pieces; their agreement can be obtained through one of these three ways. The *way of influence* is that of popular philosophy; but as we cannot conceive of material particles which can pass from one of these substances to another, we must abandon this idea. The way of the *continual* assistance of the Creator is that of the system of occasional causes; but I hold that this introduces *Deus ex Machinâ* in a natural and ordinary occurrence where, according to reason, it ought not intervene except as it operates in all other natural things. Thus there remains only my hypothesis, that is, the way of *Harmony*. From the beginning God has made each of these two Substances of such a nature that each by following its own laws, given to it with its being, still agrees with the other, just as though there were a mutual influence or as though God always took a hand in it beyond his general supervision of things. There is nothing further I have to prove, unless you wish to ask that I prove God is skillful enough to use this prearranged scheme, examples of which we see even among men. Now assuming that he can, you do see that this way is most admirable and most worthy of God. You suspected that my explanation would be opposed by the very different idea we have of the mind and body; but you see now that nobody has better established their independence. For while people are compelled to explain the communication of mind and body by a sort of miracle, there is cause for many people to fear that the distinction between soul and body might not be as real as they believe, since they have to go so far in order to maintain it. I shall not be vexed if learned persons sound out the thoughts I have just explained to you.

On the Supersensible Element in Knowledge, and on the Immaterial in Nature

(*Letter to Queen Charlotte of Prussia*, 1702)

Madame:

The letter written not long since from Paris to Osnabruck and which I recently read, by your order, at Hanover, seemed to me truly ingenious and beautiful. And as it treats of the two important questions, *Whether there is something in our thoughts which does not come from the senses, and Whether there is something in nature which is not material*, concerning which I acknowledge that I am not altogether of the opinion of the author of the letter, I should like to be able to explain myself with the same grace as he, in order to obey the commands and to satisfy the curiosity of your Majesty.

We use the external senses as, to use the comparison of one of the ancients, a blind man does a stick, and they make us know their particular objects, which are colors, sounds, odors, flavors, and the qualities of touch. But they do not make us know what these sensible qualities are or in what they consist. For example, whether red is the revolving of certain small globules which it is claimed cause light; whether heat is the whirling of a very fine dust; whether sound is made in the air as circles in the water when a stone is thrown into it, as certain philosophers claim; this is what we do not see. And we could not even understand how this revolving, these whirlings and these circles, if they should be real, should cause exactly these perceptions which we have of red, of heat, of noise. Thus it may be said that *sensible qualities* are in fact *occult qualities*, and that there must be others *more manifest* which can render the former more explicable. And far from understanding only sensible things, it is exactly these which we understand the least. And although they are familiar to us we do not understand them the better for that; as a pilot understands no better than another person the nature of the magnetic needle which turns toward the north, although he has it always before his eyes in the compass, and although he does not admire it any the more for that reason.

I do not deny that many discoveries have been made concerning the nature of these occult qualities, as, for example, we know by what kind of refraction blue and yellow are formed, and that these two colors mixed form green; but for all this we cannot yet understand how the perception which we have of these three colors results from these causes. Also we have not even nominal definitions of such qualities by which to explain the terms. The purpose of nominal definitions is to give sufficient marks by which the thing may be recognized; for example, assayers have marks by which they distinguish gold from every other metal, and even if a man had never seen gold these signs might be taught him so that he would infallibly recognize it if he should some day meet with it. But it is not the same with these sensible qualities; and marks to recognize blue, for example, could not be given if we had never seen it. So that blue is its own mark, and in order that a man may know what blue is it must necessarily be shown to him.

It is for this reason that we are accustomed to say that the *notions* of these qualities are *clear*, for they serve to recognize them; but that these same notions are not *distinct*, because we cannot distinguish or develop that which they include. It is an *I know not what* of which we are conscious, but for which we cannot account. Whereas we can make another understand what a thing is of which we have some description or nominal definition, even although we should not have the thing itself at hand to show him. However, we must do the senses the justice to say that, in addition to these occult qualities, they make us know other qualities which are more manifest and which furnish more distinct notions. And these are those which we ascribe to the *common sense*, because there is no external sense to which they are particularly attached and belong. And here definitions of the terms or words employed may be given. Such is the idea of *numbers*, which is found equally in sounds, colors, and touches. It is thus that we perceive also *figures*, which are common to colors and to touches, but which we do not notice in sounds. Although it is true that in order to conceive distinctly numbers and even figures, and to form sciences of them, we must come to something which the senses cannot furnish, and which the understanding adds to the senses.

As therefore our soul compares (for example) the numbers and figures which are in colors with the numbers and figures which are found by touch, there must be an *internal sense*, in which the perceptions of these different external senses are found united. This is what is called the *imagination*, which comprises at once the *notions of the particular senses*, which are *clear* but *confused*, and the *notions of the common sense*, which are clear and distinct. And these clear and distinct ideas which are subject to the imagination are the objects of the *mathematical sciences*, namely of arithmetic and geometry, which are *pure* mathematical sciences, and of the application of these sciences to nature, forming mixed mathematics. It is evident also that particular sensible qualities are susceptible of explanations and of reasonings only in so far as they involve what is common to the objects of several external senses, and belong to the internal sense. For those who try to explain sensible qualities distinctly always have recourse to the ideas of mathematics, and these ideas always involve *size* or multitude of parts. It is true that the mathematical sciences would not be demonstrative, and would consist in a simple induction or observation, which would never assure us of the perfect generality of the truths there found, if something higher and which intelligence alone can furnish did not come to the aid of the *imagination* and the *senses*.

There are, therefore, objects of still other nature, which are not included at all in what is observed in the objects of the senses in particular or in common, and which consequently are not objects of the imagination either. Thus besides the *sensible* and *imageable*, there is that which is purely *intelligible*, as being the *object of the understanding alone*, and such is the object of my thought when I think of myself.

This thought of the *Ego*, which informs me of sensible objects, and of my own action resulting therefrom, adds something to the objects of the senses. To think a color and to observe that one thinks it, are two very different thoughts, as different as the color is from the Ego which thinks it. And as I conceive that other beings may also have the right to say *I*, or that it could be said for them, it is through this that I conceive what is called *substance* in general, and it is also the consideration of the Ego itself which furnishes other *metaphysical* notions, such as cause, effect, action, similarity, etc., and even those of *logic* and of *ethics*. Thus it can be said that there is nothing in the understanding which does not come from the senses, except the understanding itself, or that which understands.

There are then three grades of notions: the *sensible only*, which are the objects appropriate to each sense in particular; the *sensible and at the same time intelligible*, which pertain to the common sense; and the *intelligible only*, which belong to the understanding. The first and the second are both imageable, but the third are above the imagination. The second and third are intelligible and distinct; but the first are confused, although they are clear or recognizable.

Being itself and *truth* are not known wholly through the senses; for it would not be impossible for a creature to have long and orderly dreams, resembling our *life*, of such a sort that everything which it thought it perceived through the senses would be but mere *appearances*. There must therefore be something beyond the senses, which distinguishes the true from the apparent. But the truth of the demonstrative sciences is exempt from these doubts, and must even serve for judging of the truth of sensible things. For as able philosophers, ancient and modern, have already well remarked: – if all that I should think that I see should be but a dream, it would always be true that I who think while dreaming, would be something, and would actually think in many ways, for which there must always be some reason.

Thus what the ancient Platonists have observed is very true, and is very worthy of being considered, that the existence of sensible things and particularly of the *Ego* which thinks and which is called spirit or soul, is incomparably more sure than the existence of sensible things; and that thus it would not be impossible, speaking with metaphysical rigor, that there should be at bottom only these intelligible substances, and that sensible things should be but appearances. While on the other hand our lack of attention makes us take sensible things for the only true things. It is well also to observe that if I should discover any demonstrative truth, mathematical or other, while dreaming (as might in fact be), it would be just as certain as if I had been awake. This shows us how intelligible truth is independent of the truth or of the existence outside of us of sensible and material things.

This conception of *being* and of *truth* is found therefore in the Ego and in the understanding, rather than in the external senses and in the perception of external objects.

There we find also what it is to affirm, to deny, to doubt, to will, to act. But above all we find there the *forces of the consequences* of reasoning, which are a part of what is called the *natural light*. For example, from this premise, that *no wise man is wicked*, we may, by reversing the terms, draw this conclusion, that *no wicked man is wise*. Whereas from this sentence, that *every wise man is praiseworthy*, we cannot conclude by converting it, that *every one praiseworthy is wise* but only that *some praiseworthy ones are wise*. Although we may always convert particular affirmative propositions, for example, if *some wise man is rich* it must also be that *some rich men are wise*, this cannot be done in particular negatives. For example, we may say that *there are charitable persons who are not just*, which happens when charity is not sufficiently regulated; but we cannot infer from this that *there are just persons who are not charitable*; for in justice are included at the same time charity and the rule of reason.

It is also by this *natural light* that the *axioms* of mathematics are recognized; for example, that *if from two equal things the same quantity be taken away the things which remain are equal*; likewise that *if in a balance everything is equal on the one side and on the other, neither will incline*, a thing which we foresee without ever having experienced it. It is upon such foundations that we construct arithmetic, geometry, mechanics and the other demonstrative sciences; in which, in truth, the senses are very necessary, in order to have certain ideas of sensible things, and experiments are necessary to establish certain facts, and even useful to verify reasonings as by a kind of proof. But the force of the demonstrations depends upon intelligible notions and truths, which alone are capable of making us discern what is necessary, and which, in the conjectural sciences, are even capable of determining demonstratively the degree of probability upon certain given suppositions, in order that we may choose rationally among opposite appearances, the one which is greatest. Nevertheless this part of the art of reasoning has not yet been cultivated as much as it ought to be.

But to return to *necessary truths*, it is generally true that we know them only by this natural light, and not at all by the experiences of the senses. For the senses can very well make known, in some sort, what is, but they cannot make known what *ought to be* or could not be otherwise.

For example, although we may have experienced numberless times that every massive body tends toward the centre of the earth and is not sustained in the air, we are not sure that this is necessary as long as we do not understand the reason of it. Thus we could not be sure that the same thing would occur in air at a higher altitude, at a hundred or more leagues above us; and there are philosophers who imagine that the earth is a magnet, and as the ordinary magnet does not attract the needle when a little removed from it, they think that the attractive force of the earth does not extend very far either. I do not say that they are right, but I do say that one cannot go very certainly beyond the experiences one has had, when one is not aided by reason.

This is why the geometricians have always considered that what is only proved by *induction* or by examples, in geometry or in arithmetic, is never perfectly proved. For example, experience teaches us that odd numbers continuously added together produce the square numbers, that is to say, those which come from multiplying a number by itself. Thus 1 and 3 make 4, that is to say 2 times 2. And 1 and 3 and 5 make 9, that is to say 3 times 3.

And 1 and 3 and 5 and 7 make 16, that is 4 times 4. And 1 and 3 and 5 and 7 and 9 make 25, that is 5 times 5. And so on.

1	1	1	1
3	3	3	3
—	5	5	5
4	—	7	7
	9	—	9
		16	—
			25
2	3	4	5
x	x	x	x
2	3	4	5
—	—	—	—
4	9	16	25

However, if one should experience it a hundred thousand times, continuing the calculation very far, he may reasonably think that this will always follow; but he does not therefore have absolute certainty of it, unless he learns the demonstrative reason which the mathematicians found out long ago. And it is on this foundation of the uncertainty of inductions, but carried a little too far, that an Englishman has lately wished to maintain that we can avoid death. For (said he) the inference is not good: my father, my grandfather, my great-grandfather are dead and all the others who have lived before us; therefore we shall also die. For their death has no influence on us. The trouble is that we resemble them a little too much in this respect that the causes of their death subsist also in us. For the resemblance would not suffice to draw sure consequences without the consideration of the same reasons.

In truth there are *experiments* which succeed numberless times and ordinarily, and yet it is found in some extraordinary cases that there are *instances* where the experiment does not succeed. For example, if we should have found a hundred thousand times that iron put all alone on the surface of water goes to the bottom, we are not sure that this must always happen. And without recurring to the miracle of the prophet Elisha, who made iron float, we know that an iron pot may be made so hollow that it floats, and that it can even carry besides a considerable weight, as do boats of copper or of tin. And even the abstract sciences like geometry furnish cases in which what ordinarily occurs occurs no longer. For example, we ordinarily find that two lines which continually approach each other finally meet, and many people will almost swear that this could never be otherwise. And nevertheless geometry furnishes us with extraordinary lines, which are for this reason called *asymptotes*, which prolonged *ad infinitum* continually approach each other, and nevertheless never meet.

This consideration shows also that there is a *light born within us*. For since the senses and inductions could never teach us truths which are thoroughly universal, nor that which is absolutely necessary, but only that which is, and that which is found in particular examples; and since we nevertheless know necessary and universal truths of the sciences, a privilege which we have above the brutes; it follows that we have derived these truths in part from what is within us. Thus we may lead a child to these by simple interrogations, after the manner of Socrates, without telling him anything, and without making him experiment at all upon the truth of what is asked him. And this could very easily be practiced in numbers and other similar matters.

I agree, nevertheless, that in the present state the external senses are necessary to us for thinking, and that, if we had none, we could not think. But that which is necessary for something does not for all that constitute its essence. Air is necessary for life, but our life is something else than air. The senses furnish us the matter for reasoning, and we never have thoughts so abstract that something from the senses is not mingled therewith; but reasoning requires something else in addition to what is from the senses.

As to the *second question*, whether there are *immaterial substances*, in order to solve it, it is first necessary to explain one's self. Hitherto by matter has been understood that which includes only notions purely passive and indifferent, namely, extension and impenetrability, which need to be determined by something else to some form or action. Thus when it is said that there are immaterial substances, it is thereby meant that there are substances which include other notions, namely, perception and the principle of action or of change, which could not be explained either by extension or by impenetrability. These beings, when they have feeling, are called *souls*, and when they are capable of reason, they are called spirits. Thus if one says that force and perception are essential to matter, he takes matter for corporeal substance which is complete, which includes form and matter, or the soul with the organs. It is as if it were said that there were souls everywhere. This might be true, and would not be contrary to the doctrine of immaterial substances. For it is not intended that these souls be separate from matter, but simply that they are something more than matter, and are not produced nor destroyed by the changes which matter undergoes, nor subject to dissolution, since they are not composed of parts.

Nevertheless it must be avowed also that there is *substance separated from matter*. And to see this, one has only to consider that there are numberless forms which matter might have received in place of the series of variations which it has actually received. For it is clear, for example, that the stars could move quite otherwise, space and matter being indifferent to every kind of motion and figure.

Hence the reason or universal determining cause whereby things are, and are as they are rather than otherwise, must be outside of matter. And even the existence of matter depends thereon, since we do not find in its notion that it carries with it the reason of its existence.

Now this ultimate reason of things, which is common to them all and universal by reason of the connection existing between all parts of nature, is what we call *God*, who must necessarily be an infinite and absolutely perfect substance. I am inclined to think that all immaterial finite substances (even the genii or angels according to the opinion of the ancient Church Fathers) are united to organs, and accompany matter, and even that souls or active forms are everywhere found in it. And matter, in order to constitute a substance which is complete, cannot do without them, since force and action are found everywhere in it, and since the laws of force depend on certain remarkable metaphysical reasons or intelligible notions, and cannot be explained by notions which are merely material or mathematical or which belong to the sphere of the imagination.

Perception also could not be explained by any mechanism whatsoever. We may therefore conclude that there is in addition something immaterial everywhere in these creatures, and particularly in us, in whom this force is accompanied by a sufficiently distinct perception, and even by that light, of which I have spoken above, which makes us resemble in miniature the Divinity, as well by knowledge of the order, as by the ordering which we ourselves know how to give to the things which are within our reach, in imitation of that which God gives to the universe. It is in this also that our *virtue* and perfection consist, as our *felicity* consists in the pleasure which we take therein.

And since every time we penetrate into the depths of things, we find there the most beautiful order we could wish, even surpassing what we have therein imagined, as all those know who have fathomed the sciences; we may conclude that it is the same in all the rest, and that not only immaterial substances subsist always, but also that their lives, progress and changes are regulated for advance toward a certain end, or rather to approach more and more thereto, as do the asymptotes. And although we sometimes recoil, like lines which retrograde, advancement none the less finally prevails and wins.

The natural light of reason does not suffice for knowing the detail thereof, and our experiences are still too limited to catch a glimpse of the laws of this order. The revealed light guides us meanwhile through faith, but there is room to believe that in the course of time we shall know them even more by experience, and that there are spirits that know them already more than we do.

Meanwhile the philosophers and the poets, for want of this, have betaken themselves to the fictions of metempsychosis or of the Elysian Fields, in order to give some ideas which might strike the populace. But the consideration of the perfection of things or (what is the same thing) of the sovereign power, wisdom and goodness of God, who does all for the best, that to say, in the greatest order, suffices to render content those who are reasonable, and to make us believe that the contentment ought to be greater, according as we are more disposed to follow order or reason.

The Principles of Nature and of Grace, based on Reason, 1714

1. *Substance* is a being capable of action. It is simple or compound. *Simple substance* is that which has no parts. *Compound* substance is the collection of simple substances or *monads*. *Monas* is a Greek word which signifies unity, or that which is one.

Compounds, or bodies, are multitudes; and simple substances, lives, souls, spirits are unities. And there must be simple substances everywhere, because without simple substances there would be no compounds; and consequently all nature is full of life.

2. Monads, having no parts, cannot be formed or decomposed. They cannot begin or end naturally; and consequently last as long as the universe, which will be changed but will not be destroyed. They cannot have shapes; otherwise they would have parts. And consequently a monad, in itself and at a given moment, could not be distinguished from another except by its internal qualities and actions, which can be nothing else than its *perceptions* (that is, representations of the compound, or of what is external, in the simple), and its *appetitions* (that is, its tendencies to pass from one perception to another), which are the principles of change. For the simplicity of substance does not prevent multiplicity of modifications, which must be found together in this same simple substance, and must consist in the variety of relations to things which are external. Just as in a *centre* or point, entirely simple as it is, there is an infinity of angles formed by the lines which meet at the point.

3. All nature is a *plenum*. There are everywhere simple substances, separated in effect from one another by activities of their own which continually change their relations; and each important simple substance, or monad, which forms the centre of a composite substance (as, for example, of an animal) and the principle of its unity, is surrounded by a *mass* composed of an infinity of other monads, which constitute the body proper of this central monad; and in accordance with the affections of its body the monad represents, as in a *centre*, the things which are outside of itself. And this *body* is *organic*, though it forms a sort of automaton or natural machine, which is a machine not only in its entirety, but also in its smallest perceptible parts. And as, because the world is a *plenum*, everything is connected and each body acts upon every other body, more or less, according to the distance, and by reaction is itself affected thereby, it follows that each monad is a living mirror, or endowed with internal activity, representative according to its point of view of the universe, and as regulated as the universe itself. And the perceptions in the monad spring one from the other, by the laws of desires [*appétits*] or of the *final causes of good and evil*, which consist in observable, regulated or unregulated, perceptions; just as the changes of bodies and external phenomena spring

one from another, by the laws of *efficient causes*, that is, of motions. Thus there is a perfect *harmony* between the perceptions of the monad and the motions of bodies, pre-established at the beginning between the system of efficient causes and that of final causes. And in this consists the accord and physical union of the soul and the body, although neither one can change the laws of the other.

4. Each monad, with a particular body, makes a living substance. Thus there is not only life everywhere, accompanied with members or organs, but there is also an infinity of degrees among monads, some dominating more or less over others. But when the monad has organs so adjusted that by their means prominence and distinctness appear in the impressions which they receive, and consequently in the perceptions which represent these (as, for example, when by means of the shape of the humors of the eyes, the rays of light are concentrated and act with more force), this may lead to *feeling* [*sentiment*], that is, to a perception accompanied by *memory*, namely, by a certain reverberation lasting a long time, so as to make itself heard upon occasion. And such a living being is called an *animal*, as its monad is called a soul. And when this soul is elevated to *reason*, it is something more sublime and is reckoned among spirits, as will soon be explained. It is true that animals are sometimes in the condition of simple living beings, and their souls in the condition of simple monads, namely, when their perceptions are not sufficiently distinct to be remembered, as happens in a deep dreamless sleep, or in a swoon. But perceptions which have become entirely confused must be re-developed in animals, for reasons which I shall shortly (§ 12) enumerate. Thus it is well to make distinction between the *perception*, which is the inner state of the monad representing external things, and *apperception*, which is *consciousness* or the reflective knowledge of this inner state; the latter not being given to all souls, nor at all times to the same soul. And it is for want of this distinction that the Cartesians have failed, taking no account of the perceptions of which we are not conscious as people take no account of imperceptible bodies. It is this also which made the same Cartesians believe that only spirits are monads, that there is no soul of brutes, and still less other *principles of life*. And as they shocked too much the common opinion of men by refusing feeling to brutes, they have, on the other hand, accommodated

themselves too much to the prejudices of the multitude, by confounding a *long swoon*, caused by a great confusion of perceptions, with *death strictly speaking*, where all perception would cease. This has confirmed the ill-founded belief in the destruction of some souls, and the bad opinion of some so-called strong minds, who have contended against the immortality of our soul.

5. There is a connection in the perceptions of animals which bears some resemblance to reason; but it is only founded in the memory of *facts* or effects, and not at all in the knowledge of *causes*. Thus a dog shuns the stick with which it has been beaten, because memory represents to it the pain which the stick had caused it. And men, in so far as they are empirics, that is to say, in three-fourths of their actions, act simply as the brutes do. For example, we expect that there will be daylight to-morrow because we have always had the experience; only an astronomer foresees it by reason, and even this prediction will finally fail when the cause of day, which is not eternal, shall cease. But *true reasoning* depends upon necessary or eternal truths, such as those of logic, of numbers, of geometry, which establish an indubitable connection of ideas and unfailing inferences. The animals in whom these inferences are not noticed, are called *brutes*; but those which know these necessary truths are properly those which are called *rational animals*, and their souls are called *spirits*. These souls are capable of performing acts of reflection, and of considering that which is called the *ego*, *substance*, *monad*, *soul*, *spirit*, in a word, immaterial things and truths. And it is this which renders us capable of the sciences and of demonstrative knowledge.

6. Modern researches have taught us, and reason approves of it, that living beings whose organs are known to us, that is to say, plants and animals, do not come from putrefaction or from chaos, as the ancients believed, but from *pre-formed* seeds, and consequently by the transformation of pre-existing living beings. There are animalcules in the seeds of larger animals, which by means of conception assume a new dress, which they make their own, and by means of which they can nourish themselves and increase their size, in order to pass to a larger theatre and to accomplish the propagation of the large animal. It is true that the souls of spermatic human animals are not rational, and do not become so until conception destines [*determine*] these animals to human nature. And as in general animals

are not born entirely in conception or *generation*, neither do they perish entirely in what we call *death*; for it is reasonable that what does not begin naturally, should not end either in the order of nature. Therefore, quitting their mask or their rags, they merely return to a more minute theatre, where they can, nevertheless, be just as sensitive and just as well ordered as in the larger. And what we have just said of the large animals, takes place also in the generation and death of spermatic animals themselves, that is to say, they are growths of other smaller spermatic animals, in comparison with which they may pass for large; for everything extends *ad infinitum* in nature. Thus not only souls, but also animals, are ingenerable and imperishable: they are only developed, enveloped, reclothed, unclothed, transformed: souls never quit their entire body and do not pass from one body into another which is entirely new to them. There is therefore no *metempsychosis*, but there is *metamorphosis*; animals change, take and leave only parts: the same thing which happens little by little and by small invisible particles, but continually, in nutrition; and suddenly, visibly, but rarely, in conception or in death, which cause a gain or loss all at one time.

7. Thus far we have spoken as simple *physicists*: now we must advance to *metaphysics*, making use of the *great principle*, little employed in general, which teaches that *nothing happens without a sufficient reason*; that is to say, that nothing happens without its being possible for him who should sufficiently understand things, to give a reason sufficient to determine why it is so and not otherwise. This principle laid down, the first question which should rightly be asked, will be, *Why is there something rather than nothing*? For nothing is simpler and easier than something. Further, suppose that things must exist, we must be able to give a reason *why they must exist so* and not otherwise.

8. Now this sufficient reason for the existence of the universe cannot be found *in the series of contingent things*, that is, of bodies and of their representations in souls; for matter being indifferent in itself to motion and to rest, and to this or another motion, we cannot find the reason of motion in it, and still less of a certain motion. And although the present motion which is in matter, comes from the preceding motion, and that from still another preceding, yet in this way we make no progress, go as far as we may; for the same question always remains. Thus it must be that the sufficient reason, which has no need of another

reason, be outside this series of contingent things and be found in a substance which is its cause, or which is a necessary being, carrying the reason of its existence within itself; otherwise we should still not have a sufficient reason in which we could rest. And this final reason of things is called *God.*

9. This primitive simple substance must contain in itself eminently the perfections contained in the derivative substances which are its effects; thus it will have perfect power, knowledge and will: that is, it will have supreme omnipotence, omniscience and goodness. And as *justice*, taken very generally, is only goodness conformed to wisdom, there must too be supreme justice in God. The reason which has caused things to exist by him, makes them still dependent upon him in existing and in working: and they continually receive from him that which gives them any perfection; but the imperfection which remains in them, comes from the essential and original limitation of the creature.

10. It follows from the supreme perfection of God, that in creating the universe he has chosen the best possible plan, in which there is the greatest variety together with the greatest order; the best arranged ground, place, time; the most results produced in the most simple ways; the most of power, knowledge, happiness and goodness in the creatures that the universe could permit. For since all the possibles in the understanding of God laid claim to existence in proportion to their perfections, the result of all these claims must be the most perfect actual world that is possible. And without this it would not be possible to give a reason why things have turned out so rather than otherwise.

11. The supreme wisdom of God led him to choose the *laws of motion* best adjusted and most suited to abstract or metaphysical reasons. There is preserved the same quantity of total and absolute force, or of action; the same quantity of respective force or of reaction; lastly the same quantity of directive force. Farther, action is always equal to reaction, and the whole effect is always equivalent to its full cause. And it is not surprising that we could not by the mere consideration of the *efficient causes* or of matter, account for those laws of motion which have been discovered in our time, and a part of which have been discovered by myself. For I have found that it was necessary to have recourse to *final causes*, and that these laws do not depend upon the *principle of necessity*, like logical, arithmetical and geometrical

truths, but upon the *principle of fitness*, that is, upon the choice of wisdom. And this is one of the most effective and evident proofs of the existence of God, to those who can examine these matters thoroughly.

12. It follows, farther, from the perfection of the supreme author, that not only is the order of the entire universe the most perfect possible, but also that each living mirror representing the universe in accordance with its point of view, that is to say, that each *monad*, each substantial centre, must have its perceptions and its desires as well regulated as is compatible with all the rest. Whence it follows, still farther, that *souls*, that is, the most dominating monads, or rather, animals themselves, cannot fail to awaken from the state of stupor in which death or some other accident may put them.

13. For all is regulated in things, once for all, with as much order and harmony as is possible, supreme wisdom and goodness not being able to act except with perfect harmony. The present is big with the future, the future might be read in the past, the distant is expressed in the near. One could become acquainted with the beauty of the universe in each soul, if one could unfold all its folds, which only develop perceptibly in time. But as each distinct perception of the soul includes innumerable confused perceptions, which embrace the whole universe, the soul itself knows the things of which it has perception only so far as it has distinct and clear perceptions of them; and it has perfection in proportion to its distinct perceptions. Each soul knows the infinite, knows all, but confusedly; as in walking on the seashore and hearing the great noise which it makes, I hear the particular sounds of each wave, of which the total sound is composed, but without distinguishing them. Our confused perceptions are the result of the impressions which the whole universe makes upon us. It is the same with each monad. God alone has a distinct knowledge of all, for he is the source of all. It has been well said that he is as centre everywhere, but his circumference is nowhere, since everything is immediately present to him without any distance from this centre.

14. As regards the rational soul, or *spirit*, there is something in it more than in the monads, or even in simple souls. It is not only a mirror of the universe of creatures, but also an image of the Divinity. The *spirit* has not only a perception of the works of God, but it is even capable of producing something which

resembles them, although in miniature. For, to say nothing of the marvels of dreams, in which we invent without trouble (but also involuntarily) things which, when awake, we should have to think a long time in order to hit upon, our soul is architectonic also in its voluntary actions, and, discovering the sciences according to which God has regulated things (*pondere, mensura, numero, etc.*), it imitates, in its department and in its little world, where it is permitted to exercise itself, what God does in the large world.

15. This is why all spirits, whether of men or of genii, entering by virtue of reason and of eternal truths into a sort of society with God, are members of the City of God, that is to say, of the most perfect state, formed and governed by the greatest and best of monarchs; where there is no crime without punishment, no good actions without proportionate recompense; and, finally, as much virtue and happiness as is possible; and this is not by a derangement of nature, as if what God prepares for souls disturbed the laws of bodies, but by the very order of natural things, in virtue of the harmony pre-established for all time between the *realms of nature and of grace*, between God as Architect and God as Monarch; so that *nature* itself leads to grace, and *grace*, in making use of nature, perfects it.

16. Thus although reason cannot teach us the details, reserved to Revelation, of the great future, we can be assured by this same reason that things are made in a manner surpassing our desires. God also being the most perfect and most happy, and consequently, the most lovable of substances, and *truly pure love* consisting in the state which finds pleasure in the perfections and happiness of the loved object, this love ought to give us the greatest pleasure of which we are capable, when God is its object.

17. And it is easy to love him as we ought, if we know him as I have just described. For although God is not visible to our external senses, he does not cease to be very lovable and to give very great pleasure. We see how much pleasure honors give men, although they do not at all consist in the qualities of the external senses. Martyrs and fanatics (although the emotion of the latter is ill-regulated) show what pleasure of the spirit can accomplish; and, what is more, even sensuous pleasures are really confusedly known intellectual pleasures. Music charms us, although its beauty only consists in the harmonies of numbers

and in the reckoning of the beats or vibrations of sounding bodies, which meet at certain intervals, reckonings of which we are not conscious and which the soul nevertheless does make. The pleasures which sight finds in proportions are of the same nature; and those caused by the other senses amount to almost the same thing, although we may not be able to explain it so distinctly.

18. It may even be said that from the present time on, the *love of God* makes us enjoy a foretaste of future felicity. And although it is disinterested, it itself constitutes our greatest good and interest even if we should not seek these therein and should consider only the pleasure which it gives, without regard to the utility it produces; for it gives us perfect confidence in the goodness of our author and master, producing a true tranquillity of mind; not as with the Stoics who force themselves to patience, but by a present contentment, assuring to us also a future happiness. And besides the present pleasure, nothing can be more useful for the future; for the love of God fulfills also our hopes, and leads us in the road of supreme happiness, because by virtue of the perfect order established in the universe, everything is done in the best possible way, as much for the general good as for the greatest individual good of those who are convinced of this and are content with the divine government; this conviction cannot be wanting to those who know how to love the source of all good. It is true that supreme felicity, by whatever *beatific vision* or knowledge of God it be accompanied, can never be full; because, since God is infinite, he cannot be wholly known. Therefore our happiness will never, and ought not, consist in full joy, where there would be nothing farther to desire, rendering our mind stupid; but in a perpetual progress to new pleasures and to new perfections.

The Monadology, 1714

1. The *monad* of which we shall here speak is merely a simple substance, which enters into composites; *simple*, that is to say, without parts.[4]

2. And there must be simple substances, since there are

4. *Théodicée*, § 10. [All footnote references to this earlier work, *Theodicy* (1710), are Leibniz's.]

composites; for the composite is only a collection or *aggregatum* of simple substances.

3. Now where there are no parts, neither extension, nor figure, nor divisibility is possible. And these monads are the true atoms of nature, and, in a word, the elements of all things.

4. Their dissolution also is not at all to be feared, and there is no conceivable way in which a simple substance can perish naturally.[5]

5. For the same reason there is no conceivable way in which a simple substance can begin naturally, since it cannot be formed by composition.

6. Thus it may be said that the monads can only begin or end all at once, that is to say, they can only begin by creation and end by annihilation; whereas that which is composite begins or ends by parts.

7. There is also no way of explaining how a monad can be altered or changed in its inner being by any other creature, for nothing can be transposed within it, nor can there be conceived in it any internal movement which can be excited, directed, augmented or diminished within it, as can be done in composites, where there is change among the parts. The monads have no windows through which anything can enter or depart. The accidents cannot detach themselves nor go about outside of substances, as did formerly the sensible species of the Schoolmen. Thus neither substance nor accident can enter a monad from outside.

8. Nevertheless, the monads must have some qualities, otherwise they would not even be entities. And if simple substances did not differ at all in their qualities there would be no way of perceiving any change in things, since what is in the compound can only come from the simple ingredients, and the monads, if they had no qualities, would be indistinguishable from one another, seeing also they do not differ in quantity. Consequently, a plenum being supposed, each place would always receive, in any motion, only the equivalent of what it had had before, and one state of things would be indistinguishable from another.

9. It is necessary, indeed, that each monad be different from every other. For there are never in nature two beings which are exactly alike and in which it is not possible to find an internal difference, or one founded upon an intrinsic quality (*dénomination*).

5. § 89.

10. I take it also for granted that every created being, and consequently the created monad also, is subject to change, and even that this change is continuous in each.

11. It follows from what has just been said, that the natural changes of the monads proceed from an *internal principle*, since an external cause could not influence their inner being.[6]

12. But, besides the principle of change, there must be an individuating *detail of changes*, which forms, so to speak, the specification and variety of the simple substances.

13. This detail must involve a multitude in the unity or in that which is simple. For since every natural change takes place by degrees, something changes and something remains; and consequently, there must be in the simple substance a plurality of affections and of relations, although it has no parts.

14. The passing state, which involves and represents a multitude in unity or in the simple substance, is nothing else than what is called *perception*, which must be distinguished from apperception or consciousness, as will appear in what follows. Here it is that the Cartesians especially failed, having taken no account of the perceptions of which we are not conscious. It is this also which made them believe that spirits only are monads and that there are no souls of brutes or of other entelechies. They, with most people, have failed to distinguish between a prolonged state of unconsciousness (*étourdissement*) and death strictly speaking, and have therefore agreed with the old scholastic prejudice of entirely separate souls, and have even confirmed ill-balanced minds in the belief in the mortality of the soul.

15. The action of the internal principle which causes the change or the passage from one perception to another, may be called *appetition*; it is true that desire cannot always completely attain to the whole perception to which it tends, but it always attains something of it and reaches new perceptions.

16. We experience in ourselves a multiplicity in a simple substance, when we find that the most trifling thought of which we are conscious involves a variety in the object. Thus all those who admit that the soul is a simple substance ought to admit this multiplicity in the monad, and M. Bayle ought not to have found any difficulty in it, as he has done in his Dictionary, article *Rorarius*.

17. It must be confessed, moreover, that *perception* and that

6. §§ 396 and 400.

which depends on it *are inexplicable by mechanical causes*, that is, by figures and motions. And, supposing that there were a machine so constructed as to think, feel and have perception, we could conceive of it as enlarged and yet preserving the same proportions, so that we might enter it as into a mill. And this granted, we should only find on visiting it, pieces which push one against another, but never anything by which to explain a perception. This must be sought for, therefore, in the simple substance and not in the composite or in the machine. Furthermore, nothing but this (namely, perceptions and their changes) can be found in the simple substance. It is also in this alone that all the *internal activities* of simple substances can consist.[7]

18. The name of *entelechies* might be given to all simple substances or created monads, for they have within themselves a certain perfection (ἔχουσι τὸ ἐντελές); there is a certain sufficiency (αὐτάρκεια) which makes them the sources of their internal activities, and so to speak, incorporeal automata.[8]

19. If we choose to give the name *soul* to everything that has *perceptions* and *desires* in the general sense which I have just explained, all simple substances or created monads may be called souls, but as feeling is something more than a simple perception, I am willing that the general name of monads or entelechies shall suffice for those simple substances which have only perception, and that those substances only shall be called *souls* whose perception is more distinct and is accompanied by memory.

20. For we experience in ourselves a state in which we remember nothing and have no distinguishable perception, as when we fall into a swoon or when we are overpowered by a profound and dreamless sleep. In this state the soul does not differ sensibly from a simple monad; but as this state is not continuous and as the soul comes out of it, the soul is something more than a mere monad.[9]

21. And it does not at all follow that in such a state the simple substance is without any perception. This is indeed impossible, for the reasons mentioned above; for it cannot perish, nor can it subsist without some affection, which is nothing else than its perception; but when there is a great

7. Preface, p. 37 (Gerhardt edition).
8. § 87.
9. § 64.

number of minute perceptions, in which nothing is distinct, we are stunned; as when we turn continually in the same direction many times in succession, whence arises a dizziness which may make us swoon, and which does not let us distinguish anything. And death may produce for a time this condition in animals.

22. And as every present state of a simple substance is naturally the consequence of its preceding state, so its present is big with its future.[10]

23. Therefore, since on being awakened from a stupor, we are *aware* of our perceptions, we must have had them immediately before, although we were unconscious of them; for one perception can come in a natural way only from another perception, as a motion can come in a natural way only from a motion.[11]

24. From this we see that if there were nothing distinct, nothing, so to speak, in relief and of a higher flavor in our perceptions, we should always be in a dazed state. This is the condition of simply bare monads.

25. We also see that nature has given to animals heightened perceptions, by the pains she has taken to furnish them with organs which collect many rays of light or many undulations of air, in order to render these more efficacious by uniting them. There is something of the same kind in odor, in taste, in touch and perhaps in a multitude of other senses which are unknown to us. And I shall presently explain how that which takes place in the soul represents that which occurs in the organs.

26. Memory furnishes souls with a sort of *consecutiveness* [association of ideas] which imitates reason, but which ought to be distinguished from it. We observe that animals, having the perception of something which strikes them and of which they have had a similar perception before, expect, through the representation in their memory, that which was associated with it in the preceding perception, and experience feelings similar to those which they had had at that time. For instance, if we show dogs a stick, they remember the pain it has caused them and whine and run.[12]

27. And the strong imagination which impresses and moves them, arises either from the magnitude or the multitude of preceding perceptions. For often a strong impression produces

10. § 360.
11. §§ 401 to 403.
12. Prelim., § 65.

all at once the effect of a long-continued *habit*, or of many oft-repeated moderate perceptions.

28. Men act like the brutes, in so far as the association of their perceptions results from the principle of memory alone, resembling the empirical physicians who practice without theory: and we are simple empirics in three-fourths of our actions. For example, when we expect that there will be daylight to-morrow, we are acting as empirics, because that has up to this time always taken place. It is only the astronomer who judges of this by reason.

29. But the knowledge of necessary and eternal truths is what distinguishes us from mere animals and furnishes us with *reason* and the sciences, raising us to a knowledge of ourselves and of God. This is what we call the rational soul or *spirit* in us.

30. It is also by the knowledge of necessary truths, and by their abstractions, that we rise to *acts of reflection*, which make us think of that which calls itself '*I*', and to observe that this or that is within *us*: and it is thus that, in thinking of ourselves, we think of being, of substance, simple or composite, of the immaterial and of God himself, conceiving that what is limited in us is in him without limits. And these reflective acts furnish the principal objects of our reasonings.[13]

31. Our reasonings are founded on *two great principles*, *that of contradiction*, in virtue of which we judge that to be *false* which involves contradiction, and that *true*, which is opposed or contradictory to the false.[14]

32. And *that of sufficient reason*, in virtue of which we hold that no fact can be real or existent, no statement true, unless there be a sufficient reason why it is so and not otherwise, although most often these reasons cannot be known to us.[15]

33. There are also two kinds of *truths*, those of *reasoning* and those of *fact*. Truths of reasoning are necessary and their opposite is impossible, and those of *fact* are contingent and their opposite is possible. When a truth is necessary its reason can be found by analysis, resolving it into more simple ideas and truths until we reach those which are primitive.[16]

13. Pref., p. 27.
14. §§ 44, 169.
15. §§ 44, 196.
16. §§ 170, 174, 189, 280–282, 367; Abridgment, Objection 3.

34. It is thus that mathematicians by analysis reduce speculative *theorems* and practical *canons* to *definitions, axioms* and *postulates.*

35. And there are finally simple ideas, definitions of which cannot be given; there are also axioms and postulates, in a word, *primary principles,* which cannot be proved, and indeed need no proof; and these are *identical propositions*, whose opposite involves an express contradiction.

36. But there must also be a *sufficient reason* for *contingent truths,* or those *of fact,* – that is, for the sequence of things diffused through the universe of created objects – where the resolution into particular reasons might run into a detail without limits, on account of the immense variety of the things in nature and the division of bodies *ad infinitum.* There is an infinity of figures and of movements, present and past, which enter into the efficient cause of my present writing, and there is an infinity of slight inclinations and dispositions, past and present, of my soul, which enter into the final cause.[17]

37. And as all this *detail* only involves other contingents, anterior or more detailed, each one of which needs a like analysis for its explanation, we make no advance: and the sufficient or final reason must be outside of the sequence or *series* of this detail of contingencies, however infinite it may be.

38. And thus it is that the final reason of things must be found in a necessary substance, in which the detail of changes exists only eminently, as in their source; and this is what we call God.[18]

39. Now this substance, being a sufficient reason of all this detail, which also is linked together throughout, *there is but one God, and this God is sufficient.*

40. We may also conclude that this supreme substance, which is unique, universal and necessary, having nothing outside of itself which is independent of it, and being a pure consequence of possible being, must be incapable of limitations and must contain as much of reality as is possible.

41. Whence it follows that God is absolutely perfect, *perfection* being only the magnitude of positive reality taken in its strictest meaning, setting aside the limits or bounds in things which have

17. §§ 36, 37, 44, 45, 49, 52, 121, 122, 337, 340, 344.
18. § 7.

them. And where there are no limits, that is, in God, perfection is absolutely infinite.[19]

42. It follows also that the creatures have their perfections from the influence of God, but that their imperfections arise from their own nature, incapable of existing without limits. For it is by this that they are distinguished from God.[20]

43. It is also true that in God is the source not only of existences but also of essences, so far as they are real, or of that which is real in the possible. This is because the understanding of God is the region of eternal truths, or of the ideas on which they depend, and because, without him, there would be nothing real in the possibilities, and not only nothing existing but also nothing possible.[21]

44. For, if there is a reality in essences or possibilities or indeed in the eternal truths, this reality must be founded in something existing and actual, and consequently in the existence of the necessary being, in whom essence involves existence, or with whom it is sufficient to be possible in order to be actual.[22]

45. Hence God alone (or the necessary being) has this prerogative, that he must exist if he is possible. And since nothing can hinder the possibility of that which possesses no limitations, no negation, and, consequently, no contradiction, this alone is sufficient to establish the existence of God *a priori*. We have also proved it by the reality of the eternal truths. But we have a little while ago [§§ 36–39] proved it also *a posteriori*, since contingent beings exist, which can only have their final or sufficient reason in a necessary being who has the reason of his existence in himself.

46. Yet we must not imagine, as some do, that the eternal truths, being dependent upon God, are arbitrary and depend upon his will, as Descartes seems to have held, and afterwards M. Poiret. This is true only of contingent truths, the principle of which is *fitness* or the choice of the *best*, whereas necessary truths depend solely on his understanding and are its internal object.[23]

19. § 22; Preface, p. 27.

20. §§ 20, 27–31, 153, 167, 377 seqq. [In the first copy, revised by Leibniz, the following is added: 'This *original imperfection* of creatures is noticeable in the *natural inertia* of bodies. §§ 30, 380; Abridgment, Objection 5.']

21. § 20.

22. §§ 184, 189, 335.

23. §§ 180, 184, 185, 335, 351, 380.

47. Thus God alone is the primitive unity or the original simple substance; of which all created or derived monads are the products, and are generated, so to speak, by continual fulgurations of the Divinity, from moment to moment, limited by the receptivity of the creature, to whom limitation is essential.[24]

48. In God is *Power*, which is the source of all; then *Knowledge*, which contains the detail of ideas; and finally *Will*, which effects changes or products according to the principle of the best. These correspond to what in created monads form the subject or basis, the perceptive faculty, and the appetitive faculty. But in God these attributes are absolutely infinite or perfect; and in the created monads or in the *entelechies* (or *perfectihabiis*, as Harmolaus Barbarus translated the word), they are only imitations proportioned to the perfection of the monads.[25]

49. The creature is said to *act* externally in so far as it has perfection, and to be *acted on* by another in so far as it is imperfect. Thus *action* is attributed to the monad in so far as it has distinct perceptions, and *passivity* in so far as it has confused perceptions.[26]

50. And one creature is more perfect than another, in this that there is found in it that which serves to account *a priori* for what takes place in the other, and it is in this way that it is said to act upon the other.

51. But in simple substances the influence of one monad upon another is purely *ideal* and it can have its effect only through the intervention of God, inasmuch as in the ideas of God a monad may demand with reason that God in regulating the others from the commencement of things, have regard to it. For since a created monad can have no physical influence upon the inner being of another, it is only in this way that one can be dependent upon another.[27]

52. And hence it is that the actions and passive reactions of creatures are mutual. For God, in comparing two simple substances, finds in each one reasons which compel him to adjust the other to it, and consequently that which in certain respects

24. §§ 382–391, 398, 395.
25. §§ 7, 149, 150, 87.
26. §§ 32, 66, 386.
27. §§ 9, 54, 65, 66, 201; Abridgment, Objection 3.

is active, is according to another point of view, passive; *active* in so far as that what is known distinctly in it, serves to account for that which takes place in another; and *passive* in so far as the reason for what takes place in it, is found in that which is distinctly known in another.[28]

53. Now, as there is an infinity of possible universes in the ideas of God, and as only one of them can exist, there must be a sufficient reason for the choice of God, which determines him to select one rather than another.[29]

54. And this reason can only be found in the *fitness*, or in the degrees of perfection, which these worlds contain, each possible world having a right to claim existence according to the measure of perfection which it possesses.[30]

55. And this is the cause of the existence of the Best; namely, that his wisdom makes it known to God, his goodness makes him choose it, and his power makes him produce it.[31]

56. Now this *connection*, or this adaptation, of all created things to each and of each to all, brings it about that each simple substance has relations which express all the others, and that, consequently, it is a perpetual living mirror of the universe.[32]

57. And as the same city looked at from different sides appears entirely different, and is as if multiplied *perspectively*; so also it happens that, as a result of the infinite multitude of simple substances, there are as it were so many different universes, which are nevertheless only the perspectives of a single one, according to the different *points of view* of each monad.[33]

58. And this is the way to obtain as great a variety as possible, but with the greatest possible order; that is, it is the way to obtain as much perfection as possible.[34]

59. Moreover, this hypothesis (which I dare to call demonstrated) is the only one which brings into relief the grandeur of God. M. Bayle recognized this, when in his Dictionary (Art. *Rorarius*) he raised objections to it; in which indeed he was dis-

28. § 66.
29. §§ 8, 10, 44, 173, 196 seqq., 225, 414–416.
30. §§ 74, 167, 350, 201, 130, 352, 345 seqq., 354. [In the first copy revised by Leibniz the following is found added here: 'Thus there is nothing absolutely arbitrary.']
31. §§ 8, 78, 80, 84, 119, 204, 206, 208; Abridgment, Objections 1 and 8.
32. §§ 130, 360.
33. § 147.
34. §§ 120, 124, 241 seqq., 214, 243, 275.

posed to think that I attributed too much to God and more than is possible. But he can state no reason why this universal harmony, which brings it about that each substance expresses exactly all the others through the relations which it has to them, is impossible.

60. Besides, we can see, in what I have just said, the *a priori* reasons why things could not be otherwise than they are. Because God, in regulating all, has had regard to each part, and particularly to each monad, whose nature being representative, nothing can limit it to representing only a part of things; although it may be true that this representation is but confused as regards the detail of the whole universe, and can be distinct only in the case of a small part of things, that is to say, in the case of those which are nearest or greatest in relation to each of the monads; otherwise each monad would be a divinity. It is not as regards the object but only as regards the modification of the knowledge of the object, that monads are limited. They all tend confusedly toward the infinite, toward the whole; but they are limited and differentiated by the degrees of their distinct perceptions.

61. And composite substances are analogous in this respect with simple substances. For since the world is a *plenum*, rendering all matter connected, and since in a plenum every motion has some effect on distant bodies in proportion to their distance, so that each body is affected not only by those in contact with it, and feels in some way all that happens to them, but also by their means is affected by those which are in contact with the former, with which it itself is in immediate contact, it follows that this intercommunication extends to any distance whatever. And consequently, each body feels all that happens in the universe, so that he who sees all, might read in each that which happens everywhere, and even that which has been or shall be, discovering in the present that which is removed in time as well as in space; σύμπνοια πάντα, said Hippocrates. But a soul can read in itself only that which is distinctly represented in it. It cannot develop its laws all at once, for they reach into the infinite.

62. Thus, although each created monad represents the entire universe, it represents more distinctly the body which is particularly attached to it, and of which it forms the entelechy; and as this body expresses the whole universe through the connection of all matter in a plenum, the soul also represents the whole

universe in representing this body, which belongs to it in a particular way.[35]

63. The body belonging to a monad, which is its entelechy or soul, constitutes together with the entelechy what may be called a *living being*, and together with the soul what may be called an *animal*. Now this body of a living being or of an animal is always organic, for since every monad is in its way a mirror of the universe, and since the universe is regulated in a perfect order, there must also be an order in the representative, that is, in the perceptions of the soul, and hence in the body, through which the universe is represented in the soul.[36]

64. Thus each organic body of a living being is a kind of divine machine or natural automaton, which infinitely surpasses all artificial automata. Because a machine which is made by man's art is not a machine in each one of its parts; for example, the teeth of a brass wheel have parts or fragments which to us are no longer artificial and have nothing in themselves to show the special use to which the wheel was intended in the machine. But nature's machines, that is, living bodies, are machines even in their smallest parts *ad infinitum*. Herein lies the difference between nature and art, that is, between the divine art and ours.[37]

65. And the author of nature has been able to employ this divine and infinitely marvellous artifice, because each portion of matter is not only divisible *ad infinitum*, as the ancients recognized, but also each part is actually endlessly subdivided into parts, of which each has some motion of its own: otherwise it would be impossible for each portion of matter to express the whole universe.[38]

66. Whence we see that there is a world of creatures, of living beings, of animals, of entelechies, of souls, in the smallest particle of matter.

67. Each portion of matter may be conceived of as a garden full of plants, and as a pond full of fishes. But each branch of the plant, each member of the animal, each drop of its humors is also such a garden or such a pond.

68. And although the earth and air which lies between the

35. § 400.
36. § 403.
37. §§ 134, 146, 194, 403.
38. Prelim., § 70; Théod., § 195.

plants of the garden, or the water between the fish of the pond, is neither plant nor fish; they yet contain more of them, but for the most part so tiny as to be imperceptible to us.

69. Therefore there is nothing fallow, nothing sterile, nothing dead in the universe, no chaos, no confusion except in appearance; somewhat as a pond would appear from a distance, in which we might see the confused movement and swarming, so to speak, of the fishes in the pond, without discerning the fish themselves.[39]

70. We see thus that each living body has a ruling entelechy, which in the animal is the soul; but the members of this living body are full of other living beings, plants, animals, each of which has also its entelechy or governing soul.

71. But it must not be imagined, as has been done by some people who have misunderstood my thought, that each soul has a mass or portion of matter belonging to it or attached to it forever, and that consequently it possesses other inferior living beings, destined to its service forever. For all bodies are, like rivers, in a perpetual flux, and parts are entering into them and departing from them continually.

72. Thus the soul changes its body only gradually and by degrees, so that it is never deprived of all its organs at once. There is often a metamorphosis in animals, but never metempsychosis nor transmigration of souls. There are also no entirely *separate* souls, nor *genii* without bodies. God alone is wholly without body.[40]

73. For which reason also, it happens that there is, strictly speaking, neither absolute birth nor complete death, consisting in the separation of the soul from the body. What we call *birth* is development or growth, as what we call *death* is envelopment and diminution.

74. Philosophers have been greatly puzzled over the origin of forms, entelechies, or souls; but to-day, when we know by exact investigations upon plants, insects and animals, that the organic bodies of nature are never products of chaos or putrefaction, but always come from seeds, in which there was undoubtedly some *pre-formation*, it has been thought that not only the organic body was already there before conception, but also a soul in this body, and, in a word, the animal itself; and that by means of concep-

39. Preface, pp. 40, 41.
40. Théod., § 90, 124.

tion this animal has merely been prepared for a great transformation, in order to become an animal of another kind. Something similar is seen outside of birth, as when worms become flies, and caterpillars become butterflies.[41]

75. The *animals*, some of which are raised by conception to the grade of larger animals, may be called *spermatic*; but those among them, which remain in their class, that is, the most part, are born, multiply, and are destroyed like the large animals, and it is only a small number of chosen ones which pass to a larger theatre.

76. But this is only half the truth. I have, therefore, held that if the animal never commences by natural means, neither does it end by natural means; and that not only will there be no birth, but also no utter destruction or death, strictly speaking. And these reasonings, made *a posteriori* and drawn from experience, harmonize perfectly with my principles deduced *a priori*, as above [cf. 3, 4, 5].[42]

77. Thus it may be said that not only the soul (mirror of an indestructible universe) is indestructible, but also the animal itself, although its mechanism often perishes in part and takes on or puts off organic coatings.

78. These principles have given me the means of explaining naturally the union or rather the conformity of the soul and the organic body. The soul follows its own peculiar laws and the body also follows its own laws, and they agree in virtue of the *pre-established harmony* between all substances, since they are all representations of one and the same universe.[43]

79. Souls act according to the laws of final causes, by appetitions, ends and means. Bodies act in accordance with the laws of efficient causes or of motion. And the two realms, that of efficient causes and that of final causes, are in harmony with each other.

80. Descartes recognized that souls cannot impart any force to bodies, because there is always the same quantity of force in matter. Nevertheless he believed that the soul could change the direction of bodies. But this was because, in his day, the law of nature which affirms also the conservation of the same total direction in matter, was not known. If he had known this, he

41. §§ 86, 89, 90, 187, 188, 403, 397; Preface, p. 40, seq.
42. § 90.
43. Preface, p. 36; Théod., §§ 340, 352, 353, 358.

would have lighted upon my system of pre-established harmony.[44]

81. According to this system, bodies act as if (what is impossible) there were no souls, and that souls act as if there were no bodies, and that both act as if each influenced the other.

82. As to *spirits* or rational souls although I find that the same thing which I have stated (namely, that animals and souls begin only with the world and end only with the world) holds good at bottom with regard to all living beings and animals, yet there is this peculiarity in rational animals, that their spermatic animalcules, as long as they remain such, have only ordinary or sensitive souls; but as soon as those which are, so to speak, elected, attain by actual conception to human nature, their sensitive souls are elevated to the rank of reason and to the prerogative of spirits.[45]

83. Among other differences which exist between ordinary souls and minds (*esprits*), some of which I have already mentioned, there is also, this, that souls in general are the living mirrors or images of the universe of creatures, but minds or spirits are in addition images of the Divinity itself, or of the author of nature, able to know the system of the universe and to imitate something of it by architectonic samples, each mind being like a little divinity in its own department.[46]

84. Hence it is that spirits are capable of entering into a sort of society with God, and that he is, in relation to them, not only what an inventor is to his machine (as God is in relation to the other creatures), but also what a prince is to his subjects, and even a father to his children.

85. Whence is it easy to conclude that the assembly of all spirits (*esprits*) must compose the City of God, that is, the most perfect state which is possible, under the most perfect of monarchs.[47]

86. This City of God, this truly universal monarchy, is a moral world within the natural world, and the highest and most divine of the works of God; it is in this that the glory of God truly consists, for he would have none if his greatness and goodness were not known and admired by spirits. It is, too, in relation to this divine city that he properly has goodness; whereas his

44. Pref., p. 44; Théod., §§ 22, 59, 60, 53, 66, 345, 346 seqq., 354, 355.
45. §§ 91, 397.
46. § 147
47. § 146; Abridgment, Objection 2.

wisdom and his power are everywhere manifest.

87. As we have above established a perfect harmony between two natural kingdoms, the one of efficient, the other of final causes, we should also notice here another harmony between the physical kingdom of nature and the moral kingdom of grace; that is, between God considered as the architect of the mechanism of the universe and God considered as monarch of the divine city of spirits.[48]

88. This harmony makes things progress toward grace by natural means. This globe, for example, must be destroyed and repaired by natural means, at such times as the government of spirits may demand it, for the punishment of some and the reward of others.[49]

89. It may be said, farther, that God as architect satisfies in every respect God as legislator, and that therefore sins, by the order of nature and perforce even of the mechanical structure of things, must carry their punishment with them; and that in the same way, good actions will obtain their rewards by mechanical ways through their relations to bodies, although this cannot and ought not always happen immediately.

90. Finally, under this perfect government, there will be no good action unrewarded, no bad action unpunished; and everything must result in the well-being of the good, that is, of those who are not disaffected in this great State, who, after having done their duty, trust in providence, and who love and imitate, as is meet, the author of all good, finding pleasure in the contemplation of his perfections, according to the nature of truly *pure love*, which takes pleasure in the happiness of the beloved. This is what causes wise and virtuous persons to work for all which seems in harmony with the divine will, presumptive or antecedent and nevertheless to content themselves with that which God in reality brings to pass by his secret, consequent and decisive will, recognizing that if we could sufficiently understand the order of the universe, we should find that it surpasses all the wishes of the wisest, and that is is impossible to render it better than it is, not only for all in general, but also for ourselves in particular, if we are attached, as we should be, to the author of all, not only as to the architect and efficient cause of our being, but also as to our master and final cause, who

48. §§ 62, 72, 118, 248, 112, 130, 247.
49. §§ 18 seqq., 110, 244, 245, 340.

ought to be the whole aim of our will, and who, alone, can make our happiness.

Are There Innate Ideas?

John Locke, 1632–1704 versus Leibniz

Locke appears here solely as a critic of belief in innate ideas and not in his own right. The two short passages which follow are from his *Essay Concerning Human Understanding* (published in 1690), which has always been among the most important and celebrated works of the seventeenth century. The target of his attack on innate ideas is usually taken to be Descartes but this is somewhat for want of a better candidate, since there are in general marked affinities between Locke and Descartes, and it may be that Locke is after a common contemporary opinion which had no particular champions. Nor can the *Essay* readily be classified as the empiricist work, which the eighteenth century took it to be. Nevertheless it has become usual to treat Locke as the father of empiricism and it is in this role that he takes the stage here.

From Locke's *Essay Concerning Human Understanding*, 1690

BOOK I

Chapter II: *No Innate Principles in the Mind*

1. It is an established opinion amongst some men, that there are in the understanding certain innate principles; some primary notions, κοιναὶ ἔννοιαι, characters, as it were stamped upon the mind of man; which the soul receives in its very first being, and brings into the world with it. It would be sufficient to convince unprejudiced readers of the falseness of this supposition if I should only show (as I hope I shall in the following parts of this Discourse) how men, barely by the use of their natural faculties, may attain to all the knowledge they have, without the help of

any innate impressions; and may arrive at certainty, without any such original notions or principles. For I imagine any one will easily grant that it would be impertinent to suppose the ideas of colours innate in a creature to whom God hath given sight, and a power to receive them by the eyes from external objects: and no less unreasonable would it be to attribute several truths to the impressions of nature, and innate characters, when we may observe in ourselves faculties fit to attain as easy and certain knowledge of them as if they were originally imprinted on the mind.

2. There is nothing more commonly taken for granted than that there are certain principles, both speculative and practical (for they speak of both), universally agreed upon by all mankind: which therefore, they argue, must needs be the constant impressions which the souls of men receive in their first beings, and which they bring into the world with them, as necessarily and really as they do any of their inherent faculties.

3. This argument, drawn from universal consent, has this misfortune in it, that if it were true in matter of fact, that there were certain truths wherein all mankind agreed, it would not prove them innate, if there can be any other way shown how men may come to that universal agreement, in the things they do consent in, which I presume may be done.

4. But, which is worse, this argument of universal consent, which is made use of to prove innate principles, seems to me a demonstration that there are none such: because there are none to which all mankind give an universal assent. I shall begin with the speculative, and instance in those magnified principles of demonstration 'Whatsoever is, is,' and 'It is impossible for the same thing to be and not to be'; which of all others, I think have the most allowed title to innate. But yet I take liberty to say, that these propositions are so far from having an universal assent, that there are a great part of mankind to whom they are not so much as known.

5. For, first, it is evident, that all children and idiots have not the least apprehension or thought of them. And the want of that is enough to destroy that universal assent which must needs be the necessary concomitant of all innate truths: it seeming to me near a contradiction to say, that there are truths imprinted on the soul, which it perceives or understands not: imprinting, if it signify anything, being nothing else but the

making certain truths to be perceived. But to imprint anything on the mind without the mind's perceiving it, seems to me hardly intelligible. If therefore children and idiots have souls, have minds, with those impressions upon them, they must unavoidably perceive them, and necessarily know and assent to these truths; which since they do not, it is evident that there are no such impressions. For if they are not notions imprinted, how can they be innate? and if they are notions imprinted, how can they be unknown? To say a notion is imprinted on the mind, and yet at the same time to say that the mind is ignorant of it, and never yet took notice of it, is to make this impression nothing. No proposition can be said to be in the mind which it never yet knew, which it was never yet conscious of. If therefore these two propositions, 'Whatsoever is, is,' and 'It is impossible for the same thing to be and not to be,' are by nature imprinted, children cannot be ignorant of them: infants, and all that have souls, must necessarily have them in their understandings, know the truth of them, and assent to it.

6. To avoid this, it is usually answered, that all men know and assent to them, when they come to the use of reason; and this is enough to prove them innate. I answer:

7. Doubtful expressions, that have scarce any signification, go for clear reasons to those who, being prepossessed, take not the pains to examine even what they themselves say. For, to apply this answer with any tolerable sense to our present purpose, it must signify one of these two things: either that as soon as men come to the use of reason these supposed native inscriptions come to be known and observed by them; or else, that the use and exercise of men's reason assists them in the discovery of these principles, and certainly makes them known to them.

8. If they mean that by the use of reason men may discover these principles, and that this is sufficient to prove them innate, their way of arguing will stand thus, viz. that whatever truths reason can certainly discover to us, and make us firmly assent to, those are all naturally imprinted on the mind; since that universal assent, which is made the mark of them, amounts to no more but this – that by the use of reason we are capable to come to a certain knowledge of and assent to them; and, by this means, there will be no difference between the maxims of the mathematicians, and theorems they deduce from them: all must be equally allowed innate; they being all discoveries made

by the use of reason, and truths that a rational creature may certainly come to know, if he apply his thoughts rightly that way.

From Leibniz' *New Essays concerning Human Understanding*, 1704

PREFACE

. . . Our differences are on subjects of some importance. The question is to know whether the soul in itself is entirely empty, like the tablet on which nothing has yet been written (*tabula rasa*) according to Aristotle and the author of the Essay, and whether all that is traced thereon comes solely from the senses and from experience; or whether the soul contains originally the principles of several notions and doctrines which external objects merely awaken on occasion, as I believe, with Plato, and even with the schoolmen, and with all those who take with this meaning the passage of St Paul (Romans, 2, 15) where he remarks that the law of God is written in the heart. The Stoics called these principles prolepses, that is to say, fundamental assumptions, or what is taken for granted in advance. The mathematicians call them common notions (κοιναὶ ἔννοιαι). Modern philosophers give them other beautiful names, and Julius Scaliger in particular named them *semina aeternitatis*, also zopyra, as meaning living fires, luminous rays, concealed within us, but which the encounter of the senses makes appear like the sparks which the blow makes spring from the steel. And it is not without reason that these flashes are believed to indicate something divine and eternal, which appears especially in necessary truths. Whence there arises another question, whether all truths depend on experience, that is to say, on induction and examples, or whether there are some which have still another basis. For if some events can be foreseen before any trial has been made of them, it is manifest that we contribute something of our own thereto. The senses, although necessary for all our actual knowledge, are not sufficient to give to us the whole of it, since the senses never give anything except examples, that is to say, particular or individual truths. Now all the examples which confirm a general truth, however numerous they be, do not suffice to establish the universal necessity of this same truth;

for it does not follow that what has happened will happen in the same way. For example, the Greeks and Romans, and all other peoples of the earth known to the ancients, have always noticed that before the expiration of twenty-four hours day changes into night and the night into day. But we would be deceived if we believed that the same rule holds good everywhere else; for since then, the contrary has been experienced in the region of Nova Zembla. And he would still deceive himself who believed that, in our climates at least, it is a necessary and eternal truth which will last always; since we must think that the earth and the sun even do not exist necessarily, and that there will perhaps be a time when this beautiful star will no longer be, at least in its present form, nor all its system. Whence it would seem that necessary truths, such as are found in pure mathematics and especially in arithmetic and in geometry, must have principles the proof of which does not depend on examples, nor, consequently, on the testimony of the senses, although without the senses we would never take it into our heads to think of them. This ought to be well recognized, and this is what Euclid has so well understood that he often demonstrates by reason that which is sufficiently seen through experience and by sensible images. Logic also, together with metaphysics and ethics, one of which forms theology and the other jurisprudence, both natural, are full of such truths; and consequently their proof can only come from internal principles which are called innate. It is true that we must not imagine that these eternal laws of the reason can be read in the soul as in an open book, as the edict of the pretor is read upon his *album* without difficulty and without research; but it is enough that they can be discovered in us by force of attention, for which occasions are furnished by the senses; and the success of experiments serves also as confirmation to the reason, very much as proofs serve in arithmetic for better avoiding error of reckoning when the reasoning is long. It is also in this that human knowledge and that of the brutes differ: the brutes are purely empirics and only guide themselves by examples, for they never, as far as we can judge, come to form necessary propositions; whereas men are capable of demonstrative sciences. It is also for this reason that the faculty which brutes have of making associations (of ideas) is something inferior to the reason which is in man. The association (of ideas) of the brutes is merely like that of simple empirics, who claim that what has happened sometimes will happen also in a case where that which strikes them is similar, without being able to judge whether the same reasons hold good. This is why it is so easy for men to entrap brutes and so easy for simple empirics to make mistakes. This is why persons who have become skilled by age or by experience are not exempt from error when they rely too much upon their past experience, as has happened to many in civil and military affairs; because they do not sufficiently consider that the world changes and that men become more skilled by finding a thousand new dexterities, whereas deer and hares of the present day do not become more cunning than those of past time. The association (of ideas) of the brutes are only a shadow of reasoning, that is to say, they are but connections of the imagination and passages from one image to another, because in a new juncture which appears similar to the preceding they expect anew what they found conjoined with it before, as if things were linked together in fact because their images are connected in the memory. It is true that even reason counsels us to expect ordinarily to see that happen in the future which is conformed to a long past experience, but this is not for this reason a necessary and infallible truth, and success may cease when we expect it least, if the reasons which have sustained it change. This is why the wisest do not so rely upon it as not to try to discover something of the reason (if it is possible) of this fact, in order to judge when it will be necessary to make exceptions. For reason is alone capable of establishing reliable rules, and of supplying what is lacking to those which were not such by inserting their exceptions; and of finding, finally, certain connections in the force of necessary consequences, which often enables us to foresee the event without having to experience the sensible connections of images, to which the brutes are reduced; so that that which justifies the internal principles of necessary truths, also distinguishes man from the brutes.

Perhaps our able author will not differ entirely from my opinion. For after having employed the whole of his first book in rejecting innate knowledge (*lumières*), taken in a certain sense, he nevertheless admits at the beginning of the second and in what follows, that the ideas which do not originate in sensation come from reflection. Now reflection is nothing else than attention to what is in us, and the senses do not give us that which we already carry with us. This being so, can it be denied that there is much that is innate in our mind, since we are innate, so to say, in ourselves, and since there is in ourselves, being, unity, substance, duration, change, action, perception, pleasure, and a thousand other objects of our intellectual ideas? And these objects being immediate to our understanding and always present (although they cannot be always perceived on account of our distractions and wants), why be astonished that we say that these ideas, with all which depends on them, are innate in us? I have also made use of the comparison of a block of marble which has veins, rather than of a block or marble wholly even, or of blank tablets, that is to say, of what is called among philosophers *tabula rasa.* For if the soul resembled these blank tablets, truths would be in us as the figure of Hercules is in marble when the marble is entirely indifferent toward receiving this figure or some other. But if there were veins in the block which should mark out the figure of Hercules rather than other figures, the block would be more determined thereto, and Hercules would be in it as in some sort innate, although it would be necessary to labour in order to discover these veins and to cleanse them by polishing and by cutting away that which prevents them from appearing. It is thus that ideas and truths are innate in us, as inclinations, dispositions, habits, or natural capacities, and not as actions; although these capacities are always accompanied by some actions, often insensible, which correspond to them.

From Locke's *Essay Concerning Human Understanding*, 1690

BOOK II

Chapter I: *Of Ideas in General, and their Original*

1. EVERY man being conscious to himself that he thinks, and that which his mind is applied about whilst thinking being the *ideas* that are there, it is past doubt that men have in their minds several ideas – such as those expressed by the words *whiteness, hardness, sweetness, thinking, motion, man, elephant, army, drunkeness,* and others; it is in the first place then to be inquired how he comes by them.

2. Let us suppose then the mind to be, as we say, white paper

void of all characters, without any ideas. How comes it to be furnished? Whence comes it by that vast store which the busy and boundless fancy of man has painted on it with an almost endless variety? Whence has it all the *materials* of reason and knowledge? To this I answer, in one word, from EXPERIENCE. In that all our knowledge is founded; and from that it ultimately derives itself. Our observation, employed either about *external sensible objects, or about the internal operations of our minds perceived and reflected on by ourselves, is that which supplies our understandings with all the materials of thinking*. These two are the fountains of knowledge, from whence all the ideas we have, or can naturally have, do spring.

3. First, our Senses, conversant about particular sensible objects, do convey into the mind several distinct perceptions of things, according to those various ways wherein those objects do affect them. And thus we come by those *ideas* we have of *yellow*, *white*, *heat*, *cold*, *soft*, *hard*, *bitter*, *sweet*, and all those which we call sensible qualities; which when I say the senses convey into the mind, I mean, they from external objects convey into the mind what produces there those perceptions. This great source of most of the ideas we have, depending wholly upon our senses, and derived by them to the understanding, I call SENSATION.

4. Secondly, the other fountain from which experience furnisheth the understanding with ideas is the perception of the operations of our own mind within us, as it is employed about the ideas it has got; which operations, when the soul comes to reflect on and consider, do furnish the understanding with another set of ideas, which could not be had from things without. And such are *perception*, *thinking*, *doubting*, *believing*, *reasoning*, *knowing*, *willing*, and all the different actings of our own minds; which we being conscious of, and observing in ourselves, do from these receive into our understandings as distinct ideas as we do from bodies affecting our senses. This source of ideas every man has wholly in himself; and though it be not sense, as having nothing to do with external objects, yet it is very like it, and might properly enough be called *internal sense*. But as I call the other Sensation, so I call this REFLECTION, the ideas it affords being such only as the mind gets by reflecting on its own operations within itself. By reflection then, in the following part of this discourse, I would be understood to mean, that

notice which the mind takes of its own operations, and the manner of them, by reason whereof there come to be ideas of these operations in the understanding. These two, I say, viz. external material things, as the objects of SENSATION, and the operations of our own minds within, as the objects of REFLECTION, are to me the only originals from whence all our ideas take their beginnings. The term *operations* here I use in a large sense, as comprehending not barely the actions of the mind about its ideas, but some sort of passions arising sometimes from them, such as is the satisfaction or uneasiness arising from any thought.

5. The understanding seems to me not to have the least glimmering of any ideas which it doth not receive from one of these two. *External objects* furnish the mind with the ideas of sensible qualities, which are all those different perceptions they produce in us; and *the mind* furnishes the understanding with ideas of its own operations.

From Leibniz' *New Essays*, 1704

BOOK II: *Chapter I*

1. I admit it, provided that you add that is is an immediate internal object, and that this object is an expression of the nature or of the qualities of things. If the idea were the *form* of thought, it would come into existence and would cease with the actual thoughts which correspond to it; but being its object it might exist anterior to and after the thoughts. External sensible objects are but *mediate*, because they cannot act immediately upon the soul. God alone is the *immediate external object*. It might be said that the soul itself is its own immediate *internal object*; but it is so in so far as it contains ideas or what corresponds to things; for the soul is a microcosm in which distinct ideas are a representation of God, and in which confused ideas are a representation of the universe.

2. This *tabula rasa*, of which so much is said, is, in my opinion, only a fiction, which nature does not admit of, and which has its foundation in the incomplete notions of philosophers, like the vacuum, atoms, and rest, absolute or relative, of two parts of a whole, or like the primary matter (*materia prima*) which is

conceived as without form. Uniform things and those which contain no variety, are never anything but abstractions, like time, space, and the other entities of pure mathematics. There is no body, the parts of which are at rest, and there is no substance which has nothing by which to distinguish if from every other. Human souls differ not only from other souls, but also among themselves, although the difference is not of the kind which is called specific. And according to the demonstrations, which I think I have, everything substantial, whether soul or body, has its own peculiar relation to each of the others; and the one must always differ from the other by *intrinsic characteristics*; not to mention that those who speak so much of this *tabula rasa*, after having taken away from it ideas, are not able to say what is left to it, like the scholastic philosophers who leave nothing to their *materia prima*. It may, perhaps, be answered that this *tabula rasa* of the philosophers means that the soul has naturally and originally only bare faculties. But faculties without some act, in a word, the pure powers of the school, are also but fictions unknown to nature, and which are obtained only by abstraction. For where in the world will there ever be found a faculty which confines itself to the mere power, without exercising any act? There is always a particular disposition to action, and to one action rather than to another. And besides the disposition, there is a tendency to action, of which tendencies there is always an infinity at once in each subject; and these tendencies are never without some effect. Experience is, I admit, necessary in order that the soul be determined to such or such thoughts, and in order that it take notice of the ideas which are in us; but by what means can experience and the senses give ideas? Has the soul windows? does it resemble tablets? is it like wax? It is evident that all who think of the soul thus, make it at bottom corporeal. The axiom received among the philosophers, will be opposed by me, *that there is nothing in the soul which does not come from the senses*. But the soul itself and its affections must be expected. *Nihil est in intellectu, quod non fuerit in sensu, excipe: nisi ipse intellectus*. Now the soul comprises being, substance, unity, identity, cause, perception, reason, and many other notions which the senses cannot give. This agrees somewhat with your author (Locke) who finds (in his *Essay*) a good part of our ideas proceeding from the mind's own reflections on itself . . .

Short Bibliography
Chronological Table
Index

Short Bibliography

(The items listed are canonical or especially helpful. They are the merest fraction of the whole literature)

1. BACKGROUND

E. A. Burtt, *The Metaphysical Foundations of Modern Science*, revised ed. New York 1952, pb. 1954

H. Butterfield, *The Origins of Modern Science* (esp. chs. 4, 5), revised ed. New York 1958

E. Cassirer, *The Philosophy of the Enlightenment* (chs. 1, 2), tr. F. Koelln and J. Pettegrove, Princeton N.J. 1951

F. C. Copleston, *A History of Philosophy* (vol. IV), Westminster 1959–62

W. von Leyden, *Seventeenth-Century Metaphysics*, London 1968

A. O. Lovejoy, *The Great Chain of Being* (esp. ch. 5), Cambridge, Mass. 1948

R. H. Popkin, *The History of Scepticism from Erasmus to Descartes* (esp. Preface, ch. 1), New York 1964

A. N. Whitehead, *Science and the Modern World* (chs. 1, 2, 3), Cambridge 1927

B. Willey, *The Seventeenth-Century Background* (esp. chs. 1 & 2), London 1946, 1953

2. DESCARTES

Oeuvres de Descartes (12 vols.), ed. Ch. Adam and P. Tannery, Paris, 1897–1910

Philosophical Works of Descartes (2 vols.), tr. E. S. Haldane and G. R. T. Ross, Cambridge 1911, latest ed. 1967 (pb.)

Descartes: Philosophical Writings, tr. E. Anscombe and P. T. Geach, London, 1954, latest ed. 1970 (pb.)

Descartes – Philosophical Letters, tr. and ed. A. J. P. Kenny, Oxford, Clarendon 1970

Critical Books

L. Beck, *The Method of Descartes*, London 1952

L. Boutroux, *Descartes and Cartesianism*, Cambridge Modern History (vol. IV, ch. 27)

A. Boyce Gibson, *The Philosophy of Descartes*, London 1938

H. Frankfurt, *Demons, Dreamers and Madmen*, Indianapolis 1967
E. Gilson, *The Unity of Philosophical Experience*, Sec. 2, New York 1937, 1965
S. V. Keeling, *Descartes*, London 1934, 2nd ed. Oxford 1968 (pb.)
N. Kemp Smith, *New Studies in the Philosophy of Descartes*, London 1952
A. J. P. Kenny, *Descartes*, New York 1968
J. Maritain, *The Dream of Descartes*, London 1945
W. Doney (ed), *Descartes: A Collection of Critical Essays*, London 1968
A. Sesonske and N. Fleming (eds), *Metameditations*, Belmont 1966

3. HOBBES

The English Works of Thomas Hobbes (11 vols.), ed. Sir T. Molesworth, London 1839–45, reprinted Oxford 1961
The Elements of Law, Natural and Political, ed. F. Tönnies, London 1928
Leviathan, ed. M. Oakeshott, Oxford 1947, pb. New York 1962
Leviathan, ed. J. Plamenatz, Fontana 1962
Body, Mind and Citizen, ed. R. S. Peters, New York 1962 (pb.)
Hobbes Selections, ed. F. J. E. Woodbridge, New York 1930

Critical Books

R. S. Peters, *Hobbes*, Penguin Books 1956
J. W. N. Watkins, *Hobbes' System of Ideas*, London 1965

4. SPINOZA

Spinoza Opera (4 vols.), ed. G. Gebhardt, Heidelberg 1924
The Chief Works of Spinoza (2 vols.) tr. R. H. M. Elwes, London 1883, New York 1955 and 1956 (pb.)
The Correspondence of Spinoza, tr. and ed. A. Wolf, London 1928
The Principles of Descartes Philosophy, tr. H. H. Briton, Chicago 1905

Critical Books

S. Hampshire, *Spinoza*, Pelican 1951
H. H. Joachim, *Commentary on Spinoza's Tractatus de Intellectus Emendatione*, Oxford 1940
G. H. R. Parkinson, *Spinoza's Theory of Knowledge*, Oxford 1954

5. LEIBNIZ

Philosophische Schriften (7 vols.), ed. C. I. Gerhardt, Berlin 1875–1890, facsimile reprint Hildesheim 1962
Philosophical Papers and Letters (2 vols.), tr. L. E. Loemker, Chicago 1956

Philosophical Works, tr. Gm. Duncan, New Haven 1890
The Monadology and other Philosphical Writings, tr. R. Latta, Oxford 1898
New Essays Concerning Human Understanding, tr. A. G. Langley, Chicago 1916, reprinted 1949
Selections, tr. and ed. P. Wiener, New York 1951
Theodicy, tr. E. M. Huggard, ed. Austin Farrar, London 1951
The Leibniz–Arnauld Correspondence, tr. and ed. H. T. Mason, Introduction by G. Parkinson, Manchester 1967
Leibniz–Clarke Correspondence, ed. H. G. Alexander, Manchester 1956

Critical Books
H. W. Carr, *Leibniz*, New York 1929, reprinted 1960 (pb.)
N. Rescher, *The Philosophy of Leibniz*, Englewood Cliffs 1967
B. Russell, *A Critical Exposition of the Philosphy of Leibniz*, Cambridge 1900, 2nd ed. 1937

Chronological Table

(of the principal publications of the Rationalists and some other intellectual landmarks. Publication dates are given, unless otherwise stated.)

1620	Bacon's *Novum Organon*
1624	Herbert of Cherbury's *De Veritate*
1628	Harvey's discovery of the double circulation of the blood
1628–9	Descartes' *Rules for the Direction of the Mind* (published 1701)
1633	Galileo forced by the Inquisition to abjure the theories of Copernicus
1637	Descartes' *Discourse on the Method*
1640	Hobbes' *Elements of Law* circulated in manuscript (published 1650)
1641	Descartes' *Meditations* (with the Objections and Replies)
1642	Hobbes' *De Cive*
1644	Descartes' *Principles of Philosophy*
1649	Descartes' *Passions of the Soul*
1651	Hobbes' *Leviathan*
1652	Guericke's air pump
1655	Hobbes' *De Corpore*
1659	Hobbes' *De Homine*
1661	Boyle's *Sceptical Chemist*
1662	The Royal Society founded. Arnauld and Nicole's *Port Royal Logic*. Spinoza's *On the Improvement of the Understanding* (not published until the late eighteenth century)
1665	Start of the *Journal des Savants*
1666	Newton working with the differential calculus (published 1692)
1668	Leeuwenhoek's discovery of red blood corpuscles
1670	Spinoza's *Tractatus Theologico-politicus*. Pascal's *Pensées*
1672	Newton's law of gravitation
1674–8	Malebranche's *Search for Truth* written
1675	Royal Observatory at Greenwich. Leibniz produced his differential calculus (published 1684)
1677	Spinoza's *Ethics*
1686	De Fontenelle's *Plurality of Worlds*. Leibniz' *Discourse on Metaphysics*
1687	Newton's *Philosophiae Naturalis Principia Mathematica*

1689	Locke's *On Civil Government*
1690	Locke's *Essay Concerning Human Understanding*
1693	Halley's scientific astronomical tables
1695	Leibniz' *New System of Nature*
1695–7	Bayle's *Dictionary*
1704	Newton's *Optics.* Leibniz' *New Essays*
1705	De Mandeville's *Fable of the Bees*
1709	Berkeley's *New Theory of Vision*
1710	Berkeley's *Principles of Human Knowledge.* Leibniz' *Theodicy*
1711	Shaftesbury's *Philosophical Writings*
1712	Last execution for witchcraft in England
1714	Leibniz' *Principles of Nature and of Grace*
1715–6	*Leibniz–Clarke Correspondence*

Index

Fontana Philosophy Classics

General Editor
G. J. Warnock, Magdalen College, Oxford

Leviathan
Thomas Hobbes *Edited by John Plamenatz*

An Essay Concerning Human Understanding
John Locke *Edited by A. D. Woozley*

The Principles of Human Knowledge and
Three Dialogues Between Hylas and Philonous
George Berkeley *Edited by G. J. Warnock*

A Treatise of Human Nature
David Hume *Book I edited by D. G. C. Macnabb*

Hume on Religion
Selected and edited by Richard Wollheim

Utilitarianism
Selections from the writings of Jeremy Bentham,
John Stuart Mill, and John Austin

Selected and edited by Mary Warnock

Fontana Social Science

Books available include:

African Genesis Robert Ardrey **50p**

The Territorial Imperative Robert Ardrey **50p**

Racial Minorities Michael Banton **50p**

The Sociology of Modern Britain
Edited by Eric Butterworth and David Weir **60p**

Social Problems of Modern Britain
Edited by Eric Butterworth and David Weir **75p**

Strikes Richard Hyman **50p**

Memories, Dreams, Reflections C. J. Jung **60p**

Strike at Pilkingtons Tony Lane and Kenneth Roberts **50p**

Figuring Out Society Ronald Meek **45p**

Lectures on Economic Principles Sir Dennis Robertson **75p**

People and Cities Stephen Verney **37½p**

Fontana Politics

Books available include:

Battle for the Environment Tony Aldous **45p**

The English Constitution Walter Bagehot
Edited by R. H. S. Crossman **40p**

War in Modern Society Alastair Buchan **42½p**

At War With Asia Noam Chomsky **50p**

Problems of Knowledge and Freedom Noam Chomsky **30p**

Selected Writings of Mahatma Gandhi
Edited by Ronald Duncan **45p**

Marx and Engels: Basic Writings
Edited by Lewis S. Feuer **50p**

Governing Britain A. H. Hanson and Malcolm Walles **50p**

The Commons in Transition *Edited by* A. H. Hanson and Bernard Crick **50p**

Sir Charles Dilke Roy Jenkins **52½p**

Europe Tomorrow *Edited by* Richard Mayne **60p**

Machiavelli: Selections *Edited by* John Plamenatz **60p**

Democracy in America Alexis de Tocqueville
Edited by J. P. Mayer and Max Lerner Vols I & II **75p** each

The Cabinet Patrick Gordon Walker **40p**

The Downfall of the Liberal Party 1914–1935
Trevor Wilson **60p**

Economics and Policy Donald Winch **80p**

Fontana Literature

Fontana Modern Masters

General Editor: Frank Kermode

This series provides authoritative and critical introductions to the most influential and seminal minds of our time. Books already published include:

Camus Conor Cruise O'Brien **25p**
Chomsky John Lyons **30p**
Fanon David Caute **30p**
Freud Richard Wollheim **40p**
Gandhi George Woodcock **35p**
Guevara Andrew Sinclair **25p**
Joyce John Gross **30p**
Lenin Robert Conquest **35p**
Lévi-Strauss Edmund Leach **30p**
Lukács George Lichtheim **30p**
Mailer Richard Poirier **40p**
Marcuse Alasdair MacIntyre **25p**
McLuhan Jonathan Miller **30p**
Orwell Raymond Williams **30p**
Reich Charles Rycroft **30p**
Russell A. J. Ayer **40p**
Wittgenstein David Pears **40p**
Yeats Denis Donoghue **30p**

'We have here, in fact, the beginnings of what promises to be an important publishing enterprise. This series is just what is needed by the so-called "general reader" in search of a guide to intellectual currents that clash so confusingly in a confused world.'

The Times Literary Supplement

Many more are in preparation including:

Fuller Allan Temko
Eliot Stephen Spender
Lawrence Frank Kermode
Sherrington Jonathan Miller
Trotsky Philip Rahv
Weber Donald MacRae